THE FEMALE ANIMAL

THE FEMALE ANIMAL

IRENE ELIA

A DONALD HUTTER BOOK

HENRY HOLT AND COMPANY
NEW YORK

Published by Henry Holt and Company, Inc.,
115 West 18th Street, New York, New York 10011.
Distributed in Canada by Fitzhenry & Whiteside Limited,
195 Allstate Parkway, Markham, Ontario L3R 4T8.

Library of Congress Cataloging in Publication Data
    Elia, Irene.
        The female animal.
        "A Donald Hutter book."
        Includes index.
        1. Reproduction.   2. Females—Physiology.
3. Females—Evolution.   4. Parental behavior in animals.
5. Sexual dimorphism (Animals)   I. Title.
QP259.E45   1988   155.6'463   87-28714
ISBN 0-8050-0702-4

First United States Edition
An earlier version of this book was published in
Great Britain by Oxford University Press.

Designed by Susan Hood
Illustrations by Muntes

Printed in the United States of America
10 9 8 7 6 5 4 3 2 1

ISBN 0-8050-0702-4

I dedicate this book to the two angels
who were always at my side:
my grandmother, Ida Haimowitz, and
my father, Fred Cohen

CONTENTS

INTRODUCTION

BY ASHLEY MONTAGU

In *The Female Animal*, Irene Elia has written a brilliantly original book which throws a flood of light upon the origins and evolution of human physical and behavioral traits. It is also an important, as well as highly readable, book: important because it approaches the subject from a wholly new perspective—that of the mother and the female principle flowing from her—and highly readable because Dr. Elia writes so clearly, simply, and eloquently.

Not only is this a book for the general reader, but there isn't anyone with an interest in anthropology of whatever kind who would not greatly profit from reading this exemplary work. Indeed, the book should be required for all students of anthropology at whatever level—school, college undergraduate, even graduate—and the sooner in the course of their studies they read it the better they will be prepared for the rest of their careers. This is very high praise for a book which, from its title, one would judge to be devoted to the female from a biological point of view. And so it is, but embracing much more.

Dr. Elia's interest is to discover how it came about that females were selected to be the more parenting sex in almost all species of insects, higher invertebrates, and vertebrates in which parenting occurs. Such discovery leads to revelations of the great influence that the female has had on biological and social evolution. As a biological anthropologist, and a mother herself, Elia understands a number of things that most male anthropologists have failed to perceive—such as (although she is too polite to say so) the large underlying fact that the male is a mere *additus naturae*, that the family really consists of a female care giver and her offspring. Even in more civilized societies throughout the animal "kingdom," she demonstrates that the male of the family is really the constitutional monarch, while the actual power behind the throne, the prime minister, is the female.

Irene Elia is by far the most knowledgeable biological anthropologist I have ever encountered, and therefore it was an enriched pleasure to read her masterly handling of the biological and social evolution of the many species she examines. She is especially good and enlightening on the primates, where in the space of twenty-one pages it seems to me she has more to say of genuine relevance than many an entire textbook.

The Female Animal is a book that was in search of an author. It has found its perfect author in Dr. Irene Elia.

Princeton, New Jersey
August 1987

PREFACE

There is a plague of greenflies in Cambridge. When I speak, they fly into my mouth; when I inhale, they waft toward my nose. Strollers crossing Magdalen Bridge swat the air, not knowing that the clouds of insects, rising from the river, are all female aphids. Eager to seize the windfall of tender July greenery, they are tumbling out of their virgin mothers in rapid generations. As they are born, their own daughters are already formed inside them. They seem to have been caught in a hall of mirrors, each one sending an endless line of reflections into space.

In the afternoon, I watch worker bees in the rose garden. They are all females, all sterile, and all surpassingly successful at placing their genes into future generations. Their flower work paints patches on the park and fills the air with perfume, as if to atone for the aphid pest. But the bees are not our servants; they work for themselves, sheltering and feeding their sister embryos so that three times as many females as males will emerge from their waxy dormitories each spring.

In the early evening, speckled frogs cross the gravel path to reach the swamp near the college. I pick one up. It seems to be a slender male. Perhaps he is off to court an egg-fat female—to squeeze her in the pond, until she is dazed, eggless, and carefree for another season.

At night, a friend and I share a sea bass at a Chinese restaurant. "Did you know that some species in this family of fishes are females first and become males later?" We poke around in the soy sauce for evidence of transformation, but, being hungry females with eggs of our own to support, we soon eat whatever biology lesson may be on the plate.

Female fishes, frogs, and flies spend the day unperturbed by, and seemingly unaware of, their gender. Why, I wonder, are these females free, abundantly fertile, and biologically fit, while others—the nervous robin in her nest, the masculinized hyena at her den, the human mother delighted or bored with her brood in the playground—buy their fitness so dearly? Why has the number of offspring per female decreased and maternal responsibility increased with the evolution of species?

I add together all the species of invertebrates, fishes, reptiles, birds, and mammals that show disproportionate female parenting, and find that they account for less than 10 percent of the animal kingdom. The prominence of the female-as-mother among birds and mammals has overshadowed its rarity among animals. Mothering seems so important to the survival of the young that few people realize it is a trait that has existed for only a six-hundredth part of life's history.

Why is it that the more elaborate the mother care, the more sociable the species? Even among the notoriously lonely spiders, the few species with outstanding mothers are the only ones that can tolerate each other's company for long enough to munch on a moth together.

And why is good mothering apparently linked to a higher level of communication and intelligence, or at least to greater complexity of behavior? The answer seems to be that good parenting, wherever it occurs in the animal world, requires keen senses, advanced motor skills, and emotional control. Females with these traits have been better equipped to build shelter, find food, keep away the wily predator, or simply to sit patiently on a pile of eggs through all kinds of weather. The young have consequently been more likely to survive, males and females alike inheriting these broadly adaptive components of good mothering. This selection process caused an accumulation of characteristics—greater alertness, good judgment, and love—that put mothering species on the road to high intelligence and behavioral versatility.

Similarly, even something as basic as maintenance of constant body temperature was selected for in connection with mothering—the cold-blooded python mother coils around her eggs and quivers to keep them warm. Gradually, natural selection integrated warm-bloodedness into the inheritance of certain species; constant body temperature greatly improved the survival chances of the young and was also one of the most important bases of a high and uniform level of responsiveness, which in itself disposes an organism toward intelligent behavior.

The fact that the component traits of good mothering were inherited by both male and female offspring explains why males in highly mothering species can assist in or, in the absence of females, try to take over parenting. Why then were females selected to be the more parenting sex in almost all species of insects, higher invertebrates, and vertebrates in which parenting occurs?

The answer to this question begins with the shape of the egg and ends with the shape of animal societies. It is an answer that started to evolve in the sea, spread over land, went back to the sea, shot to the moon, and now stands swatting greenflies beside an ivory tower.

Irene Elia
Cambridge, England
1987

Acknowledgments

The first person I must thank is my former agent, Charlotte Sheedy. It was her confidence in the importance of having a popular biology book written with a "female slant" that first gave this project its publishing credibility. While she was not able to see me through the distressing prolongation of the work, due to my emigration and marriage, the birth of my daughter, and the deaths of my beloved grandmother and father, I thank her sincerely.

I am most grateful to all the field, laboratory, and theoretical workers in natural history for the facts and insights that helped form this view of the female animal. Treatment here of their complex findings and arguments is necessarily brief, but I have always tried to report accurately and not distort the emphasis of their work.

My husband, Marinos, has sacrificed his dream of married life for this book, as I worked through the nights in all but the second year of our marriage, when our daughter required nocturnal breast-feeding. Except for this last duty, he has participated lovingly in all child-care tasks. His intelligence, sense of humor, and affection have made these years of hard labor bearable. For such things there are no adequate thanks.

I thank the Radcliffe Science Library in Oxford and the University Library in Cambridge for access and advice.

I thank the users of the Cambridge University Computer Centre for teaching me how to use a word processor.

I thank Professors George Hemingway, Jack Cohen, and E. C. Amoroso, and Dr. Elliott Haimoff, for reprints, photographs, and discussions.

I thank Antoinette Stadler for reading and making notations on an early draft of the first six chapters, and Gay Palmer for her thorough criticism of the section on lactation.

I thank my parents and parents-in-law for their loving support.

PART 1

1 | THE EGG

Female animals produce eggs. This seems an obvious statement, but if we take the converse statement—eggs produce female animals—which is also obvious and true, we have a problem: which came first? The answer is that the egg did, both in the lifetime of one female animal and in the lifetime of evolving species. Thousands of millions of years ago there were microscopic plants and animals that had no ovaries but were nevertheless able to produce eggs. In other words, eggs evolved before females, before ovaries, before almost all the species we know today, and certainly long before the chicken in the age-old question.

When we think of eggs, we usually do think of smooth, brown or white chicken eggs. And although it may be natural for a species that eats birds' eggs, as ours does, to symbolize the entire set of eggs with a chicken's egg, this gives only a limited picture. There are myriad eggs of different colors and textures, unshelled and shelled, suited to diverse environments.

Whatever misconceptions or limits our symbolization of the noun *egg* has placed on our understanding of the female gamete (sex cell; egg), the verb *to egg* offers a number of appropriate, although linguistically accidental, meanings that might be applied to females and their sex cells. "To egg," meaning "to goad" or "to incite to action," is often a female property. Her presence or the presence of her eggs may attract males, instigate competition among them, and provoke spawning or copulation. It might be said that females and eggs egg on life.

In their twin capacities to engulf and nurture genetic material from sperms, eggs are unique. No cells except eggs incorporate and support the genetic material of other cells. Although they have stood for the past six hundred million years as the most apparent identifiers of female gender, we still do not know the source of their conservatism or of their capacity to integrate new genetic material.

Some theories, however, suggest precedents for incorporative behavior in eggs. Certain ancient symbiotic (mutually beneficial) relationships between cells may have resulted in one cell incorporating its partner. When we look at chloroplasts and mitochondria, in plant and animal cells, we may be observing the descendants of such united symbionts. Chloroplasts, like flecks of blue-green algae, and mitochondria, like Archeozoic bacteria, are caught and carry on their own replications within the larger cell.

Another theory is that of predation. Perhaps some early predaceous cell swallowed another cell, only to find that its prey remained viable within it. This model may well describe the earliest fusion of gametes, a union of cells in which both genetic complements continued to function. With this model, the egg can be visualized as a simple predator, consuming the sperm to initiate production of a new individual.

Lack of motility (the cell's ability to move itself across relatively large distances) in eggs must not be equated with lack of activity. Eggs are very active. After taking in the tiny sperm, they supply energy and genetic data for embryonic development, and may also repair chromosome damage in sperm-cell genes. In the time between fertilization and the first cleavage, enzymes in the eggs of certain strains of mice seem able to repair chemically induced mutations in sperm chromosomes.

Just after fertilization, the vitelline membrane (a transparent membrane around the egg) alters in most eggs in order to bind other sperms that try to penetrate. In mammals, follicle cells of the ovary, which surround the egg as it grows and after it moves out of the ovary at ovulation, will trap sperms to prevent further penetration after fertilization. Thus, the egg consumes, but it "knows" its limits and usually admits only the genetic material it can sustain.

In addition to their abilities to consume, nurture, and possibly repair sperms, eggs can produce the first stages of embryonic development without resorting to nuclear directives. Egg cytoplasm (the cell matter that is not nucleus) contains special mRNA (messenger RNA), a nucleic acid similar to DNA that makes up the chromosomes in the nucleus. Ordinarily these mRNAs lie dormant, but after fertilization they become the template for the first ten to twenty hours of embryonic life. It is possible that the mRNA codes also control later stages of embryo differentiation by determining which genes in the nucleus will be activated in the cells of different parts of the embryo.

All animal eggs also contain special DNA in the cytoplasm, in structures called mitochondria. Maternal mitochondrial DNA is inherited by every individual, male and female, only from the mother. The maternal DNA carries important proteins and maintains mitochondrial function, vital to energy production in the cells. Recently, Rebecca Cann and her colleagues have used mitochondrial DNA as an evolutionary clock to determine that the most likely ancestor of all of us was an African woman who lived between 140,000 and 290,000 years ago.

For a long time people have been trying to explain why females are often left "holding the baby," why they frequently produce relatively few offspring, which they tend well, while males may produce many offspring, which they may not tend at all. Keeping in mind that the exploited-female-versus-carefree-male view applies principally to birds and mammals, which comprise less than 2 percent of all animal species, we can look to eggs for the beginning of an explanation of female parental bondage.

Eggs are larger than sperms. Cows' eggs are about 20,000 times larger than bulls' sperms by volume. A human egg *could* house about 250,000 sperms, but it normally takes in only one. Egg volume is greater than sperm volume because eggs have yolk and much more cytoplasm than sperms.

Whether it develops outside or inside the female that produces it, an egg always provides nutrition (yolk, abundant in most eggs, meager in those of mammals) and cytoplasmic guidance for the developing embryo. In addition to the greater amount of cytoplasmic genetic material in eggs compared to sperms, there is also more *nuclear* genetic material in eggs of many species. This is because the sex-determining pair of chromosomes is XX in females and XY in males, meaning the chromosome pairs roughly form the shapes XX or XY. The little piece of DNA forming the lower right leg of the second X gives the XX female a "few" more genes than the XY male. (This does not happen among species with heterogametic, or XY, females, i.e., all moths, many fishes, newts, salamanders, frogs, snakes, and birds.) These genes are often the difference between health and severe disability, especially in a mammal that carries deleterious genes on one of its X chromosomes. (See chapter 6.)

Because, in her gamete, the female gives more than her half share to a new life, it has been said that the large egg is "parasitized" by the small sperm. As Richard Dawkins has put it,

> Even in humans, where the egg is microscopic, it is still many times larger than the sperm. . . . it is possible to interpret all the other differences between the sexes as stemming from this one basic difference. . . . eggs contribute far more in the way of food reserves: indeed sperms make no contribution at all. . . . Since each sperm is so tiny, a male can afford to make many millions of them every day. This means he is potentially able to beget a very large number of children in a very short period of time, using different females. This is only because each new embryo is endowed with adequate food by the mother in each case. This, therefore, places a limit on the number of children a female can have. Female exploitation begins here.

In reality, however, female exploitation can and usually does end here at the gametic level. In the vast majority of female animals no incubation, gestation, or aftercare is required. Most female fishes, marine invertebrates, and insects, for example, squander eggs with no more effort or care than males do sperms. They may even spawn first, leaving males to deal with fertilization and brood care. Females in certain species of insects, fishes, and reptiles dispense with males altogether, and virgin birth—the parthenogenetic development of eggs—occurs regularly.

Why, then, have higher vertebrates—certain reptiles, birds, and mammals—gone down the road toward supermothering? Why have the social insects taken a different path to arrive in almost the same place—that is, spectacular female parenting by sterile sisters rather than biological mothers? What change in eggs initiated these evolutionary journeys?

The answer seems to lie in the adjustment to life on land. Animals, whether vertebrate or invertebrate, that came to land had to protect their eggs from dessication and sharp temperature changes. To make their eggs sturdier, land vertebrates "tried" leathery shells, hard shells, earth nests, and twig nests, and finally internalized the nests, moistening, protecting, and feeding embryos within their own bodies. Progressively, there was a reduction in the number of young produced each season, as females prepared eggs for land or became gestators.

Perhaps it was a lack of understanding of the union of gametes and the process of gestation that historically made people see the extra efforts of gamete reception as exploitation of females rather than control by them. With only a superficial knowledge of female biology, a pregnant animal could be thought of as nothing more than a moving eggshell. Indeed, men have held that females are only the ovens in which the bread is baked, and the word *fornication*, coming from a Latin root meaning arched like an outdoor Mediterranean oven, extends the presumed female passivity in gestation to copulation.

It was believed that the only seeds for growth of a new offspring came from the male and that the female was merely the germinal ground for their maturation. Thomas Aquinas thought it was the father's sperm that "cooked" the menstrual blood of the mother into a new human being. At least in this culinary metaphor the input of some ingredient by the mother is acknowledged. Now we know that females supply larger, more directive gametes than males and, in addition, they often supply the anatomical and physiological equivalents of an oven and fuel for sustaining the fire of each new life.

Social insects solved the egg-shelter problem without having to sacrifice high productivity and without having to gestate. By using protective mansions—mounds and hives, rather than shells—which were durable and extendable, they could keep the number of eggs high. This meant that insects could combine a large number of progeny with prolonged care, while vertebrate females had to follow a few-eggs-well-tended strategy. In both cases, egg tending meant that females, as the source of these large, nurturant gametes, were most easily selected to hold, feed, teach, and control "the baby."

Whether this state of affairs is called female exploitation or female ascendancy depends very much on our point of view. If this view is formed by an extension of mammalian or human standards to other species, we, like many natural historians in the past, might expect that mothering is an exclusively female activity and that males automatically reject an extremely mothering role for themselves. But mammalian and human standards are not universal. For example, until the late nineteenth century, zoologists thought that female giant water bugs (Belostomainae) back-brooded eggs. Even when Florence Slater published the discovery that it is the male of these species that back-broods, it was not without the expressed conviction that the job was foisted upon him by the female and that he found it objectionable. Slater in 1899 and de la Torre Bueno shortly after suggested that activities ranging from stroking to violent shoving of the eggs on their backs were male attempts to be rid of a demeaning burden. However, Robert L. Smith revealed by experiment and thoughtful observation that stroking is a normal behavior, which cleans and oxygenates eggs to keep them fungus-free, and violent attempts to dislodge the egg pad are crisis behavior brought on by laboratory conditions. When brooding males are kept in jars of water without vegetation, they have no way to support themselves near the water's surface, where they can replenish their air supply. The heavy eggs weigh them down, and they drown unless they can kick off the egg pad.

So, is the mothering one an exploited being or just one that human societies have exploited? As I hope to show, while the genetic and social constraints that force certain animals to mother may make them vulnerable to exploitation, the complex of traits called mothering usually gives an individual extra control over its reproductive success and that of others. Through mothering, an individual may apply its endurance and intelligence to extend the existence of itself and others through time.

What I hope to explain in this book is how mothering evolved and came to be associated with female animals. We will see that mothering is so advantageous that selection for its component traits has strongly influenced the evolution of species, to the point whereby the disruption or loss of a mothering legacy may extinguish an individual, a species, or in the case of humans the female sex.

In order to clarify the taxonomic organization of this review, the following simple explanation of taxonomy, a science of classifying plants and animals, is supplied. Modern taxonomists have assembled organisms into a hierarchy of groups within groups, like the colored boxes within boxes of a child's nested toy. The kingdom corresponds to the largest box and contains the phylum, class, order, family, genus, and species, in descending scope of inclusiveness.

The species, then, is the most exclusive group, or taxon. It contains the most closely related organisms, those that generally mate only with each other and not with members of other species. The larger taxa are groupings of species based on anatomical and behavioral similarities, shared habitats, and major evolutionary acquisitions. For instance, all individuals in species of our subphylum, Vertebrata, have a bony or cartilaginous column housing the spinal cord.

There are five major classes of vertebrates—fishes, amphibians, reptiles, birds, and mammals, although the forty thousand or so species of fishes are often divided into three classes. Most members of vertebrate classes are male or female for life, but there are exceptions, including regularized patterns of transformation or reversal of sex. Most vertebrates reproduce sexually, but there are some that can reproduce by self-fertilization or parthenogenesis (development of an unfertilized egg). Most fish and amphibian females spawn in water, and reptiles lay eggs on land, but there are also species in these classes that are viviparous.

Classes are human categories, which, in nature, are composed of species that grow and evolve around each other, sometimes following parallel paths through time, sometimes surpassing each other in length and breadth of change. Fishes are the most numerous in terms of species; they are the oldest class, the one from which amphibians and possibly reptiles arose directly.

Thus, taxonomic hierarchy implies evolutionary pedigree. The smaller the taxon to which two species belong, the more closely they are related—that is, the more recently they should have shared a common ancestor in the past. (Of course, species may be wrongly categorized and their pedigree relationships therefore misunderstood.)

It is worth noting that modern taxonomy, which emphasizes the branching and organic relatedness between species, is just one of many invented by people. We believe this system reveals more about animal relationships than other systems, which may have classified animals by their sacred properties or zone of residence: sea, land, or air. But our system, like all previous ones, is based on a view of the world—in this case, organic change through genetic processes—that forces selective observation and oversimplification. These observations and simplifications fit into and reinforce the kind of order we imagine is natural to the world—that is, hierarchical order, the order of the nested toy, the barnyard hens, and the political pyramid. Sometimes the consistencies within animal groups that a neat hierarchical system would lead us to expect are absent. This is especially true of reproduction in a large taxon such as the class.

Nature does not restrict herself to man-made categories. The taxonomic scheme may be used to organize data about females in a general way, but the categories may never be considered absolute. Therefore, while the groupings of modern taxonomy are used here to present information about female animals, the structure is not seen as a natural hierarchy but as one imposed for the convenience of study.

Let us look at the general progression of sex-cell evolution, which is now thought to be from no gametes, to similar gametes, to two kinds of gametes. Today several all-female species of insects, fishes, and lizards have gone a step further and again rely on one kind of gamete only—the egg.

About one billion years ago, the first eggs were evolving in the taxon of one-celled plants and animals called the kingdom Protista. Furthermore, as fossil remains of marine algae from that time seem identical to modern green algae that produce distinct gametes, it is inferred that the fossil forms could also. Therefore, anisogamy—the production of eggs and sperms—is an ancient trait that developed against a background of asexual reproduction, which includes binary fission, or mitosis (though some reserve the term *mitosis* for body cells of multicellular organisms) and budding.

Asexual reproduction is the process that allows one amoeba to become two and that underlies growth in everything from microscopic cell colonies to complex plants and animals. During asexual reproduction the cell passes (usually) exact copies of its chromosomes to its daughter cell.

The geographical and historical scope of fissioning organisms was not inconsiderable. Through various forms of asexual reproduction, bacteria and algae have persisted for 2.5 billion years. In fact, blue-green algal colonies along the western coast of Shark Bay, Australia, have built giant monuments to the success of asexuality. These huge mushroom- and loaf-shaped stromatolites are formed as algae filaments trap shells and sand. Broad stromatolite fields, like those of Shark Bay, are unusual for modern seas, but they represent asexual forms that were widespread six hundred million years ago.

Why did sexual reproduction evolve at all, if asexual modes were so successful? Why, if genes are really selfish, in the sociobiological sense of behaving so as to put the most possible copies of themselves into the next generation, did they not resist sexual reproduction? After all, sexual reproduction requires the presence, cooperation, and simultaneous passage of genes from other organisms in order to achieve perpetuation. It would seem that truly selfish genes should try to get out of this dependent arrangement and reestablish asexual reproduction whenever possible. Perhaps the species in which asexual and sexual reproduction alternate through time or are simultaneously applied, as among honeybees, are examples of a certain degree of success in *regaining* asexuality. It is not surprising that these examples occur most frequently in the oldest classes of sexually reproducing organisms, such as insects, for the genes in some lines of organisms in these classes would have had the most time to fight the tide of sexual reproduction.

But why should the tide of sexuality have flowed so strongly that we and most of the vertebrates are still carried by it? The most likely answer is that although sexual reproduction originally occurred by chance, and most certainly not to meet any need of organisms or their genes, it created conditions that favored the survival of cells (and colonies of cells) that could produce low-chromosome-number gametes, capable of fusing with each other.

These first sex cells, or isogametes, all looked alike. They were produced by a new process called meiosis, which halved the chromosome number of the parent cell (leaving N, or the haploid, number of chromosomes). Fusion of two isogametes regained the complete set of chromosomes (called the 2N, or diploid number of chromosomes). As will be explained, the processes of meiosis and gamete fusion proved advantageous to the survival of the individuals in which they occurred and so were passed on.

Probably the most important chance advantage of sexual reproduction was that it increased genetic variability in offspring. Firstly, at the cellular level the process of meiosis enables chromosomes to cross over each other and exchange or reorder parts of their gene sequences. Then, at the organismic level, mating (that is, the fusion of gametes from two different genetic endowments) gives sexual reproduction its second degree of genetic mixing power. At the population level, sexual reproduction may involve the migration of groups, which further mixes and redistributes genes geographically.

The advantage of increased genetic variety is that it helps organisms cope with changing environments. In 1946, J. Lederberg and E. L. Tatum were the first to demonstrate this in the protosexual activities of the bacteria *Escherichia coli*. Although there are no gametes, two cells of different strains of the bacteria can come together, exchange genetic material, and produce a new strain, which, because of its new genetic constitution, can survive on a substrate that neither of its "parents" could have lived on. Yet, as G. C. Williams points out in *Adaptation and Natural Selection*, any advantages that may have been conferred by sex—genetic diversity, rapid adjustment to new conditions, and increased population size—were *effects* of sex and possibly reasons for its continuance as a trait in populations. Such advantages should never be designated as functions that sex evolved to serve.

Meiosis and fusion of gametes removed organisms from the realm of straight replication and genetic sameness. Except for occasional mutations, asexually reproducing organisms had been clones. Sexually reproducing organisms, though sharing a basic blueprint, could now become more individualistic. Their offspring were not identical to them, and, in this sense, gametic production gave the organic world *individual* mortality. It was through the struggle for survival implicit in this variety and "complete" death that the sexes and the species evolved.

Dying before reproducing means that a gene, cell, or organism has failed its fitness test. Sexual reproduction made reproducing, without dying in the process, more difficult. It entailed risks at every level: the possible incorrect division of chromosomes during meiosis, the efforts of courtship, and the dangers of mating and migrating. So why did it become the dominant mode of reproduction among animals?

It seems that although sexuality makes passing the fitness test more difficult, organisms that do pass are rewarded with a form of continued existence, with faster adaptability to changing conditions relative to asexual organisms, and sometimes with aggregation into societies that may amplify the adaptations of individual organisms. While sexual reproduction made survival dependent on contact and cooperation between at least two cells and usually two organisms, it was competition for perfection of such contact and cooperation that spurred rapid evolution, through the proliferation and rearrangement of genes. Thus the differentiation of the gametes and sexes gained momentum.

It may seem paradoxical that sexual reproduction preceded the strong differentiation of the sexes, which biologists refer to as sexual dimorphism. At first there were asexually reproducing organisms, then isogamous ones that reproduced sexually but employed only one sort of gamete. The margin of new genetic variability provided by isogamous mating set the stage for the gradual but striking morphological divergence of gametes into eggs and sperms. Sexually dimorphic species came much later.

Even now, females and males are sometimes not crisply defined, either to our eye or to the eyes of other members of the species. Male flatbugs in certain genera, such as *Afrocimex* and *Hesperoctenes*, do not seem to discriminate male from female, for they inseminate either. With the aid of a scimitarlike penis, sperms are deposited right through the carapaces of both sexes, and sometimes into the larvae as well.

Not only may sexual differentiation be visually and behaviorally indistinct, it may be gametically ambiguous. Thus there are hermaphrodites, with the reproductive organs of both sexes, in almost every class of invertebrates and vertebrates. Such organisms may fertilize themselves or each other, simultaneously or sequentially. For example, two blue female sea bass (*Serranus subligarius*) may mate and produce young in spite of the fact that they are both female. One of them becomes a male on the spot, changing from blue to a brilliant orange streaked with white. Both are hermaphrodites and can switch gender in a matter of minutes, serving each other alternately with a clutch of eggs or a stream of milt.

There are also scores of cases in which an individual of one sex slowly turns into its opposite and remains so for the rest of its life. This is called serial hermaphroditism—protogyny when a female gradually becomes a male, and protandry when a male gradually becomes a female. Serial hermaphroditism is the norm in several species of coral reef fishes, and, surprisingly, a mock form of protogyny exists as an anomaly in our own species.

In May 1979, Julianne Imperato-McGinley and her coworkers reported that four sons among ten children in a Caribbean family began life looking, behaving, and being treated like girls. While internally and genetically they were boys from birth, these children did not complete the process of external genital masculinization until puberty. At about age twelve their vaginas spontaneously closed and two testicles descended. The clitoris grew into a full-sized penis, and, from that point on, the boys matured and behaved as males. Later they were able to marry and have children.

On the island where these boys lived, there are twenty-two families with thirty-seven children having this syndrome. Cases of protogyny have been occurring there since 1930. The genealogies of all the affected families lead back to one common female ancestor in the mid-nineteenth century, who must have carried a mutant gene for the condition. Since an individual cannot manifest the "protogyny" unless he inherits the gene from both mother and father, several generations, during which the gene lay dormant, had to intervene before a male and female carrier married and produced the first "protogynic" hermaphrodite on the island.

In other species, complete or periodic absence of the male sex is a consistent variation. When this happens, females may reproduce parthenogenetically.

It is therefore no more accurate to think that all species have clearly defined sexes for life than it is to think that all eggs look like chicken eggs. The rule with sexual dimorphism, as with any biological character, is that its expression is determined through natural selection and may vary with the pressures within and around species members.

Although eggs from different species vary in size, shape, and yolk distribution and content, there are general characteristics that typify the eggs of each class. For instance, in insect eggs the yolk fills the whole cell, except for a rim of cytoplasm all around, and the nucleus stands at one end of the cell. Most other invertebrate eggs are about one-quarter yolk granules, distributed fairly uniformly throughout the cytoplasm.

Large yolk granules, called yolk platelets, mass at one end of vertebrate eggs, excluding those of mammals. Yolk makes up about half of the egg volume in amphibians and up to 90 percent of the volume in fish, reptilian, and avian eggs. The cytoplasm in the latter is stretched thin over the yolk, and the nucleus resides in the cytoplasmic layer. Mammalian eggs, like those of invertebrates, have a small amount of yolk, but their development, assisted by placental nourishment, resembles that of other vertebrate eggs.

In general, invertebrates, bony fishes, and amphibians have shell-less eggs, and since these eggs often contain too little yolk to support full development, the offspring must go through a larval stage intermediate between the embryo and the young adult forms. From reptiles on, the yolk supply or internal nourishment from the mother's body is sufficient to bring the egg through relatively full development, and the larval stage drops out. (In species of birds in which nestlings are totally dependent on parent[s] for food and protection, and in mammals, especially marsupials, in which newborns are "exterogestates," it might be thought that the young are so far from adults in appearance and activity that they qualify as larvae. But larvae are *self-feeding*, while the young of birds and mammals are not.)

Reptilian and avian eggs have shells that are formed in the oviducts (tubes from the ovaries to the uterus or cloacal opening). Shelled, fertilized eggs are deposited; the embryos therefore develop in the eggs but outside the mother's body. Species that reproduce in this way are called oviparous.

Except for the egg-laying platypus and the pouched marsupials, mammalian eggs and embryos are nourished entirely within the female body cavity, inside the uterus. These mammals are viviparous. Quite a few bony fishes, sharks, reptiles, insects, and arachnids, like the scorpion, also have internal gestation in either the ovary or oviduct, and in some cases in a uterus. Eggs that develop on their own yolk, while still inside the mother, are typical of the ovoviviparous sharks and snakes. Alternatively, the embryos of certain species form directly within the body cavity or uterine sac, taking nourishment from extensions of the gut or of the uterine wall, as in the viviparous scorpions and the placental mammals, respectively.

Why, with such a wide variety of methods of development, are all eggs larger than their sperm counterparts? One theory is that, given a certain range of size of gametes among the primeval sex cells, some would have succeeded in making a viable zygote (first cell of offspring formed from the union of the two parental gametes) because of their large size, and some would have succeeded because they were small but able to link up with a large gamete. The large gamete had the fitness advantage of a substantial cytoplasmic supply, and the little gamete had the advantage of motility. In addition to nurturing, which was further enhanced by the acquisition of yolk, the large gametes probably also contained more genetic instructions to guide the development of the zygote. This is still true of eggs today. These specialist cells did better than intermediate-sized cells by dividing the nurturing and motility functions. A gamete laden with yolk that also tried to be mobile would have required more fuel than a streamlined, yolkless one. And if the whole purpose of movement was to meet and fuse with another gamete, the heavier gamete would have had fewer opportunities. Either it would have been spending time gathering the extra fuel it needed, thereby losing chances to meet and join with another gamete, or it would have missed gathering extra fuel and been rendered less mobile. Thus, over a period of a thousand million years, natural selection favored eggs and sperms that diverged sharply in size, shape, and behavior from each other.

Not only do eggs have a history of phylogenetic development, having gradually differentiated in form and function from isogametes and from each other according to species, they also have an ontogenetic history of development within the female organism.

Mature eggs are fundamentally different from all cells of the body because they may come to have half the number of chromosomes that body cells have. They reach this state through the process of egg maturation, or oogenesis, from precursor cells (oogonia) to oocytes to mature eggs. The speed of oogenic metamorphosis is geared to the life span of each species. In minute insects, the eggs are small, rapidly produced, and short-lived. In human beings, an egg can wait more than forty years before it completes oogenesis.

Meiosis is the process through which the egg chromosomes duplicate, recombine, and twice divide, while the maturing gamete is changing its size and shape, usually enlarging with fatty food molecules of yolk. Fertilization is almost always needed to trigger the completion of meiosis in eggs, bringing their chromosome number down from the diploid or 2N number (for example, forty-six in human body cells) to the haploid or N number (for example, twenty-three in human egg cells).

Unfertilized *human* eggs do not complete meiosis; most oocytes just die. For example, the oogonia in the ovaries of ninety-day-old human embryos become primary oocytes when they enter the first phase of meiosis. Then they halt. The human female is born with about four to five hundred thousand primary oocytes in her ovaries, although estimates range as high as two million. In any case, hundreds of thousands, perhaps millions, of oocytes will already have degenerated during her gestation.

From about thirteen to fifty years after birth, approximately forty oocytes per month complete the first meiotic division, after which usually just one of these is ovulated (i.e., passes through the ovarian wall). At about this time, the first meiotic division is completed, and the oocyte still contains forty-six chromosomes, like all human body cells. During its apparent suspended animation, the oocyte has been receiving contributions to its cytoplasm from surrounding cells and, after the first meiotic division, from its own nucleus. Like some super silicon chip, the maturing egg comes to be etched with extra information, stored in proteins, ribosomes, mitochondria, and DNA.

The result, then, of the first meiotic division, at around the time of ovulation, is a small cell, called a polar body, that degenerates and a secondary oocyte that is moved into the fallopian tube, where it may be fertilized and undergo the second division of meiosis. The completion of the egg's meiosis, triggered by the entry of a sperm, expels another polar body and leaves the egg nucleus with only twenty-three chromosomes. This unites with the sperm nucleus, which also has only twenty-three chromosomes.

What potent, youth-retaining, forces must surround the few primary oocytes that wait in the ovaries from infancy until ovulation! Only about forty to four hundred eggs are ovulated in a woman's lifetime, depending on the number of pregnancies, lactation, and type of contraceptive used; even fewer eggs are fertilized and complete meiosis. In contrast, as Martin Daly and Margo Wilson point out, a man produces about as many sperms every half-second as the woman ovulates eggs in her entire life.

Male and female mammalian gametes differ also in length of time they remain viable. While oocytes can lie dormant in the ovaries for many years, they are ripe (fertilizable) for only about twelve hours. Sperms, on the other hand, do not wait in the gonads; they are constantly produced to order, but they often remain viable (able to fertilize) in the male reproductive tract for long periods. Early this century, an embryologist found spermatozoa alive three days after the execution of a prisoner from whom they were obtained. While vitality and motility may not ensure the human sperm's ability to fertilize, other organisms do retain sperm viability for long periods. In ferrets, sperms are viable for 126 hours, in horses even longer, while it is reported in Lamming and Amoroso's *Reproduction in the Female Mammal* that sperms of certain bats can wait inside the *female's* reproductive tract up to five months before fertilizing eggs.

We still do not know exactly why the egg and sperm went down separate evolutionary paths or how meiotic gametogenesis came about. It is clear, however, that the phylogeny and ontogeny of eggs dictate female existence, and that when we manipulate the egg by freezing, enucleating, artificially fertilizing, or shutting off its normal cyclic production with contraceptives, we touch the source and possibly change the course of evolution.

As far as we know today, organic evolution is the unifying theme in the tale of the female animal. It is the dynamic process that produced everything from the submicroscopic amino acid arrangements that build the protein components of gametes to the macro arrangements of sexual complementarity and antagonism.

Time, variety of traits, and their differential perpetuation are the key elements in the theory of organic evolution. According to this theory, differentiation of species, variability within and among them, and maintenance of population numbers that can be supported by the environment are all beads held together by the single explanatory thread of adaptation through natural selection. Just as human selective breeding and operant conditioning can shape the structures and behaviors of other animals, so natural selection shaped the form and activity of all species. However, while human breeders and trainers proceed consciously, natural selection, so far as we know, proceeds mindlessly through the agencies of death and inviability (failure to reproduce for physical or social reasons).

Traits of individuals that survive and produce the greatest number of viable young will be passed on more often than those of individuals that survive and reproduce less often. Thus, structural and behavioral traits are selected or eliminated in proportion to the reproductive success of individual organisms. Such success is called biological fitness or, simply, fitness. An organism's fitness is measured by its ability to stay alive, reproduce, and sometimes to support its offspring and close kin, until they in turn reproduce.

In other words, an organism's fitness may be measured by its success in perpetuating its own traits (and hence its own genes and sometimes its own culture). Traits that assist individuals in their pursuit of biological fitness, or at least do not unduly interfere with this pursuit, will be passed on. The same is true of the gene(s) that code for these traits. They stay in the population.

Of course, there are arbitrary events that can wipe out genes, traits, organisms, and populations, but such bad luck is necessarily subsumed in the process of organic evolution. There are forces that can wipe out excellent adaptations, and whatever organic forms remain may continue to evolve.

Evolution could be compared to a business. There is the basic capital resource (genes), which, through proper management (individual and group structure and behavior), may expand (produce copies). However the business runs (with whatever degree of adaptation its form and function allow), it is always open to windfall or ruin for reasons beyond its control. The biological counterpart of windfall is called radiation— the proliferation of individuals and sometimes of species. The biological counterpart of ruin is, of course, extinction.

So, according to the modern theory of evolution, traits and genes that work toward the survival and reproduction of their carriers are naturally selected; they find themselves inside new carriers. This means that *any* genes or traits that work stay, even if they create organisms that are ugly, cruel, or immoral by our standards. The female mantis cannibalizes her mate; the mite *Pyemotis* is raped by her brother the moment she is born; the hornbill helps her mate imprison her in the hollow of a tree trunk for the period of incubation; and Indian langur babies may be killed and their mothers left with no better survival option than to submit to the murdering male.

In the case of our species, culture adds another dimension to natural selection. The tests placed upon people by society may be as critical to their fitness as tests that arise from the physical environment and biological heritage. The same criterion of fitness may be applied to a cultural trait as to a biological one—if it helps its bearer to survive and reproduce, it persists. The selective pressures of culture merge with those of the internal and external environments of human beings. While we can clearly distinguish a cultural injunction behind the wide-

spread Afro-Arab custom of infibulation (in which surgery creates a
smooth, sealed, and featureless area in place of the genitalia of girls
and women), it is no longer clear what combination of social and
biological pressures may have selected for a heritable feature like the
steatopygic (huge, fat-storing) buttocks of the Hottentot and Kalahari
Bushwomen of southern Africa.

The reader may well wonder how removal of the external reproductive organs of millions of women could help them survive and
reproduce. In the complete form of infibulation, only a tiny opening
for urine and menses is left, making intercourse, not to mention childbirth, a near impossibility. Repeated incisions and suturings are necessary, and death and disability due to shock and infection are common.
Saying that men in certain societies would shun the uninfibulated
woman, leaving her effectively sterile and, so, biologically unfit, does
not explain the initial imposition of this apparent barrier to female
fitness.

Fully infibulated women wear a chastity belt made of their own
flesh. The ultimate explanation for their nearly complete sexual re-
nunciation is probably to ensure a high degree of paternity certainty.
A male's investment in his genuine offspring can favorably affect not
only his fitness and theirs but that of the mother also. Another, not
incompatible, ultimate explanation is that human societies can judge
that their survival depends on population limitation. Infibulation and
female infanticide are dramatic forms of such limitation. Barriers to
male fitness are created less often because the female is the rate limiter
in population growth.

The more an individual woman's survival depends on the survival
of her group and her retention of a place within it, the more easily
she will submit to harsh cultural pressure upon her fitness. She, like
each of us in our particular cultural context, relies on proximate explanations to help her believe that what happens to her, what she in
fact wants to have happen to her, is necessary. In the case of infibulation, such reasons may include pleasing parents by showing proper
modesty; attractiveness to prospective husbands; and pride in surviving a rite of passage. In contrast, women who can survive and reproduce
without close community ties or an extended family find it difficult
to understand the acceptance of cruel options by women in other
societies.

Although it is impossible to set down with absolute authority how
organic evolution through natural selection defined the stages of female

development, from egg to fully differentiated female, the following is one plausible phylogenetic sequence.

At first, all animal life was unicellular and reproduced asexually by splitting into two identical cells. Then, certain cells became able to join and mix their genetic material; among these were the isogametes. Eventually, isogametes differentiated in form and function to become distinct gametes which, however, were still derived from identical precursor cells. Later, the egg developed from a special precursor cell called the oogonium, which was produced in a specialized part of the organism called the gonad or ovary.

In multicelled plants and animals, the gonads evolved the ability to secrete hormones. These influenced the growth and reproductive viability of the entire organism through their chemical impact on other tissues. Hormones literally shaped the organism and coordinated reproductive activity with internal and external cues. Female and male matured in response to the different hormone ratios within them. In this particular evolutionary view, the development of femaleness can be seen as a byproduct of the evolving abilities and requirements of the massive egg.

At this point some basic definitions of femaleness may be cautiously proffered. At the cellular level, a female is usually distinguished by something in her chromosome makeup, often a pair of X chromosomes. The gametes in her ovaries are further distinguished by development-initiating cytoplasm, plus the energy-loaded nutritive component called yolk.

At an organismic level, the female assumes many roles according to her age and species, but the one that often becomes ascendant is centered on her ability to produce eggs and to guard and nurture young. In fact, her parenting seems to be both a cause and an effect in the progressive development of a complex nervous system, advanced forms of communication, and sociality.

At the level of population, female-young interactions may be lifted out of context and used by all members of the species, serving as cohesive gestures that bind individuals into functioning groups. Thus, the female is the builder of populations, both numerically and socially. On the one hand, the number of females limits population size, and on the other, the amount and type of female parenting helps to structure a population.

It is the behavior of females toward their young that is often imitated and carried by the offspring into adult life. Interactions in which the female feeds, protects, warms, comforts, and restricts the movements of the young are important to the creation of groups, first of which is the nuclear family: a female and her young. Beyond family groups there are larger aggregations (the shoal, the troop, the hive, etc.), but it is only the human species, with its growing comprehension of the link between female-tending-young behaviors and the development of communication and rapport between members of society, that can begin to aggregate these smaller groups—from family to nation-state—into units approaching the species level.

While we can understand what a female animal is at each of these levels, definitions extended to human beings are always modifiable, even those that appear most fundamental: for example, females are the ones that produce the costly eggs, that bond with and care for the infant. People tend to think that biologically based sex differences are unchangeable facts of life. But faith in the immutability of organisms is as wrongly placed as faith in the immutability of the heavens before Galileo's observations of variable sunspots. Who would have imagined that it would be possible for a female to give birth to an offspring that was genetically unrelated to her? But this is exactly what has happened, in our species and others, with in vitro fertilization and surrogate pregnancy. In *human* biology especially, the "facts" are not stable: culture can alter appearances and behaviors vastly more rapidly than organic evolution. We tend also to view the type of sex differentiation found in our species as standard for other species. This is bound to be misleading, since we (or forms like us) have existed for only about three million years, while certain fish lineages have existed more than a hundred times longer.

The trend toward greater mothering, from fish to mammal, fostered and was fostered by three other evolutionary trends: the elaboration of the nervous system and of the endocrine-exocrine glands, and the development of two highly differentiated sexes. The first of these three trends provided the basis for greater sensory acuity, alertness, and novel behavior. The second trend, toward a network of internal and external secretions, enhanced the first. It amplified nervous system activity within and between organisms, thus making possible elaborate communication and communities.

Plaited together, like Rapunzel's long braid, these trends must be unwound and examined to tell the story of female origin and heritage. Like Rapunzel, our species has been cloistered from the rest of the animal kingdom in a tower of imagined superiority, and the female of the species has been surrounded by a tangled forest of theory. Ideas about the evolution of the sexes are still obscured by cultural over-growth, and, so, all facts and theories presented here are offered with the strong sense that they must be taken in the spirit of a tale that varies with each retelling.

2 | A SEA OF FEMALES

The story of females began in the sea, in the ancient kingdom Monera, where bacteria and colonial algae reigned together. While algae turned the world on to photosynthesis, bacteria specialized in the equally important task of decomposition, escorting organic matter to the dark world of decay.

Today bacteria live virtually everywhere: 35,000 feet under the ocean's surface, 90,000 feet up in the air, in the soil, in food, water, on clothing, skin, teeth, and in the intestine. Some may cause disease, but others provide soil with the nitrogen essential for plant growth. Bacteria have illuminated our understanding of the genetic code, and it is among them that we can study the origins of sex. In their various modes of genetic exchange, bacteria may reveal the activities that disposed (preadapted) early cells toward sexual reproduction.

Normally, when a bacterial cell replicates, its chromosome complement (that is, its ring of DNA) doubles. The duplicated chromosomal material is pinched off with the new cell produced. Sometimes, when bacteria grow on a rich substrate, their chromosomes start duplicating more rapidly than new daughter cells get pinched off. In this situation, cells can end up with multiple chromosome complements.

Under suitable conditions, *E. coli*, a bacterium that lives in the human intestine, will multiply in an exponential way. This means that every cell may divide every twenty minutes and produce a daughter cell that contains from two to four identical ring-shaped chromosomes. If nutrients and oxygen are not depleted, one bacterium can produce 250,000 new ones in six hours.

This bacterial fissioning is not exactly like mitotic replication in plant and animal cells, because bacteria have no real nuclei in which to form the spindle apparatus where duplicated chromosomes line up and are drawn to opposite poles of the cell. Bacterial ring chromosomes simply congregate in one area of the cell, attach to its wall, and get pinched off into separate cells. While nucleated plant and animal cells can regulate their divisions, synchronizing chromosome replication and cell division so that each daughter cell receives the same number of chromosomes, bacteria cannot. Their divisions and chromosome number vary with external conditions. Occasionally the gametes of vertebrates can also end up with extra sets of chromosomes, a fact that may have had a profound effect upon vertebrate evolution (see chapter 4).

In a process distinct from binary fission, bacterial cells sometimes mix part of their chromosomal material; this happens especially in harsh environments. Instead of gametes joining to form a zygote, as in sexual plants and animals, two cells of different strains of bacteria may combine some of their genes without forming a separate organism. This protosexual process, called conjugation, permits bacterial strains that would not have survived on a minimal medium to form hybrids that can. The rare and adaptive process of bacterial conjugation entails the formation of a tube of cytoplasm between two cells. Through this tube the donor cell transfers part or all of its ring chromosome to the recipient cell, where enzymes "snip open" its ring chromosome to enable the new piece to be added.

Conjugation is considered to be somewhat analogous to sexual reproduction because, as in zygote formation, it provides new genetic combinations that may help organisms cope with difficult or changing environments. The analogy is extended to the labeling of the donor and recipient cells as male and female, respectively. In keeping with the tradition that designates the male as the one with something extra and the female as the one with something missing, a bacterium that has the fertility factor (F+) which allows it to form a tube is called male, and a bacterium that lacks the factor (F−) is female. While this is a convention applied to everything from bacterial conjugants to electric plugs and outlets, it is not a law of nature. Sometimes either sex may be lacking a quality or ability that the other has. Bacterial "females" lack a fertility factor, just as human males lack some genetic material when compared to human females.

The tradition of designating the female as "lacking" is widespread and misleading. Even Aristotle called honeybee queens kings; queen bees did not lack great size or attention from other members of the hive, so, of course, they were thought to be male. In most natural histories, males are assumed to be the primary members of a species and females their appendages for reproduction. Simone de Beauvoir discussed this problem of the female as "other" in *The Second Sex* (1949), and Antoinette Brown Blackwell stated in 1875 (!) that "The older physiologists . . . interpreted facts by the accepted theory that the male is the representative type of the species—the female a modification preordained in the interest of reproduction and in that interest only or chiefly." Since this view has not changed, I have decided to discuss species with reference to the female. Therefore, when you read "frogs" think "female frogs." See the last sentence of the second paragraph on page 69 for this example of my reversed convention. I am not asking the reader to "think female" out of a desire to get even with previous writers who took the male as standard, but because male-as-standard-for-the-species natural history has made people think that a female is usually similar to the male of the species in her environment, diet, behavior, etc., except in the case of reproduction. But this is often untrue. Females are not just males with different gametes. Femaleness may arise from the egg, but it does not cease with the egg. Females often use different parts of the environment in different ways from males for survival, and females may show behaviors with respect to other members of their species and other species that are deeply divergent from those of males. Hopefully, the facts and reflections in this book and their presentation in female-first prose will go some way toward correcting the mistaken assumptions of male-as-standard natural history. But I also hope that readers and I will not perpetuate the converse error by assuming that because females are being focused upon, males are subsumed in the description or secondary in any sense. Revenge is not the brief, just rectification.

Traditions aside, bacterial cells are no more male or female than electric plugs and sockets. Although they differ in their chromosome makeup and behavior during conjugation, bacterial cells are not stable in their identities as donor and recipient. If the F+ factor is passed through the tube to the female, she instantly becomes male by definition. The sex identifier has been transferred.

The sex of a multicellular animal like a fish, amphibian, bird, or mammal can sometimes change. Hormones and stimuli such as heat, light, pressure, infection, or the absence of more dominant species members may be responsible. But, so far, no one has ever shown sex to be genetically transferrable in metazoa (multicelled animals), as it is in bacteria.

In addition to conjugation, bacteria may change their genetic makeup by means of lysogeny and transduction. These processes require the intercession of viruses and are worth looking at because they show that genetic communication between cells is not limited to the fusion of gametes; it may even occur between cells of vastly different species.

A virus is a tiny piece of DNA stored in a protein capsule. Certain viruses called bacteriophages can attach themselves to the outer surface of a bacterium and release enzymes that "drill" a hole in the cell wall. The viral DNA can then enter and replicate itself repeatedly until it ruptures, or lyses, the cell. If the new viruses take with them a fragment of the host chromosome, they may infect other bacteria and transduce them. This means that the new host exhibits new properties due to the extra genetic material forced upon it by the virus.

It is probable that transduction through infection played some part in the evolution of the gametes, as it is just another means, beside mutation, recombination, and irregular divisions of the chromosomes during meiosis, by which the genetic makeup of the gamete may be altered. As we will see, certain bacterial, viral, or fungal infections may cause change of sex (usually from female to male) or alter the sex ratio at birth. Examples of this potentially important evolutionary action are noted for species of insects, fishes, and birds in chapters 2, 3, and 5, respectively.

The sea is the earth's constant womb. It gestates the embryos of more than two hundred thousand species, thus performing a function that relatively few marine females can accomplish in their own bodies.

Gametes exposed to changes in current and temperature and to predation are produced in huge numbers. The oyster may lay from five hundred thousand to five hundred million eggs. These must be fertilized by chance meeting with sperms in surrounding waters, where the majority of chanceling zygotes are eaten, chilled, or dehydrated if washed ashore. Females that produce millions of eggs in order that just a few may survive are called r-strategists, r standing for the rate of increase of population size, and it is this rate that r-strategists try to maximize. Females that use this strategy make a small parental investment.

In many cases the option of producing myriad eggs is not available, and an aquatic female must employ a different strategy. Eggs that are fertilized externally may be held on the body surface or in the mouth or gills until they hatch. The obstetrical catfish carries her embryos embedded in her back. In other species of catfishes, the male mouth-broods the embryos and may even permit the hatchlings to return there for refuge. The male Brazilian catfish lipbroods his young in an enlarged lower lip. While it is often the male fish that builds and guards a nest or carries embryos in mouth or gill chambers, it is almost exclusively the female that holds the embryos when they develop inside the body proper. The great exceptions to this rule are the seahorses, seadragons, and pipefishes, in which males are impregnated. They are discussed in chapter 3 together with other gestating fishes, including sharks, rays, and the live-bearing bony fishes such as guppies and surfperches.

In contrast to r-strategists, females that are internally fertilized usually produce fewer embryos but gestate or tend them assiduously. These females are trying to maximize K, the carrying capacity of their habitat, by altering their body or environment to sustain and protect the developing young. For example, the K-strategist octopus receives a sperm packet from the outstretched arm of her mate. Fertilized internally by this inserted packet, the eggs are then deposited in a sheltered place. The embryos within them are aerated and guarded by the mother as they mature in seawater.

Other reproductive strategies found in the sea include serial sexuality (as described for the sea bass in chapter 1), hermaphroditism, and parthenogenesis. Many marine invertebrates are hermaphrodites, capable of producing both female and male gametes. They may fertilize themselves or each other. The shell-less snail called the sea hare (species of *Aplysia*) can be fertilized while fertilizing its partner. Long chains of sea hares thus engaged can later release strands of millions of fertilized eggs. A count of eggs clustered inside capsules of one specimen showed forty-one thousand eggs were deposited *per minute*.

A type of parthenogenesis called gynogenesis, which produces only females, is the strategy followed by the fish species known as Amazon molly (*Poecilia formosa*). Like the mythological Amazons, these fishes form an all-female community and produce only female offspring. The first Amazon molly was probably formed from a diploid (2N) egg (one that never completed meiosis) and a haploid (N) sperm. All the cells, including the eggs, of this fish were therefore triploid (3N).

The triploid eggs are amazing. They can be triggered by a sperm from a closely related species (*P. latipinna*), but they need not incorporate the sperm's genes in order to develop into young. In other words, Amazon mollies have sex in order to reproduce asexually! This tactic ensures production of offspring whose genetic variability is small.

Although parthenogenesis is extremely rare as a vertebrate mode of reproduction (regularly present only in certain fishes, salamanders, and lizards), it points out a distinction between the sexes that is obvious but profound. In sexually reproducing species, no new life develops without an egg. No sperm that we know of has ever been able to create a new life without an egg. The closest thing to male parthenogenesis occurred in an experimental manipulation of newt eggs, in which a fragment of the egg containing a sperm nucleus but no egg nucleus was separated from the rest of the egg, just after fertilization. At least one specimen developed from this doctored sperm and survived to maturity. However, an egg was still necessary for its formation.

Even a hydroid (species of *Obelia*), which is an animal that looks like seaweed and spends its life anchored to a rock, shell, or piece of wood, has eggs. During the asexual phase in its life cycle, the hydroid sprouts polyps. Buds break off these polyps and grow into tendrilly female or male medusa jellyfish, the free-swimming, sexual components of the hydroid. These release eggs and sperms into the water where they unite and form a ciliated larva, which swims to a new anchor point and begins the branching "seaweed" stage again.

Another marine invertebrate, the annelid worm (*Eunice viridis*), also drops "buds," which in this case are really the sexual organs of the worms. Every autumn, off the coasts of Samoa and Fiji, the buds of mature worms split off and rise to the water's surface. While Samoans come out to harvest these gyrating delicacies, the eggs and sperms, which the buds have released in the water, unite to form new worms.

A more familiar invertebrate, the octopus (e.g., *Octopus briareus*), also has two distinct sexes. Although it would be difficult for an untrained eye to distinguish the female from the male, she is behaviorally well differentiated from him throughout life. Soon after the octopus blushingly (they show emotion by changing color) accepts a packet of sperm from a male, she jets off to find a suitable rock shelter for her eggs. The sperm package in her mantle can remain unopened for days or months, until she finds conditions that will support embryos. Then she allows the eggs to be fertilized internally and glues them to the nest site as they emerge. Guarding, oxygenating, and cleaning the eggs by suction, so that they are not smothered by parasitic fungi, exhausts the female. She eats nothing and will not leave her brood for up to three months.

When the young hatch, she blows them away from the nest. Only one or two out of a possible brood of two hundred thousand may survive. The octopus is a K-strategist in spite of her relatively large number of fertilized eggs. Her great parental commitment to the brood was illustrated nicely by a sequence in the observation tank of marine biologist G. L. Voss. While trying to remove octopus eggs from a nest, Voss saw the guarding mother change color. She pushed his hand away with two of her arms, and when he hesitated, wondering how to approach the eggs while avoiding her poisonous bite, the octopus broke her mature egg capsules with a sharp poke of one of her "elbows." About 120 little octopuses sped away in a cloud of their mother's ink and were thus saved by her decision.

It may seem that worms, oysters, snails, and octopuses are too far removed in habit and habitat to be relevant to our own identity and role problems. But even this small sample from the marine invertebrates emphasizes that sexual flexibility goes far beyond our concept of physical gender identity and gender role.

The higher invertebrates, like the octopus, begin to show the trend toward more intense mothering coupled with greater intelligence. Whether or not selection for traits that permit good mothering provides the background for elaboration of intelligence remains to be shown conclusively. The link between excellent parenting and complex, purposive behavior seems strikingly clear in the behavior of some of the first females to live on land—the insects.

While life continued to evolve in the sea, what was to become the largest, most diverse class of the animal kingdom evolved on land. Long before any other animal life had approached the challenges of survival on dry land, wingless insects explored the forests of the Devonian period, some four hundred million years ago. Since then, the class Insecta has come to express a vast array of female form and behavior in its nearly one million species. Genetic intercession of bacterial and protozoan parasites and symbionts plus the enormous length of time and number of environments covered by insect evolution have produced a range of adaptations next to which human inventiveness, industry, strength, and cooperation pale.

Within the basic insect plan there are a few fundamental adaptations that necessarily influence the behavior of almost all females in the class. As an adaptation to living without surrounding water for support, insects evolved an external skeleton of a rigid material called chitin. This material protects against injury and loss of water in addition to providing support, but it also means that insect growth must occur in stages, separated by moults of the chitinous exoskeleton. Higher insects of both sexes must go through three stages—larva, pupa, imago—which correspond roughly to embryo, juvenile, and adult. The worm-like and voracious larval stage is linked to the winged, sexually active imago by the deceptively dormant pupa. Sometimes female, and more rarely male, adult insects will feed and protect offspring through the first two stages.

In order for an insect to move while wearing its exoskeletal armor it is divided into parts. The underlying nervous structure is also segmented. In a small animal, such a system can operate efficiently with only a few large fibers. While the nervous system of an insect is simple compared to that of a vertebrate, some insects have the capacity for full-scale mothering, including building brood chambers, hunting for food to supply larvae, mouth-to-mouth feeding, and attacking would-be predators.

Because the insect nervous system is made up of small neural fibers, it carries less detailed information but permits very rapid transmission of messages and consequent rapid movement. Each segment of an insect has its own local nervous control so that rapid, coordinated movement of some parts can often occur, even if another part is missing. For instance, during intercourse, the praying mantis always relieves her mate of his head, yet he proceeds undeterred to copulate even more vigorously. Likewise, a headless fly can groom itself and continue to live until its internal food stores are exhausted. Its bodiless head can even eat for a short time after separation. The survival advantage of this is unclear, but certainly it would be adaptive if a female, minus her head, could still participate in one last reproduction. This has been found to be the case for some insects like the silkworm, whose isolated abdomens may continue to lay eggs efficiently.

Neural economy and segmentation endow insects with these astounding properties. Their automaticity and often very short generations make them seem a frightening horde of personality-less existence. As economically and epidemiologically important as insects are, their relentlessness has forced our threatened species to cover them with a security blanket of anthropomorphic interpretation.

Everything we have done, insects have done better, or at least first. Aerial flight, solar navigation, elaborate community architecture, and farming were mastered by their species more than one hundred million years before our primitive reptilian ancestor laid its first leathery egg on land. Even with simple nervous systems, insects have been able to get a lot of highly specialized work done. Certain species have professionalized some of their members; bees, ants, and wasps have baby-sitters, construction engineers, and warriors. Some insects use tools, keep pets, and entertain houseguests, follow each other on pheromonal food trails, and beguile each other with subtle perfumes.

Because of the diversity of the class, general statements about female insects are not easy to make; it may be true, however, that this most successful of classes is dominated by females. From the ferocious mating mantis to the altruistic spinster honeybee, insects of every disposition challenge our preconceptions about sexual roles and ratios.

One of the most difficult things to explain about insects is why several important species produce mostly or only females. Throughout the sexually reproducing animal world, a female:male ratio of approximately 1:1 prevails. This balance is naturally selected, in species where both sexes are diploid (have 2N chromosomes in all their cells except gametes) and both gametes are haploid (have N chromosomes), in the following way: When either sex becomes less numerous than the other, natural selection will favor its proliferation simply because the scarcity of that sex ensures that its average member will have more offspring, and hence pass on its sex more often than the numerically superior sex. As the scarce sex proliferates and evens out the ratio, its differential reproductive advantage disappears.

But an insect sex ratio can be maintained indefinitely with females outnumbering males by several thousand to one. How can they defy the natural selective cycle governing sex ratio just described? The answer lies in modification of the sexual reproductive process, through mutation or infection, which either introduces parthenogenesis or selectively kills males. Most often, the capacity of certain insect species to use both parthenogenetic and sexual reproduction is their source of female numerical ascendancy.

Insects often live in long-lasting relationships with bacterial and protozoan parasites or symbionts (mutual assistants). These relationships may change the functioning of the genetic material of the host or partner species and shift its sex ratio toward females. For instance, certain strains of the sexually reproducing fly *Drosophila* can lose their ability to produce males if the blood and the egg cytoplasm are infected with spirochete bacteria. These kill almost all male embryos, but a few may be born, sparing the strain from extinction.

Sometimes, in spite of the exclusive production of female progeny, the ability to produce males lies dormant in the genome (chromosome makeup). Some parasitic wasps, for example, reproduce parthenogenetically; the eggs do not undergo meiosis, so there is no need to unite egg with sperm. No males are born unless the eggs are exposed to X-rays, in which case a perfectly formed male may be among the offspring. He is not, however, reproductively viable, and like a eunuch in a harem he lives out his life as one of the girls and is not inclined to be sexually active with them or they with him.

Among honeybees (*Apis mellifera*), the sex ratio favoring females results from the mixture of parthenogenetic and sexual reproduction. The queen can yield eggs that either develop parthenogenetically into haploid males (drones) or that develop after fertilization into diploid females (workers). Because the queen can store sperms in an internal chamber, called a spermatheca, she is reproductively self-reliant after a single mating. Males and mating are not needed for the maintenance of the hive.

(Perhaps an enterprising reproductive biologist/engineer will recognize the value of developing a long-term sperm storage unit for women. Such a visionary would change the life-style of her species as much or more than the developers of the pill. Sperm storage would place more control over the time of fertilization and the choice of father in the hands of women.)

The incredible social order that may develop when females control fertilization and the sex ratio of offspring is reviewed below for the order Hymenoptera—social bees, wasps, and ants. The avid work and paradoxical altruism of females in a haplodiploid system, with sperm storage and contraception governed by one central figure, the queen, is exemplified by the honeybee colony.

The bulk of hive citizenry are female workers, who are effectively sterilized by a substance secreted by the queen. The workers' main job is to suck nectar, drop by drop, through their strawlike proboscis (nose). Taking a thousand to fifteen hundred sips from as many clover flowers to fill their tiny nectar stomachs, they may release a valve to permit some nectar to pass into their gut, when hungry, but they bring the bulk of the collection to the community stores.

That honeybees can deposit two pounds of honey on a good summer's day in spite of the fact that it takes them sixty refills of the nectar stomach to collect a thimbleful of honey testifies to their industry and to their enormous numbers. A queen lays an egg a minute (about fifteen hundred per day) all spring and summer. One thousand or more workers emerge daily during summer, and just as many old workers die.

Although a queen may live four or five years, workers live only months. In their brief life span they not only gather honey but clean and feed larvae and maintain the best brood-cell temperature of 95°F by watering and fanning to cool or by huddling together and merging their furry coats to warm the chambers.

The queen determines the sex of new bees. If she releases a sperm from her spermatheca to fertilize one of her eggs, a female worker or new queen will develop, depending on the size of its brood-cell and what it is fed as a larva. If the queen releases an unfertilized egg, a male drone will develop.

The workers determine the sex ratio. By building different numbers of different-sized cells—large ones for future queens and drones, small ones for future workers—and by feeding the embryos different diets, they control the proportion of workers and queens to drones.

Embryos that will become queens must be fed the protein-rich and B-vitamin-rich royal jelly, which workers secrete from their head glands at certain times of the year. Worker and drone embryos do not receive royal jelly. Although drones are particularly pampered by workers, who feed them honey even after they are hatched, they remain small brained and sluggish. They live for the nuptial flight, during which they compete with each other to mate with a virgin queen.

The future queen can accept only one drone. After he gives her his sperms, his penis breaks off inside her, plugging sperms in and keeping other drones out. The drone that was lucky enough to mate then bleeds to death.

At the height of summer, when a "pregnant" queen has taken some workers with her to establish a new nest, workers start to build cells and brood larvae. They will also kill any drones that try to enter the colony.

A combination of pheromones (secreted chemicals that control the behavior of other members of the species) and agitated dancing serves to organize all this activity. The queen secretes an organic acid that is both an attractant to drones during the nuptial flight and a birth control agent for workers. Although the ovarian function of workers is suppressed by this substance, one may occasionally lay an unfertilized egg that develops into a drone. This may mean either that the worker is so distant from the queen that she has not received the substance in sufficient quantity or that one of the nurses accidentally dosed her cell with a bit of royal jelly when she was an embryo.

The building, cleaning, feeding, temperature controlling, and guarding that are part of a worker bee's repertoire are not focused on her own or her offsprings' survival. Behavior that does not seem directly adaptive, in the selective sense of increasing the reproductive success of the actor, is called altruistic. But honeybee altruism is more apparent than real. In bringing up sisters and brothers, rather than daughters and sons, workers do serve their own genetic continuity.

Since the female workers of social insect colonies are diploid and the male drones haploid, workers turn out to be three times more likely to share a gene with another worker than with a drone. Hence, workers do better, genetically, to tend the larvae of future sisters than of future brothers, or even their own offspring, were it possible for them to lay eggs.

Another way of looking at this is that workers raise other workers to sustain the queen, for only she can pass worker genes to the next generation.

The worker is one-fourth related to the drone, what with their having zero chance to share a gene from their father (since drones are fatherless) and a one in two chance of sharing a gene from their mother the queen (since she is diploid and therefore has eggs containing a random mixture of genes from her mother and father).

In contrast, the worker is three-fourths related to another worker, because they have one whole chance of sharing a gene from their father (since they all come from identical sperms from the same haploid drone), and a one in two chance of sharing a gene from their diploid mother, the queen. This not only means that sister bees are 300 percent more related to each other than they are to their brothers but that they are 50 percent more related to each other than they are to their own mother. Put another way, in the honeybee system, any female that is a mother (usually just the queen) is less related to her offspring than to her sisters (because the average chance of the queen sharing any gene with a daughter is only one in two).

The parthenogenetic production of males and consequent system of relatedness is what skews the honeybee sex ratio so far in favor of females. Sperm storage and pheromonal contraception appear to have been selected because they serve the bee's haplodiploid system so well. Mutation and infection remain possible physical initiators of this system millions of years ago.

The same system prevails for ants and wasps. Since the female in these groups also is three times more related to her future sisters than to her future brothers, she favors her sisters, and thereby her own genes, by building more small cells to hold worker larvae than large cells to hold drone larvae. She thus feeds more future females than males. Sociobiologists Robert Trivers and Hope Hare compared the total weight of female and male progeny for twenty-one species of ants. The bulk of female progeny exceeded that of male progeny in a ratio very close to 3:1. This shows that workers are altruistic in proportion to the number of genes they stand to secure in the next generation!

Further confirmation of the link between extra effort and extra genetic relationship was provided by raider ants. These enter other colonies and capture slaves. Raiders put the slaves to work tending larvae. Since slaves are foreigners and therefore have no vested genetic interest in these larvae, they raise equal numbers of males and females. If the raider ants are forced to tend their own larvae, the skewed ratio favoring females, 3:1, reappears!

The duties of worker bees are synchronized to their age. In the first ten days of life, they are cell cleaners, foragers, and nurses. Their head glands, which supply protein-rich "milk" derived from pollen, are at the peak of their development.

From ten to twenty days, another set of head glands takes over and secretes the wax to build new cells. While the milk and wax glands mature at fixed times, they can be called back into service, even after they have atrophied, if the needs of the hive require it. When nurses or builders are removed from a colony, bees at other stages of development assume the absentees' responsibilities. Their bodies cooperate by providing the necessary glandular modifications, and milk and wax start to flow again. Hormones and pheromones seem to compensate for neural simplicity, allowing the social insects to vary their behavior and organization in adaptive ways.

The bees' distant relative, the wasp, shows behavioral flexibility of a similar kind. If an experimenter makes a hole in a queen wasp's clay brood chamber, she patches it up. (Wasp colonies are begun annually by the queen, starting with one brood cell in which she lays her first eggs. Unlike the honeybee queen, the wasp queen does not remain immured in the brood chamber or hive, and she does not live for several years, attended by her daughters.) Although nest repair is not part of the queen wasp's standard behavior, she can improvise. Even if her species always builds from the outside, a queen confronted with an inside repair job may pause for several hours, as if to consider her problem, and then repair the cell from inside.

Strangely, the mason bee (subfamily Eumeninae), a much closer relative of the honeybee, cannot improvise a cell repair. There is no hive in this subsocial species of bee. The female builds a separate honey-filled clay chamber for each of her eggs. Although the mason bee will examine a hole made by an experimenter, she will not repair it. Instead she makes as many trips to fill the broken cell as she would to fill an intact one. She then proceeds to lay her egg in it. All the honey and the egg fall straight through the hole, but she proceeds to seal the chamber as if nothing unusual had happened. In general, insect behavior is stereotyped as this. Even Karl von Frisch, great admirer of bee culture and behavior, avers "there is . . . not one example on record of a really intelligent action having been performed by a honeybee." (But see S. J. Gould's "Do honeybees know what they are doing?")

At the ten- to twenty-day stage, some workers become hive guards. Their stingers are designed to kill other insects, like ants and wasps, that come by to rob honey. If a mammal lingers near the nest, it will be attacked also. Since bee stingers evolved in response to the selective pressure of insect intruders with chitin "skins" (long before soft-skinned animals existed), assault on mammals turns out to be more dangerous for the bee than for the (nonallergic) victim. The stinger embeds in soft flesh and rips out of the bee as she tries to withdraw it. Still she never hesitates to sting a loiterer, although this means certain death.

From the twentieth day to her death, four to five weeks later for a spring/summer worker to several months later for an autumn/winter worker, the bee is most useful to plants and man. In this period, she gathers nectar and pollen, places these commodities in storage cells, and then dances out a message of flying directions to the other foragers. At the food source, she secretes an organic alcohol that supplements the dance in drawing other bees to the ambrosial target.

Because we so strongly associate "active" with "male" in our language, it is difficult to remember that all these active bees are females. Thus, where nature shows an outstanding elaboration of cooperative care of the young, plus economical engineering of communal shelter and elegant, profitable interaction with surrounding resources and species, females have been chosen. On the other hand, there are no all-male, or almost all-male, societies.

Many accounts of social insects characterize queens as egg factories. Pictures of the egg-engorged ant, wasp, honeybee, and distantly related termite queens show that they are prisoners of "pregnancy." Sometimes this unseemly bondage may last fifteen or twenty years, as in the case of the termite queen, who can produce more than two hundred million eggs in her lifetime. The queen honeybee may lay as many as three hundred thousand eggs annually. How do they maintain their incredible gamete output, and also elicit care for themselves and their young offspring (and, in the case of termites, for their husband too) from their mature daughters (and sons, in the case of termites)?

The answer is inside a pair of glands, called corpora allata, found in the queen's brain. They secrete a hormone that enables immature eggs to consolidate yolk by picking up blood proteins. Interestingly, neural-secretory control of the ovaries in insects is analogous to that in vertebrates. Like the corpora allata in insects, the mammalian hypothalamus, composed of nerve cells in the base of the brain, secretes factors that direct the pituitary to release gonadotrophins to stimulate the ovaries.

This hormonal control of egg maturation is closely coordinated to environmental conditions, because the corpora allata (just like the hypothalamus) will not secrete hormonal instructions to the ovaries (or pituitary) unless they first receive neural messages stating that external conditions of nutrition, sunlight, and temperature are adequate. An undernourished queen bee will not lay eggs, just as a very undernourished girl probably will not ovulate or menstruate. Although vertebrates, especially the mammals, seem so much more highly evolved than insects, analogous neuro-endocrine safeguards work to prevent production of young in times of scarcity or severe stress. Among mammals, extreme anxiety (a hormonal state which may accompany inferior status due to youth, physical handicap, or behavioral insufficiency) may not only inhibit ovulation but also prevent embryo implantation in the uterus and lead to spontaneous abortion.

In order to maintain her reign, the queen's mandibular (lower jaw) glands secrete a pheromone that is distributed and eaten by all the workers. If a queen dies or is aged and produces too little of this pheromone, workers are no longer inhibited from producing new queens and will cause them to form by enlarging certain cells and feeding royal jelly to larvae already in larger cells.

Only one new queen will take over the vacant throne. She will mate, and, then, if the old queen (her mother) is still alive, she will kill her and any other young queens (her sisters) that may not have flown off to found new hives. The killing of sister queens appears odd at first. Why should the new queen kill off sisters that are three-fourths related to her in order to produce offspring that are only one-half related to her? The answer is in numbers; the loss of the portion of similar genes carried by a few sisters is enormously offset by the production of thousands of progeny, albeit each with a smaller individual ratio of relatedness than a sister.

Development of all the different types of individuals in a colony—various stages of larvae, workers, reproductive females, and males—is also controlled by hormones from the corpora allata and by pheromones emitted by workers. The corpora allata secrete a substance called juvenile hormone that governs maturation. In some species it prevents the appearance of sexually competent adults.

Although hormonal control constitutes the operational means of producing a multicaste, multiactivity social insect colony, it does not explain how such a system evolved. One hypothesis visualizes the evolution of complex insect societies as a gradual increment and diffusion of parenting behavior—from a female's simply staying with her eggs until they hatch, to her building a brood chamber or cluster of cells to receive the larvae, to producing several generations, and finally to creating the caste of sterile females, bound to each other and to her for mutual survival.

How can such mutual dependence and support be communicated? In part, as already explained, it is communicated through queenly secretions that are ingested by workers. Among social insects a lot of mutual begging and feeding goes on. This mouth-to-mouth communication is a binding social force and may be derived from brood-tending behavior. Since all workers feed "milk," royal jelly, honey, and other foods (for example, cultivated fungi in the case of certain ants) to their larvae, they easily carry over this familiar behavior to their interactions with each other. Antennae touching and feeding serve as greetings, peace offerings, and methods of identifying caste and age of another member of the society. While we chiefly use vision and hearing to make assessments of others, insects rely on a chemoreceptive sense, which is probably a combination of smell and taste.

Bees, wasps, and ants independently evolved societies that require chemoreceptive communication, using behaviors derived from brood-tending for social interaction and bonding. It seems that the clustering together and mutual assistance of animals almost always goes back to an intensified relationship between females and their young or foster young. Females, whether they be mother, grandmother, sister, or aunt, supply the basic model for socialization. This can be seen in human society too, where every culture has its adult pacifiers—cigarettes, cigars, pipes to suck on; tobacco, gum, and fingernails to chew on—that reduce tension and help people socialize. They all recapture the oral aspect of the mother/young situation. In an outstanding survey of the congruence of parenting, courting, and social-bonding behaviors called *The Sexual Code*, Wolfgang Wickler suggests that kissing, on the hand or lips, is a socially bonding gesture derived from nursing. So, even in human groups, bonding behaviors reveal a reliance on touch and partially on the senses of taste and smell, the same senses that social insects use when they tip their antennae to each other.

Although the Hymenoptera are famed for their female-dominated colonies, it must be noted that most species in this order are subsocial, which means that females live independently, not in a hive or hill. They are internally fertilized once and build their nests alone in soil, wood, or clay, then feed their larvae unaided.

Subsocial species of wasps provide occasional examples of cannibalization of the mother. Ordinarily the female deposits her fertilized

eggs in the corpse of a spider or in the larva of an insect. If she finds
no spider or larva, the eggs grow and hatch inside her, and the larvae
chew their way out of her, as they would have done had they been
deposited in the corpse of a prey. Unfortunately, the tissues of the
mother wasp do not provide enough protein to sustain the hungry
larvae, and they die in spite of her sacrifice.

Another group of insects, the gall midges (such as *Mycophila speveri*),
shows a pattern of cannibalization of the mother that maximizes their
reproduction to enable them to take advantage of temporary surfeits
of their favorite food, mushrooms.

Short, all-female generations of gall midges are produced parthenogenetically. Each wingless female reproduces while still in the larval
or pupal stage, depending on the species. Wingless females develop
and live within their mother's tissues, growing to fill her entire body,
devouring her from within. They hatch out of her empty chitinous
exoskeleton. Each wingless midge female thus has become a "burst"
of new wingless females. Within two days each member of the burst
will begin to be eaten alive.

These truncated generations, in which immature individuals reproduce, allow the species to increase at its maximum possible rate while
food is superabundant. When the windfall declines, the midges meta-
morphose completely, become sexually mature, and fly off to find
more mushrooms.

Aphids (species of *Macrosiphum*) that live on the sap of leaves and
stems also adjust their reproductive methods and female forms to
utilize available food. In a single year, six different types of females
may appear in rapid succession in one species. One generation of
females has mouthparts able to deal with a woody host, another with
a herbaceous one. One may be bisexual, the next parthenogenetic,
another oviparous, and the last viviparous! Overwintering eggs produce
wingless, parthenogenetic females that remain larvalike in appearance
and rapidly give birth to more like themselves. Instead of going through
several moults, these females go through several abbreviated lifetimes.
When this happens, especially when combined with immediate cannibalization of the mother, it almost seems as if one individual is
growing and maintaining itself rather than giving birth and dying. In
fact, the generations are so short that if all the offspring of each generation survived and reproduced, a single aphid female would give
rise to 524 billion aphids annually.

The primary occupation of all these aphid generations is eating.
When leaves and stems are used up by the busy eaters, winged females
are produced that fly to new food, where they revert to rapid repro-

duction of wingless forms. The last generation before winter includes males and females that mate, each female leaving about six fertile eggs to overwinter in a dormant state.

The attine ants (species of *Atta*), which sometimes keep aphids as winter guests in their hills, bring us back to consideration of colonial hymenoptera. These remarkable communities may number in the millions. The queen and brood live in a well-tended garden, guarded by female soldiers and groomed and fed by female workers. The queen, who may live up to fifteen years, is fertilized by several males and packs away a store of about three hundred million sperms in her spermatheca. She starts a colony alone by digging an underground room and raising her first workers there. She feeds them and herself on her own eggs, until there are a sufficient number of mature workers to begin brood-tending and cultivation.

Although there are two hundred species of attine ants, each with its own sort of nest—hills, burrows under rocks or into tree trunks— their life patterns are quite similar. In spring, winged females and males fly up for midair mating. When they fall to the ground, the males die, and the fertile females shed their wings and try to begin new colonies. If a colony is successful, its workers will begin to forage for base materials for their fungal crops. They use a variety of substrates and fertilizers—wood particles, bits of leaves, stems, and flowers, caterpillar droppings, decomposing vegetation, and insect corpses. Each piece of substrate is chewed to a pulpy mash and coated with a drop of clear anal fluid that prevents the growth of fungal spores other than the ones preferred by the ants. One species even uses the silk of its own larvae, passing the larva between them like a shuttle, to weave leaf fragments together for a superb fungal substrate. While the miniature underground plantations of the ants serve tropical ecosystems well by enriching the earth with organic material, this is incidental to the feeding of workers, larvae, and queen.

Ants also enjoy a taste of honey occasionally. And this is why they come to entertain aphids in their colonies. Since aphids suck leaf and stem sap, they excrete a sweet fluid called honeydew. When an ant meets an aphid, it says hello in the usual insect manner, by tipping its antennae. Sometimes the ant greets the wrong end of the aphid, which responds with a drop of sweet dew. A colony of red ants can eat more than 220 pounds of this fluid in a year. They like the dew so much that they sometimes carry aphids down to the nest to visit over winter. The following spring, ants and aphids together ascend to the leaves, where tired worker ants once more refresh themselves with sips of sugary aphid dew.

Termites (order Isoptera) are older, evolutionarily, than ants, wasps, and bees. They date back to Triassic times, about 230 million years ago, when the age of dinosaurs began. The earliest hymenopteran fossils are found in the next period of the Mesozoic Era, the Jurassic, about 50 million years later.

Like attine ants, some termites build elaborate nests with fungal gardens, using leaves as substrate. There are about eighteen hundred species of termites, some (species of *Cryptotermes*) of them preferring a wood-frame house in North America, others (species of *Bellicositermes*) building a fortress of clay on the East African plain.

Like other social insects, termites swarm in nuptial flight, but only to disseminate the species. Intercourse occurs on the ground after the female has led the male down a pheromone path to a new nest site. When they have built a nuptial chamber underground, they mate and care for the young larvae together.

A termite queen cannot store sperms like honeybee and attine queens because she has no spermatheca. Therefore, she always needs a male around to fertilize her eggs. The king and queen remain together, reproducing and being attended by many generations of their offspring. If they die, it is the absence of their larvae-inhibiting pheromone that permits new soldiers (females) or a new monarch to develop. It was this unseen control by the royal pair that E. Marais called "the mysterious power that governs" when he characterized the termite colony as a single organism in *The Soul of the White Ant*, written in 1937, long before pheromones had been identified.

The "white ant" is a termite larva, although it looks like a miniature adult. Thousands of them are tended by minor workers who are male. If the nest is disturbed, the workers carry the larvae in their mouth pincers to safety. Major workers, also male, forage for food—grass, bone, dung, paper—and maintain the mound, which can stand ten feet high and remain functional for half a century. The major and minor soldiers, who are all females, are equipped with pincer jaws and syringe beaks that squirt a paralyzing chemical on prey or potential invaders. In some species, both workers and soldiers are females.

How much meaning can the structure of female-run insect societies have for the structure of vertebrate societies? Is the femaleness of an insect comparable to the femaleness of a mammal? In the social hymenopteran colony, mating is minimal, as is individual competition. Such factors permit a unity of function, efficient mothering, high productivity, and peace. Evidence from laboratory and field studies is beginning to show that varying degrees of sexual suppression of younger/less dominant females by older/more dominant ones also contributes to the smooth running of certain mammalian societies, especially among social carnivores such as wolves, and primates such as macaques. So far, however, the mole rat is the only mammalian species that has a single reproductive female for each "colony," with all other females being effectively sterilized by the "queen." Very little is known about the naked and blind mole rat, apart from the fact that it eats roots and never emerges in light of day. Females of the colony ingest or inhale a contraceptive from the urine or feces of the queen, a true analogue of the queen-substance among honeybees.

Hymenoptera and isoptera show many patterns of social organization, many sex role expressions, and sex ratio options, but it seems that whichever pattern is followed, if an individual is used as a vehicle for reproduction only—as are the queen, termite king, and drone—its chances for developing other behaviors are small. Life span reduction, as in parthenogenetic aphid nymphs and short-lived drones, or imprisonment or immobilization, as in hive, hill, or mound royals, can make reproduction very expensive for insect parents. To the extent that either sex remains sterile, it can participate in a variety of activities—nursing, building, farming, hunting, and guarding.

This is not so different from the situation in other classes. Becoming a reproductive severely restricts an individual's options. Thus, wherever in the animal kingdom females (or more rarely males) have evolved into (or voluntarily restricted themselves to being) reproductives, they may perform less of their species' repertoire. In this view, mothering is seen as an activity distinct from reproducing, and excessive reproduction is seen as excluding full, active mothering.

While it may overwhelm our sense of choice and security in the distinctiveness of our personalities to know that we too are governed by hormones, pheromones, and the behaviors of those around us, such knowledge is essential to any program for changing the status and activity range of females in our species. I think we may be encouraged by the idea that the same inexorable process of natural selection that produced the insects and their all-powerful parenting females simultaneously created their enormously productive and cooperative societies, societies in which females are liberated from producing eggs and finding mates.

3 | FISHES

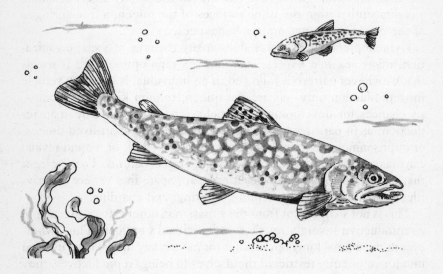

Fishes have a history almost as long as that of land insects. Nearly five hundred million years of evolution have permitted the fish class to encompass such a diversity of femaleness—including the only vertebrate females that internally fertilize males—that any generalization can only be tentative.

Seventy-five percent of the earth is covered with water. The vertical range of water is from Lake Titicaca, at about 2 miles above sea level, to the bottom of Pacific Ocean fissures, about 7 miles below sea level. It is not surprising that the ponds, lakes, rivers, and oceans of the world accommodate more different fish species than the land does all other vertebrate species combined. As a class, the fish are exceeded in numbers of species and numbers of individuals only by the insects.

The forty thousand or so different species of fishes are divided into three groups. The two most ancient are the Cyclostomi, including hagfishes and lampreys, and the Elasmobranchs, including sharks, rays, and chimaeras. Living species of the first group are thought to resemble forms that existed almost five hundred million years ago. The third group of fishes is called the Osteichthyes, or bony fish group; it contains some thirty thousand species, again divided into three groups: lungfishes, lobe-finned fishes, and teleosts. The last group holds the majority of species, which are familiar as food, sport, and aquarium favorites. Osteichthyes have bony skeletons, whereas elasmobranchs have cartilaginous ones.

Forebears of the modern coelacanths, or lobe-finned fishes, are regarded as the stock from which the first land-dwelling vertebrates, the amphibians, evolved some 400 million years ago. Most modern species of bony fishes (that is, the teleosts) have evolved in the past 150 million years, the same period of time in which our own class, mammals, has been evolving. So, although a certain small branch of the enormous Osteichthyes group did contain our most distant vertebrate ancestor, bony fishes, elasmobranchs, and cyclostomes as we know them were not ancestral to any land-dwellers. Therefore, the adaptations of female fishes belong to another world, incomparable at all levels to our own except by broadest analogy.

Because its sexual identity may be plastic, often depending on the action of environment and genes other than the XX or XY sex pairs, a fish's strategy for obtaining reproductive success may vary through its life. Pressure, temperature, and the presence of more dominant species members may influence when and into which sex a fish matures.

Considering that fishes range in size from the smallest vertebrate—the pygmy goby of the lakes of Luzon in the Philippines, weighing only 0.0002 ounce and measuring 0.33 inch—to the whale shark, weighing up to 12 tons and measuring about 70 feet, it is amazing that they have almost universally evolved the trait of two distinct sexes (gonochorism). Most fishes are born male or female or mature from an indifferent stage into a stable gender.

The age at which a fish will reach sexual maturity depends on the size range of its species. Tiny fishes are generally shortlived and therefore mature early. The tropical reef perch (*Micrometrus aurora*) and the dwarf perch (*M. minimus*) are sexually competent just after birth, but although females in these species accept sperms at this time, they do not bear until one year later. Many of these species are found in home aquaria, where they can sometimes be seen giving birth to their young. Most species in the less than 6-inch range come of age at about one year. Those that grow to one foot or more may take two to five years to mature.

The eel and the sturgeon are very late developers, consistent with the fact that they can grow to about 2 or 3 feet average, and often to 10 feet or more. They are full grown at fifteen or more years. Eels take so long to mature and are so private about their reproductive functions that people were at a loss for centuries to figure out how they propagated. Aristotle and Pliny thought that an eel was sexless and procreated spontaneously from "the bowels of the earth" or vegetatively from "cuttings" of itself, obtained by rubbing against rocks.

The reproductive habits of numerous species of fishes have given man several mysteries to ponder. More hermaphrodites, both normal and anomalous, occur among bony fishes than among any other group of vertebrates, with the possible exception of the lampreys and hagfishes (cyclostomes).

In a heroic review article on intersexuality in fishes, James Atz summarizes the great range of sexual dimorphism and reproductive patterns in fishes, from hermaphrodites that fertilize their own eggs with their own milt to females that turn into fully functional males, and males that turn into egg-laying females. Most of the time these changes are genetically programmed for the species, but sometimes they occur only in particular individuals that have a fungal infestation.

Just as spirochete infection in the fruitfly *Drosophila* causes only females to hatch, so the fungal infection of guppies (species of *Lebistes*) and swordtails (*Xiphophorus maculatus*) can make females turn into males. Apparently the fungus (*Ichthyophonus hoferi*) can either cause the female to start producing androgens (male sex hormones) that transform part of her ovaries into sperm-producing testes, or it can produce these hormones itself. This is just another example of how the integration of other organisms and their DNA into unrelated species can alter the behavior and number of females in a population and thereby potentially set the group on a new evolutionary course.

Before looking at individual species, the methods of reproduction prevalent in each of the three major groups of fishes—cyclostomes, cartilaginous, and bony fishes—can be reviewed.

Cyclostomes, or roundmouths, have long, slender bodies and are jawless. They look somewhat like but are not related to eels. They are bottom-dwelling scavengers or parasites that latch onto other fishes and suck their blood. Cyclostomes are synchronous, or true, hermaphrodites, with fully developed female and male gametes in each organism; eggs or sperms may pass from any individual's gonads to unite and develop externally.

Elasmobranchs, species of sharks, skates, and rays with cartilaginous skeletons, show internal fertilization. Small numbers of young may be born live or hatch from horny egg cases, according to species.

Bony fishes show a full array of reproductive arrangements: gono-choristic species with external or internal fertilization, to hermaph-roditic species with external or internal fertilization, and gynogenetic all-female species with internal fertilization but no inclusion of the sperm's genetic material in the offspring. While most bony fishes hatch from unguarded eggs, some are protected, aerated, and cleaned. In certain species the fry are also guarded and fed. Most often it is not the female fish that builds the nest or guards and feeds.

Among live-bearing fishes, however, the female must invest ma-terially in the production of young that develop within her. If she carries embryos that are at different stages of development, it means the eggs of successive ovulations have been fertilized at different times, possibly by different males. This condition is called superfe-tation. It has also been suggested that when different batches of eggs develop simultaneously in the ovary, some of them may break down and serve as food for the other maturing embryos, a sort of intraovarian cannibalism.

Genetic studies have not helped much to sort out the diverse sexual identities and parenting strategies of fishes. This is partly because fish chromosomes are small and difficult to spread out and study under the microscope. They are not easy to arrange by size and shape into match-ing, or homologous, pairs, a procedure called karyotyping. Most bony fishes have about 36 to 50 chromosomes in each cell, depending on the species. The salmonids have 72 to 84 chromosomes. (Human cells have 46.)

Consistently sex-linked features, like certain color patterns or be-haviors, imply the existence of X and Y chromosomes, even when these cannot be seen. Fishes can develop as normal males and females, even when they do not have visible XX or XY pairs. The sexual identity instructions seem to be distributed over all the chromosomes, and clearly distinguishable sex chromosomes have been seen in only a few species. When X and Y chromosomes have been identified, the usual XX-female and XY-male situation is not always found. A YY or XY genotype can develop into a female, an XX into a male. This flexibility extends so far that swordtails, guppies, and Japanese ricefish show XX males in some populations and YY males in others. Clearly, external factors working on the entire genome (that is, ordinary chromosomes plus sex chromosomes) determine the sex.

"Clear-cut differentiation of sexes came about very gradually through evolution," says Wolfgang Wickler in *The Sexual Code*. Even now, differentiation of the sexes among fishes is rarely immediately apparent (at least, to us); therefore we say that they show little dimorphism as a class.

Clarity of differentiation between the sexes is partly attributed to the process of sexual selection, a corollary of natural selection described by Charles Darwin in *The Descent of Man and Selection in Relation to Sex*. Sexual selection shapes anatomical, physiological, and behavioral characteristics that are involved in mating. By helping attract members of the opposite sex and defeat members of the same sex, certain traits are more immediately responsible for sexual acceptance. These traits may include bright color, large size, appendages (such as barbels in fishes), sound, strength, and agility. Other traits that may sexually recommend an individual involve interactions, both friendly and competitive. Females of most species seem less likely than males to have traits for courtship that would put their lives in jeopardy, but while they have traditionally been seen as the selectors of males, they too compete with same-sex peers in order to be chosen by opposite-sex peers. Overall, females seem to have less ostentatious ways of competing for the chance to mate than males (but see pages 61 and 131), especially when they are munificent K-strategists.

Since most fishes do not have difficulty locating mates, do not need intimate contact for fertilization, and do not show large parental investment, sexual selection has not been a potent force in creating strong divergences between the sexes in most species. Whether a fish is female or male is rather incidental to the rest of its existence. There are a few outstanding exceptions, however, and some of these occur, as in species of the deep-sea angler, where lifelong differentiation of the sexes ensures successful mating under difficult conditions. Temporary sexual dimorphism in the breeding season is more common.

Can the fishes themselves distinguish female from male? The answer is "not always." Zebrafish, some kinds of angelfish, and herring cannot. The higher incidence of interspecific and intergeneric hybrids among fishes than among other vertebrates is testimony to their frequent inability to detect an opposite-sexed member of their own species and to their generally unconfined method of fertilization in water.

Still, females in many species are distinguishable in several ways. Visually, they often register as larger, more pot-bellied (especially in the spawning season), and quieter in color than the male.

Females, in turn, use color, shape, and even movement cues to identify males of their species. This helps to avoid hybridization that may result in partial or complete sterility of the offspring of one or both sexes and in a disturbed sex ratio (that is, differing markedly from 1:1).

Among fishes in which courtship, intercourse, or very intimate, synchronized spawning occurs, it is important for the sexes to recognize each other, and although it has taken scores of ichthyologists years to discriminate and describe the features that separate fish sexes, most dimorphic fishes have been clear about the separation for a long time. The form of the fins, mouth, lips, and snout may all be sex identifiers. Males have "whiskers" and fleshy tentacles (barbels) more often than females.

Proof that these visual cues are linked to sex recognition and mating is the fact that many of them appear only in the courtship and breeding seasons. Usually it is the male that changes drastically. In salmon, for example, the male develops horny tubercles or large, hooked jaws on its upriver, spawning run.

Females change internally, as the ovaries fill with mature eggs, but externally, they change less from the juvenile form of the species than do males.

Another modality for sex detection among fishes is the equivalent of smell and taste. Chemical factors released by one sex diffuse through the water to the nasal openings and on to the olfactory brain region of the other sex. With nasal organs larger, relative to body size, than any other vertebrate, dwarf males of some anglerfish species appear well equipped, in the dark depths of the sea, to find females by smell. Other dark dwellers—catfishes in muddy waters, and blind fishes that live in caves and grottos—also depend on this modality. Sometimes males of certain species will mouth the urogenital area of another fish to determine its species and sex by taste and smell. Laboratory experiments with the jewel fish have shown learning to be important in recognition of taste-smell cues from the opposite sex. Chemoreceptive sensors are also used to identify home territory, eggs, and fry.

Sex identity begins in the embryo, with the formation of the gonads. In bony fishes, these develop from one tissue layer instead of two as in all other vertebrates. This partially accounts for the less apparent separation of sexes and the high incidence of anomalous hermaphroditism in most fish species. The bony fish's gonad can go through three stages: indifferent, bisexual, and heterosexual, which are analogous to an individual fish with no sex, with the gametes and behaviors of both sexes, and finally with the gametes and behavior of just one sex. If the gonad contains a mixture of ovarian and testicular cells, it is called an ovotestis. Its function as either an ovary or a testis will depend on many factors: light, temperature, presence of females or males, infection, and, in the case of experiments, surgical intervention.

When fish ovaries are fully developed, they are elongated sacs, lying just over the kidneys and just beneath the swim bladder (an organ that is filled with gas in nearly all species to regulate buoyancy). The ovaries are light pink or yellow and granular in texture. When they are egg engorged, they fill most of the body cavity and may account for 70 percent of the body weight. Generally, females mature later than males, and their gonads ripen later. This may be due to a higher rate of metabolism in males.

Environmental conditions have a lot to do with when a female fish will mature and how frequently she will be ready to spawn. Seasonal changes in light and temperature may induce marked activity in the pituitary and consequently the ovaries. In spring spawners, increased light and rising temperature stimulate ovulation, and in fall spawners the reverse conditions will do so.

Egg laying in small freshwater fishes (*Oryzias latipes*), under study in a Japanese laboratory, is synchronized with sunrise and the hours just after. The daily ovulation cycle begins at about four in the morning. If a male is present and the mating ceremony is completed, the eggs waiting in the oviducts will be expelled. In spite of the strong seasonal rhythmicity of egg production, eggs will be retained if the male is not present. The female probably needs to be stimulated by both the sight of, and the water currents created by, the male's courtship dance. The low vibrations of his movements are detected tactilely via the lateral line organs, tiny sensory structures set into deep pores that run in a line from head to tail on either side of the fish.

The immediate mediator of gonadal changes necessary for full gamete production is the pituitary. In response to brain messages telling it that all environmental factors are favorable, the pituitary, like the corpora allata in insects, sends hormonal commands to the ovaries and secondary sex tissues. The pituitary-gonadal axis, as this system is called, is common to all vertebrates. The basic chemistry of the individual hormones—gonadotrophins plus estrogen and prolactin in females, or testosterone in males—is similar in fishes, amphibians, reptiles, birds, and mammals. This is why injection of prolactin (the milk-stimulating hormone) and other pituitary extracts into a fish may induce ovulation, sexual behavior, or parenting in many species, just as it would in a woman.

In short, it is not fish reproductive endocrinology (the secretions of the pituitary or gonads) that would predict the high incidence of hermaphroditism, maturational sex change, and delayed sex identity that exists in this class. Rather these would seem to result from the unique gonadal embryology of fishes and their reliance on many environmentally triggered chromosomes.

Environment may determine not only how fish sexes develop, but how many of each sex will develop. Among vertebrates in general, a variety of adverse conditions, such as crowding, starvation, social stress, and temperature extremes may promote the development of males. For example, *low*-ranking yellow baboon mothers produce more male than female offspring. Since males fight for higher rank but females inherit their mother's rank, males are more likely to escape the adversity of their mother's low status. Excess males are also produced by red and gray kangaroos during severe drought. However, in a few species, including ours, females may be produced in adversity. Apparently no unified theory of sex ratio variability exists for all vertebrates.

Among fishes, in particular, there are many examples of more males resulting from conditions of adversity and aging. This may be due to a higher birthrate of males, to the more frequent differentiation of uncommitted individuals into males, and to a gradual, partial, or complete transition of females into males. It is not that females die more easily in difficult circumstances but that male formation is favored. In fact, in certain species, females resist adversity better than males and their disproportionate maturation into males during such times may be an adaptation that ensures there will be enough males left for them to mate with.

In contrast, sex ratios shift toward females in times of food windfall or extreme stability. The aphids that appear in a green and rainy summer, the lizards in the rich, dead tree margin of the scrubland, the Amazon mollies of steady tropical inlets are all females. Being parthenogenetic reproducers, they propagate quickly and thereby fully utilize the assets of plenty and security.

It is difficult for us to comprehend that a newborn or just-hatched fish may not be one sex or the other. Development of its gonads and secondary sexual characteristics remains indifferent until conditions and maturation force an identity decision. In eels, for instance, the crucial factor may be whether an individual migrates upstream or stays in warmer waters along estuarine shores; a trip upriver can be a feminizing experience.

There is no natural law that demands there be just two sexes in every species or that individuals retain one sex identity for life. In assuming a new sex, an organism may take on only the secondary sex features and behaviors of the new sex, or it may also take on the full sexual duties of the new gender. If a female fish only looks and acts like a male but cannot fertilize eggs, she is called arrhenoid.

Natural sex changes, those that occur regularly as part of normal maturation, most frequently go from female to male, since femaleness, as a physical state, is often closer to the youngster or adolescent of the species. Assumption of male features with maturation is not unusual. (Even human females are physically neotenic [like juvenile] relative to males, until well after menopause. Then women may begin to show some maturational maleness: facial hair, coarsening of facial features and skin texture, and sometimes deepening of the voice.)

Not only may particular fishes change sex, but they may merge their sexes into one being. This is different from true hermaphroditism, in which the individual contains both sex potentialities from birth. A symbiotic hermaphrodite is formed from two formerly distinct sexual beings. Some bugs, spiders, a parasite of the sea cucumber, and several species of anglerfishes do this to keep a mate where conditions make it difficult to find one.

The Greenland, or Holboell, angler (*Ceratias holboelli*) is about 45 inches long and is named for the wormy lure that sprouts from the top of her head. The male Holboell, only about 0.5 inch long and about a millionth the weight of the female, sinks his jaws into the skin of her flank and becomes her permanent sperm-producing organ. Thus the female will be essentially a self-fertilizing hermaphrodite and the male (or males, as several may attach to one female in some species) becomes completely dependent on the female for movement and for nourishment through her circulatory system. His viscera atrophy, and one large testis fills his body cavity. He, like certain male-dependent females in the history of our own species, has become a reproductive convenience, with virtually no freedom of mobility or behavioral choice. (Only a minority of the nearly one hundred ceratioid species have males that fuse permanently. In some species males attach temporarily.)

In certain fish species it is normal for every member to be female first and become male later. Many tropical reef fishes show this pattern, called protogyny, in response to the loss of the male leader of their harem. The swamp eel is also a protogynist. Female for the first thirty months of its life, it then begins to grow cords of testicular tissue that eventually replace the degenerating ovaries. Starvation accelerates this process; again the female becomes a male sooner under adverse conditions. Any stressor, like *Ichthyophonus* fungal infestation, X-ray exposure, or incomplete removal of the pituitary will hasten masculinization.

Ichthyophonus, the masculinizer of guppies and swordtails, may not only interrupt ovarian function but may produce androgens itself. Atz reports Stolk's observation that a female swordtail, isolated from birth, produced an all-female brood. No sperms or testicular tissue were found in her ovaries, but *Ichthyophonus* was. The observer believed that androgens from the fungus created this isolated example of apparent parthenogenesis. Normally, the swordtail, native to Guatemalan and Mexican streams, reproduces sexually. It is a protogynous species in which females that have already spawned several broods may grow the typical male sword extension of the tail and replace ovaries with testes. Both male and female gametes are needed for reproduction; although they are serial hermaphrodites, swordtails are not self-fertilizing. Therefore, the ovaries observed by Stolk must either have been induced by the fungus to transform partially (for which there is no evidence), or the fungus produced androgens or other substances that stimulated the development of unfertilized eggs.

All females, fish or other, do many things besides produce eggs, mate, spawn, and occasionally brood-tend. They all must eat, move about, and protect themselves from predators and environmental change. They must choose where they will stay, day and night, where they will look for food, where they will rest. They must eliminate wastes, fight disease, and communicate with members of their species and occasionally with members of other species.

Sometimes females do these things the same way that males of the species do them; sometimes they do them differently. Ethologists are just beginning to describe the sexual dimorphism of behaviors other than mating and parenting. Further study of behavioral divergences between the sexes will reveal more about how organisms divide their time and energy between securing their immediate survival and perpetuating themselves through the production of young.

A few of the things that certain female fishes are doing besides spawning include breathing air, climbing trees, and fishing with a lantern and bait. The first two activities are shared by males of the species; the last is exclusive to the female deep-sea angler.

Fishes of the genus *Anabas* are partly built for land. They are less than 8 inches long and have an accessory breathing device that permits them to breathe in air. Their skins are tough to retard body water loss when they are on land, and their dorsal (back) and anal fins have sharp points that protect them from the jaws of hungry land snakes. With the aid of their spiked gill-covers, fins, and tail, *Anabas* move overland from one shallow pool to the next, covering about 10 feet per minute.

The mudskipper, or tree-climbing fish (*Periophthalmus barbarus*), of Borneo also comes out of water for extended periods and moves overland with the aid of modified fins. The oxygen it breathes must come through the water medium, even when it is halfway up the tangled roots of a mangrove, so mudskippers fill their branchial chambers, where the gills are located, with water. Thus supplied, they can remain out of water, searching for crustaceans with independently rotating, bulbous eyes.

At the midpoint over her upper lip, Holboell's deep-sea angler (*Ceratias holboelli*) has a slender appendage that wiggles like a worm. Attached to the end of this lure is a light that glows in the dark at depths of 400 to 600 feet underwater. The light is a product of bioluminescent bacteria, living symbiotically in the fish and helping her draw prey to her long-toothed jaws.

Of course, these are very special female fishes, and they each have a way of breeding consistent with their unique life-style and the environment in which they function.

Anabas drift through the warm waters of India, Sri Lanka, and the Philippines, leaving most of the breeding work to the males. Occasionally darting to the surface to gulp a mouthful of air, females wait until they are literally tackled by males and brought to prepared bubble nests before they begin laying eggs. The male catches in his mouth most of the two thousand eggs laid by a female. Then he shoots them up to the bubble nest at the water's surface or onto the underside of a leaf. The female moves off, and he guards the fertile eggs, and later the young fry, until they swim away.

The mudskipper has a completely different breeding plan based on the mud of the mangrove swamp. She must do all the work in this case and so digs funnel-shaped holes in the mud, deposits the eggs in them, and then stands guard.

Certain deep-sea anglers, like Holboell's discussed above, do not guard or gestate their young. Instead of nourishing their young with a placentalike attachment, they sustain their husband(s) in this way. In effect, the male has become the female deep-sea angler's testes. (Imagine a woman with a tiny birthmark that supplies sperms but does not masculinize her, enabling her to fertilize an egg whenever she is ready. Not very romantic, but practical!) The angler and her attached male(s) spawn together in the summer. Fertilized eggs float to surface waters and mature to about one-third of an inch before sinking to depths of 3000 feet or more, where metamorphosis is completed. A female may grow to 3 feet in length, while a male to 6 inches or less.

Anabas, mudskipper, and deep-sea angler begin to show some of the diverse accommodations of bony fishes. These three groups live in different environments—shallow tropical waters, muddy swamps, deepest oceans—and have different methods of obtaining prey: pursuit in water, on land, and with a patient lure. They also have different female roles in breeding: passive with no parenting, active with parenting, and functionally hermaphroditic with no parenting, respectively. But unfortunately no consistent correlations between way of earning a living and breeding can be deduced from the above examples. While *Anabas* females wander carefree and leave the nest to the male, another tropical female might be steadfastly monogamous and tend the brood herself.

While reiteration of nonreproductive female activities is necessary to counteract centuries of equating the female with reproduction, it is still true that eggs are the single common characteristic uniting females of all classes. At ovulation, the fish's enlarged follicle ruptures and contracts so that the egg rolls out through the rupture. In most cases, the eggs pass from the ovary to the genital aperture via the oviduct, which may be directly connected to the ovary or separated from it by a small gap. Contractions of the muscular oviduct and adjacent body wall propel the eggs to the external opening. A sphincter is often present at the oviduct opening. It may suddenly relax in coordination with an ovarian contraction, sending the eggs out in a forceful spurt. In cyclostomes, trout, and salmon there are no oviducts; the abdominal muscles must provide the main force for extrusion of eggs from pores around the urinary and rectal openings.

The ovaries themselves may contract during the spawning season. The little Japanese ricefish starts its egg-laying period in April and continues to show ovarian contractions daily, from six at night to four in the morning, through August. This timing coincides with the female's daily resting period. When she is active, the ovaries are relaxed, and no contractions occur during the day to interfere with her swimming and feeding.

Among species that leave their spawn floating free, the numbers of eggs produced must be enormous to counter the risk of nonfertilization, destruction by temperature change, or predation. A 54-pound open-sea sunfish (*Mola mola*) can broadcast twenty-eight million eggs into water where males are swimming. A turbot weighing 17 pounds can leave nine million eggs; the cod of about the same weight lays more than six million, and it is estimated that only one egg in every million ever reaches maturity. Among more territorial species that defend their eggs and fry, fewer eggs are liberated.

The urogenital aperture, or cloaca, of the female is not markedly different from that of the male. Through it pass the eggs and kidney excretions. In the four-eyed fish (*Anableps*), the aperture is covered by a shield of scales, open on one side. The intromittent organ of the male is turned to the left in some individuals and to the right in others. This means that only certain males will match certain females, and intercourse must occur sideways. There are species of scorpion fish and cardinal fish in which a protruding oviduct is introduced by the female into the male's cloaca. This oviduct, or urogenital papilla, gets coated with sperms and is drawn back by the female into her body, where the sperms can fertilize her eggs.

The bitterling also has a remarkable oviduct, which is modified into a 2-inch tube that deposits her eggs in the exhalant siphon of a fresh-water mussel. At the same time, her mate deposits sperms near the inhalant siphon. These are sucked in as the mussel "inhales," and they fertilize the eggs. (Incidentally, the mussel may release her eggs just as the bitterlings are depositing their gametes. So, while the eggs of the fish find safety and mature in the aerating respiratory currents of the mussel's mantle, the mussel's eggs may be doing the same thing in the gills of the bitterling!)

In addition to live-bearers and the bitterling, there are several female fishes that invest time and effort in protecting their eggs. Some build and guard nests; others carry their maturing eggs in their mouths or branchial chambers.

There are two groups of nesting fishes: those that build a nest and desert it after spawning, like lampreys, trout, and salmon, and those that build and stay to guard, like fathead minnows, sunfish, and black bass. In the last group, it seems that it is the male that most often watches the nest. In certain South American species of lungfishes, the males that attend the eggs in nests seem to feed them oxygen with special gill-like structures that grow out of their pectoral fins. It is rare to see a female gathering materials for nests, fanning and cleaning the eggs, or plucking the young fry out of danger.

Many species of cichlids and the false pipefishes include females responsible for the safety of the brood. In about 5 percent of cichlid fishes the mother is a "mouther." This means she ensures the safety and aeration of her eggs by carrying them in her mouth. The young fry remain in her mouth after hatching and later stay close by to take shelter when necessary. Blind cave fishes (such as species of *Amblyopsis*) have males that carry the embryos in their gill chambers. Females of these species have an oviduct opening at a point on their underside above the pectoral fins. This unusual chest position of the oviduct may be linked to spawning ceremonies that bring the heads of mates together and thus the eggs close to the male's gills.

Another variation on this theme of internal protection of the embryos is found in the catfish genus *Platystacus*. At breeding time, the bellies of females turn soft and spongy, enabling the externally fertilized eggs to be pressed into the swollen skin. Each egg develops in a small cavity rich in blood vessels that help nourish the embryo. Among the false pipefishes, the eggs remain in a pouch formed by the female's pelvic fins. Filaments line the walls of this pouch and keep the eggs inside.

In general, species that guard their eggs and young are not pelagic—that is, they do not swim and feed in the open waters of the ocean, but inhabit mudflats, coral reefs, and shore shallows. In such environments, which are more crowded, the need for protection increases, and territories may be aggressively defended. Such brood-tending and territoriality are often accompanied by elaborate courtship.

Sociobiologists say that males perform courtship ceremonies to repel other males or outrank them in competition for the female resources of eggs and parenting. But since males are most often the brood-tenders among fishes, they cannot be competing for female parental investment. Rather, their aggressive displays and courtship serve to discourage other males from entering the territory and to attract and prepare females for synchronized spawning.

The need to possess territory in crowded habitats directly increases interaction between the sexes at the time of breeding. Environments that encourage competition and cooperation supply the basis for social grouping. In addition, the parental defensiveness that these species are forced to show may provide behaviors that can be lifted out of the care context and applied to courtship and territorial displays.

The thing to notice is that crowded environments seem to force individuals to interact more frequently. This is true for fishes and insects. They become more social and are more parenting in small habitats. Spatial confinement also demands that an animal group control its numbers. This is just what happens with fishes. When their space is small and their courtship and parenting patterns strong, fewer eggs are deposited. The relationship between fewer offspring and greater parenting seems to hold, whether it is the female or the male doing most of the parenting.

What attracts a female fish to a particular male? The chemistry of a male secretion; the vibration of his swimming; the property of a well-built nest are all attractants for certain female fishes. Conversely, it may be the female's chemistry, or movements, or provision of a nest that stimulates male display or spawning.

Among gobies of the genus *Bathygobius*, the female leads the male around by the nose. When she is ripe with eggs, she releases a chemical into the water that stimulates his full courtship display. In other tropical species, the male releases a chemical attractant that will synchronize the ovulatory cycles of females.

Auditory as well as olfactory cues are attractants. There are mating calls in species of gourami, seahorse, drum fish, and toadfish. In some species, modified fins, pharyngeal (in pharynx) teeth, and gill covers help emit sounds which may serve as mating and congregating calls. Weakfish (*Sciaena aquila*) are equipped with special drumming muscles that are attached to the swim bladder and to special bony processes extending off the fourth vertebra. When they contract, they make the bladder vibrate to produce a humming noise. Weakfish are abundant in Mediterranean waters, and their drumming was probably the basis of the Homeric song of the Sirens.

Attractants bring the sexes together but not always on a one-to-one basis. Sometimes a single female is attended by many males, sometimes one male by many females. Often among nest builders, where males build and attend the nests, a female will go from nest to nest depositing her eggs. This is the reverse of the situation among many other vertebrates in which a male territory overlaps that of several females, and he visits all of them.

Unlike most vertebrates, in which active male courters are competing for the female's parental investment, male fishes may be very active courters yet still tend the eggs and broods. Males may be forced into the parenting role because fish gametes are almost always released in water and because sperms are lighter and diffuse more rapidly than eggs. This means that a male cannot spawn until after the eggs have been deposited; by then the female can disappear and leave him holding the baby. This plausible explanation of why male fishes are more often the parenting sex was provided by a student of sociobiology, T. R. Carlisle. Her view fits well with the modern biological belief that each organism will try to get the most for the least: the most genes into the next generation for the least investment of time and energy that will ensure their passage. This is exactly what the female fish is doing, in effect, when she swims away from her eggs.

Modes of fertilization are as various as the attractants. Most are external, with a minimum of contact between pairs or groups of individuals. Some external fertilizations, however, require elaborate physiological preparation and long migrations to spawning grounds.

Internal fertilization occurs in all elasmobranchs and some bony fishes. It may occur without gestation. Many fishes are internally fertilized but shed their eggs, so they develop outside the mother. Amazon mollies and certain strains of minnows show coitus-dependent parthenogenesis, called gynogenesis. Their all-female broods, formed by the stimulus but not the inclusion of sperms, are live-born. Also, there are the scorpion fish and cardinal fish that accomplish internal fertilization when the specialized oviduct enters the male's cloaca. Some mouthbrooding *Haplochromis* species follow a unique method of internal fertilization. The female picks up both eggs and sperms in her mouth. The eggs are fertilized and incubated there. In many species, both gonochoristic (two-sexed) and gynogenetic (all-female), females may accept sperms of successive copulations with different males. Therefore, these females carry broods at different stages of development and may give birth every eight to twelve days. Also sperms may be stored for three to four months. Superfetation and sperm storage may make it seem as though a fish is a hermaphrodite, when in fact she is a gynogenetic or sexual reproducer.

Eggs and sperms expelled into the water perish unless they unite. Compromises have arisen in which external fertilization occurs but is followed immediately by internal protection or gestation. Oral and branchial (gill) incubation evolved separately in six different families of fishes. In some species it is always the females that mouthbrood; in others it is always the males, and in certain cases both or either may take up the eggs. During the incubation, the responsible parent cannot eat.

In the majority of fish species, however, the embryos develop in the water where fertilization occurs. Two interesting groups of fishes that conform to this ancient mode are eels and salmon. The former are catadromous, meaning they swim downriver to spawn in the sea. The latter are anadromous, meaning they return from the sea and swim upriver to spawn in fresh water.

In order to travel from the river mouth to their home lakes and streams, salmon seem to retain a memory, or smell-print, of the odor of these waters. If the olfactory sense is intact, migrating salmon will be able to make the correct choices at forks in the rivers by picking up the scent of the home stream, even when it is diluted to one part per billion of water. Before they get to the rivers salmon must set their course in the sea. They probably do this by taking cues from the sun and electrical currents produced as seawater flows through the earth's magnetic field. Using these guides, fifty million Pacific salmon (*Oncorhynchus*) arrive in Alaska's Bristol Bay early each July.

On the trip up the Canadian river system, a 300-mile journey lasting about eighteen days, the salmon undergo several sexually dimorphic changes. Their color changes from silver to red or to red with green heads. The male grows a humpback, and the female's eggs mature. During this migration no food is taken; there is no time for predation. All energy is drawn from internal fats and oils stored from the rich diet in the sea.

At the end of this difficult journey and fast, Pacific salmon spawn and die. The decaying bodies of the salmon parents fill the pure, clear waters with minerals that sustain the embryos and fry. These thrive in the almost predator-free waters, which their parents sought so skillfully. In fact, some say that the very timing of death right after spawning is a trait that has been selected for, just to sustain the young in this way. Were it not for the necessity of spawning in waters so devoid of food that they are also free of predators, salmon might make their run again.

A few Atlantic salmon (*Salmo salar*) can spawn more than once. Slightly less than 10 percent of the females can return to the sea to eat and restore themselves, but hardly any of the males. Females sometimes spawn three or four times before dying, but males never more than twice. Although only females make the nests, using their tails to scoop out shallow ditches in the river bottom gravel, males bear a heavier burden of prespawning physical and physiological changes. These include growth of hooked, sharp-toothed jaws that they use to defend the egg pits, or redds. Males are often wounded in the spawning season.

The mating pattern is intimate and well synchronized. After the female has scooped out the egg pit, about 6 inches deep, she crouches in it with the male beside and slightly behind her. The pair quiver rapidly, then shoot forward in the redd, leaving eggs and sperms behind. Although sperms survive less than one minute, they succeed in fertilizing 98 percent of the eggs. The female will dig five or more redds in her travels upstream. Usually the same male follows her throughout the journey.

Gravel nests are excavated by female salmon in such a way that they take advantage of the river's flow. The current carries small stones and silt over the embryos, keeping them secure until the winter, when inchlings emerge. After two years in rivers and lakes they will be about 5 or 6 inches long and will begin traveling down to the sea. There they grow and travel for thousands of miles. Pink Pacific salmon cover 3000 to 4000 miles in a year, and Atlantic species cover about 2000 miles.

Eels are the other great migrators of the fish class. Like salmon they travel huge distances, 3000 to 4000 miles, from Europe to waters around Bermuda. Also like salmon they have incredible olfactory acuity; it has been shown experimentally that they can detect the equivalent of one teaspoon of alcohol dissolved in Lake Superior.

In autumn, mature yellow eels, males of eight to ten and females of ten to eighteen years, prepare for their catadromous journey. They change to a silvery color, and their eyes alter for deep-sea vision. Inside, their reproductive organs reach maturity. The drive to reach the sea to disperse gametes is so powerful that eels in ponds and lakes cross wet, grassy land to enter rivers that will carry them down. After spawning, they die. The fertilized eggs are left floating to hatch into elvers, which mature for about three years and then begin to ascend the rivers where they will live for seven to fifteen years, growing to lengths of more than 5 feet. With salmon and eels, K- and r-strategies are interwoven. They shed many eggs into water, like r-strategists, but they literally kill themselves to spawn in the right setting.

The only well-observed cases of shared parenting combined with pair-bonding are among the many species of South American cichlid fishes. The discus fish (*Symphysodon aequifasciatus*) is one of these. Both parents care for the embryos and then supply the young fry with food in the form of mucus, which covers their bodies. The aquarium-raised fry of this species will eat from their parents' bodies for five weeks.

In another species—the Indian orange chromide (*Etroplus maculatus*)—observed under natural conditions, the young were seen foraging for other foods, then returning to their parents for a bite of mucus every ten minutes or so. There is something vital in the mucus; young deprived of it die or are handicapped in development.

The mucous secretion is stimulated by pituitary prolactin, the same substance that makes avian crop-milk and human and all other mammalian milk flow. In fact, prolactin has been called the mother love hormone because it stimulates lactation and mothering behavior, even in certain males. (The male penguin, for example, will experience an uncontrollable urge to sit on an egg, after being given prolactin. If he cannot find one, he will sit on an egg-sized stone.)

These special cichlids could be called mammal fishes. Like certain mammals, they show much interaction between members of the group and strong pair-bonding. Again, marked parenting and much social interaction between adults seem to be linked.

Snapping at their parents' flanks for a vital bit of mucus every ten minutes for five weeks evidently cements the flank-touching behavior into the young fry. Even when they grow up, they approach each other with this friendly bump and nip. Smaller members always greet larger members of the species in this way. The flank-touching behavior is seen between equals only during courtship. Wickler uses this behavior as an example of his concept of the emancipation of brood-tending behaviors for achievement of pair-bonding. (Brood-tending behavior is used here in the broadest sense to include what young do to parents as well as what parents do to young. What works for an offspring with its parents is what it is likely to try in other social interactions. By "what works" I mean that which makes the all-powerful parent behave gently, give food and comfort.)

All internal fertilization and gestation in fishes, except for scorpion fishes and cardinal fishes, pipefishes, and seahorses and seadragons, occur when the male introduces sperms into the female via her cloacal opening. The most common form of internal fertilization in teleosts occurs when the male's anal fin, which may be modified with a hook or claw and elongated to form a gonopodium (fertilizing appendage), enters the female. During internal fertilization, the female's ovarian fluids penetrate the male's gonopodium and reduce the viscosity of the sperm-binding matrix. Thus she causes sperms to flow into her.

The most uncommon way for teleost eggs to be internally fertilized is the method adopted by the marine tarpon (*Megalops*). She bites off and swallows the sperm-bearing segments of several males. The sperm must enter her gut, penetrate its wall, and swim through the body cavity to reach the ovaries.

Another unusual mode of internal fertilization is that of *Haplochromis*, one of the mouthbrooders. First, the female scoops up her unfertilized eggs in her mouth. Then she darts at and tries to swallow the spots on the underside and tail of any nearby male, for these spots look just like eggs to her. Simultaneously, the male releases sperms, and she picks up these instead of the spots she had aimed at. The female soon has a mouthful of embryos to incubate.

The evolutionary antecedents of mouthbrooding behaviors, in *Haplochromis* and other species, probably existed in the form of moving eggs from one nest to another by mouth to avoid predators. Another possible antecedent may have been transferring embryos by mouth to a nest of bubbles to keep them afloat and aerated.

The exceptional cases of internal fertilization in which females take the penetrating role occur among the cardinal fishes, seahorses, seadragons, and pipefishes. Inserting the genital papilla into a slit in the male's belly, the seahorses, seadragons, and pipefishes do not draw out sperms, as do cardinal fishes, but actually impregnate their mates by pumping eggs into the male brood pouch, where they are fertilized and retained for about ten days. When the embryos have become miniature adults, the male gives birth to them with strong, muscular spurts. The 10-inch seadragon (*Phyllopteryx taeniolatus*) male looks like a surrealist's sketch of a skinny yellow and purple dog as he carries two hundred gaudy pink eggs under his tail. For three to five weeks, he takes on the parental commitment that females fulfill in other live-bearing species.

Like males in other species, the female seahorse is the colorful, competitive member, courting the male for his parental investment. Her contribution to the offspring ends with her gametes, while the males must gestate the embryos using a placentalike structure to feed them. Sociobiologists say there is a general lesson here. The more parenting sex is the courted sex. It has the "right," perhaps the "duty," to be coy (reluctant to mate), a tactic which may serve to test the prospective spouse, to see if he or she is interested enough to provide a nursery territory or invest in a continuing relationship that will probably include shared parenting. The prospective spouse also benefits from the coyness of the courted sex because a courtship interval may give the gamete donor (usually male) time to learn whether or not the gamete receiver (usually female) has already been impregnated by another. In this case, the courter would be wise to pursue another partner, so that his (or her) genes will have a chance of passing to the next generation.

These explanations do not apply to seahorses and seadragons because they are not monogamous. Still, it is true that the females court the shy males. Maybe coyness is just an adaptation to secure adequate preparation of the gametes via hormones released during courtship.

In any case, the reluctant partner of either sex must be induced to mate. Because of this, the coy partner automatically becomes the selector of attractive features and successful courting tactics in the pursuer. When the reluctant partner acquiesces in the presence of certain traits, it puts any genes that may be associated with these traits one step closer to entering the next generation via offspring. (If one sex's reluctance to mate is reduced for some reason—as some say the woman's has been by birth control and liberation—then that sex loses some of its selector powers and its ability to obtain parenting commitment from the partner.)

The viviparous and oviparous sharks, skates, and rays are all internally fertilized. They have glands at the beginning of the oviducts that store sperms and also secrete mucus and a horny shell around the fertilized eggs in egg-laying species. In order to copulate in shallow water, the male shark gets the female's attention by grabbing one of her pectoral fins (the shark's counterpart of an arm) in his mouth. But the female, who is larger, usually pulls away, letting part of her fin be torn off. The male grabs her again and again, until he has a firm enough hold to flip her on her back and insert his cartilage-reinforced claspers (modified pelvic fins) into her cloaca, breaking her hymen if she is a virgin. Their embrace may last twenty minutes.

Eggs then pass into the uterus and gestation lasts several months. In smooth dogfish (*Mustelus canis*), for example, the embryos mature for ten months. This species, also aptly known as "nursehound," has very yolky eggs, in spite of the fact that the young are gestated. First the embryo lives off the egg, and then a yolk-sac placenta forms a close attachment to the uterine wall. A fully developed umbilical cord containing an artery, vein, and segment of intestine begins to carry nourishment to the fetus.

Rays have no such placenta, but they nourish their embryos internally with up to seventy thousand villi (fingerlike outgrowths) lining the uterus. These tiny projections supply an albuminous uterine milk, which is aspirated by the unborn rays through their breathing spiracles.

Selachians, as sharks, rays, and skates are called, sometimes nurture enormous embryos, and generally, the larger the female, the larger her live-born young or her externally hatched eggs. Large females, large embryos, and long gestation periods go together. For example, the surface-cruising basking shark, grown to 12 tons (the equivalent of two elephants) on a diet of tiny plankton, gestates her embryo for two years or longer. But the basking shark is not the largest fish; that honor is reserved to the whale shark, which can weigh as much as 20 tons and measure up to 75 feet, an average specimen being "only" about 10 tons and 32 feet. Whale sharks are oviparous, and each of their eggs is encased in a horny shell that could easily house a set of human quadruplets.

The number of embryos gestated at one time by selachians can also be astonishing. A pregnant 18-foot tiger shark when cut open contained a brood of eighty-two young, each clothed in the brightly striped birth membranes that give the species its name.

Compared to their size the rays carry the largest embryos of all fishes. A 2-foot-wide ray can contain two embryos, each more than a foot wide when unrolled. Babies may be ejected if the mother is frightened or injured. A harpooned ray was seen to vault from the sea and give birth in midair. While she died, her offspring was saved when it landed on the water's surface and was swept to safety under the wing of a male ray.

A giant manta ray caught off the shore of French Somaliland required twenty-two boys to lift and drag her carcass to a butchering platform. She contained an embryo weighing 50 pounds. This big baby was found curled up in its own wings, and when it was placed in the sea, it spread them and gracefully floated away.

Amazingly, however huge, numerous, hard, pointy, or abrasive the young or the egg cases may be, they do not injure the mother as they are delivered. In addition to the thick skin around her cloaca, the female is protected by special birth adaptations of the emerging young. For instance, the quills that cover the skin of all spiny dogfish are tipped with soft cartilage at birth, so they will not tear her. These tips slough off immediately, so the baby shark is fully armed. Hammerhead babies are born with the sides of their wide heads folded back. This arrangement prevents injury to the mother, although the litter may number twenty pups or more.

Skates are the other major selachian group, and they are just as prolific as sharks and rays. They copulate, but unlike many of their viviparous relatives, skates are all egg laying. Their black, rectangular egg cases, with long curving projections at each corner, are familiar sights on the Atlantic beaches of North America. Each case may shelter and nourish about seven embryos for four to fifteen months. This system permits skates to reproduce abundantly. In fact, they are so numerous that a trawler off Long Island Sound once reported taking in an average of about 100 pounds of little skate *per hour*.

Complex internal gestation and, alternatively, hard egg cases, as durable as any land eggs, existed three hundred million years ago. This makes us wonder if viviparity and shelled oviparity can be labeled advanced characteristics, found only in more recently evolved birds and mammals. Although we think of "higher" animals as having internal gestation or much mothering, there are many invertebrates, including certain land snails, scorpions, and the tsetse fly that give birth to their young live, and many "lower" vertebrates, like the selachians, that do also. Internal gestation and mothering are specializations that have arisen in many parts of the animal kingdom. They did not await the development of "higher" or "more advanced" organisms; they were called out by natural selection when needed and where possible. It is only in the broad overview that we see these special adaptations—gestation plus mothering—accumulating in the classes of vertebrates after reptiles.

Among bony fish there are many species of perches, blennies, and rockfishes and three whole families in the cyprinodont order (small spindle-shaped fishes) in which females gestate: the live-bearer, topminnow, and four-eyed families. (The last gets its peculiar name from the fact that the lower half of its eye is accommodated to underwater vision, while the upper is accommodated to seeing in air.) Naturally, all these females are internally fertilized.

Guppies (species in the live-bearer family) give birth to their young headfirst. Many of them are expelled together by peristaltic waves passing down the reproductive tract wall. A remarkable form of population control and sex ratio balance, two females for each male, is practiced by guppies. They eat their offspring in just sufficient numbers to ensure that they each end up having at least half a gallon of water to swim in. Laboratory experiments have shown that even when food and oxygen resources are sufficient in a smaller volume of water, cannibalism will occur, thereby giving each survivor more space.

An experiment conducted by C. M. Breder, then curator of fishes at the American Museum of Natural History, illustrated how "crowding" of guppies triggers the eating of newborns. When he placed a pregnant female in a tank for six months, she gave birth four times to a total of 372 young. (The impregnated guppy can store sperms, so one copulation will suffice for several births during a six-month period.) In spite of the fact that there was food and oxygen sufficient for five hundred guppy-sized fishes in the tank, the mother ate all but a few of her young after each birth. Therefore, by the end of six months, only nine fishes remained, six female and three male.

Another tank, similarly supplied, into which seventeen males, seventeen females, and seventeen juveniles had been placed, contained the same proportion (2:1) of females and males after a six-month period. Young guppies were eaten immediately by their mothers, and some of the original adults died. The tank population was down to nine again by the end of six months. How the guppies eat males and females in just the right quantities to produce the 2:1 sex ratio is not known.

In many of these viviparous bony fishes, the embryos develop inside the follicle of the egg, which becomes vascularized (enriched with blood vessels) and develops feeding villi. This arrangement is just one variety of ovarian gestation; in other cases, leafy extensions of the ovarian wall may grow directly into the embryos' mouth and gill cavities, or the embryos may have anal, urogenital, or fin extensions that interdigitate with the ovarian surface.

Between the two ends of the reproductive spectrum—internal fertilization and parthenogenesis—stands the phenomenon of gynogenesis.

It is a method of reproduction that includes both copulation and formation of an organism from an egg alone. Sperms received during copulation with males of closely related species stimulate but do not fertilize eggs to form all-female broods. So it is said the eggs are sperm dependent, but not sperm incorporative.

If females carrying sperm-dependent eggs were to become so numerous as to crowd out the females of the closely related gonochoristic (two-sexed) species, they would assure their own extinction, because there would be no more males left to mate with (since the females that produce them through sexual reproduction would be gone).

Males of closely related species must guard against mating with gynogenetic females, if their genes are to survive. Laboratory experiments have shown that males using a mouth-to-genital-region "smell" test can detect and mate preferentially with females of their own sexually reproducing species. In nature, however, a scarcity of normal females, such as in a drying pool, where there are mostly gynogenetic females, may leave males little choice but to mate with them and form offspring that contain no male genes.

Although many fishes have been mistaken for hermaphrodites because of sperm storage and delayed fertilization, or slow maturation into distinct sexes, the only ones that are hermaphroditic are those that possess both male and female gamete-producing tissues at some time in their lives, either synchronously or sequentially. Whether they are external or internal fertilizers, normally occurring hermaphrodites are fairly common among fishes. In certain species every individual is both a male and female, simultaneously or serially. Hermaphroditism may also be induced in some fishes by partial surgical removal of the ovaries or by fungal infestation. Such interference may cause the ovotestes to release sperms, allowing former females to father broods.

The most dramatic hermaphrodites are the ones that change sex rapidly. The serranid (sea bass), sparid (sea bream), scarid (parrot fish), and labrid (tropical reef fishes and wrasses) families have this ability. Sometimes a pair of fishes will change sex back and forth, reciprocally serving each other with the appropriate gametes. Within a few seconds, the sea bass (*Serranus subligarius*) begins to change from male to female or from female to male. The partner that assumes the male role wears what is known as a nuptial dress, consisting of the bright colors and patterns on its flanks and fins.

When the female has yielded her eggs and the male his milt, they may reverse roles, and the female, who is indigo, will turn fiery orange.

It is as quick as a blush. Even if there is no partner, a *Serranus* female can lay her eggs, quickly change into a male, and release a stream of fertilizing sperms.

V. B. Dröscher supplies a vivid description of *Serranus subligarius*, which he concludes by saying, "This fish reveals the following fact about the history of evolution. The existence of males may prove beneficial to a given species, yet it is by no means necessary that the two sexes be embodied in separate individuals." Hermaphroditic fishes are a reminder of the dual sexual potentiality in each individual of almost all vertebrate species, even human beings.

The sparid family, containing species of porgy and sea bream, shows the most complex expression of hermaphroditism in the order of perch-like fishes, to which all the normally hermaphroditic fishes belong. In some species an individual is female first and grows to be a functional male in time. Fishes of the species *Sparus auratus* have male gonads that mature in the second year and are supplanted in the third to fifth years by functional ovaries. In another species, *Pagellus acarne*, there are some females that were male first and there are others that were female from birth. In other words, there are two ways of being female in one species. Sparids also contain gonochoritic species. So, there is a spectrum in this family from species that are serial hermaphrodites of both the protogynous and protandrous variety, to species in which all members are rudimentary hermaphrodites until conditions call forth one or the other sex, and to species that are structurally and functionally dimorphic.

It is just another step to the interesting expression of hermaphroditism that occurs in species whose members arrange themselves in harems, the leaders of which may be females that have become males. This social pattern is typical of the Great Barrier Reef "cleaner" fishes, which remove parasites from the skin of other fishes.

One male leads three to six females around a single territory. They lay their eggs only in his nest. There is usually one dominant female. Sometimes there are two codominant females, and they will generally be the oldest members of the harem. Within hours of the death of the male cleaner fish, the senior female begins to show aggressive displays typical of a male. If her territory is not immediately invaded by an outside male, she becomes fully masculine within two to four days. She then courts the rest of the harem, particularly the new top female. Her ovaries, which contained crypts of tissue capable of sperm production, have turned into fully functional testes.

Species of another order (the cyprinodont) often show simultaneous hermaphroditism. They are small spindle-shaped fishes of many colors, including the Amazon mollies; guppies; blind, translucent cavefishes that live in underground waters; and high-jumping, golden Rivulus. They can live in fresh water or seawater, depending on the species, and are often kept in aquaria.

One species of *Rivulus* was raised for three generations from a single female whose ovotestes could produce both viable eggs and sperms. A few males developed from her self-fertilized eggs, but they did not seem to be reproductively functional. The ability to self-fertilize is adaptive in this genus because members of it often find themselves alone in isolated bodies of water. But tropical fishes that are hermaphroditic, like many of the sea bass family mentioned before, live in populous waters. Why, then, have they evolved simultaneous hermaphroditism? Could their habitat have changed?

No general correlations between habitat and hermaphroditism have been established. Some hermaphrodites are benthic, others pelagic. Some are internal fertilizers, others external. The only thing that bony-fish hermaphrodites seem to have in common is the undifferentiated ovotestis. Description of any single natural selective pressure or complex of pressures that favor the development of hermaphroditism in fishes awaits future ichthyologists.

The complexity of fish sexuality challenges the concept of a simple progression from asexual to sexual animal forms. Clearly it is more complicated than that. Sometimes animals we consider to be lower on the evolutionary scale, like snails and spiders, may have well-differentiated sexes or give birth to small but fully formed young, while animals we consider to be higher, like fishes, amphibians, and reptiles, sometimes are not well defined into two sexes or may spawn asexually produced carbon copies of themselves.

Perhaps it is better not to think of animals as "lower" and "higher" than each other but as earlier- and later-evolved. Perhaps it is better to think of the mutual dependence of asexual and sexual processes, both within and between organisms, rather than of a simple progression from asexual to sexual.

The story of the female animal has fanned through the class of Fishes, revealing that dimorphism and mode of reproduction are more variable and may be involved with the evolution of group formation and the development of behaviors that appear intelligent. Sexuality is not just a perpetuator of life; it is an organizer of life.

4 | FEMALE VERTEBRATES CONQUER LAND

Amphibians and reptiles are collectively called herptiles. Being a female herptile means having taken another evolutionary step toward the female-mother identity. Again, there is no smooth progression from "simple" to "complex" organisms, from amphibians with shadowy sexual dimorphism, many eggs, and little or no mothering to reptiles with clear sexual dimorphism, relatively few eggs, and careful mothering. But this is the overall trend that appears when the two classes are compared.

All amphibians derive from an ancient fish lineage that lived in the Late Paleozoic era, about 375 to 400 million years ago. The first amphibians probably developed from a fish that looked something like the heavily scaled coelacanth, which is the only living representative of land vertebrates' ancestral fossil fish family, the Crossopterygii (lobe-finned fishes). Until 1938, all members of this family were thought to be extinct. Then a coelacanth was drawn up by the nets of a trawler off the coast of South Africa. With its stumpy fins, ability to breathe air for long periods, and internal gestation, the coelacanth, or, rather, an ancient fresh water relative of it, would seem a most plausible model for a pioneer inhabitant of land.

Although early amphibians displayed a triumphant radiation into many species by the end of the Devonian period, when they had no other vertebrate competitors on land, they are now overshadowed by more successful forms: reptiles, birds, and mammals. But these forms owe their current dominance to the first tentative steps of the amphibians, who, even today, divide their time between water and land. Generally, an amphibian is born and matures in water before it moves onto land. Although it passes most of its time on land, it usually returns to water to spawn.

Amphibians form the smallest class of vertebrates, only 4000 species, 3500 of which are frogs and toads, the rest being salamanders, newts, sirens, and limbless subterranean caecilians (described on p. 93). Amphibian reproductive habits are the most varied and their sexual determination the most delicately balanced of all land-capable vertebrates. This is not surprising, considering their evolutionary proximity to Fishes, the most sexually diverse class of vertebrates. Because of the many reproductive experiments pursued by amphibians during the period when they flourished long ago, no generalization about any aspect of their modern methods of reproduction can be invariably true. Their sexual behavior and even the type of gametes an individual produces can change with age or a sharp rise in temperature. For example, although their genetic sex is not altered, certain frogs (species of *Rana*) that have grown old or have been exposed to heat can behave like males and even produce sperms.

According to the species, an amphibian may participate in simple or elaborate courtship; shed her eggs for external fertilization or obtain sperms for internal fertilization; deliver eggs that may or may not pass through a larval stage; or give birth to live young. She may deliver in water or on land, her clutch may be large or small, and she may or may not show parenting commitment.

In each pair of possibilities above, the trend, among vertebrates in general and among herptiles specifically, has been from the former to the latter. Of course, we would have no way of judging the direction of these trends in reproduction, and we would have to say each method was a separate, species-specific adjustment unrelated to the rest, if we did not have the other vertebrate classes as reference points. Insofar as an amphibian method of mating, delivering young, or parenting approaches the general mode of fishes, it is labeled more primitive. Insofar as it approaches that of "higher" land vertebrates, it is labeled more advanced. Because we believe animals evolved from water to land habitats, we believe that reproductive trends proceed from minimal courtship, external fertilization, egg laying in large clutches, water spawning, and parental indifference toward the opposite situation in each case.

The move onto land seems to have pressured species to evolve from large clutches and r-strategies to small broods and K-strategies, and from simple courtship and minimal parenting to complex forms of both. The need for extra protection of the young helped distill out many new adaptations: homeothermy (maintenance of fairly constant body temperature), gestation, and finer sensory discrimination. These adaptations moved vertebrates away from stereotyped and automatic behavior toward a capacity for learning and producing novel routines; away from solitary individualism and toward social interdependency.

The changes required to create such adaptations imply genetic plasticity: an innate property of some organisms that enables them to grow in new directions and give rise to new lineages. The genetic foundation of this plasticity may lie in the trait of polyploidy, the presence of duplicate sets of chromosomes in the cells of an organism.

Amphibians as a group have more DNA per cell than any other vertebrate class. According to Claude Villee and Vincent Dethier, the amount of DNA per cell, measured in picograms (1/1,000,000,000,000 gram), ranges from 2 in Fishes and Birds to 5, 6, and 7 in Reptiles, Mammals, and Amphibians, respectively.

There are many ways to beget polyploidy in fishes and amphibians; sudden temperature drops or changes in mineral-salt and oxygen concentrations in the water may allow duplication of chromosome sets without separation into new cells. When salmon and carp eggs are stopped from completing meiosis by chilling, they remain diploid and form triploid zygotes if artificially fertilized. Stickleback zygotes have been made triploid (see Glossary) by exposure to cold also. These zygotes have developed into apparently normal males and into females that have some rudimentary testicular tissue.

Temperature fluctuations, low oxygen, and high salt content were conditions typical of the pools out of which the first amphibians crept. They were also the conditions that could have produced polyploid cells and individuals, as C. J. and O. B. Goin suggest in *Journey onto Land*. Fresh water ponds and swamps that are rich in vegetation trap minerals, like phosphates, which are leached out of the soil. Bacteria break down the vegetation, further increasing the concentration of salts. As plants decay, oxygen is used up. So the muddy waters, rich in minerals but poor in oxygen, may retard metabolism and cell division. The resultant polyploidy, whether in groups of cells or in whole organisms, may have lain completely dormant, destroyed the cell or organism, or aided its survival in less than optimal conditions. (Compare bacteria in which extra chromosomal material, derived from conjugation, helps the organism survive on deficient media; see chapter 2.) The extra sets may have supplied the uncommitted DNA needed by early amphibians to make their radical move onto land.

The Goins admit that their view is speculative, but laboratory experiments and observations in nature do support the idea that polyploidy develops in muddy waters. The fishes and amphibians of swamps and shallows choked with mud and vegetation are the ones with more DNA in their cells. Most fishes have about 1.7 picograms of DNA in their cells, but mudminnows have 5.4; goldfish in stagnant, muddy pools have 4.0; catfish in the Mississippi River (also known as the Big Muddy) have 8.8; and Congo Eel swamp salamanders have 284, more DNA per cell than any vertebrate in the world. (Interestingly, lungfishes, close relatives of and sometimes considered the subsuming group for lobe-fins [our amphibian ancestor's group], also have an enormous amount of genetic material in their cells.)

It has been said that the rarity of polyploidy in vertebrates is due to its incompatibility with the formation of two consistently different sexes. For instance, a triploid species (XXX females, XYY males) might produce five different types of gametes: X or XX eggs; Y, XY, and YY sperms (or vice versa, if the females were the XYYs and males the XXXs). Several sex-chromosome combinations in the progeny would be the result: XY, XXY, XXXY, XXYY, XYY. Who would be the females, who the males? Sexual ambiguity, infertility, and incompatible gamete combinations could lead to the extinction of the species. (Triploid sex chromosomes are not necessarily incompatible with survival and reproduction; witness XXX women and XYY men who are sexually well differentiated and fertile. However, they do normally reproduce with diploid mates.)

Tetraploid organisms (XXXX females and XYXY males, or the reverse in species with XY females) present an especially interesting picture, for they are apparently doomed if Y typifies males, but are potentially viable if Y typifies females, as it does in many diploid species of invertebrates, fishes, herptiles, and birds.

In the first case, XXXX females produce XX eggs. XYXY males produce XY sperms. (It is assumed that they do not form XX or YY sperms because XY assorts to the gamete as a unit.) The union of XX and XY is always an XXXY offspring. If having a Y makes an organism male, in this hypothetical species, then all the XXXY offspring would be male. These males might produce a few XY sperms that could unite with the XX eggs of normal females of the species, but the result would again be all male XXXY offspring. After some time there would be no more females, no more eggs, and no more species.

In the second case, where Y makes the organism female, XYXY females produce XY eggs, and XXXX males produce XX sperms. The union of XY eggs and XX sperms is again always XXXY, but now all the offspring are females. If these females were able to reproduce parthenogenetically, either because of a mutation or a viral, fungal, or bacterial infection, then an all-female (XXXY) species might form from eggs that did not complete meiosis. Or, if the eggs could complete meiosis to produce XX or XY gametes, then the parthenogens would be diploid XY females and XX males. Thus, the possibility of sexual reproduction would arise again!

Could it be that periods of apparently rapid evolution are assisted by phases of polyploidy and parthenogenetic reproduction? Susumo Ohno believes that the different reptilian ancestors of both birds and mammals were tetraploid and that at some point diploidy was regained. The implication is that the tetraploid interlude boosted the pace of evolution at these class junctures.

While the spiny anteater (*Tachyglossus aculeatus*) is a modern species, it possesses traits that may have characterized organisms in the transition from reptile to mammal: an insect diet, brief gestation followed by egg laying, and "rudimentary" suckling. The female anteater has XXXX sex chromosomes and the male XXY. Karyotypes (photographs of chromosomes in descending size order) of this and other monotreme species have by no means been finally analyzed, and it may even turn out that the female anteater is XXXY, but it is seductive to speculate that this species suggests, in its polyploid sex chromosomes as well as its anatomy and physiology, the role that extra chromosomes may play in massive evolutionary change at class "boundaries."

Duplicate sets of chromosomes may have allowed cells of certain ancient amphibians to experiment with novel codes, and hence with new enzymes and processes needed when conditions forced them onto land. "Once the invasion of land began, evolution took place very rapidly," say Goin and Goin ("rapidly" here being in spans of millions rather than billions of years). While it took about 2.5 to 3 billion years after the formation of the earth for the first cells to appear in the sea, and more than another 1.5 billion years for fishes and amphibians to appear, the first reptiles evolved in less than 100 million years. It then took them just 70 million years to not only spread across land but also to reenter certain aquatic habitats as well. It was as if a herptilian tidal wave had hit the shore, infused the earth with new being, and been pulled back into the sea.

We do not know exactly how many species of reptiles there were, but their scope was remarkable: from the long-necked, herbivorous dinosaur to the less familiar, upright carnivores, which ran quickly over land and grabbed their prey with stunted arms; from the flying *Pteranodon* with its 25-foot wingspan to the long-snouted, blimp-shaped ichthyosaurs of Jurassic seas.

How much polyploidy really can be credited with permitting the reptilian radiation remains to be shown. Still, the curious correlation between uncommitted DNA and rapid evolution remains. Even today polyploidy is part of the picture when all-female, pioneer species of reptiles, such as whiptail lizards, move rapidly into a new niche.

The boundary between the quiet amphibian estate and the sumptuous reptilian empire, known as the Age of Dinosaurs, was an eggshell. Eggshells allowed reptiles to master land, and only females could produce them.

Even reptiles that have returned to an aquatic life, like some of the turtles, come back to land to deposit their shelled eggs. And inside every shell is a special sort of gamete called the amniote egg, which can support an embryo until it has become a miniature adult. Avian and mammalian females branched off from different reptilian ancestors millions of years ago, but the legacy of their amniote eggs still recalls the basis of reptilian supremacy on land throughout the Dinosaur Age.

The surviving remnants of the glorious reptilian past include four orders: Squamata, the snakes and lizards; Testudinae, the turtles; Loricata, the crocodiles and alligators; and Rynchocephalia, containing only one species, New Zealand's unique tuatara. These reptiles derive from females that began to shell their eggs some 350 million years ago.

A solid shell meant reproduction could be independent of water. Eggs were safe from aquatic predators, which outnumbered land predators, and from droughts and floods. A solid shell also meant that fertilization had to take place inside the female in order for the shell to consolidate around the embryo and its food supply. No sperms could pass through a solid shell, as they had always passed through the jelly coatings of fish and amphibian eggs. This is why all modern reptiles and their avian and mammalian descendants copulate. Obviously, reproduction on land, the hallmark of the reptilian class, radically changed female existence.

Since internal fertilization was a necessity, efficient methods of copulation were selected for. In terms of behavior, this meant clearer recognition of other individuals in the species, some of which could be future mates. Cooperation between conspecifics, at least during the time of copulation, became mandatory.

In terms of structure, internal reproduction among reptiles was facilitated by the evolution of the penis. Although certain male fishes have anal or pelvic fins modified into sperm conduits and claspers, the penis of reptiles was an innovation. Only the tuatara was left without one, and all the snakes and lizards have two. Fertilization via the penis always means that the female is left holding the zygote. Whether she shells the fertilized egg, passes it and leaves the scene, or retains and nurtures it internally, she is left with more work. This is the reptilian heritage that we and other postreptilian females retain.

Thus, acquisition of a hard shell changed the female role and, thereby, the evolution of all species on land. While lungs and limbs were critical to the development of amphibians, and the bony spinal column and jaws had been crucial to the development of fishes, the most stately mansions ever to be built by vertebrate species rested on an eggshell.

Reptilian, avian, and mammalian eggs are all amniote eggs, named for the amnion membrane, which surrounds the growing embryo and its cushioning fluid. (It is this fluid that is tested in the procedure called amniocentesis, which may reveal a defective embryo.) A separate membranous sac in the egg contains yolk that passes directly to the primitive gut of the embryo. There is more yolk in the reptilian egg than in most fish and amphibian eggs because it supports the embryo until it looks like a tiny adult. This means there is no self-feeding larval stage in reptiles or their descendants, the birds and mammals, which use yolk or placenta to nourish the immature organism. The third membrane, the allantois, forms a sac for gaseous exchange, a function it performs cooperatively with the all-surrounding, protective chorion membrane in reptile and bird eggs. In mammals, blood vessels in the allantois-chorion placenta carry food molecules as well as oxygen to the embryo and carbon dioxide and waste molecules from the embryo to the mother's blood.

A few characteristics of reptiles as a group will be reviewed before considering the changes that living on land brought to females specifically. The skin of reptiles is not coated with mucus, like that of fishes and amphibians, but is protected by a layer that prevents water loss and sloughs off periodically. Reptiles must keep their skin cool at an ideal temperature of about 90°F. This is much warmer than the fatally cold point but not much cooler than the fatally warm point. In other words, reptiles can die from overheating with only a small rise in temperature, but they can bear quite a drop in temperature without suffering permanent damage.

In cool weather, internal hormonal as well as external temperature cues stimulate most reptiles to eat more in order to store fat for a period of quiescence and fasting underground. The cold reptile's heart slows down, and its lungs (or lung in the case of certain snakes) fill less frequently with air. The torpid reptile is still mentally alert, however, and will react to handling by squirming feebly, opening its mouth and biting, or possibly by voiding an evil scent. The rest, fast, and retardation of metabolic and physiologic processes, enforced by cooling, may contribute to the longevity of certain reptiles, but they are not immortal, as some legends have stated. Reptilian females are distinguished from amphibian females by all these attributes and by the necessity of copulation. (Except for caecilians, no *amphibian* group consistently employs copulation.)

Copulation not only gets the sperm to the egg before the hard shell is sealed, it prevents gametes from drying out, as they would be if they were deposited on land. But the question arises as to why the female wet interior was selected to be the repository for male gametes, and not the other way around? As seen for the seahorses, seadragons, and pipefishes, the wet interior of the male is just as capable of sheltering gametes and embryos. Even among mammals it is possible to fertilize eggs outside the female body, as is done in the conception of test-tube babies. Here the early embryo is injected into a uterus, but considering that there are recorded cases of pregnancies coming to term in the body cavity and not the uterus, it is not unimaginable that males might have been chosen by evolution for gestation. However, the reptilian stage of depositing eggs on land did not offer gestation as an option to early reptiles, female or male.

Because their eggs had to be shelled and had to carry sufficient yolk to bring the encapsulated embryo through its metamorphosis into a little landworthy animal, reptilian females, and consequently their avian and mammalian descendants, had to become the gamete repositories. Only the egg had the "genetic tradition" of consolidating nutrients around its nucleus, so it was selected to enlarge with yolk. In addition, only females possessed the oviduct apparatus for jelly-coating eggs that could be modified to lay down shell.

Like so many fishes, herptiles are only faintly dimorphic, which means the sexes are difficult to distinguish because their external features are similar. Usually the amphibian is larger than her mate, but among reptiles, only turtles and certain lizards are consistently larger than their males.

W. T. Neill, who gives a thorough account of alligators, crocodiles, and their kin in *The Last of the Ruling Reptiles*, says that sexual dimorphism in size is an adaptation that reduces competition between males and females for food. For instance, among the American alligators only the full-grown males of more than 10 feet take large prey like hogs and cattle. The females eat catfishes and garfishes, frogs, turtles, birds, and some insects. (Formerly, both sexes enjoyed an even broader menu: beaver, capybara, tapir, wolf, bear, horse, jaguar, and sabretoothed tiger. These species have disappeared from the habitat.)

The most reliable mark of sexual identity among mammals, the genitalia, will not differentiate female from male in most herptiles. The external sex organs of frogs are similar, and only a few lizards and snakes have evolved a structure like the clitoris, which is found in some birds and most mammals. Although certain snakes have evolved elaborate penises, they keep them closeted in the base of the tail between matings, making sex determination on this basis very difficult. (During copulation the snake or lizard penis, with its barbs, warts, calyces, and hooks, anchors in the female, but she is not injured when it is removed because it draws in on itself, like a glove finger turned inside out.)

One amphibian that is difficult to sex lives in equatorial West Africa. It is the giant Goliath frog (*Gigantorana goliath* or *Conraua goliath*), which lolls in the spray of waterfalls, waiting for scorpions, insects, and smaller frogs to pass within range of its sticky tongue. The largest Goliath ever found was a female that measured nearly 33 inches and weighed more than 7 pounds. The only thing that distinguishes the male from the female is a slight lump on each of his thumbs. This lump, called a callosity, helps him grip the female during coordinated spawning.

In fact, males of almost all water-spawning species of frogs show this dimorphic feature, knitting their fingers and hooking their thumbs together when embracing the female from behind. Watching mating frogs spiral and spin, it becomes clear why the little male needs hefty thumbs to be reproductively successful. He needs all his digits to hold on as his larger mate swims around the pond looking for a place to lay her eggs, and as rivals try to pry him off her back.

The female, who is at the center of each mass of scuffling males, has been described as passive. But swollen to twice her normal size with eggs and imprisoned in a chest-lock by her mate, while surrounded by gouging suitors, she is incapacitated rather than passive. Actually, when male rivalry is not fierce, females are active in the mating sequence. They not only take the lead in finding the spawn site but also give the male his cue to spawn.

Among frogs that do not spawn in water, the male does not have calloused thumb pads. This is the case in the midwife toad (*Alytes obstetricans*) that spawns in private mud burrows. There is no piggyback swimming routine for the male to go through, and there are no rivals to resist. The female comes to a burrow, which has been prepared by the male, and lays her long strands of beadlike eggs, which the male fertilizes and wraps around his hind legs. He is the midwife; she hops away.

A dramatic change in the size and shape of the anuran (frog or toad) female occurs after spawning. Without her eggs she is slender, and she begins to croak, registering as a male to other males, so they do not grasp or torment her with futile mating.

With herptiles, it is often true that what does not register as male will be regarded as female. This is why a male frog sometimes can be seen embracing a stone or lump of mud, and the male gecko lizard will mate with an anesthetized male, whose suspended activity makes him look female. Similarly, if the blue cheeks of the male Mexican fence lizard are painted over, males will assume they have found a female and try to mate. In each case, when the critical male marker is gone, the object automatically becomes female.

Conversely if a male marker is placed on a female, she will be regarded as a male. Thus, the favorite wife of a fence lizard will be attacked by her husband if blue stripes are applied to her cheeks. Even in our species, females with male markers, such as extreme height or athletic development, may find it difficult to evoke sexual responses from males and may even provoke their scorn or competition.

Females, in turn, are susceptible to male marker wiles. Certain lizards with color vision will literally wilt at the sight of blue patches on a male's cheeks and throat, or at the sight of a bright pink throat balloon, and will fail to respond sexually if they are absent.

Sexual markers serve other ends in addition to mating. They help animals divide the resources of their niche and their activities. The most effective sexual markers may not be visible at all. Individual aromas (many of them undetectable by human noses), electrical fields, and vibrations that are beyond our senses can assist the sexes in their complementary survival.

Temperature and humidity often control sexual differentiation in herptiles. For instance, Bufo frogs will develop as females at 50°F, as females and males (that is, with the normal sex ratio of 1:1) at 64° to 70°F, and as males at 80°F. Drying the eggs for 50 to 75 hours produces a ratio of almost three females to each male.

Temperature variations in the spawn waters also account for certain populations of common frogs remaining undifferentiated when they are tadpoles, while other populations of the same species are clearly differentiated into female and male. There is evidence that certain frogs are protogynic—female first and male later. Although the mechanism of this maturational masculinization in frogs is unknown, temperature may play a role if females and males are found to occupy different parts of the habitat, where they may be exposed to contrasting water temperatures at different times in their lives.

A review of the structure and embryological development of the reproductive system in herptiles will show how vertebrate female sexual identity arises.

The general plan of the vertebrate reproductive system is bilaterally symmetrical. In females it consists of two ovaries and two horn-shaped openings (ostia) which pass eggs into their respective fallopian tubes (oviducts). Oviducts empty into one or two uteri or directly into the cloaca. Ovaries are attached to the body wall by ligaments but are *not* attached to the oviducts. The small gap between each ovary and ostium means that an egg from either ovary may go to either duct. Although this generally does not happen, it ensures that if only one ovary and one oviduct on opposite sides are functioning, fertilization is still possible. There is a disadvantage, however. Sperms usually fertilize eggs in the oviduct, but since there is a space between the ovary and the ostium, a sperm may occasionally fertilize an egg before it enters the oviduct. This means that an embryo may start to grow in the abdominal cavity, causing internal bleeding, pain, and sometimes death.

In some herptilians the enlargements of the ends of the oviducts nearest the cloaca are scarcely noticeable, and fertilized eggs seem to pass directly into the cloaca. Gradually, in evolutionary history, the female cloaca came to be divided into urinary and reproductive passages. The passage from the uterus to the external opening is the vagina, and the passage from the bladder to the external opening is the urethra.

Nestled on the outer side of each kidney, the ovary, or one small area of the ovary, will enlarge with several eggs, or just one egg, according to the species. Most fishes and amphibians have ovaries that

ripen seasonally, with all the eggs maturing at once for external fertilization. Fewer eggs mature when they must develop in the oviduct;
fewer still, if they are to gestate in the uterus. Reduction in numbers
of eggs fertilized at one time begins among the copulating reptiles and
is the foundation of the fewer-offspring-well-tended strategy that characterizes postreptilian females.

The eggs are swept into the openings of the oviducts by cilia (little
hairs), which cover the body wall, liver, and other structures adjacent
to the ovary. Then the eggs begin their peristaltic journey down the
long oviduct, which, in frogs, coils under the ovary like a tiny pile of
spaghetti. Interestingly, as the egg is being conducted down the tube,
sperms may be conducted up. In some herptiles there are even cilia
inside the oviduct that specifically direct the gametes in opposite directions, as if they were on up and down escalators.

Passing down the oviducts, eggs acquire their jelly coats and/or
shells. Those eggs that will be fertilized externally do not get hard
shells and collect in the widened ends of the oviducts, or uteri. In
certain frogs, the ends of the oviducts merge and the eggs collect in
one space.

Among salamanders that are internally fertilized, a female can take
a packet of sperms, called a spermatophore, into her cloaca, and the
eggs will be fertilized there instead of in the oviduct. There is also a
small pouch in the cloaca for sperm storage, which means that a female
may fertilize her eggs at a later date. An Alpine salamander (*Salamander
atra*), for example, can wait as long as two to three years before fertilizing her eggs with retained sperms. Each season, only two eggs of
the sixty to two hundred released by her ovaries mature. The others
degenerate in the oviducts, forming a soup on which the salamander
larvae feed. (In certain sharks, the young are also fed at the sacrifice
of siblings, but in their case it is not the fertilized eggs that embryos
may feed upon but other well-developed embryos.) The gestation
period of the Alpine salamander varies with altitude. From about 4500
feet to 9000 feet, "pregnancy" lasts thirty-seven to thirty-eight months,
which is even longer than that of elephants. At elevations under 2000
feet, *S. atra* gives birth in about twenty-four to twenty-six months.

Determining the sex of a herptile is not a matter of finding an XX
pair of chromosomes in her cells, as it would be in mammals. In
herptiles, there are no visible X and Y chromosomes or characteristics
consistently linked to either an X or Y chromosome. Indirect experiments (see p. 80), which change the anatomical but not the chromosomal sex of a frog or newt embryo, have shown that female
amphibians are often the XY, or heterogametic sex. This means it is

the female (not the male, as in mammals) that can produce gametes with either an X or Y chromosome and thereby determine the sex of the young. Male embryos that had their gonads feminized by hormones produced eggs at maturity. When united with sperms from normal males, these eggs always produced males. This indicated that males were almost certainly homogametic (XX). By deduction, females were seen to be heterogametic (XY). In humans and other mammals, it is the other way round: females are XX and males XY. (If a human female fetus could ever be so masculinized that the man it became produced sperms, then those sperms united with normal eggs could produce only girls [XX]. If a male fetus could ever be so feminized that the woman it became produced eggs, then those eggs united with sperms could produce either girls or boys [XY].)

R. R. Humphreys supplied further proof that many female amphibians are XY in chromosome constitution by grafting male gonads onto female embryos. When he mated a masculinized female axolotl (aquatic salamander) with a normal female, her X and Y sperms mixed with the normal female's X and Y eggs, producing both XY females and XX males. (Axolotls look like big tadpoles with legs and frilly gills. They remain larval looking all their lives and breed in this state.) Another type of offspring was also produced: YY females. These were laboratory creations not found in nature. Still, they were fertile and when mated to normal XX males produced all-female (XY) broods. Only after Humphreys dissected the females with the grafts and saw their ovaries in the process of becoming testes could he be certain these specimens were females with an XY constitution.

In order to understand how the early embryonic gonad can have dual potential, developing into either an ovary or a testis, it is necessary to know that it consists of two parts: an inner core called the medulla and an outer shell called the cortex. The ovary develops from the cortex, the testis from the medulla. Any embryo is also capable of producing two sets of ducts, the Mullerian and the Wolffian, which become the oviducts and sperm conduits, respectively. Usually, only one set of ducts forms fully; the other regresses. In female amphibians, however, both sets are used: the Mullerian ducts carry eggs and the Wolffian are retained to carry urine. (Mammals evolved more of a separation between excretory and reproductive functions; therefore, the Wolffian ducts disappear in female mammals, and ureters develop to carry urine.)

The bipotentiality of the vertebrate gonad makes it easier to understand how sexual ambiguities and apparent reversals can occur, even in postembryonic life. Some female frogs, for instance, can change into males when food is scarce, when they are exposed to heat, or in old age. Similar changes may occur in species of fishes and birds.

It is not known why there are consistently XY females in many species of fishes and herptiles, including certain frogs, newts, salamanders, and poisonous snakes such as vipers, rattlesnakes, cobras, kraits, and mambas. What significance, if any, can be attached to the fact that there is a clear division between birds and mammals on this point—female birds being XY and female mammals being XX? Perhaps, three hundred million years ago, that "cleavage plane" between the lines that would become birds and mammals was formed as the (presumed) XX reptilian ancestor of female mammals sheared away from the (presumed) XY reptilian ancestor of female birds.

Grafting experiments not only show that there is no fixed law that females be XX, but they also demonstrate that the (usually early embryonic) gonad and other reproductive structures are dual potential. This means that although the chromosomal sex of a female, be it XX or XY, is determined at the moment of her conception, her reproductive system may become male or female depending on hormone exposure during embryonic life and afterwards. Normally, female hormones bathe female embryos, but not always. Inconsistencies between genetic sex and hormonal exposure occur more frequently than we realize. The freemartin (in cattle, the female masculinized *in utero* by her twin brother's hormones) and the human male with testicular feminizing mutation (see chapter 6) are just two among many examples of apparent (phenotypic) sex being different from the chromosomal (genotypic) sex.

In contrast, the only thing that can alter chromosomal sex, which is fixed for each species, is a mutation or a mistake in the allocation of chromosomes, during meiosis, to the gametes of one or both parents. Thus instead of an egg contributing just an X it may contribute an XX, or a sperm an XY pair. When one of these misformed gametes gets together with its normal counterpart, it produces an embryo with cells containing XXX or XXY. If it unites with an abnormal counterpart, it can produce a zygote with XXXX or XXXY cells. In certain species, individuals with such unusual chromosome makeups may die, or, if they survive, be infertile and have ambiguous sexual identity.

Eggs mature in the ovaries, gathering yolk until they are ready to pass into the oviduct. There they acquire jelly and membranous coverings under the guidance of hormonal messengers. These messengers link the formation of eggs to environmental conditions, so that their appearance will be coordinated with the availability of sperms and the season of best survival for embryos and young. This important link is accomplished by the hormones of the front portion of the pituitary gland, which dangles from the base of the brain like a grape on its stalk. The pituitary is in constant two-way communication with the brain via its stalk, which carries messages along nerve and blood vessel connections. Since the brain is constantly taking in information from the outside world, it can always convey to the pituitary some "sense" of conditions: presence of potential mates or competitors, relative temperature, humidity, and light.

The part of the brain that forms a crescent of tissue over the pituitary is called the hypothalamus, and although it is made of nerve cells like the rest of the brain, it can secrete protein messengers, called releasing factors, just like an endocrine gland. These factors flow down the blood vessels in the stalk leading to the pituitary and cause it to release various hormones, one of which is gonadotrophin, which travels in the bloodstream to the ovaries.

The ovaries themselves are endocrine glands, which may be stimulated by gonadotrophin to release estrogen, progesterone, and a few other female hormones. Remembering their dual-potential origin, it is not surprising to find that they also produce small amounts of male hormones. In fact, it is testosterone, the so-called male hormone, that normally stimulates female sex drive.

Whether a female is a salamander, snake, horse, or human, the relationship between her hypothalamus, pituitary, and ovary is basically similar, and the chemistry of her hormones is too. This is why females of the amphibian class can help a woman determine whether or not she is pregnant. A woman may inject a small amount of her urine into a clawed toad (*Xenopus*), and if the toad ovulates within twelve to twenty-four hours, she knows she is pregnant. This is because the placenta, forming inside the woman, secretes gonadotrophin similar in structure to that given off by the pituitary; some of this gonadotrophin is excreted in her urine. When the urine reaches the ovaries of the frog, the gonadotrophin in it causes them to release eggs. That gonadotrophin from a human can make a frog ovulate shows the similarity of the hormones and the system operating in both of these vertebrate females.

In spite of this basic similarity, there are vast differences among species in the number and size of eggs. These differences are largely determined by the amount of yolk, which is formed in the liver under the influence of female hormones, and which is transported to the ovaries by the blood. Overall, reptilian and avian eggs contain more yolk than do fish or amphibian eggs. The eggs of fishes and amphibians that are fertilized in water go through a self-feeding larval stage and, therefore, are less yolk dependent. When internally fertilized, the eggs of fishes such as those of sharks may develop outside the mother's body in egg cases and so need an exceptionally large amount of yolk.

The fact that yolk granules exist at all in mammalian eggs may mean that yolk sustains the embryo in the earliest stages before the placenta is formed and/or that yolk accumulation is linked to the transfer of genetic directions from the nucleus to the cytoplasm.

Jelly, which is secreted by the oviduct, coats, protects, and helps most amphibian eggs adhere in a mass for collective fertilization and warmth. Some say that the jelly also acts like a magnifying glass to concentrate rays of light on the growing embryos. However, the jelly itself is not a heat conductor; rather it insulates the eggs by holding in the heat produced by their metabolic processes.

The number of eggs produced depends on many factors: the species, the method of reproduction and parenting, and the size and age of the female. For instance, Alpine salamanders that carry their embryos in their oviducts have only two eggs that develop into young, while European water frogs each spawn up to ten thousand eggs. Of these only one or two survive to maturity. In spite of the drastically different strategies of these females, they do not differ in the number of new adults they produce.

In general, the number of eggs produced decreases as the amount of care after fertilization increases, regardless of whether mother, father, or both parents are supplying this care. This is why the nonparenting common toad will lay several thousand eggs per season, but the mid-wife toad, with her assiduously parenting mate, will lay only about a hundred.

The development and deposition of frogs' eggs can serve as a general example of amphibian ovarian processes. From late summer, through fall and winter, the ovaries are filling with eggs, stretching the female's belly until it is plump with two thousand to twenty thousand ripe eggs. Each one looks like a little waning moon, with a dark portion containing the chromosomes at the top, called the animal pole, and a light well of heavy yolk below, called the vegetal pole.

The development of these two-tone eggs occurs between two membranes that coat the ovary—the theca externa and the theca interna. The internal membrane is lined with muscle fibers that contract and force the egg through the theca externa at ovulation. As the eggs grow in their sac formed by the two membranes, yolk, or vitellus, is consolidated and a noncellular, transparent film, called the vitelline membrane, forms around each egg.

Deposition of yolk is important not only in terms of accumulation of a food supply but also in terms of transfer of genetic information from the nucleus of the egg to the cytoplasm. Yolk, synthesized in the liver from the fats and proteins of digested foods, concentrates around very special fragments of the egg nucleus, called nucleoli, which break off and pass into the egg cytoplasm. The yolk blobs, or platelets, congregate around these nucleoli and form the food source of the future embryo.

Ovulation, which is the rupture of the ovarian wall by the ripe egg or eggs, takes several minutes. The eggs get slightly squashed as they pass through the ovary wall, but when the cilia roll them over to the ostia, they regain their spherical shape. By the time an egg has moved down an inch of frog oviduct, it has acquired its jelly coat and can be fertilized from that point on. Fertilization, which among amphibians normally occurs externally, sends the egg through its second meiotic division, and cleavage begins two to twelve hours after fertilization.

The frog can expel all her thousands of eggs in five seconds. In other words, she can shed them into water in less time than it took for them to emerge from the ovary. She assists this forceful expulsion by pressing down on her belly with her hands. Just as she is about to release her eggs, she signals her mate to release his sperms. The signal is different in different species. Sometimes she taps him on his pubic bone with her back foot; sometimes she arches her back; and in other cases, the swift rush of the stream of her eggs will touch the male on his pubic bone, feet, or legs and make him spawn. Simultaneous ejaculation by the mating pair ensures formation of zygotes and may jet-propel the couple around a pond or piece of vegetation.

Once the eggs have been deposited in spring and summer, immature egg cells, or oogonia, start to grow in the ovaries for the following season. A frog can pass through four and sometimes more reproductive seasons. Other herptilians, with longer life spans, pass through many more. Some salamanders can give birth seven or more years in a row.

Light seems to be an important factor in egg ripening, migration to breeding places, and sexual readiness. When vertebrates came to land they were exposed to more light. It became a cue to seasonal change, with lengthening or shortening of the day. Increasing light, both in spring and during the early morning hours, seems to be a releaser of frog spawning behavior. With light, algae in ponds proliferate, and R. M. Savage, the tireless frog watcher, believes it is the odor of these algae that attracts the common frog to breeding ponds.

Temperature does not seem to be as significant a releaser as light. Frogs spawn at low temperatures as well as at higher spring and summer temperatures. But increasing light could be cueing the frogs to a long-term trend in temperature rise. Savage feels that the relatively late readiness of female frogs in industrial areas is due to reduced light in these zones. (It must be remembered that Savage did much of his research for *The Ecology and Life History of the Common Frog* in England in the 1930s, when coal was used and the quality of the air in industrial areas was even worse than it is now.)

Frogs and many other vertebrates detect light not only with their eyes but also with an organ called the pineal gland, which acts somewhat like an eye in herptiles. It rides on the top surface of the brain, and in some species there is a thinning or absence of skull bone and a translucent region of skin over the pineal to increase light's access to it. In the spiny reptile of New Zealand, the tuatara, there is even a lenslike focusing device over the pineal. (In humans the pineal is drawn deep into the brain between the two hemispheres, but it still receives information about light via nerve tracts that are distinct from the optic nerve and, paradoxically, give no visual perception of light. This information about light affects egg ripening and related hormonal maturation in women, p. 234.)

Among herptiles the pineal has a triple function: temperature control, pigment alteration, and sexual cycling. Through its sensitivity to light, the pineal helps warn the cold-blooded herptile of overheating conditions. If it can get out of strong light, it can get out of the heat. Pineal light sensitivity also helps many herptiles vary their camouflaging skin color. In fact, the pineal originally attracted experimental interest when it was found that an extract of it could lighten skin. Indirectly, skin color alteration related to light could play a part in reproduction, because pigment patterns are often sexual releasing signals among herptiles.

Probably the most important effect of light on the pineal is that it suppresses the pineal's production of melatonin. Since this hormone inhibits ovarian activity, light, via its suppression of melatonin, must stimulate ovarian activity. Thus, increasing light in springtime could prepare the ovaries in diurnal (day-active) species for their reproductive work.

The development and deposition of alligator eggs can serve as a general example of the reproductive "advances" seen in reptilian compared to amphibian females. Alligator eggs, which are shelled, are somewhat larger and less ovoid than chicken eggs, and much larger than typical amphibian eggs, which are unshelled and only about an eighth of an inch in diameter. They illustrate the basic difference between the more invested strategy of female reptiles and the generally less invested strategies of almost all females that came before. When an alligator deposits her clutch of thirty to fifty eggs, they are pure white and covered with a slick mucous coat. They contain a very thick, albuminous jelly, which corresponds to egg white and supplies water to the embryo. As in all amniote eggs, there is also a yolk sac and an allantois, which is the site of oxygen and carbon dioxide exchange. The egg that is laid contains an already well-developed embryo, which, after several weeks more growing in the nest, exits from the egg by breaking the shell with one little buck tooth.

Before this occurs, however, the female has made a nest of vegetation scraps, which she finds on the ground and gathers with side swipes of her tail. She heaps dirt over the nest, turning the eggshells a yellowish brown. Decay of nest vegetation, which stains and spots the eggs, also produces heat. Although we associate incubation with an increase in heat, it is often important for an alligator to ensure that her eggs stay cool. The female seems to consciously counteract increasing heat by soaking herself and allowing the water to pour off her body onto the nest. This cooling procedure may be the fortuitous result of her needs, both to maintain her own body temperature under 95°F and to stand by her nest.

We scarcely comprehend the female's guarding need, which in crocodiles may last eighty days or longer. Needs supposedly exist to help an animal survive. We can understand her need to stay cool; this helps her survive. But standing by the nest, foregoing opportunities to eat and relax in the water, does not help her survive.

Mothering behaviors are too self-sacrificing to fit into an evolutionary scheme based solely on individual survival. They are more understandable as part of an individual's pursuit of survival in posterity through the passage of genes into the next generation. All organisms, according to this sociobiological view, behave as if they possess the need to transcend individual mortality. Such a need, in this view, is the grand effect of natural selection, which by definition culls genes that collectively cause organisms to reproduce and thus place copies of these genes in offspring. Land environments selected supermaternalness as the operant expression of the need to transcend individual survival, in the following way:

1. Because land embryos had to be shelled or gestated to avoid drying out, the number of embryos produced each season was limited.
2. Therefore, parents (usually females from higher reptiles on) had to ensure that these few survived.
3. To do this their strategy had to be "give more care." They did

not have enough embryos to trust to chance. The environmental demand for care was satisfied by natural selection of traits that improved the guarding and nourishing of offspring.

Because it was the female that was the site of fertilization and shell deposition or gestation, it was no accident that passage of genes from one generation to the next came to rest more and more upon her altruism. I think that it was from this inherited need and capacity to care for young that the ability to love, unselfishly, evolved in several vertebrate species. I believe our concept of moral altruism also derives from this mothering care.

Fertilization and birth methods in herptiles vary. Except for caecilians, a few toads, and several newts and salamanders, amphibians show external fertilization. Therefore females do not have contact with the zygotes, except in the relatively rare instances of external fertilization followed by internal incubation, in the skin, mouth, or vocal pouch of certain frogs. And here it may be either the male or female that has contact with the zygotes.

There is a form of internal fertilization, practiced by nearly all salamanders, which does not include copulation. Females pick up sperm cases with the lips of their cloaca.

In contrast, all reptiles show internal fertilization via copulation, except for the tuatara, a relict of the early dinosaur period (225–195 million years ago). According to K. R. Porter's *Herpetology*, nothing is known of tuatara courtship, and since the males lack a penis, it is surmised that insemination occurs by cloacal contact. Lizards, snakes, turtles, and crocodiles take sperms into their bodies directly from the penis. Copulation is followed by egg laying or live birth. With either method of delivery, it is rare for the female to have much to do with offspring once they have left her body. The constant guarding of nest shown by female crocodilians and the incubation of eggs shown by certain giant snakes are exceptions.

Frogs and toads, like fishes, spawn in water or on nearby stones and vegetation, and must ensure fertilization by immediate contact of sperms on eggs. This is why the female's spawn signal to her mate is vital. Anurans are similar to fishes in preferring to lay their eggs in the early morning hours, and they must make sure the male is also ready then.

Another way in which herptiles control the success of external fertilization is by placing their spawn correctly. If the eggs are held in the uteri or cloaca too long or laid in waters that are too cold or too warm, many embryos can die and the equality of the sex ratio will be disrupted. This is why frogs in temperate climates will spawn in one short period of the year, when water temperatures are closer to optimal (64° to 70°F). In tropical zones, they can reproduce more than once a year.

Because timing and temperature are so important to the survival of their zygotes, frogs have become masters of coordinated external spawning. But even within the limits of extreme cooperation between the sexes, courtship, spawn sites, and aftercare remain variable. This permits many species to occupy one locality. M. L. Crump reports that she found eighty-one frog species coexisting in 2 square miles along an upper Amazon tributary, each species employing a variation on the external fertilization theme. Some shed eggs directly into water, and the embryos develop in water. Some lay eggs out of the water, and the larvae (tadpoles) must be transferred to water in order to survive. Others lay eggs on land, and the larvae develop in a nest or in the parent's skin.

Regardless of the site of egg development, cooperative external spawning is almost always the case among anurans. Internal fertilization is a rarity but does occur in the West African toad, *Nectophrynoides occidentalis*, and in *Eleuterodactylus jasperi* of Puerto Rico, which gives birth to fully formed young. In the latter species, gestation is complete after nine months in specially vascularized oviducts. While there is no placenta, there is not much yolk in the eggs either, suggesting that the mother's bloodstream is sustaining the embryos in some way. Gestation, even in these anurans, is partially dependent on progesterone secreted by the empty egg follicles (corpora lutea) in the ovaries, a situation usually thought of as strictly mammalian. Birth is achieved as the mother's inflated lungs push her babies out of her cloaca.

If the female chooses an out-of-water egg site, it may be on overhanging leaves. In one group the male rides on the female's back while she hops around looking for just the right leaf. Depending on the species, she may deposit near the leaf tip or at its base, where eggs nestle in the cup formed by the furl of the leaf. In some cases, she regularly returns to the nest to deposit unfertilized eggs, which the tadpoles eat. So, even among anurans there are examples of females feeding young.

Entirely land-breeding species have the smallest clutches. From five to about forty eggs may develop directly into little frogs, omitting the larval stage. It seems that whether the entire vertebrate subphylum is considered or an order within it, females that breed on land cannot afford to be r-strategists. Their broods become smaller.

One of the most unusual methods of anuran reproduction is found in the muddy bottom waters of the Amazon and Orinoco rivers. Here the Surinam toad (*Pipa pipa*) is grasped in the same desperate embrace (called amplexus) used by all water-breeding anurans, the difference being that her fertilized eggs are pushed onto her back by the male, who steers her protruding cloaca to direct the eggs upward. These fifty to sixty eggs encyst in little pockets on the female's skin, and after six weeks toadlets emerge from her back.

There are also certain salamanders that employ external fertilization in water. These are the giant salamanders of Japan and China (species of *Andrias*) and the hellbender (*Cryptobranchus alleganiensis*) of the United States. The largest specimen of this group was found in China and measured 5 feet. The male hellbender waits in a depression under stones to grab a passing female, so that she may spawn in his nest. After she releases her eggs, he releases her. His sperms and cloacal secretions then mix with the eggs in water. After several females have spawned in his nest, he stays with the embryos until they hatch, ten to twelve weeks later.

Except for the giants just mentioned, all female newts and salamanders acquire sperms from the capsules known as spermatophores. They may insert these or expel egg cases to join the spermatophores. If they follow the insertion pattern, they may store sperms or use them immediately to fertilize eggs, which may be deposited quickly. Some salamanders gestate embryos.

Courtship of caudata (tailed amphibians) ranges from impersonal to intimate and may take place on land or in the water. In the aquatic modes, males ignore females, except to snatch their new-laid egg cases. Both egg and sperm packets are then attached to submerged stones, where their sheaths dissolve, allowing the gametes to mingle and form zygotes. Females may not see their mates or their offspring.

In contrast, land newts and salamanders often communicate with their males via visual, olfactory, and tactile cues. The crested newt (*Triturus cristatus*), for example, is mesmerized by the scent that arises from the base of her mate's tail. Some salamanders straddle and sniff the male's "hedonic glands" as if they were roses. Others inhale the perfume at a distance, as the male swishes his tail to spread his scent. This usually puts a female into the mood to follow a trail of spermatophores, pressing them into her cloaca, where there are tiny storage crevices for sperms. If the aromatic courtship ceremony is not long enough and the female is not ready, she may skip right over the spermatophores or even eat them. Male caudata sometimes discourage female noncooperation with a gripping amplexus, which may last several days.

Mating on land does not always ensure a more intimate courtship pattern. For instance, if an Asiatic salamander (species of *Hynobius*) is attaching her eggs to stones in a snow puddle, a passing male will push her aside and wrap strands of his sperms around the eggs. Technically the mates are on land, but they are following an aquatic fertilization pattern.

Similarly, an aquatic environment does not preclude courtship for caudata. For example, the Congo Eel salamander (species of *Amphiuma*), distinguished holder of more DNA per cell than any other vertebrate, will court a male by rubbing her snout along his body and taking sperms directly into her cloaca. The only other amphibians that have internal fertilization are caecilians and a few anurans that breed in swift-running streams, which would wash away the spawned gametes.

Over the millennia, herptiles gradually moved more firmly onto land and simultaneously toward gestation and live birth. Physical contact during courtship, which became extensive even among some of the externally fertilizing amphibians, was an evolutionary step toward copulation and viviparity. The phenomenon of delayed fertilization after sperm storage may have preadapted (predisposed) certain Devonian herptiles to retain embryos for ovoviviparous or viviparous development. The numerous modern species of ovoviviparous snakes and lizards shelter, in their oviducts, embryos which are sustained by yolk alone until they are born.

While the cloaca, oviducts, and ovaries were very responsive to selective pressure to become incubatory sites, they were by no means the only possible ones. The most unexpected organs became incubators in amphibians: the mouth, the vocal pouch, and the skin of the back or abdomen. It is not always possible to predict which part will be preadapted to a new function like gestation because selection for new functions may have occurred in habitats no longer occupied by the species.

Hormone systems also had to be shaped by natural selection to permit pregnancy to be maintained, but evolution of such hormone systems did not restrict pregnancy to mammals or even to females. As mentioned above, seahorses, seadragons, and pipefishes impregnate their males, who give birth to live young. Among nonmammalian vertebrates, certain fishes, lizards, snakes, frogs, and caecilians gestate their young. Among invertebrates, there are hundreds of gestating species, including the feared tsetse fly. Pregnancy can occur in the ovary, as in many bony fishes, in the oviduct, as in certain snakes, or in the uterus, as in mammals. Both E. C. Amoroso and P. J. Hogarth point out that among amphibians, the olm (*Proteus anguinis*) may produce either live young or lay eggs. This blind cave salamander may not be the only herptile with an oviparous-viviparous option. The lizard *Lacerta vivipara*, viviparous in most of its range, as its name implies, sometimes lays eggs, which develop and hatch.

The hormone that finally became central to pregnancy maintenance (in mammals) was progesterone, a steroid hormone which, in addition to its many effects on the female reproductive system, is the precursor of both estrogen and androgen (testosterone) and of all the vital steroid hormones produced by the adrenal cortex. (The adrenals are small yellow glands that cap each kidney in humans and are found in different positions with respect to the kidneys in other species. The cortex is the outer layer of the gland, and its hormones include the glucocorticoids [such as cortisol and corticosterone], which govern the body's use of sugar, and the mineralocorticoids [such as aldosterone], which control salt balance.) So, in its chemical structure and some of its functions, progesterone is related to these hormones that control alertness, blood pressure, and the ability to cope with stress.

In *Hormones and Evolution*, T. Sandor and A. Z. Mehdi observe that steroids are formed in all vertebrates, not just mammals; they are also formed in invertebrates, microorganisms, and higher plants. The evidence presented for the universality of the adrenal cortical hormones, including the sex hormones (which are produced by the adrenals as well as the gonads), strongly suggests that steroids have been operating in vertebrates for at least five hundred million years. Since progesterone is the common link in the different chains of chemical events leading to the formation of all the steroid hormones, it is logical to infer that progesterone is also very ancient.

Thus, hormones that may have preadapted certain herptiles to gestate, back in the Late Paleozoic, were probably those that had long been involved in the maintenance of arousal through sugar formation and utilization. It is possible that the links between arousal, awareness, intelligence, and gestation were forged early in the endocrine systems of mammal-like reptiles. Of course, internal fertilization does not have to be followed by gestation, as the enormously successful bird class proves, but if the reptilian ancestors of mammals were preadapted to extended embryo protection by sperm storage, delayed fertilization, and progesterone, then there would have been increased probability of selection for improved viviparity, reduction in birth numbers, and consequent intensification of mothering.

Internal fertilization, followed either by external or internal incubation, is controlled by the hypothalamus, pituitary, and ovaries. These control a female's egg ripening, receptivity to copulation, and in some cases readiness to care for offspring; the adrenal glands and thyroid are also involved.

Adrenal hormones help make sugar rapidly available to tissues and consequently control a battery of arousal reactions, like rapid heartbeat, heavy breathing, muscle tension, pupil dilation, inhibition of digestion, sweating, etc. Although these reactions are associated most with the flight or fight in the face of danger, they may also typify courtship: fluttering heart, sighing, wide eyes, etc., and naturally, typify the arousal of a mother defending her endangered eggs, hatchlings, or newborn.

Thyroid hormones regulate the use of nutrients and output of energy. If the iodine necessary for proper thyroid function is lacking, sexual maturation and function can be impaired. The tiger salamander (*Ambystome tigrinum*), which inhabits a broad geographical range over the continental United States and Mexico, serves as an example. In the eastern part of its range the species goes through complete metamorphosis, but in the west and south, where breeding lakes are deficient in iodine, the salamanders never complete metamorphosis. Somehow they are able to reproduce in their larvalike form. These neotenic salamanders are like the axolotls mentioned earlier in the embryonic grafting experiments.

(Women are also dependent on thyroid activity for sexual maturation and full fertility. In mountainous and inland areas, like the Himalayas, iodine was scarce and underfunction of the thyroid was common. This meant the age of first menstruation was delayed and normal cyclicity often not achieved. Nowadays, the addition of iodine to table salt protects against deficiency hypothyroidism.)

In addition to proper endocrine function, which is dependent on genetic integrity and good health, females need sensory contact with males in order to achieve maximum fertility. Squamata (snakes and lizards) were probably the first group of *land* vertebrates to consistently require active contact courtship for achievement of copulation, not just for locating an egg site and spawning in synchrony. (Some *aquatic* vertebrates, such as certain sharks, had already evolved this courtship requirement.)

Just as female snakes can eat at long intervals, so they can take in sperms at long intervals. Sperms collected in one intercourse can last two to five years in species of garter, night, and indigo snakes. Delayed fertilization ensures that even if a female does not come across a male for several breeding seasons, she is still reproductively viable. According to Goin and Goin in *Herpetology*, a diamondback terrapin (*Malaclemys terrapin*) had clutches containing fewer and fewer fertile eggs in the four years following a single copulation. In the first year, 123 eggs out of the total 124 deposited were fertile; in the second year, 102 out of 116 were. By the third year, only 39 out of 130 eggs were fertile, and in the fourth year, just 4 out of 108 were. The female's stored supply of living sperms had dwindled.

It is not known if female crocodilians can store sperms the way snakes, lizards, and turtles do, but it is likely, since alligator broods often develop after the usual hatching season. The incubation or gestation periods of internally fertilized herptiles vary according to environmental temperatures. Just as the embryos of certain snakes and turtles will overwinter in their shells, if their usual summer hatching season has been cold, and hatch the following spring, so the embryos of vipers and the slow worm lizard will overwinter inside their mother, if they miss the summer birth season.

We may close this section on internal fertilization with a summary of what little is known about reproduction among the caecilians, the least familiar order of amphibians. These are the only *amphibians* that achieve internal fertilization via an intromittent organ. Whether their eggs are deposited and incubated or retained for gestation in the oviduct, females invest much energy in the embryos. Copulation and care may have become elaborate in this group because living and breeding in burrows instead of in water placed their eggs in some danger of dessication and predation by carnivorous conspecifics (members of the same species). Coiling her body around the eggs or gestating them, the mother would have helped secure the embryos from these dangers.

An eyeless caecilian, like *Typhlonectes*, that measures about 1 foot, can bear young that are up to 60 percent of her length. She may gestate as many as nine offspring simultaneously. After using up their yolk supply, they rely on the secretory cells lining their mother's oviduct to feed them. Embryos have tiny teeth, which rasp at these oviduct cells, causing them to secrete a fatty food substance.

The parenting of female caecilians may seem inconsistent with their stage of evolutionary development, but it is not inconsistent with their survival needs. As far as is known, however, mothering has not been able to overcome the effects of an isolating environment and make caecilians social or highly communicative, as is the case in most other land species with disproportionate female investment.

There is one other method of reproduction available to certain herptiles. This is parthenogenesis. The only natural parthenogenesis among herptiles occurs in certain species of lizards. The first of these to be discovered was the rock lizard (*Lacerta saxicola*), in the Caucasus Mountains of Russia. Now it is known that several desert lizards of the southwestern United States are also parthenogenetic.

Artificial parthenogenesis in herptiles has been accomplished in many laboratories. Pricking a frog's egg with a pin can produce a haploid frog, which has half the normal number of chromosomes, just like honeybee drones and, under certain conditions, aphids, weevils, and walking sticks. (Induction of parthenogenesis has also succeeded with turkey eggs, giving rise only to male birds. Among mammals, chemical agents, heat, and shock have induced partial parthenogenetic development of rabbit and mouse eggs.)

Apart from Insecta, the reptilian class shows the greatest number of parthenogenetic species, including more than two dozen species of lizards. All members of these species are females, and all of them remain virgins, giving birth only to female offspring. These lizards are not gynogenetic like Amazon mollies. They do not need a sperm cell to trigger egg cleavage.

Some species of these unusual parthenogenetic land vertebrates have males and females in certain localities and only females in others. The all-female forms of the species seem to occur in areas of ecological disturbance, where there is a sudden windfall of good breeding places, like piles of dead logs and stumps, lush with insects for the lizards to feed on. Females with a mutation for parthenogenesis are able to reproduce fastest and take advantage of a rich zone for growth. Even a single female could start a colony before decaying woods turned into growing trees again.

After many years of trial and error, scientists learned how to breed all-female species of New Mexican whiptail lizards in captivity. Completely isolated from males, these females produced generation after generation of all-female young. Since the eggs of whiptails do not undergo complete meiosis, they remain diploid, if the female herself is diploid; triploid, if she is triploid; tetraploid, if she is tetraploid; and so on. In other words, in these lizards the egg chromosome number is no different from that of the female's body cells. The way in which the "ploid" is raised will be explained shortly. Barring mutation, all the female offspring are genetically identical to their mother.

The diploid egg that develops without the inclusion of a sperm can arise in several ways: by not undergoing the process of meiosis at all; by missing one or the other of the two divisions of meiosis (see chapter 1); or, in cases of sperm entry, by segregating all the paternal chromosomes in the first polar body, which then degenerates. It is not known which way lizards of the *Lacerta* genus produce the eggs that grow to maturity without sperms. I. S. Darevsky, who wrote the first reports on parthenogenetic lizards in Russia, believes the diploid eggs develop by skipping division II of meiosis.

There are two ways in which females with such eggs can arise:

1. The mating of a male and female from two closely related species usually forms sterile hybrids, but an occasional female hybrid can have the parthenogenetic trait. This female not only has adaptive traits from each of her parents' species that will help suit her to an environment intermediate between both parental environments, but she also has the ability to start a colony immediately. She does not have to wait for a mate to arrive on the scene.
2. The offspring of a gonochorist (male-female) species are usually dependent upon each other to achieve reproduction. Sometimes a gonochorist lizard species will produce a mutant female with the parthenogenetic trait. She resembles her parents' single species in all features, except that she has the ability to reproduce alone.

Amazing things can begin to happen once a unisexual female species arises. Apparently, certain females can still reproduce sexually with a male from a closely related species, as well as parthenogenetically. Since the female gives a diploid egg and the male a haploid sperm, their offspring are triploid. If any of the triploid females reproduces parthenogenetically, her offspring are triploid, but if one of the triploid females mates with a male and reproduces sexually, her young will be tetraploid. Charles J. Cole documents that several all-female species of lizards are triploid and that two specimens of tetraploid lizards have been found in southern Arizona. While polyploid hybrids of two closely related species may be mostly sterile, the existence of parthenogenetic females among such hybrids circumvents the problem of sterility or nonmatching gametes in females and males. Parthenogenetic females can continue to reproduce alone, and there is a real possibility that just such females pioneered the vertebrate conquest of land four hundred million years ago. Diploidy and sexual reproduction could have been regained, as discussed earlier in this chapter (see p. 72ff).

Parthenogenesis is a detour (perhaps a very important one) in the vertebrate trend toward dual-sex (gonochoristic) courtship, copulation, and care. Now we return to the main route of development by looking at courtship.

Usually a period of courtship helps the herptile form a pair-bond that lasts a maximum of a few days in the case of certain lizards and snakes, and up to a few weeks in crocodilians. Of course, there is a deficit of firsthand field observation of herptiles, and it may be learned that consort bonding, single or cooperative parenting, and social communication are more extensive among herptiles than previously thought.

The courting habits of tailless amphibians are sometimes annoying to humans. Anyone who has lived near ponds or bushes where certain frogs breed will notice their voices and understand why God sent frogs as one of the ten punitive plagues on Egypt. For the most part, females are not responsible for the noise. They only begin to croak after spawning, and even then they are not as loud or as constant as the males.

Each night in springtime, females arrive at ponds a few at a time. They are greeted by a full male chorus, which differs in volume from one species to another. Females probably do not follow the "love" calls to find the ponds, as is popularly believed; they are more likely to follow the odors of algae growing in the breeding pools. But chorusing may be a stimulant once the females are on the scene.

Although chorusing may arouse female frogs, it has a long history of being tiresome for human listeners. Savage mentions that when the extra loud continental frogs (such as *Rana esculenta*) kept eighteenth-century French nobles awake in their chateaux, the nobles forced the peasants to beat the ponds all night to make the frogs scatter. Understandably, peasants kept awake by nobles get just as irritable as nobles kept awake by frogs. In this way, courting amphibians may have contributed to the resentment brewing between social classes prior to the French Revolution.

Certainly, the frog has no time to deal with human displeasure. Gripped in amplexus that can last for days, she must find a spawn site. Sometimes, mating is so brutal it approximates rape. Even when the female is twice the size of the male, as is the African clawed toad, she can be squeezed so energetically that she faints, the male pressing out her eggs after she has lost consciousness.

There are more than two thousand species of frogs, and most of them mate less violently and more quietly. In some, the male chooses the egg site and prepares a nest or burrow. As in fishes, when there is some care of the embryos it is usually the male that provides it. The "rule" that the partner that spawns last in external fertilization can be left holding the baby applies to amphibians as well as to fishes. While most spawning is simultaneous among frogs, the male sometimes fertilizes the eggs a few moments after they are shed, as does the male midwife toad, who then carries the embryos wrapped around his legs for the next six weeks.

Among newts and salamanders the females come to the water looking for mates, but unlike frogs they usually do not stay in the water throughout courtship. On land, the female follows the male around, attracted by his scent. She waits for him to "lay" a spermatophore, the shell of which is composed of a solidified secretion from cells lining his cloaca. Deposited on the ground, it stands like a miniature modern sculpture, displaying the design of the interior folds and furrows of the male's cloaca. The female inserts the upright capsule.

Lizards may look like certain caudata but they belong to the reptilian class and should not be confused with the amphibious newts and salamanders. Lizard females are internally fertilized via the penis, not the spermatophore. They have their own distinct courtship patterns and can either lay eggs or give birth to live young.

Some lizards recognize males of their species by a specific pattern of head bobbing. Combined with other signals, like throat-sac enlargement, mouth opening, and tongue showing, head bobbing can alternate between a threat and a courtship display. Even with these primitive copulators, courting and fighting are closely associated in the general heightening of arousal. This is the beginning of male threat display being used as an attractant. Sometimes male lizards get carried away and nip the female on her neck and sides.

As herptiles evolved to a more consistent use of internal fertilization, cooperation for mating may have been built upon existing arousal reactions related to confrontation of predators. Aggression and lovemaking have long been mixed. Dinosaur fossils show that during courtship females received painful love bites, around the head, from their giant, herbivorous mates. Courtship became a cameo of chase and escape, with males and females assuming (and sometimes alternating) their attenuated roles as "predator" and "prey." Vitus Dröscher believes that early land-based copulation was accomplished by rape, and many females were injured or died in the contact.

It is not uncommon for the hormonal wires of strong emotions to get crossed, even in our species. From the boastful shadow boxing of a little boy in front of his girlfriend to husbandly cuffings, which wives in some cultures have come to equate with affection, women inherit a long tradition of finding just the right amount of threat mixed with tenderness, sexually compelling. That this is true does not mean females are masochistic or want to be raped. In fact, male aggression during courtship may have been accentuated by natural selection for aggressiveness in nesting female reptiles, birds, and nursing mammals.

Females would have passed any genetic disposition to be aggressive and territorial at breeding time to their male, as well as their female, young.

Eventually, males recycled the aggressivity and protectiveness of mothering into a sort of pseudoparenting with respect to the female in courtship. Just like a mother, the male came to defend his breeding area from intruders, to corral his females as if they were his children, to gently touch, groom, and even feed the female during courtship. Occasional slaps, shoves, or bites applied to females were no more than those a mother might have to use to gain the attention of her young in order to teach them something or direct them away from danger.

Since it was among the copulating reptiles that female care of the young probably first developed among vertebrates, it is not surprising that reptiles were also the first group to show widespread and elaborate courtship. Birds and mammals that evolved from different reptilian ancestors extended courtship and care even further.

Snake courtship involves gentle paired slithering and entwining. When more than one male shows interest in a female, the wooing gets less dignified, and several snakes can form an ungainly knot. Snake courtship shows that it is not only the female that can suffer bodily harm during mating. Once linked in coitus, a pair must remain together for hours or days, the time it takes for the male to pump out all his sperms. The female may drag him around, as he is anchored inside her. If the partners decide to flee in opposite directions from an enemy, the penis can break off. But since every male snake has two penises, one such accident will not necessarily disqualify him from future courtship and copulation.

Tortoises are slower than snakes in their actions, but they are still injury-prone during mating. Like her snake and lizard cousins, the tortoise must suffer male bites on her neck and front legs. At first she "runs" away, but after the male has inflicted several bleeding wounds, she is exhausted and tries to take cover under her shell. When she pulls in her head, her rear is exposed, and the male walks around her and climbs halfway up her shell to position himself for intromission. At this point, he is more likely to fall off his mate than to be rejected by her.

Marine turtles that migrate long distances from their feeding waters to their breeding beaches arrive quite reduced in weight after their long journey and fast. Green turtles swim 1400 miles from Brazilian coastal waters to Ascension Island in the South Atlantic. After they finish laying and covering their eggs, they swim out to mate with the waiting males. Thus they ensure that eggs for the following season will be fertile. These huge turtles are quiet courters, not as competitive and boisterous as other mass migrators and breeders, like salmon and walrus. The male turtle, who attracts a female's attention by swimming backwards, strokes her cheeks with his long fingernails, until she moves her tail to one side to receive him.

Alligator and crocodile courtship is noisy and much more ostentatious than that of tortoises and turtles. Their season begins in April, and their bellowing grows even louder after eggs have been laid. Both sexes roar to announce their arousal and to space individuals once they arrive in a territory. Their arrival, as with frogs at a pond, is probably dependent upon olfactory cues, rather than upon the roaring calls.

Females seem to favor males with more territory. One way males simultaneously show the borders of their territory and impress females is by raising the front half of the body out of water and then crashing down with a resounding wallop. This display is called head slapping.

Females can visit males in several territories and mate with all of them. Although bull alligators in captivity may mate with only one female, L. Garrick and J. Lang, who studied wild alligators (*Alligator mississippiensis*) in the coastal marshes of Louisiana, report that a male with a large territory in a lake had "priority access to females." This means more females choose to visit or chance to visit the male with more territory.

If a female decides not to mate with a particular male, after preliminary nose-touching ceremonies and a bit of muffled conversation, she swims away from his territory with a brief bellow of goodbye. It is impossible to tell what may have displeased her. Although humans cannot detect any odors arising from male alligator throat or anal glands during courtship, it is probable that female alligators can. (When an alligator is butchered, even humans can smell the scent of anal glands at a distance.) The female alligator who meets a male for the first time can probably pick up some olfactory information from him. There is no reason why scents cannot convey as much about the age, status, confidence, or sexuality of their producer as can vocal or visual cues. If a female turns up her nose at the scent of a suitor, she may have smelled good reasons for avoidance. She may have detected that he was not mature or virile enough to be a good mate, in which case he must remain in his territory, waiting for another female to visit him.

If the female decides to stay in a male's territory, he may proceed to court her by slipping under her body to give her a ride. Later, assisted by buoyancy in water, she will carry the much heavier male. Surprisingly the Loricata respond to very tender handling, although most of their skin is covered by thick bony plates. Stroking is however focused under the chin and on the "shoulder," where their armor is thinnest. That both mates obtain gentle caresses from each other, in spite of their normal habit of devouring prey or rivals, is proof of the absolute necessity of contact and patient arousal for crocodilian reproduction.

After anything from a few days to a couple of weeks of courtship, the partners face each other, and the male butts the female under the chin with his long, flat head and blows bubbles, which rise up and tickle her cheeks. She arches her back and raises her head with jaws open to signal her consent. Copulation takes place in shallow water, as the tails of the pair entwine for a few minutes. Then the female is off again, her courting visits to last six weeks, with most activity focused in the second week, which is about one month before she will build her nest.

Patterns of parenting often reflect the patterns of courtship. It is not surprising, for example, that the crocodilians show cooperative parenting after such prolonged and attentive courtship. Adult males as well as females tolerate hatchlings crawling over their heads and backs. Both sexes react to the distress calls of the young. Although more field observation is needed, alligators seem to show less dual parenting than crocodiles. This means that the American alligator is more solitary during brood-tending than her crocodile relatives in Africa. In both families, however, females stay close to their nests. The alligator's is formed of ground vegetation piled over a foot high, and the crocodile's is formed with mud and sand as well as vegetation.

Nestlings give high-pitched cries as they break through their shells. Nile crocodile females respond by opening their nests. They may even carry some hatchlings in their jaws. Female alligators apparently do not open their nests, but there are differing reports about their behavior at the time of hatching.

In places where there is a long history of human predation upon alligators, females will not assist hatchlings from the nest. The fact that some observers say that mother alligators guard their nests and assist departure of their young, while others claim that they do not, merely reflects that females in high poaching zones will behave differently from those in protected areas.

Even animals we consider primitive and incapable of thought or intention adjust their behaviors to circumstances. Observers who see alligators only in high poaching areas may think that defense of the nest by charging or by opening it to liberate the hatchlings is simply absent from the species' repertoire, and thus rate alligator mothering as minimal. But there is a range of expression of maternal care in each species. Perhaps the mothering norm for American alligators once resembled that of Nile crocodiles, but has been abolished by human hunters in some areas. Although eggs and hatchlings remain as vulnerable as ever to other predators—such as the black bear, raccoon, otter, turtle, and heron—fear of the gun may have made the alligator too timid to provide the traditional protection. Hence, man's presence in an area can cause a rapid drop in population not only through killing but through altering reproductive patterns.

Normally, young alligators stay near their mother at least the first half year of life, and contact may last from two months to two or three years, according to the species and the part of its range. By three years of age young alligators are 3 to 4 feet long, but they do not mature sexually until they grow to adult size, which is 6 to 8 feet for females and 14 feet for males.

Like alligators, Nile crocodile mothers guard their nests constantly. For twelve to thirteen weeks, they discourage monitor lizards, mongooses, baboons, hyenas, and warthogs that may come by looking for eggs to eat. Examination of stomach contents shows that the three-month incubation period is virtually a fast. Starvation or semistarvation among incubating or brooding females is not just a consequence of their need to guard the nest attentively. Selection to curb maternal appetite at this time also may have helped prevent predatory females from eating their own eggs or offspring.

The defensive and patient waiting of the Nile crocodile contrasts sharply with the behavior of turtles that lay their eggs in deep sand pits. The marine leatherback turtle, for example, shovels sand away with her hind legs and then buries dozens of her eggs so well that almost no predator can find them. Her cache is so secure that she does not have to stand guard and returns to the sea immediately to obtain sperms for the following year's brood.

The giant snakes (pythons, rattlesnakes, boa constrictors, and anacondas) and the American mud snake all show maternal care, while Indian and king cobras show dual parenting—the parents alternately guard the fertile eggs. Rattlesnakes, boa constrictors, and anacondas are all egg retainers. The "gestation" period ranges from 141 to 295 days. The Indian, reticulate, and African rock pythons are all egg layers, and many species of these snakes guard their clutches by coiling around them. Only the Indian actually incubates the eggs, raising their temperature with warmth from her quivering body. These snakes grow to from 20 to 35 feet long, and the python mother can coil her long body around as many as a hundred eggs at a time.

Python reproductive habits have been observed closely in captivity. Their copulation lasts only about ninety minutes, while, in nature, other snakes couple for an average of six to twelve hours. When the female is ready to lay her eggs, she shows signs of pain. She rolls, twists, and contracts lengthwise and tongues her cloaca; she rests on her back or side, avoiding pressure on her enlarged belly. She will cease eating up to one month before laying her eggs and will become very irritable, hissing or moving about excitedly if anyone approaches.

She lays twenty to sixty eggs on average; older females have larger clutches. Since it takes ten to twenty seconds for one egg to emerge, and the female rests for five to twenty-five minutes after every one or two eggs, her labor may last for several hours. Eggs are ovoid, about 4 inches long, and weigh 5 to 10 ounces. They are covered in a tough, leathery shell that can be dented but will not break.

The Indian python, whose brood-tending has advanced to the point of incubation, raises her body temperature by shivering and thus keeps her eggs within 1° of 90°F. Even if the temperature of the environment fluctuates between 78° and 90°F, the incubating female can compensate with variation of her body temperature.

There are other ways for snakes to ensure that their eggs stay warm: building the nest in a sunny spot, building it under bamboo, in hollow logs, or under brush where slow decay of vegetable material will provide some warmth. But the method of the incubating Indian python is remarkable because it contains at least two features found consistently only among birds and mammals: maintenance of high, constant body temperature, and extreme breeding-time territoriality. Even if her eggs are removed, she will coil around the empty space and quiver constantly, as if she were keeping the eggs warm. One egg-robbed female was observed to keep up her brooding and incubating for over one month.

There are in all about eight to ten thousand species of herptiles: about three thousand five hundred amphibians and six to seven thousand reptiles. Only about one-tenth of these consistently show considerable parental investment, but naturalists are finding that, in this small fraction of "invested" herptilian females, internal development is not unusual. Nest building, incubation, and gestation plus posthatching or postbirth protection of the young emerge as strong trends at the evolutionary level represented by the herptilian double class. This is not surprising since herptiles brought vertebrates from water onto solid ground, a move that made internal fertilization mandatory for deposition of landworthy eggs.

The avian class, an offshoot of one of the reptilian lines, took the next evolutionary step in the Late Mesozoic, about 150 million years ago. How avian females took flight, capitalizing on courtship, copulation, and care, is the next chapter in this tale.

5 | BIRDS

The position of this chapter after reptiles and before mammals should not imply that there is a chainlike order of evolution of the classes or that mammals evolved after or from birds. Like separate leaves in the furl of a blade of grass, the classes of vertebrates each evolved from some indiscernible seam within the other(s). It is possible, but controversial, that the reptiles had a dual origin: some from an amphibian ancestor, others from a form similar to the partially land-capable fishes described in chapter 3. Birds and mammals grew out of the reptilian line, and both these classes, sometimes collectively called the higher vertebrates, evolved around one another during approximately the same period of time.

When they appeared, about 150 million years ago, birds existed on the periphery of a strong ongoing biological dynasty. Just as fishes arose against the thriving diversity of plant and invertebrate life in the sea, and amphibians developed as a specialized branch of the fish hegemony, so birds evolved from one of the many hundreds of reptilian lineages that dominated the Jurassic period, from about 200 to 150 million years ago.

As dinosaurs wandered over land and other reptiles became adapted to the sea and air, a few of the first avian skeletons were sealed in the fossil record. One of these skeletons is that of the earliest known bird, *Archaeopteryx lithographica*, so named for its near perfect imprint on soft limestone. This cast clearly shows that the bird had feathers that are indistinguishable from those of its modern descendants. Were it not for these feathers, *Archaeopteryx* would have been classified as a reptile. In virtually every feature it resembled the dinosaur *Ornitholestes hermanni*. Its three-fingered hands, its four-toed feet with back-pointing big toe, its shoulder and hip girdles, its skull and upright posture were all similar to those of the small predatory reptile. In other words, if *Archaeopteryx*'s feathers were plucked and its wishbone overlooked, it would be mistaken for a reptile.

Once it was thought that birds arose from the order of reptiles that gave rise to crocodiles, which are the *living* reptiles that share the greatest number of traits with birds. But, now, reevaluation of simi-

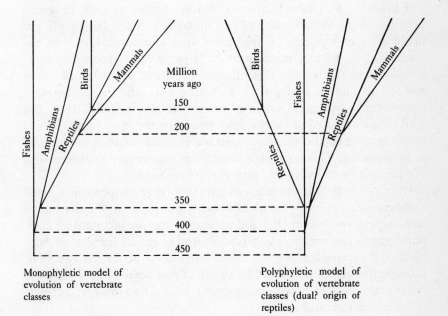

Monophyletic model of evolution of vertebrate classes

Polyphyletic model of evolution of vertebrate classes (dual? origin of reptiles)

Two ways of viewing vertebrate evolution. (Chart by Dr. M. Elia)

larities between the little bipedal dinosaur *Ornitholestes* and the first bird, *Archaeopteryx*, points to a dinosaurian and not a crocodilian ancestry for birds. This may turn out to be significant not only to understanding the anatomy of birds but also to understanding their behavior. As far as female avian behavior is concerned, a crocodilian origin might have meant more dimorphism in parenting, with the female taking on a very mothering character. But with evidence pointing toward a dinosaurian ancestor, there is, so far as we know, no heritage of a tendency to weight the female with all of the parenting responsibility. This may be part of the reason why we see more joint parenting in the bird class than in any other vertebrate class.

Although it is true that the closest living reptilian relatives of the birds are the crocodiles, it must be remembered that the reptilian ancestor of birds looked nothing like a crocodile, but like a lizard that scurried about on its hind legs, with its short arms and long tail extended. A completely different reptilian stock gave rise to mammals, fifty to one hundred million years *prior* to the emergence of birds. These mammal-like reptiles of the Triassic period looked neither like crocodiles nor little dinosaurs. They are called therapsids and will be described in the next chapter.

While birds and mammals are structurally highly differentiated classes, it is surmised that they had an extremely ancient common ancestor, predating both *Ornitholestes* and the therapsids. Since both birds and mammals had reptilian origins, they share the triple legacy of the amniote egg, internal fertilization, and rudimentary control of body temperature. Apart from this inheritance, birds and mammals were and are distinct; as biologist D. E. Carr points out, "birds represent a profoundly divergent class that never was in our family tree." So, while the discussion of birds cannot bear directly on mammals, it can show amazing parallels in the sexual and parental strategies of females in both classes. These parallels arose from similar confrontations with the necessities of living and reproducing on land.

Homeothermy (maintenance of constant body temperature), small numbers of completely helpless young, the dialectic of competition and cooperation in courtship and parenting, the use of sound for communication, territoriality, and sexual display are all features of both birds and mammals. Overall, the females of both classes also show juvenile (neotenic) traits, and by virtue of this neoteny they are more behaviorally malleable, with the greater potential for growth and change in both structure and behavior.

In the various families into which the approximately 8600 species of birds are divided, females differ considerably in their anatomies, abilities, and reproductive strategies. The ratites—ostrich, rhea, and emu—are thought to be the oldest, or most primitive, birds. Females in these families are sexually aggressive and may share a male (gynopoly) or take several of them (polyandry) in one season, sometimes leaving them to guard and control the temperature of the eggs.

Even among the more than four thousand species of passerines, or perching birds, which are considered more advanced than the ratites, there are examples of polyandry and of females leaving clutches of eggs in the care of several males each breeding season. This arrangement, whether in primitive species or advanced, seems to be a response to environments that, for reasons of harsh climate or predators, put eggs at greatest risk. The vast majority of female birds, however—whether passerine, ratite, raptor, or waterfowl—share incubation and/or care of hatchlings with their mate (monogamy). This is fortunate because avian eggs and offspring require more care than those of almost all herptiles.

While avian eggs are landworthy, like those of reptiles, they must be kept warm in almost all cases. Because homeothermy and the ability to fly helped birds enter cooler habitats than those occupied by reptiles, birds had to evolve new methods of nest building and incubation to thrive in these zones.

Although different avian females can do many things—build and decorate shelters, use tools, baby-sit, sing, speak, and, of course, fly and migrate—none of them can gestate. It is interesting, therefore, that we who are heir to a highly evolved form of gestation have found so much in the behavior of birds to imitate and exploit in the service of our own survival. We have not only used birds in the obvious way—to supply us with eggs—but also to hunt and fish, and carry messages, to supply down to warm and comfort our babies, and to supply us with decorative feathers so important in ceremonies of courtship and rank in many human societies.

Since all modern genera of birds had evolved about sixty million years before the first representative of our genus shambled through Olduvai, it is surely we who mimic birds and not the reverse. Clearly the most important aspect of our aviomorphic behavior is language, which was inspired by and partly based upon birdcalls. We first imitated birdcalls to disguise ourselves in order to catch birds for food or to follow them to their nests for eggs. Later, we used birdcalls to communicate among ourselves, especially when secret codes that would not be recognized as human language were needed.

Nowadays, birds imitate our calls. We can only speculate about the reasons for this. It may be due to the fact that in certain species birds mimic each other for mate identification. A goldfinch, for example, solicits food from her mate only after she has heard his shibboleth, a replica of her own call. Similarly, birds trapped in a human flock may mimic voices in order to gain recognition from or even to court the human callers.

Sexual differentiation for most birds begins on the fifth day of embryonic life. All embryos begin with the same early tissue cells for formation of the organs of either sex. According to J. Welty, author of *The Life of Birds*, the sex of a bird embryo is determined by enzymes produced by the sex chromosome genes. The enzymes control the growth of hormone-releasing cells, which, in turn, direct the early tissue cells of the reproductive system to differentiate as male or female. After hatching, some avian females reach sexual maturity within two weeks. Others of longer life span, like the California condor, which can live to fifty years, mature after five or six years.

Behaviorally, female birds differ from their males more in the degree than in the essence of activity. The endocrine and nervous inheritance of each species determines just how much female and male identity will diverge. The only absolute criterion of femaleness remains the egg. Even so, the avian female reproductive equipment sometimes transforms through life and starts to put out sperms instead of eggs.

Sexual reversals occur only from female to male in the bird class. This may have something to do with the fact that avian females are XY, or heterogametic (producing X and Y gametes) like most reptilian and mammalian *males*, requiring an embryonic dose of estrogen from their fetal ovaries to make them female and further estrogen to keep them female throughout life. If this dose wanes with age or because of infection, certain avian females begin to "revert" to the male type.

Male birds are always XX (homogametic); all their sperms contain an X chromosome. Therefore, it is the female bird, with eggs containing either an X or Y chromosome, that determines the sex of the offspring. This is precisely the opposite of the situation in mammals, where males are XY and require a hormone dose from the fetal testes to induce their development, take on female form in the absence of fetal androgen, and produce the sex-determining gametes.

The XX pair seems to be associated with whichever sex the basic embryologic program of the species runs toward unless otherwise instructed—female among mammals and male among birds. The XY pair seems to call forth the variant, requiring fetal hormonal induction—male among mammals and female among birds.

Many female and male birds do not differ in appearance at all. Adelie penguins look alike all year round. The only way one field-worker could be sure of their sex was to check the vent (opening of the cloaca) after eggs had been laid. The birds with traces of blood on their feathers were the females.

Some birds differ in appearance only during the mating season. Often, while the female remains cryptically colored for protection during the egg-laying and incubating season, the male puts on his courting clothes. This does not necessarily mean that the male will not be active in incubation. Even with his bright plumage, the male may take the added risk of attracting predators by helping to incubate or feed his young. The advantage of attractive courtship colors seems to outweigh the danger they may entail at the nest.

Only "primitive" birds, like the ostrich and emu, and some ducks, geese, and land fowl, like chickens and turkeys, show clear external genital differentiation. Females have a cloacal clitoris, and males have a grooved penis like that of male reptiles.

Usually, birds of both sexes have similar cloacas that are pressed together for gamete transfer, as the male stands on the female's back. As a bird may receive fewer or many more sperms than the average woman, size of the organism is not a good guide for predicting the number of sperms received. Pigeons take in two hundred million sperms per copulation, while chickens receive four billion. A woman receives about three hundred million sperms per ejaculation. Sperms live longer in the female bird's cloaca than they do in the mammalian oviduct or uterus. Hen turkeys, for example, can retain enough sperms to fertilize 83 percent of their eggs one month after copulation.

Except for the falcon family in which both ovaries are alternately active, only the left ovary is active in avian females. The right one is vestigial. If the active left ovary is removed, the right one may start to function as a testicle. Degeneration of the left ovary occurs spontaneously as certain birds age. Their right ovary then becomes a pseudo- or completely functional testis that puts out male hormones. These females will grow a comb and wattles and crow at dawn, if these be the masculine traits of their species. A fifteenth-century French saying about crowing hens, which in those days were condemned to death for their devilish imitation of cocks, sums up human distaste for sexual interchangeability:

C'est chose qui moult me deplaist,
Quand poule parle et coq se taist.

The thing that to me seems most ill,
Is when hens speak and cocks are still.

Present-day understanding of sex differentiation in birds and mammals is still incomplete. One thing that is known about ovarian degeneration and the development of a testis in female birds is that it
is more likely to occur if the female is infected with tuberculosis or
cancer. This recalls the fungal infections in fishes that cause females
to change to males. It would seem that study of this phenomenon
could improve our understanding of tissue differentiation and of the
degree of male potential hidden inside every female, and even help
clarify the mystery of the origin of two variably divergent sexes.

Although it is well known that male birds are generally more colorful
and vocal in courtship than females, there are a few species—phalaropes, hairy woodpeckers, dotterels, jacanas, and quails—in which
the female has the brighter plumage and song. These exceptional
females are polyandrous; that is, they have several husbands. They
show less parenting than almost all other birds and mammals; the
males of their species take over most or all of the incubation and
feeding duties. It is believed that the display paraphernalia of colorful
female birds is used to compete with other females of the species for
the large parental investment of the males. This is analogous to the
male-male competition that occurs in most other species in which the
females' exceptional parenting is sought.

In phalaropes it is known that a hormonal reversal underlies female
display and male parenting. E. Otto Hohn reports that females have
more of the male hormone testosterone than males, and males have
more prolactin than females. Prolactin is a hormone, produced by the
pituitary, that stimulates broodiness in both male and female birds.
It is the same hormone that makes mammals produce milk and, in
many species of pigeons and penguins, prepares the lining of the
throat, or crop, to secrete nutritious "crop milk" for the young.

The cycling of prolactin and ovarian hormones is often related to
light, and, as in herptiles, the pineal plays some role in linking light
and reproductive activity. The pineal's sensitivity to light is nonvisual.
Even if the animals are blind or their eyes are covered, light will affect
their reproductive readiness. Because of this light-sensitivity, poultry
breeders can keep their hens laying eggs by lighting the coops continuously, and Japanese bird fanciers can keep their songbirds singing
by putting candles near their cages.

When the amount of daylight is almost invariable all the year round,
as it is near the equator, female birds may take their sexual cycling
cues from other changes in the environment, such as temperature,

humidity, and rainfall variation. The singing and display antics of males—including fancy flight, special postures, and courtship feeding—can also stimulate the female. A house wren's nest box was electronically monitored, and it was found that every time the male sang, the female's heart rate increased. Such emotional stimulation may help start female hormones flowing and thereby prepare the ovary for ovulation. In some species, just the sight of the male courting is enough to provoke egg shelling and laying, even prior to copulation; these eggs, naturally, are sterile.

The mediator between the sound and sight of the male's behavior and the proliferation of oviducts and eggs is the female's endocrine system. Her emotions are nervous translations of what she sees and hears. These nerve messages trigger endocrine glands to release their hormones, which in turn travel via the blood to target tissues such as the oviduct, ovary, and eggs to alter their size, shape, and activity. Some species have females that are more independent of male stimulation for their sexual cyclicity. Their eggs mature and are laid at a fixed pace, regardless of male performance.

Most birds lay a fixed number of eggs at one specific time of the year, but a few are indeterminate layers and will replenish eggs in a nest as they are removed. Humans have selectively bred domestic chickens for this trait, and so have achieved the daily laying pattern that is not seen in nature. Of course, dimorphism and patterns of sexual activity vary according to the selective pressures that acted upon each species during its evolutionary development, not according to human selection.

Detailed studies of avian female form and function are needed. For instance, how might the extreme oxygen requirements and metabolic rate changes experienced during flight affect a female's reproductive activity? When a house sparrow's respiratory rate increases from 50 to 200 breaths per minute in flight, what is happening to the hormones that govern her eggs and mating patterns? What are the consequences of the 800-foot dives of the emperor penguin and of her fifteen-to-twenty-minute underwater episodes, when breathing stops, carbon dioxide increases, and metabolic rate plummets?

In addition to species-specific patterns of coping with different habitats, social habits play a large role in the synchronization of female reproductive activity. This is especially true when thousands of birds, like the black-headed gull, breed in dense colonies. Mating couples seem to set off a breeding chain reaction in one another, with the result that all females in the colony lay their eggs at about the same time.

An important result of this synchronization is monogamy. All the females are ready to mate at the same time, and their span of readiness is short. Therefore, a male must spend all his time choosing, wooing, and mating just one female. After that, there will be very little time for or profit in promiscuity because the females will no longer be receptive or fertile.

One of the strangest traits of certain domestic fowl is parthenogenesis. Occasionally, unfertilized turkey or chicken eggs, placed in an incubator, will develop and hatch. The parthenogenetic offspring (parthenogens) are diploid, like normal chicks, and they are all male, but their genes come only from their mother.

The method of formation of fowl parthenogens is uncertain. S. Ohno suggests, in an essay in Austin and Short's series on reproduction, that parthenogens are formed from an oocyte and polar body after the second division of meiosis. Why both of these haploid cells should contain X or both Y, when the normal mechanics of meiosis would ensure that one contains an X and the other a Y, is not clear from his explanation. I think the XX or YY "zygote" may be formed if the haploid egg undergoes mitosis and immediately reunites with its daughter cell. In this way, the egg, whether it is X or Y, will join with an identical haploid cell and produce either XX males that survive, or YY embryos that die. Females (XY) never form, to the chagrin of egg and poultry farmers who would welcome an all-female strain.

Parthenogenesis in chickens and turkeys is facilitated by viral infection, either that administered in the vaccine for fowl pox or that found in a cancer-causing infection. It is not known how a virus can affect the formation of gametes, but that it or some other factor induces the rare avian egg to parthenogenetically create a *male* is unique among vertebrates.

The four main functions fulfilled by avian courtship are:

1. *bringing the sexes together:*
The female is either attracted to a male's territory, or both females and males congregate at great mass breeding grounds.

2. *preventing hybridization:*
Not only must the sexes get together but individuals of the same species must get together; this prevents the birth of stillborn or sterile hybrids.

3. *suppressing nonsexual responses:*
Aggression and heightened sexual activity are often mixed together. Females have evolved courtship signals that are especially effective

in disarming the male. Many of these signals mimic juvenile behavior; they tell the male he is not confronting one of his own sex and that he need not compete or fight with the female. Sometimes courtship is not totally successful in preventing overflow competition, and fighting enters the mating routine.

4. *forming a pair-bond for cooperation:*
Pair-bonding enables mates to incubate their eggs in shifts, or it allows the male to forage for the female as she incubates. When eggs hatch, the bond continues, allowing male and female to alternate in feeding the young.

Since so many birds are monogamous, their courtship, unlike that of mammals, is not simply a process of males fighting fiercely with other males, and females selecting from a few winners or being forced to take a single victor. Although there are bird species whose courtship proceeds in this way, most avian courtship takes place on a one-to-one basis. It is much more like our own romanticized vision of human courtship, in which partners devote themselves to each other and form a lasting attachment.

Monogamous birds court to achieve pair-bonding and hormonal readiness for mating. Monogamous females will not flock to mate with one showy male, for they each require a loyal mate to help share brood care. Females get what they need by resisting promiscuity and, in many cases, by the synchronization of their fertile periods. Similar tactics, incidentally, have been used by women. In some societies (such as the Yurok Indians), groups of women achieved menstrual synchronization, perhaps by pheromonal cues or exposure to moonlight, thus making monogamy the better fitness option for their men. With monogamy, a female (bird or mammal) avoids the problem of exclusively holding the baby and the possibility of producing far fewer offspring than particularly successful males. With monogamy, males avoid the problem among themselves of great variation in, and therefore fierce competition for, reproductive success.

Among polygamous birds, courtship does become a matter of one sex, usually the male, competing among its own members to impress and secure a mate or several mates, and of the other sex, usually the female, discriminating among rivals. Such choice by females may cause the appearance and behavior of males to change over generations. By mating only with certain males, females permit only certain male traits to enter future generations. In *The Origin of Species*, Darwin said that he could "see no good reason to doubt that female birds, by selecting, during thousands of generations, the most melodious or beautiful males, according to their standard of beauty, might produce a marked effect."

Females not only select the male plumage, song, and display they prefer, but they genetically bias the population for these traits. Since males that are attractive to females get to pass on their genes more often than other males, the females are materially encouraging the passage of qualities that they enjoy and that may also help sustain them and their broods. Also, anything a male has incorporated into his courtship repertoire that enhances a female's comfort or feeling of readiness would be sexually selected for.

The result of strong male-male competition and selection by females is usually a pattern of polygyny: one male inseminates several females. While the females usually have just one sexual encounter per season and focus their energy on their single brood, males concentrate on getting as many females as possible to allow them to mate. Some species, like ostriches, express polygyny in a harem pattern: three or four females sharing one male. This is what I call gynopoly because, unlike an ordinary harem, this group of females and their male are controlled by one or two chief females, not by a harem master.

As mentioned above, the opposite of polygyny may also occur. In this case polyandrous females mate with several males, leaving each of them to care for a clutch of chicks. An uncommon form of polyandry is shown by the American jacanas. The female has a large territory that encompasses two or more male territories, and she lays four eggs in the nest of each of her males. Afterward she continues to copulate with all her males, maintains a pair-bond with each, and helps them defend their territories. Only among jacanas is there such a perfect reversal of sex roles, as we are accustomed to think of them. Instead of a male mating with several females and protecting them, the female mates with several males. Instead of the females being jealously guarded by the male and caring for the young, the female jealously guards the males, and they take care of the young.

In other species, such as tinamous and rheas, several females visit a male in his territory; then he cares for all their eggs in a communal nest. The reason this pattern is rare among birds is that it may leave an individual male with too many eggs to watch. This cannot happen in the polyandrous situation in which a male is left with only his clutch to care for. Also, there is no way a female can ever be burdened with too many eggs (apart from being tricked by parasites, like cuckoos or cowbirds) because she will care only for the eggs that have been fertilized during her mating; thereafter, she will either produce no more fertilizable eggs or strenuously resist attempts to copulate with her while she is incubating. If this were not the case, female birds in species in which males are promiscuous would have nests overflowing with fertilized eggs, all of which could not possibly be incubated successfully, no matter how diligent the female or how ideal the territory.

We do not know what the female looks for in the courtship display of males in order to select one above another. We can only deduce, from the conditions that are needed for survival of dependent young, that there are certain things a female *should* be looking for, if the male is to play any role at all in the survival of her young. Unless it is a species in which the female raises the young alone and forages outside the mating territory, she should select a male for his ability to provide a territory with sufficient nesting material and cover, and adequate food. The female can select a male for his territory indirectly, if fine appearance, voice, and a generous feeding ritual are consistently correlated with a male's possession and defense of a good territory. She need not assess the real estate, only be responsive to his signals.

It is not farfetched to think that courtship rituals and male appearance can reveal something to females about male reproductive "talent." As castration experiments have shown, males can lose or fail to develop the plumage, postures, odor, or song typical of their sex if they are hormonally deficient. A female cannot risk being attracted to males that do not have the right physical features, lest these males be deficient also in sperms and leave her eggs unfertilized after mating.

Marlene Zuk and W. D. Hamilton have recently made the ingenious suggestion that female choice, or sexual selection as it is formally called, is connected to resistance to parasites. If a female mates with males of bright color, good feather condition, and robust song and display, she is likely to be selecting healthy males with high resistance to parasites. If this resistance is genetically based, then any offspring she may have with such males should enjoy the advantage of better health.

According to sociobiological theory, courtship can also be informative to the partners in another way. It can tell the female if the male is going to stay with her and help her raise the brood. If a male perseveres, he will have invested so much time in her that it would not be worth his while, in terms of successfully passing his genes to the next generation, to leave her without helping her incubate the eggs or feed the chicks. In short, the female can trust a persistent courter to improve her fitness by fathering rather than philandering. Of course, this applies only to monogamous species.

It is not known which are the most critical innate and learned behaviors that keep almost 98 percent of all birds in monogamous pairbonds, with only 6 percent of these slipping into occasional promiscuity. It is not known how song, display such as wing stretching and neck stretching, feather fluffing, mock feeding, and cooperation in nest building may combine to make a pair physically and emotionally dependent upon each other. Canada geese, for example, have longlasting bonds, and widowed individuals may stay single for many years or never mate again.

In contrast, some birds may pair just long enough to copulate, as in lekking. In this mating pattern, males display on contiguous territorial plots called leks. A female can visit one or several males. If she visits just one male, she may go off to build her own nest and tend her eggs alone. If she visits several males, she may leave her eggs in a communal nest along with those of other females that have visited the same male; he takes care of all the various broods he has sired.

More frequently avian pair-bonds endure until the eggs are laid, whereupon one mate leaves the nest for the duration of the first incubatory shift. This mate returns after a day or more, sometimes bringing a token piece of nesting material or food and giving a characteristic call or gesture to release the sitting mate from its incubating posture. The bond can last for weeks, months, or years, depending on the species. Golden eagle couples have been observed returning to their giant nests year after year. Some say that a pair can remain mated for twenty to fifty years in succession.

Broadly, there are two types of courtship and two types of relationship that can develop between a pair. (Actually there are more than two types of relationship that can develop, but for the sake of simplicity of contrast, I will lump the monogamous varieties together in one group and the polygamous varieties in another.)

In one sort of courtship, the male is a fighter; he competes with his own sex for territory and females. He is the bringer of trophies. The females are usually docile, and their submissiveness soothes the aggressive male they choose or are forced to take. The sexes in this system of mating are very different behaviorally and also in appearance. The female is quietly colored; the male is showy.

The result of this "vive la difference" courtship is a brief union, sometimes for a mating season, sometimes just for copulation. The female does all or most of the parenting; the male may continue courting other females. This pattern occurs in a small minority of avian species—about 5 percent.

In the other sort of courtship, the male and female court each other mutually and may defend a territory together. The sexes look alike and perform similar courtship ceremonies toward each other. They are inclined to share their responsibilities and form a longlasting monogamous bond. This is most typical of long-lived birds, such as the golden eagles.

The result of this "vive le confluent" courtship is a long, sometimes lifelong, relationship. The female is not left alone to care for eggs and hatchlings. If there is any polygamy, it may be in the form of serial monogamy, the changing of mates in the following season. The reason for a divorce is usually failure to produce offspring.

Obviously, there are parallel forms of these two types of courtship and relationship among mammals, and among different groups of humans. The reason for the similarities is not closeness of ancestry and, therefore, some common genetic program, but a closeness of ecological pressures and permissive conditions. Although people are just beginning to understand the connections among ecology, mating systems, and character of the sexes, some consistencies are already evident.

The "vive la difference" system seems to arise when there is a scarce resource that all members of the species depend on, like beeswax to the honey guide or nectar to the hummingbird, or when one sex (usually the female) is scarce, either in absolute numbers or in availability (as when females are well dispersed). In such a situation, one "strong" male or group of males can monopolize materials and females. The same background applies to mammals, including people, that adopt this system and "choose" to differentiate the sexes sharply in appearance and role.

The "vive le confluent" system, on the other hand, seems to arise when there is a more plentiful supply of essential resources. No strongman monopolizes materials or females. The females are not totally dependent on male territorial defense or the courtship cues that attend defense. Females and their young can survive without male defense and assistance, although male provision of these can much improve their chances of survival. There is little emphasis on competition or individuality, and there is no great variation in life-style between the haves and have nots.

Human societies lean one way or the other with respect to mating and dimorphism, probably for the same underlying ecological reasons. In urban Western culture, we can see both mating systems in action, sometimes simultaneously. We would have to admit, however, that in the West recently there has been an overall trend away from "difference" and toward "confluence." It is reflected in the convergence of clothing fashions for the sexes and in the tendency for females to be less resource dependent on males and less monopolized by a few bringers of trophies.

Females, both avian and mammalian, may blur the border between monogamy and polygamy by choosing whichever pattern best serves their fitness. Where resources are more uniformly distributed throughout the breeding area and among potential mates, females do better to choose a monogamous relationship with a remaining bachelor than to choose an already mated male. Where resources are less uniformly distributed or deliberately monopolized by a few males, females do better to mate, even polygynously, with a male possessing a choice territory. This is how certain marsh-nesting songbirds behave. Confronted with the variable habitat of the marsh, females are much more likely to cluster around a few males with good territories than to mate monogamously. Their non-marsh-nesting sisters are more monogamous.

It is interesting to look at promiscuity among normally monogamous species to learn the occasions on which it may occur and to see that a female's resistance to it is adaptive. In fact, female reluctance to mate after her eggs are laid is the most primitive form of birth control. It is her strategy for ensuring the survival of the maximum number of offspring she can care for.

Promiscuity, which is rare among all birds that bond to raise young together, is resisted by colonial seabirds—egrets, blue herons, herring gulls, and albatross. In their reproductive pattern a male must occupy a territory and begin to build a nest, closely packed in with others made by fellow colonists. The female comes to assist in its completion, and the pair then brood the eggs together. There is an optimal number of eggs for each species—for the albatross it is one; for the gulls one to four; for herons three to seven—that can be reared successfully in one nest by two parents. Therefore, females resist copulation after they have deposited a batch of eggs.

Extra mating usually occurs only if a strange male forces himself on a female sitting on eggs. D. E. Gladstone delicately describes such rapes among colonial birds as "forced extra pair copulations." He observed that a female sitting on a full clutch might be mounted and her neck grabbed in the male's bill. Sometimes another male scared off the assailant, only to proceed to rape the female himself. She would call her protest loudly and become extremely agitated. Since rape is really maladaptive for both sexes that breed in colonies, the male that forces himself upon a mated female is anomalous, unmated. In contrast, mated males are rarely promiscuous; they try to maintain their pair-bond and concentrate on their single clutch of eggs. If a mated male were promiscuous, any eggs he might fertilize would be added to an already occupied nest and have little chance of surviving, and, in addition, his own clutch would be put at risk by his absence.

As the pair-bond is developing, females are scrutinized by their potential mates. Behavioral scientists are just beginning to document the conditions for rejection of a female by a male during courtship. Carl Erickson found that if a female ringdove had recently been courted by a male, her hormonal state changed, and she could be spotted and rejected by other males. Because courtship causes the release of ovarian hormones, female ringdoves are impelled to show nest-soliciting behavior. If this behavior is shown too soon by the female after she meets a male, he acts as if he suspects that she has already copulated with another male. He scolds and pecks her as if the scarlet "A" were embroidered on her bosom and thus avoids the risk of caring for eggs that have been fertilized by another male.

David Barash showed that mountain bluebirds (*Sialia currucoides*) are also rejected if they are suspected of adultery. He put a male decoy near the nest before the eggs were laid. When the male bluebird returned from feeding, he attacked the decoy and then his mate. This experiment was repeated with several bluebird couples, and the females were unjustly accused in every case. One male attacked so vigorously that he injured and drove away his innocent wife. Suspicion of female adultery was better tolerated once eggs had been laid. Returning males battered the decoys less forcefully and did not attack their wives once incubation had begun. It appears that if a female's previous behavior has assured a male that he is helping to care for his own brood, he is more tolerant of her suspected flirtation. (Of course, as Gould and Lewontin point out, Barash also should have shown the decoy suitor for the first time after the eggs had been laid. If the male then attacked the model, it could not be for fear of being cuckolded. Another control test run outside the breeding season could show [a] whether a male attacks a decoy unrelated to female and/or egg presence, and [b] whether he stops attacking after one or two exposures, upon noticing the decoy is inanimate.)

Females show no comparable intolerance of male adultery or previous courtship. Females have nothing to lose by male dalliance, as long as promiscuity does not interfere with fathering. A female is looking after her own eggs; her mate's occasional polygamy will not destroy her fitness by preventing her from passing her genes to the next generation. Still, a female may resent *any* stranger at the nest for fear of predation. Morton et al. repeated Barash's experiment with a

closely related species, the eastern bluebird. Females were more bel-
ligerent than males to both female and male models. One female
attacked a male decoy and began singing (unusual for females in this
species) at the observer's approach.

Nest building, like mate assessment, is usually part of courtship.
In about 55 percent of avian species nest building is shared equally
between the sexes. In 25 percent of the species, the female works
entirely alone. Ovenbird females, who build tidy, dome-shaped, mud-
sealed nests, work alone, as do sunbird, red-eyed vireo, and hummingbird females. Only 6 percent of bird species have males that build
nests alone, either for show, like the wrens and bowerbirds, or for
eggs, like the males of some shrike and many weaverbird species. And
15 percent of all birds have a variable nest-building pattern, in which
female, male, or both participate to varying degrees in supplying material and building the nest. In all, females are active builders in 80
to 95 percent of all bird species.

Even when there is no nest, as with many colonial seabirds and
shorebirds, there can still be a strong, enduring bond between mates.
In these cases, something other than nest building must bind a pair
together and enable them to recognize each other after long periods
of separation. The emperor penguin, for example, after two months
at sea, supposedly can recognize her mate from among thousands of
males wearing the same black-and-white uniform. Sometimes actual
or ritualized sharing of food cements a union. It seems that species-
specific displays of the young that trip off feeding behavior in the
parent may be carried over into courtship, bonding, and recognition
salutes. Thus, one or both sexes may beg and feed alternately.

Feeding, protecting, and keeping hatchlings warm are the activities
that must follow successful mating in 90 percent of the 8600 species
of birds. In the overwhelming majority of these species both parents
share these duties. There are only a relatively few species in which
the male assumes full responsibility, and there are somewhat more
species in which the female parents alone. The most common pattern
is cooperation between the sexes, and selection for this pattern is so
strong that cooperation sometimes extends to activities other than
parenting, such as building shelters, catching fish, and hunting.

In general, passerine (perching) birds show more elaborate nest
building and care of their young than primitive birds or waterfowl. In
many passerine families, the female incubates alone, but the male
assists her with feeding the young. Incubation is extremely important
because in some four thousand passerine species eggs would cease to

mature if not incubated virtually constantly. There are relatively few birds, even outside of the passerine category, that have precocious young, able to shift for themselves from the beginning.

"Primitive" birds and waterfowl often make simple nests by scooping out an area on the ground. Sometimes they make no nest at all. The emperor penguin egg rests on the webbed feet of its father for sixty-five days while its mother is at sea feeding. The webbed feet and the fat, feathered fold of the father's white shirtfront are its only nest. The mother returns just after her hatchling has emerged from the shell. Her crop (throat) is rich with milk, which she feeds to her offspring as the male goes off to sea to restore his starved body.

Certain hummingbirds, grouse, ducks, crows, wrens, thrushes, finches, and birds of paradise will tend their eggs and young alone. A female's taking on the total responsibility for nest building, brooding, and raising the hatchlings is usually correlated with a male's spending a great deal of time and energy on competitive display, territorial defense, and wide-ranging copulation. The more promiscuous the male, the more burdened the female with care of the young.

Raptors bring fresh food to their young in their claws; smaller perching birds bring little offerings in their beaks. Many bird parents feed their young by regurgitation, especially the fish eaters, like penguins and gulls. Pelicans hold food in their dangling pouches; the young just dip into the parent's chin bag and pull out small fishes.

Pigeons and doves provide cheesy crop milk for the first few days after hatching and then supplement this with solid foods. It is interesting that the crop of both males and females is sensitive to prolactin, which is released by a combination of male and female hormones, testosterone and progesterone. Therefore, both parents can feed the young with crop milk. In *The Second Sex*, Simone de Beauvoir points out that "Male and female pigeons secrete . . . a milky fluid . . . [to] feed the fledglings . . . [and] where the male takes part in nourishing the young, there is no production of sperms." Although the milk, in this case, comes from the crop and not the breast, it is still linked with a period of infertility, even in males.

Both crop milk and mammalian milk contain similar proportions of water, protein, fat, and vitamins, but crop milk lacks the calcium that is found in mammalian milk. Although male mammals do not now provide milk for their young, their breasts are sensitive to prolactin, just like the crops of male pigeons and doves. In certain diseases, like acromegaly, in which prolactin secretion is elevated, a male may produce milk. Such inducibility shows that the sexes are not as fixed in demarcation of function as we may imagine.

The inborn patterns of soliciting food are as varied in the young as are the foods supplied by the avian parents. Each species has its juvenile call for food. Open-mouth begging is the most common. Sometimes prey is dropped in; sometimes it is regurgitated down the chick's throat. Young may also peck at the parent's bill and thus trigger release of food from the beak or crop. In addition to its immediate survival value, feeding may teach species recognition, as the young focus on the features and sounds of the vital adults. It may also imprint the pattern of cooperation. This early dependency relationship is reenacted during courtship and bonding in more than 90 percent of avian species.

Copulation (which for birds is by cloacal contact) becomes part of the pair-bond repertoire at different points in the reproductive sequence, according to the species. Sometimes copulation begins months in advance of egg laying, in which case it seems to be an important factor in creating the bond. It may continue during incubation and even after the eggs have hatched. Since adding more fertile eggs to the nest would be maladaptive, matings that occur after the clutch has been set are usually infertile, either because the female no longer contains any ripe eggs or because the male's sperm production or viability declines. The maladaptiveness of copulation during incubation may explain why females usually take the first shift on the eggs or are the sole incubators, even in cases where the male comes back to assist with feeding the hatchlings. Males may stay away from females just after the eggs have been laid, in order to avoid "temptation," and then return when the peak of sexual arousal and fertility has passed.

When various copulatory postures are part of the play that precedes mating, the female may be seen mounting the male. House finches, red-bellied woodpeckers, and starlings show this playful exchange of positions, just like the courting alligators that ride on each other's backs as a prelude to intercourse.

Play, as well as display, is an important part of avian courtship. Play not only creates new patterns of interaction, it fills in time while waiting for a mate to arrive or consent. Special spiral flights, fast flying, and stooping are courtship-play activities, especially in predatory birds. Play stimulates the nervous system and keeps suitors fit. One seagull was seen flying and hovering over the beach, holding a small piece of driftwood in her beak. At intervals she dropped the piece and then swooped to catch it before it could touch the ground. Play strengthens skills and reflexes that will be needed in territorial defense, food gathering, and tending the young.

In courtship, play and display are often difficult to separate, but a rule of thumb is that display—whether it be singing, posturing to show off special plumage, or threatening rivals—may be said to be more ritualized and repetitive, compulsively performed with an aggressive edge, while play is usually much more variable and under more voluntary control. Play probably can escalate into display as sexual arousal increases.

After courtship, copulation, and egg deposition, the female almost always begins a period of fasting and incubation. Regardless of whether the eggs are glossy enamel like those of woodpeckers; pitted like those of storks; rough, greasy or chalky of shell; with orange, yellow, or tangerine-red yolks; a quarter of an inch in length like the hummingbird's or 3 feet around like those of the recently extinct elephant bird of Madagascar, females must follow certain routines to ensure the survival of their eggs.

Egg turning is performed by almost all incubating birds. Apart from sitting on the eggs, this is the activity that females must perform most often during the incubation period. The early embryo floats to the top when the egg is turned, and the yolk and amniotic fluid (the white) stay below. If the eggs are not turned, the embryo adheres to the shell, the membranes are pinched, and the fetus dies.

If the eggs roll away from the nest, many incubating birds can awkwardly draw them, between bill and neck, toward the nest. The retrieval pattern grows weaker after the eggs hatch. In other words, young are not retrieved as anxiously as eggs.

A female must be able to recognize her mate during incubation, and must heed his change-of-guard signal (as he must later heed hers), so that she may stop incubating and find food for herself. This does not happen, of course, in species in which the female incubates alone. In such cases, she may have to endure a period of protracted starvation, or take very brief breaks for food.

If the eggs do not hatch on time, most females will sit on them for up to 50 percent longer than the total normal incubation period. By that time, the eggs should have hatched or died.

The incubating female must also protect her eggs from predators. If the occasion arises, she may defend by direct attack or by decoy display, distracting a predator by feigning a broken wing, for instance, at some distance from the nest. If an egg eater does destroy part of the clutch, a returning mother will try to drive it off. If she is successful, she resumes incubation and eats the remains of any embryos and shells that have been damaged. The response of finishing off the remains of broken eggs is probably due to the pattern of keeping the area near the nest clean. This prevents the development of odors that would attract more predators and retards the development of vermin in the nest.

Cleaning the nest is accomplished by throwing out or eating bits of any broken eggs or debris from feeding. Feces of nestlings are eaten or tossed away. The cleaning response is so strong that robins sometimes hurl their own banded offspring from the nest when they detect the silvery ankle ring fitted by an ornithologist. As young grow, the nest is cleaned less frequently, making it less comfortable for them, thus encouraging them to fledge.

Tossing out the eggs of parasites like cowbirds and cuckoos also comes under the heading of cleaning, but only a few species like catbird and robin can distinguish the parasite's eggs as foreign matter. This ability seems to be based on color vision; catbird and robin eggs are blue, while cowbirds' are brown. Most females are duped by alien eggs, possibly because of an inability to reject them on the basis of shape. Experimenters have found that as diverse as the egg-tending and nest-tending abilities of the incubating female are, they do not include fine discrimination of shape. Herring gulls, for instance, will incubate experimental eggs of several shapes—prisms, cubes, cylinders—as long as there are no sharp edges. Rejection of eggs for eccentricity of shape was probably not selected for because females must also brood the hatchlings, which are not egg shaped.

In order to incubate efficiently, most females and some males lose the feathers in a small abdominal zone called the brood patch. The skin of this area is rich in blood vessels and may be covered with special soft feathers called down. Ducks and geese pluck their own down to create a patch and to line the nest. The brood patch is an essential part of incubatory care.

The enormously varied adaptations of avian females for their own survival as well as that of their young can be examined for three main categories of birds: raptors, land and water fowl, and colonial species.

Although thousands of species of birds are technically predators because they eat other animals, like insects, worms, and other invertebrates, the raptors are the true avian hunters. They take fishes, birds, and small mammals. Many colonial birds, such as the pelican, osprey, heron, penguin, and kingfisher, catch fishes, but the raptors, including falcons, hawks, owls, and eagles, are lone hunters.

Raptorial birds are remarkably good parents, and they teach their young to hunt and fly well. "Stooping" is a dive-bombing technique used to fall upon prey suddenly; it must be learned and practiced to perfection. Female raptors are almost always larger than their males, and they do the heavier hunting. Presumably, they have the greater role in teaching the young to hunt, as do female carnivores, such as lions and cheetahs.

In almost every case, eagles lay only two eggs per season. These virtually always hatch into one male and one female. The young do not get equal portions of food, although the eyrie, as an eagle's nest is called, is kept well stocked during the first six weeks after hatching. For some reason the female, which is always born larger, is fed first and most. The male is a runt. Parents probably feed the bigger female chick first because its food-request signals are louder, larger, or brighter than those of the other chick. When food is scarce, a runt may die and serve as well-kept food for its sibling.

During an early study of the golden eagle (*Aquila chrysaetos*), S. Gordon and his wife observed that "[The hen] gorged Cain [the female offspring] before paying the slightest attention to Abel [the male] who all the time lay in the cup of the eyrie cheeping miserably for his share." The female eaglet is stronger and aggressively attacks her weak brother and may even kill him. The adaptive advantage of this sexual competition is still a mystery, but certainly the female repays her species by hatching her many broods, and by feeding and protecting her young under all weather conditions.

At six weeks of age, the white down that is the first dress of eaglets has only just been replaced by dark brown feathers, and the eaglets are stretching and exercising their wings. As summer progresses, they feed themselves from the carcasses left by their parents. Gradually the parents bring less and less food, the nest becomes less livable as summer flies hatch, and the eaglets begin to test their wings. At about ten weeks, they go off with the adults to learn superior flying and hunting skills.

The female eaglet eventually grows to be about 3.25 feet from head to tail, with a wingspan up to 8 feet. The male, if he survives, will be about 2.66 feet, with a wingspan up to 7 feet.

Perhaps the larger size of the female raptor compensates for the aggressiveness of the male during courtship. M. Everett suggests that large raptors cow their males and thus achieve the balance necessary for mating. As will be seen for certain mammals such as hyenas, civet cats, some rodents, insectivores, and primates, large size and even mimicry of male genitalia may play a role in mating with a potentially very aggressive male.

Another theory about the adaptiveness of sex-related size differences in raptors is that it permits male and female to use food resources efficiently. They will hunt for different prey without competing with each other and will be able to supply their young with different sorts and sizes of prey. For example, when the offspring are newly hatched, the males of goshawk and larger falcon and eagle species do most of the hunting for the family. Males bring in suitably small prey, which, in the case of eagles, they feed directly to the young. When the young have grown and need more to eat, the female starts to hunt and bring them larger meals. She may feed the eaglets bits of hare and eat the bones herself. She also may bring in larger game, such as weasel, fox cub, or roe deer calf.

In a report on the sexual dimorphism of food habits in three North American hawk species—the sharp-shinned, Cooper's, and goshawk—Robert Storer accumulated evidence from many studies to support the idea that male and female raptors utilize different parts of their habitat consistent with their difference in size. Females, on average, take larger prey, and their prey is primarily other birds.

Among the smaller raptors, where there is the most marked difference between the sexes, female/male feeding differentiation is greatest. When prey were divided into groups by weight, females were found to have taken only two items from the lowest weight group (about 0.1 to 0.3 ounces), while males took fourteen items from this group. Females took six items from the highest weight group (3 to 4 ounces), while the males took only one. This sex-related hunting difference was less pronounced in the largest raptor in this study, the goshawk, as would be expected from the smaller size difference between female and male in this species.

The reason smaller raptors have relatively much larger females may be that the female spends more time at the nest during incubation and after hatching, and her larger size makes her somewhat less vulnerable to predators. Her large size might even help her protect her young from males of her own species.

The reality of the threat of predators to nesting raptors was well illustrated during the field study of Cooper's hawk (*Accipiter cooperi*) conducted by Helen and Noel Snyder. One morning the mother hawk was missing from her nest. Some of the eggs she had been brooding were cracked, and it looked as if she had been pounced upon by a goshawk or great horned owl. All that remained were a few of her feathers at the foot of the tree that held the nest. Her mate, who had built most of the nest with sticks, bark, moss, and grass, tried to hatch the eggs himself, but without a brood patch on his underside he failed to keep them warm enough. The human observers replaced the dead eggs with nestlings, and they watched the father hawk foster them. He learned to tear off small pieces of chipmunk, instead of presenting his empty beak. He also learned to hold his head higher when feeding in order to protect his red eyes, which were mistaken for food. The young learned that they would receive a morsel of meat if they pecked at his beak and not at his eye.

One thing the cock did not do was keep the nestlings warm at night; the naturalists had to do this. The young birds were finally fledged, and the incident showed the extent of male accommodation, in this species, to parenting alone. Evidently there are strong nurturing tendencies, but they are inadequate without the female. This is not to say that a male of another species or even another individual of the Cooper's hawk species might not be a successful single parent. There is a wide range of parenting ability among the species, and an individual's success probably increases with experience.

The modern species of land and water fowl, such as ducks, geese, rheas, emus, and ostriches, have been thriving since the early Pliocene, about twelve million years ago. In spite of dissimilarity in their habits and habitats, all females in these groups, and those of modern domestic fowl, have a well-developed cloacal clitoris and their males a penis. Intromission is achieved by these birds. In all other avian species, cloacal contact transfers sperms to the female.

Land and water fowl and the large flightless ratites are similar in another respect. They all lay more eggs at a time and/or larger eggs than other birds. Note, however, that relative to its body size, the ostrich lays the smallest eggs: they are about 5 inches wide and 7 inches long. Average clutch size for this group of species ranges from about eight to fifteen eggs. The clitoris may play some role in the enormous delivery responsibilities of these females. Like the penis, which is its homologue (that is, derived from the same embryonic tissue), the clitoris is used in the rituals of ostrich courtship. Much more study is needed to explain the homologies of the female and male reproductive systems, the divergence in function of which seems to be the source of much past and potential evolution.

Although it is usually the ostrich (*Struthio camelus*) hens that finish their nuptial moult and begin courtship activities first, the males do catch up and become as sharp-tempered as the females. Both sexes court by standing erect, hissing, snorting, and threatening younger, weaker animals. Females peck and kick other females and even males that come too near the male they are courting. In both sexes, ceremonies include tail raising for genital display, followed by urinating and defecating.

In their natural South African habitat, the most common ostrich family unit is a male mated to one major hen and two minor hens. The females not only share their mate; they share the nest in which fifteen to twenty-five eggs are deposited.

The male guards the eggs until the whole clutch has been set. Then the major hen incubates all of them. She sits on them and stretches her long neck flat on the ground. The huge eggs are turned as she swivels in her position on the nest. If the temperature goes above 130°F, the incubating hen must adopt tactics of cooling the eggs, standing above them with wings slightly spread as shade umbrellas.

Monogamy is rare among ostriches, but associations between a female and male may endure for years, even without reproductive relations in a particular season. A male seen accompanying a female and a flock of chicks, therefore, may not be the father of any of them.

Although colonial birds, such as penguins, pelicans, and flamingos are all associated with water, they span a wide range of approaches to that medium. Penguins are bullet-shaped divers, pelicans are long-beaked dippers, and flamingos are stilt-legged filter-feeders. Penguins take deeper water prey, pelicans more surface prey, and flamingos strain the murky shallows. In spite of these differences and their obviously disparate feather-, body size, and shape adaptations, all these species mate in large colonies, and this is the basis of certain consistencies in relations between the sexes and their care of the young.

The eighteen species of penguins are all inhabitants of the southern hemisphere, but only three species live on or mate on snow and ice. Most species are temperate-zone dwellers, and there are even a few tropical species on the Galapagos Islands. All penguins spend more time in the sea than on solid ground.

Because pursuit of a seafaring way of life is the top priority for both sexes, their general courting adaptations are similar and there is little sexual dimorphism. Male and female are virtually indistinguishable, which may reflect that there is no pressure on them to divide scarce food resources, for the sea is an abundant provider. It also suggests that both parents invest heavily in the survival of offspring.

In comparison to prolific fowl, penguins are paltry egg producers. A couple may fledge only two chicks every three years, if they are lucky. Still, this is remarkable productivity, given the conditions under which king and emperor penguins (*Aptenodytes patagonica* and *A. fosteri*, respectively) must breed. Immediately after her egg is laid, in the dead of the antarctic winter, the emperor penguin goes to sea for about two months. She is 60 to 100 miles from her male and her egg during the entire period of incubation. While she is gorging on fishes, her mate is losing up to 40 percent of his body weight and huddling with other males in colonies of millions.

Incredibly, the little egg, tucked under the male's shirtfront, stays at 90°F, when the air and surface temperatures may drop as low as −20° to −60°F. In spite of their weight loss, the males can produce some crop milk for any chick that hatches before its mother's return.

When she does return, no one really knows how (or if?) she picks out her mate and her chick from the uniformly tailored crowd. Although it may not be fair to compare animals so different as bats, lions, and hyenas to penguins, it is worth noting that mothers of the three mammalian species will feed any nearby infant. Perhaps penguin mothers do the same. G. C. Williams (in *Adaptation and Natural Selection*, p. 191) says, "Marking experiments have shown that when adults return from the sea they recognize their young by vocal signals." But this must apply to the second and subsequent returns because on her first return the mother has never seen the chick or heard its voice and vice versa. She probably recognizes the call of her mate, and then takes over and feeds the chick on crop milk for two to three weeks while the male revives himself with food and swimming. Then follows more frequent alternation of the guard, with each parent bringing back fresh seafood.

Another feature of parenting in a large penguin colony is the creche. This is a grouping of many youngsters with one adult, usually a female. Such a baby-sitter will sometimes defend and warm offspring that are not her own, but she will not feed them.

The creche is also found in flamingo (*Phoenicopterus chilensis*) colonies. For the first few days both parents feed the hatchling beak-to-beak with a special formula, thought to be pumped out from the lining of the upper digestive tract. It contains much glucose, fat, and about 1 percent whole blood. Annelid worms, small molluscs, crustaceans, and insect larvae, which the parents strain through their bills from the feeding waters, make this "milk" a bright red-orange and rich in the same substance that gives carrots and autumn leaves their color: carotene.

After a few days the chicks are covered in gray fluff, and they begin milling around the long legs of their elegant pink parents, scavenging bits of shell, feathers, and even mud, the material of which the nests are made. Since the breeding colony is highly synchronized, the chicks are all about the same age, and when they are one week old, they begin to form creches of one hundred to two hundred individuals. The creche walks over the lagoon nesting site as a unit, and drinks or bathes at freshwater springs.

It is not known exactly why a female or male will become a baby-sitter or "aunt" of a creche. The aunt may have lost its egg or missed mating in a particular year. She or he will herd the young together by patrolling the edges of the group. From time to time, incoming parents find their chick and feed it, and then may take over a shift so the aunt can feed. By fifty days, the chicks are beginning to filter-feed on their own. A few weeks later, they are learning to fly.

Synchronicity of activities is the outstanding feature of colonial breeding. It is not perfect; there can be many casualties, both due to greater exposure to the elements and predators and to mistimed be-havior among members of the colony.

The backfiring of colonial synchrony was observed by F. Knopf, who studied white pelicans (*Pelecanus erythrorhynchos*) on an island in the Great Salt Lake. One chick was mature enough to wander about, and it strayed near an incubating adult. The adult killed the chick with one swift stab of its long bill. Unlike flamingo aunts that watch over creches, incubating pelicans are very territorial. It is safest if all the chicks mature at the same time and begin to wander about together, once their parents' territorial defensiveness has abated.

Pelican chicks delve in the parents' pouch for a meal of regurgitated fish. In addition to being a fish net, the pouch is used when mates greet each other after an absence. Sideways display of the distended pouch helps pelican spouses recognize each other.

The reproductive cycle of the colony begins when courting females start charging groups of unmated males. Females are slowed down by bill jabs from the males, and, periodically, the females stop to bow. Males bow in return, but no copulation occurs. Alternating pushing and bowing brings the aggressive females to the center of the flock. After a few days, the entire group is sexually excited by the charging and bowing displays. (Mass displays also seem to heighten arousal in flamingo colonies; instead of shoving and bowing like pelicans, they neck-stretch, head-wag, and march in stiff-legged unison.)

Then, each male attends one female and fights off other males with his long bill. Pelicans dissipate sexual aggression by crossing bills. Both sexes have evolved horny shields on their bills to take the jabs of agitated neighbors. The shield falls off when the birds quiet down during the month-long incubation period.

Because both sexes are committed to parenting it is not surprising that females are as active as males in courtship. The pelican female is neither left with the whole parenting job, nor does she ever leave all the work to the male, as do females in species of polyandrous birds.

Phalaropes, dotterels, and certain species of quails, snipes, and pheas-ant-tailed jacanas are unusual in that females mate with more than one male and leave each with a clutch of fertile eggs to care for. Consistent with their polyandrous mating, these females are more brightly marked than males, and they are more aggressive in courtship.

Wilson's phalaropes (*Steganopus tricolor*) in northern Canada are shorebirds that feed on aquatic larvae and mate in late May. At that time females have ovaries and oviducts that are ten- to twentyfold heavier than they were in the nonbreeding season. Like the courting female ostrich, phalaropes defend, with threatening postures, an area around the male of their choice. When an experimenter tricked a female phalarope into courting a male decoy and chasing a female decoy, which naturally would not fly away, the frustrated female pre-tended to go to sleep. She tucked her bill under her shoulder feathers but kept peeking at the stubborn decoy.

Normally, the female can pursue the male she has chosen until his interest slowly turns from feeding to mating. Apart from a short threat-ening posture directed at other females, there is little display by the female. However, just before coitus, she displays to the male by run-ning in front of him with an outstretched neck. After this signal, the couple mate on land or on the water, according to their species.

While the males are sitting in a grassy scrape, incubating the four eggs under their brood patch for about twenty days, the females are not to be seen near the eggs. They do not help raise the downy chicks or lead them to water. This role reversal is fostered by an excess of testosterone in females and of prolactin in males.

Since it is the phalarope's pattern to leave her eggs with her male, it is adaptive for her to have some way of checking beforehand that the male will not desert her just after fertilization. Sociobiologist Rob-ert Trivers suggests that a phalarope uses courtship to estimate her male's capacity to care for eggs. He interprets N. Tinbergen's obser-vation of a red-necked phalarope, which courted a male vigorously and then ran away repeatedly as soon as he advanced, to be a test of the male's willingness to brood. The female rejected this male continu-ously until Tinbergen destroyed the clutch he was brooding. After that, the female mated with him. Something in the courtship proce-dure seemed to help her determine when the male would be free to brood her eggs.

Dotterel (*Eudromias morinellus*) hens also leave incubation to the males, and they are even more territorial and display oriented than phalaropes when competing for a male. The courting female threatens her rival by standing upright, puffing out her breast, and showing the black patch on her belly. Then she may hunch forward, draw in her neck, and run toward her rival in stops and starts. Just before she actually assaults her victim, the angry dotterel ruffles her back feathers and partially spreads her tail.

All the female-female animosity of the courtship phase passes after the eggs are laid and the males are installed on the nests. Then the dotterel hens form friendly groups of about half a dozen members. They eat together and warn each other of a predator's approach. They eat foods that are not used by the cocks and broods and so do not compete with their own young for resources.

No one knows exactly how the female courter and male incubator roles arose in just these few species. One speculation is that a mutation occurred in a shore-dwelling species in which both parents were good brooders. The mutation reduced the amount of prolactin produced by females, and the males simply had to carry on alone.

Another explanation given for the dotterel females' behavior is that the species, which is now a mountain bird, evolved in cold pre-Pleistocene tundra regions and was exposed to heavy snow cover, low temperatures, and drought. The females, unable to both replace lost eggs and share parental duties, came to concentrate on winning a territory and mate and on producing three eggs per day. All other responsibilities fell to the males.

Male and female dotterels have elaborate courtship ceremonies in which they scrape the ground and make shallow mock nests. This may be why pair-bonding among dotterels is sometimes stronger than it is among phalaropes and why the hen dotterel occasionally assists in brooding.

The issue of who will help whom in bird societies is an interesting one and is closely related to the evolution of deception, shown by parasitic species like the cuckoo (*Cuculus canorus*) and cowbirds (such as *Molothrus ater*), which deposit their eggs in nests built by other species and so contrive to have the eggs incubated by others. Where there is cooperation, as there is in almost every avian species, or where one sex gives most of the care, there is fertile ground for exploitation.

A helper is a bird of either sex that assists in feeding or guarding hatchlings and sometimes in nest building or mobbing a predator. The outstanding point about helpers is that they are not feeding, guarding, or building nests for their own young but for those of someone else. A helper is almost always a member of the same species as the ones she/he helps, but sometimes the helping "urge" is so strong (that is, the signal prompting the response is so strong) that a bird of one species helps a member of another species. Alexander Skutch observed young captive birds feeding fledglings of other species. A six-week-old eastern bluebird helped nourish nestlings of six different species. A young black-shouldered kite adopted a day-old buzzard chick and fed it until it was three times her size. A cardinal was photographed crossing *class* lines to feed a goldfish, probably because the fish's gaping, red mouth acted as a feeding-behavior releaser, just as the mouth of a baby bird does.

In nature, helper birds appear to be those that are mature but not yet mated, or they are surplus birds of the outnumbering sex. That is to say, if there are too many females or males in a group, those that do not find mates may become helpers. It seems that the urge to build nests and feed young is very strong in most species, and the rudiments of these behaviors are seen even in nestlings. If an adult is frustrated by missing the natural opportunity to mate and breed, it may become a helper or pursue routines that do not help anybody but do no harm either. Thus, a bachelor penguin has been seen building a huge nest of stones, 5 feet across and 2 feet high, as if to underline the pathos of his condition.

Because of a prolonged association between some birds and their parents, the young may still be present when the parents start their next brood. These juveniles may help their parents raise a new brood and thereby indirectly improve their own fitness. First, helpers gain experience that they may later apply to raising their own young, and second, they help their siblings or half-siblings survive and pass on genes that are one-half or one-quarter identical to their own. (Remember, any individual of an exclusively sexually reproducing species shares as many genes with a full brother or sister as with an offspring.) It has been found that sibling helpers increase the reproductive success of their families. Each mated pair of scrub jays that is assisted by helpers can fledge an average 2.1 young per incubation period; couples that receive no help raise only 1.1 to fledgling.

There are also examples of birds keeping injured or handicapped but unrelated "friends" alive. For example, in a reversal of the usual pattern of nuptial feeding, a female black-headed grosbeak fed a male with a deformed bill. This sort of altruism is more difficult to explain according to the cost-benefit mathematics of fitness, as friends do not necessarily share any of the same genes. Perhaps the only survival-adaptive explanation for helping a friend is reciprocity.

The great risk attached to the cooperation and altruism typical of pair-bonded and gregarious birds is exploitation. Animals (including people) that can get others to do their work for them, either because the helpers are slaves to irresistible drives or because some threat or ethic forces them to help, may be getting free fitness tickets into the next generation. However, since most altruism is directed at close kin, an individual may increase its overall fitness by helping for a season before reproducing.

Much more field study of avian helpers and exploiters is needed. It would be especially useful to know how genetically similar the birds in colonies with well-established creche systems and helpers are. They look very similar to each other; more similar perhaps than birds of noncolonial species? Are two unrelated flamingos or penguins more genetically similar to each other than two unrelated eagles? Or does it just look that way? J. L. Brown mentions that altruistic and communal-breeding Mexican jays are so highly inbred that "members of a flock become . . . nearly genetically uniform." Are there some species in which genetic endowment is so universal that helping a nonfamily member is as fitness enhancing as helping a daughter, son, sister, or brother?

Could stringent female synchronicity in colonial breeders delete the usual benefits of the different mating strategies of the two sexes? The males and females not only come to resemble each other but help equally in producing small numbers of young each season, homogenizing the genetic makeup of the population as they do so. No other vertebrates can match certain species of birds for helping and homogeneity or for the absence of the usual structural and behavioral differences between the sexes.

Avian species offer many lessons. One of the most important is that sexual identity alone is not a predictor of altruism, cooperation, or parenting. The same lesson cannot be drawn from the next class to be considered: the mammals, where mothering is almost exclusively a female job and helpers are almost always close female kin.

PART 2

6 | MAMMALS

By now it is clear that the fate of females was directed by a few momentous evolutionary "decisions" over the past four hundred million years. The decision to use rudimentary limbs and lungs to come out on land and breathe air for extended periods piloted the amphibians out of the sea. For some of them this meant the first experience of not releasing their eggs into water before fertilization. Although most amphibians did and do return to water to spawn, a few experimented with a hands-off form of internal fertilization via sperm capsules. For the first time females were left holding the baby (or at least the embryo), if only for the short interval until the fertile eggs were deposited.

This direction was extended when the reptiles decided to live permanently on land and to reproduce via shelled amniote eggs. Females were now consistently the gamete repositories, and their reception of male gametes was through copulation—no more egalitarian release of eggs and sperms into water, no more pristine spermatophores.

While becoming warm-blooded helped early birds and mammals stay alert and energetic in order to avoid an assortment of reptilian predators, it demanded that young, both in and out of the shell, be nourished and kept warm until they could independently find sufficient food, at regular intervals, to maintain a constant high body temperature. Female freedom was curtailed, through satisfying the needs of the young. Even airborne avian females, who kept their baggage light by never gestating, had to accept the task of fertile egg care, for they too were warm-blooded.

As tetrapods (animals with four feet) became more complex and their embryos needed more time for development, no shelled egg with a limited supply of yolk could be sufficient. The only solution was internal retention of the embryo(s). Before vertebrates lived on land, gestation had been used by females of many species (such as scorpions, sharks, rays) to spare their young from hostile environments and ferocious conspecifics.

Mammals not only succeeded with gestation, diversifying into many species, they grew larger and required abundant food. This nutritional requirement applied to babies as well as adults so that there came to be a great evolutionary demand upon parents to supply this food. For mammals, the requirements of warm-bloodedness (homeothermy) eventually obliged females to spend the bulk of their lives gestating and lactating.

This devotion enabled mammals to live in a broader range of environments than other vertebrates. The intelligence and cooperation needed for extended mothering eventually brought mammalian life to levels of higher sentient and finally self-conscious being. It was as if mother's milk made such an impression upon the individual that each one, female and male alike, made attempts to communicate with other species members just to discover whether or not they would be as warm and nurturing as that first-known being. Mammals, always sniffing and searching for mother, put on a show of independence and separation as adults but were ever ready for close communion with kin, even if it meant manufacturing them in the form of babies. Our class owes its uniqueness to mothering and lactation; indeed, this is why it is called Mammalia, after the mammae or mammary glands.

With substitution of placenta and maternal nutrition for yolk, the female became an extension of her own egg. She could not escape the responsibility or power that natural selection had conferred upon her. Although it may seem unfair that gestating females should inherit a larger share of risks and stresses related to reproduction than males, in almost all cases, they evolved to be able to perform this job *alone*.

Parenting, like any other trait, evolves in response to natural selective pressures. One pressure is always economical utilization of matter and energy. If the efforts of one parent were sufficient, then both parents would not evolve to make a large investment in the young. The fact that (1) female mammals do not possess, so far as is known, physiological ways to force males to participate in parenting—which would have been possible with traits like selective abortion or fertilization—and that (2) most male mammals show no spontaneous need or compulsion to parent means that male parenting is not usually vital to the survival of the young. Sociobiological reasoning connects these facts to the relative uncertainty of paternity among male mammals; they did not volunteer to care for young because they could not be sure which of them they had sired. Since organisms profit most by investing in similar-gene carriers (self and close kin), only females, who are virtually always certain that their young are their own, made a marked investment in them. This may be one of the reasons lactation evolved in females and not in males. This is not to say that male lactation could not potentially give a differential boost to the survival of a male's offspring. Were he quite sure that the young were his, as in monogamous pairing, he would do well to lactate. This is exactly what certain monogamous male birds are doing when they produce crop milk.

As the presence of lactation in the modern egg-laying mammals *might* suggest, lactation probably preceded gestation. Gestation would have been most viable in those females that already possessed the "insurance" of lactation. Only they were ideally equipped to feed newborns, if other foods were difficult to obtain and males unavailable for assistance in care. So, female mammals came to concentrate on offspring maintenance (more K-type strategy) and males to concentrate on maximizing the number of offspring (more r-type strategy).

Since the oldest known fossil remains of mammals date from the beginning of the Mesozoic era, some 200 million years ago, the first mammal-like reptiles lived much earlier, in Late Paleozoic times, about 320 million years ago. Even as the lines that produced the dinosaurs were evolving, a reptilian offshoot, with links to an amphibian past and a mammalian future, was beginning to eke out its existence. Like the modern salamander *Proteus* and the lizard *Lacerta vivipara*, some mammal-like reptiles may have had the option of retaining eggs for internal development or of depositing them on land. Like mammals today they probably had the capacity to lactate and regulate body temperature.

The therapsids, as mammal-like reptiles are called, evolved a complex of traits focused on the skin, its glands, and its hairy covering, which permitted them better body temperature control. It is thought that the glands that produced sweat (to offset the warmth retention of fur) and oil (to make the coat water-repellent) eventually became modified to produce milk. While true mammals with fully developed mammary glands probably existed by 200 million years ago, it was only after the mysterious downfall of the dinosaurs, about 130 million years later, that our inconspicuous mammalian ancestors inherited the earth.

It seems logical for gestation to have been favored in females that already could lactate and control body temperature. Gestation and homeothermy are linked through endocrine changes that affect the maintenance of both these states. As mentioned in chapter 4, the steroid hormones, including progesterone, are probably among the most ancient substances produced by plants and animals. The pathways to their synthesis are identical in all vertebrates studied, but their functions vary from group to group. In mammals, progesterone plays a key role in pregnancy. The hypothalamus, which, in most vertebrates, has centers for regulation of hunger, thirst, satiety, sexuality, aggression, etc., is sensitive to progesterone in the context of both temperature regulation and ovulation in mammals. Ovarian and adrenal progesterone set the hypothalamic thermostat up, just after ovulation. In addition, the extension of the progesterone-secreting ability to the corpus luteum, derived from the follicle cells that surround the egg before ovulation, opened the way to gestation. When the corpus luteum became sensitive to a hormone from the pituitary, and, in response, pumped out increasing amounts of progesterone after ovulation, it was as important a step in mammalian development as the evolution of hair and milk.

With their constant body temperature, their high rate of metabolism, their brain bathed in well-oxygenated blood, and limbs tucked under the body for efficient support and forward motion, early mammals were more continuously active than their reptilian predecessors. Desmond Morris calls the first mammals "animated thermostats," and, as such, they penetrated hotter and colder zones than other vertebrates. By entering these harsher environments, mammals automatically assumed the burden of extra protection of their young. Egg retention was a solution to the problem of protecting developing young from excessive heat and cold.

The taking of this "small" evolutionary step of egg retention astronomically accelerated mammalian females in the direction of mothering. Its consequences could be compared to those of receiving a challenging gift. For example, suppose your friends give you a custom-made bowling ball that instantly raises your average score. This, in turn, gets the tournament team interested in you. You practice more, win more, and are reinforced by prize money and praise. But after a while, the bowling activities take up a lot of your time, and people are starting to think of you as Dolores, the bowler, instead of Dolores, the banker. You're speeding toward a new identity.

In the same way, mammalian females began snowballing toward their present identity of Mother more than two hundred million years ago. They swept the males of their species along with them in this trend, imparting the traits that facilitated good mothering to all their offspring, female and male alike. These traits included greater sensory acuity for detection of predators, also for assessment of temperature and satiety condition of the nurslings. Patience was needed to wait out pregnancy, strength and courage to endure the discomforts of birth, good judgment and gentleness for effective care of young. Female gentleness, the hallmark of maternalism, was probably evident even before the step of egg retention had been taken. The modern Nile crocodile (*Crocodylus niloticus*) may suggest the antiquity of this adaptation when she gingerly picks up her young in the same jaws that have slaughtered and dismembered large prey. Although the crocodile is a modern species, it resembles in form certain reptiles from the age of dinosaurs, and behavioral resemblance may be cautiously inferred from structural resemblance.

Since gentleness can be the judicious restraint of physical strength, intelligence, when defined as the ability to judge situations and choose appropriate behaviors, was probably perfected from maternal gentleness. Just as it was important to discern when to use and when to restrain her physical strength, it was important for her to compare risks and choose correct strategies when mating or avoiding predators. Females with appropriate gentleness and good judgment left more young than females without these traits, and so these traits were perpetuated.

Selecting, building, planning—the pieces of intelligence coalesced in the good mother and were passed on to her young. The young, in turn, embodying the traits that constituted their species' accommodation to environmental demands for good mothering, themselves became the natural selectors for good mothering. It was a spiral: environments that required good mothering selected for traits that led to intelligence; intelligence demanded complex organ systems to bring in information; and these complex systems, whether the eye of the octopus, the antennae of the ant, or the brain of the dolphin, selected for good mothering that would provide a sheltered period of time for their development in each new organism. Whether in the egg, the larval chamber, the oviduct, nest, or womb, the female animal supplied the time, space, and energy for the ontogenetic expression of the phylogenetic potential of intelligence.

As females invested more in their young, males began to compete with each other for this valuable sacrifice without which they could never pass their genes to the next generation. At the same time, males began to express their inherited mothering traits in uniquely masculine ways. While females showed maternal nesting or denning territorialism, males expressed their territorialism in preparation for courtship. Males of many mammalian species became jealous, protective, and disciplinary with the females they courted, just as their own mothers had jealously defended them when they were small. Both sexes sought to enhance their fitness by using maternal traits; females used them to spare the young, and males used them to vie for and retain mates.

The mammalian male is doubly dependent on females to secure his fitness. Not only must he, like other land males (reptiles and birds), gain access to eggs by copulating with females, but unlike most other land males he must pass through a stage of complete reliance upon his mother. No mammalian male reaches the task of finding eggs for his sperms unless he already has received the gestational and lactational investment of a female—his mother or mother surrogate. No male mammals, not even men, have yet been liberated from this primeval dependency.

At present, there are three types of mammals in the world—the monotremes, marsupials, and eutherians.

Female monotremes—the duck-billed platypus, spiny anteater, and echidna of New Guinea—lay eggs, but all other mammals give birth. Although marsupial females do give birth, it is only to a tiny embryo which finds its way to the pouch unassisted by its mother. Once there, the embryo fastens onto a nipple for several days or weeks until it has grown to term. In contrast, eutherian, or placental, females give birth to young that range from the fairly embryonic, like those of mice and men, to the fairly precocious like those of wildebeest and giraffe. All eutherian young are fed via the placenta during gestation and by milk after birth. This arrangement holds even for marine mammals, such as whales, dolphins, and porpoises, whose young are born and suckled underwater. The eutherian method of gestation and milk delivery seems to have provided a better foundation for the development of the brain than did either the monotreme or marsupial modes.

More than 150 million years ago the monotremes stopped short of becoming truly viviparous. Their embryos still develop externally in leathery shelled eggs, and their young still lap milk from the fur surrounding the opening of each mammary duct. Monotreme reproductive adaptations lie somewhere between those of the mammal-like reptiles and the eutherian mammals, and they show that the mammalian investment in the young was substantial even before the stage of internal retention of the eggs.

The duck-billed platypus, spiny anteater, and larger echidna resemble other mammals in their fur and activity, but the structure of their shoulder girdle, ribs, and spine reveals their closer relationship to reptiles. Like reptiles and birds too, the monotremes have only one exit for their intestinal, urinary, and genital tracts, hence their name: *monotrema*, meaning "single hole." They have no separate vagina, and their oviducts do not join a central uterus. Once their eggs have been fertilized, shelled, and coated with slippery albumen in the oviducts, they simply pass out of the ducts, into the common urogenital sinus, and through the cloaca, as do the liquid and solid wastes.

Spiny anteaters (*Tachyglossus aculeatus*) lay one egg that contains a two-day-old embryo. This is the largest mammalian egg, roughly the size of a large kidney bean. It is transferred by the mother from her cloaca to her belly pouch, where, after about ten days, it hatches. The baby anteater sucks milk from a hair tuft or nipple, depending on the species. When the youngster starts to sprout its spines, its mother wisely transfers it from her pouch to a nest.

The duck-billed platypus (*Ornithorhynchus anatinus*) does not have a temporary pouch in which to put her eggs or young. She incubates one to three eggs in the tight space between her abdomen and the base of her flat, beaverlike tail. She and the eggs inhabit a burrow, which she has dug and lined with wet leaves. During the ten-day incubation period, the eggs are in continuous contact with the female's body, except when she emerges to wash and defecate. When the hatchlings break their shells, they are ready to climb on to their mother's belly as she rests on her back, and to lap milk from the mammary hairs around her abdominal pores. The young do not leave the burrow until about four months of age, at which time they take up the twilight-active life of their species, hunting snails, crayfish, shrimp, and worms on river bottoms. In this way they survive for ten to fifteen years.

The best-known marsupials are, of course, the kangaroos, but the subclass includes pouched versions of many of the placental mammals we know. There are marsupials that look something like cats, rats, dogs, hamsters, chipmunks, lorises, moles, skunks, flying squirrels, and little bears. The reason for this parallel diversity with eutherians is that marsupials evolved unchallenged by placental mammals during the course of several millennia in the Australian archipelago and parts of South America.

The pouch, or marsupium, is a gestating organ, an alternative to an expandable uterus. It may be a permanent feature or develop seasonally, around the mammae. Opening toward head or tail in different species, it regulates the temperature of the growing offspring, which receives a constant flow of nourishment from the nipple.

Not only do the pouches of marsupial females differ from group to group, but the sexual "inner plumbing" also shows a wide range of design among the 250 or so species in this subclass of mammals. The typical marsupial has two slim vaginas that branch off either side of the urogenital sinus, which connects them to the cloaca or vent. Sperms travel up and urine and embryos travel down the sinus. The vaginas arch up toward each other to join either side of a central, split uterus. The mates of some marsupials have a bifid penis, which efficiently sends a stream of sperms to each side of the female reproductive system.

Surprisingly, there is no straight connection between the uterus and the outside world, until the firstborn excavates a birth canal by tearing through the solid connective tissue separating the uterus from the urogenital sinus. Once formed, this birth canal remains open in kangaroos, but it must be reopened by the passage of each new offspring in other species.

The red kangaroo (*Macropodus rufus*) fetus that passes through the canal weighs only about 0.025 ounces; the fetus may be smaller in other species. Its tiny forelimbs are strong and sometimes equipped with temporary claws for the arduous journey from urogenital opening to pouch. When safely at its destination, the claws of the fetus gradually fall off, and it attaches itself to a nipple for several more weeks or months of development.

The kangaroo female, who would seem unfortunate enough just to have to undergo the extemporaneous construction of a birth canal, also comes into estrus (the period when the egg is ripe) just after she gives birth. Luckily, she does have the sparing adaptation called diapause. This is the ability to hold an embryo that has grown to the stage of about one hundred cells (the blastocyst) in suspended animation in the uterus, while another offspring develops in the pouch. If the pouch youngster dies or is grown up enough to be out most of the time, the blastocyst automatically implants itself in the uterine wall, where it grows until it is born.

If an older sibling is still nursing intermittently, the newborn embryo will attach itself to another nipple from which it will receive a low-fat milk. The older brother or sister receives a high-fat formula. How the marsupial mother dispenses different milks from different nipples is not known. All that is known is that the presence of a continuously nursing offspring suspends growth of the embryo and makes the marsupial uterus sustain the blastocyst without implantation. (As will be discussed, the presence of a continuously nursing youngster acts as a contraceptive for eutherian mammals. Instead of preventing implantation, however, nursing in eutherians prevents ovulation. Unfortunately, in modern women who nurse, dietary and feeding schedule factors may combine to negate the contraceptive effect.)

Thus, diapause is a birth-spacing mechanism that works for female marsupials. However, since these females come into heat immediately after giving birth and are presumably impregnated at that time, diapause will provide only the minimal interval between offspring. It effectively prevents more than one infant from growing in the pouch at the same time. Still, three offspring, at different stages of development, can be supported simultaneously by the mother kangaroo: the "suspended" embryo inside her, awaiting its 27-to-38-day uterine gestation; the embryo in the pouch, attached to a teat for 235 days; and the out-of-pouch "joey," returning for meals. With this system the kangaroo can average 1.5 full-grown offspring per year.

Most marsupials elaborate the membrane of the yolk sac into a placenta. In this they differ from eutherians that use the fetal chorion and allantois membranes to form the placenta. Perhaps this is a way in which marsupials show their primitive character and closeness to a reptilian stock, for among modern snakes and lizards, which retain eggs for internal development, the yolk sac and its contents nourish the embryos. There are a few species of marsupials, such as wombats, bandicoots, pouched cats, and koalas, that do form the placenta from the chorion and allantois. The marsupial native cat forms her placenta in this way, and the fact that her babies are born more mature than those of any other marsupial, in spite of having the shortest gestation period (twelve days), seems to indicate that the chorioallantoic placenta is more efficient than the yolk-sac placenta.

The mating and parental habits of all the marsupials have not been thoroughly studied, but for better-known species, like the red kangaroo, it is true that the female is the sole governor of her olympian reproductive system and of her young. She may even sacrifice her baby by jettisoning it from the pouch, if she is being chased by a predator. At 20 to 30 miles per hour, she can relax her pouch muscles, and the unlucky infant may fall to the ground, never to find its mother again.

Female red kangaroos are ready to mate at two years, when they have grown to about half their final adult size, which is approximately 5 feet tall. The males, although mature at two and a half years, may wait months or years before reaching a status in the mob hierarchy that empowers them to mate. The dominant male sires most of the young but has no contact with them as they grow.

Eutherian females can gestate their fetuses until they are much larger than those born to marsupial females, one of the reasons being that they have evolved a larger uterus and a spacious, permanent vagina for the passage of young. Urinary and reproductive systems share no exits. In addition, the more efficient eutherian placenta helps to maintain gestation longer by supplying more nourishment, carrying away more wastes, and secreting hormones that sustain the pregnancy by inhibiting the mother's immune rejection of the embryo. With long uterine gestation and nursing, eutherians, from the least shrew to the blue whale, assume their great maternal role and at the same time release the growth potential of the mammalian brain. The liberation of mammalian brain potential was bought, however, at the expense of female bondage in pregnancy, nursing, and extended parenthood. For the expansion of their brains, mammals also had to pay the price of the biological double standard and fierce male-male competition.

It has taken over 150 million years since the development of the placental mammals, over 65 million years since the appearance of primates, and over 15 million years since the existence of the earliest hominids to evolve a female that can finally end the harsher aspects of her mammalian heritage. In our species, where the ecological-cultural background permits monogamy or equal polygamy for both sexes, the double standard may be eschewed and excessive competition and territoriality be recognized as undesirable consequences of the mammalian accretion of mothering. Perhaps an evolutionary view of female mammals will help us use all the intellectual and emotional assets of mothering to temper human competitiveness and territoriality.

Now that we have achieved the milestone of taking a human egg out of the ovary, fertilizing it in vitro (that is, in a glass tube or dish containing a growing medium), and inserting it back into the womb for full, normal development, it is rather alarming to realize that most people have no notion of how ovulation occurs or how the environment for pregnancy is established inside the female body.

The estrous cycle is the period in which an egg (or eggs) gathers yolk, moves to, and ruptures the ovarian wall. Ovulation is the process by which the egg ruptures the ovarian wall, falls into the abdominal cavity, and is coaxed into the oviduct by the beckoning fringe of the duct's funnel-shaped mouth. In most mammals, ovulation is closely tied to a time of high sexual drive, receptivity, and attractiveness to males. This part of the cycle is called estrus, "heat," or the luteal phase.

While all female mammals ovulate, only marsupials and eutherians become pregnant, and only eutherians gestate for comparatively long periods. Ovulation may be spontaneous or induced by copulation. In some spontaneous ovulators, such as dogs, cows, goats, monkeys, and humans, the cycle from one ovulation to the next is relatively long, several days or weeks. In these animals, the corpus luteum (see pp. 150–152) assumes its secretory function spontaneously and starts to pump out the hormones that will help prepare the body for pregnancy. In other animals with spontaneous ovulation, such as rats, mice, and hamsters, their corpus luteum does not begin secreting unless mating has occurred, and their cycle is short, fewer than seven days. In animals with induced ovulation, such as cats, rabbits, and camels, the corpus is also induced by copulation, and the female will stay in heat for days or weeks while mating occurs.

Some mammals, usually small ones in year-round mild climates, with equal day lengths through the seasons, are polyestrous. This means that one breeding cycle follows immediately upon another. There can be several matings and pregnancies each year. The egg ripens and is fertilized during estrus. Then pregnancy, birth, lactation, and the next estrus follow like clockwork. Humans and other primates, having evolved from an order closely related to that of small, polyestrous insectivores and rodents, have retained the trait of repeated cycling, with the addition of one significant variation: the menses.

Each ovulation and estrus in primates that is not followed by pregnancy and lactation is followed by menstruation, which is the sloughing off of the thickened surface of the uterine lining, or endometrium. Depending on the degree to which the species resorbs the shed endometrium, a bloody discharge, called the menses, will be more or less visible each month. The menstruation of New World monkeys is only microscopically visible.

Sometimes menstrual bleeding occurs in a cycle without ovulation.

The regular monthly rise in estrogen seems to be sufficient to induce changes in the uterine lining that will make it detach. For example, macaque monkeys may menstruate without ovulating during most of the year. Ovulation occurs only during the breeding season when food, light, temperature, and humidity are favorable. Exposure to males in this season may also contribute to induction of ovulation. The menstrual cycle in most Old World monkeys and humans is about twenty-eight days, in chimpanzees it is about thirty-four days, and in baboons thirty to forty days.

Whether or not women also experience estrus as a period of heightened sexual drive, around the time of ovulation, is still debated. Some women are aware of an estruslike state; others are not. A rise in body temperature is nevertheless detectable in all women at the time of ovulation. It is literally a "heat."

In other mammals this heat can be more insistent and disturbing. Restlessness and increased sexual solicitation in some mammals can approach frenzy. The restlessness may be mixed with pain or irksome discomfort, which causes impatience and may supply the proximate explanation of why females, even when most excited, sometimes run away from sexual suitors. The less immediate explanation for coyness may be that it gives a female time to assess the vigor or loyalty of a prospective mate.

Some women can understand the tribulations of estrus in animals better than others because they have the pain at midcycle called *mittelschmerz* (middle pain). It can vary from a stabbing sensation for fifteen to thirty minutes as the egg ruptures the ovarian wall, to a diffuse abdominal pain caused by a small amount of blood released along with the egg. Blood in the body cavity is an irritant, which can make the ovulating female feel discomfort of the bowel, urinary and genital tracts. Accompanying sensations of urgency are only exacerbated as she seeks relief through repeated futile evacuation or sexual stimulation. All of these symptoms may be similar to or compounded by those of urinary tract infection.

For most women, this estrous situation does not arise, and they do not know when they ovulate, nor experience any peak of discomfort or desire. Although women ovulate spontaneously at midcycle and do not require males or intercourse, as some female mammals do, in order to release a ripe egg, this does not mean that arousal, copulation, and orgasm cannot play an important part in making the human egg burst from its ovary at midcycle or other times.

Mammals that live in variable climates with variable day lengths through the seasons, or that have long gestation periods, are frequently monestrous, ovulating once during an annual breeding season. The ruminants, such as deer, are monestrous. When food is scarce in winter, the fat portion in these animals declines. The females are infertile during this period partly because of this decrease in fat. The period of infertility proves to be adaptive because mating does not occur or embryos do not implant until more food becomes available, and the young are then born in favorable season.

Although our domesticated ruminants—cattle, sheep, and goats— are polyestrous, they are descendants of wild ruminants and retain a disinclination for food in winter, even when it is available. They too produce young in good season, but, in the case of the long-domesticated sheep and goat, whose nine-thousand-year-old remains appear in the rubble of Jericho, pregnancy, rather than eggless cycles, spans the winter. Sheep and goats conceive in autumn and gestate for five or six months.

Carnivores are monestrous in the wild but may become polyestrous in captivity. A change in light exposure and increased year-round nutrition in captivity probably promotes multiple cycles.

Our own self-imposed captivity or "domestication" in cagelike apartment dwellings and offices, with abundant food and artificial lighting constantly charging the pineal to disinhibit the ovaries, may well have increased human sexual receptivity and fertility. The age of menarche (first menses) has decreased steadily in the past one hundred years (from fourteen or fifteen years to twelve or thirteen years). At the same time, the adolescent period of reduced fertility, which normally follows menarche, shrank from about six years to three or four years in duration. We cannot, therefore, assume that women always ovulated every month or that they were able to be as continuously sexually interested or interesting as the well-fed, long light-exposed women of today. This does not mean that women on other diets and light schedules were or are not sexually potent, only that they probably had or have fewer fertile ovulatory cycles in their lives.

Theories about the development of human society and interpretations of "primitive" human understanding of the role of sex in conception should not therefore rest too heavily on the assumption that female cycling and receptivity was always what it is now. It is probable that prehistoric women and those who lived or live in physically and nutritionally harsh conditions were and are irregular ovulators, just as the gregarious monkeys and social carnivores are today. Knowing this will make us skeptical of theories that suggest that human monogamy was selected for by the riveting effect, on the male, of continuous female receptivity. There may well have been no such receptivity for him to be riveted by. While humans, chimpanzees, gorillas, and certain Old World monkeys *may* continue to copulate throughout the menstrual cycle and even during pregnancy, this may be less an indication of biological receptivity (or arousability) than of social receptivity used to enlist the protection and assistance of male group members or to befriend male invaders.

Whether a female animal is monestrous or polyestrous, there must be a way of shutting off ovulation once pregnancy begins, lest embryos start to pile up in the uterus. This is so obvious that we rarely stop to consider how it happens. To protect herself from simultaneous pregnancies (a condition called superfetation, encountered in certain viviparous fishes), the eutherian female needs the assistance of all the different hormones released from her pituitary, ovaries, corpus luteum, the fetal membranes, and placenta.

When she first becomes pregnant, her fertilized egg has not arrived in her uterus, and there is no placenta to secrete hormonal messages to the ovary telling it to cease egg preparation and start pregnancy maintenance. In many species, the follicle from which the egg is extruded at ovulation assumes the task of announcing the pregnancy to the female's body. When it is bombarded by the luteinizing hormone (LH), which comes from the pituitary, the follicle is transformed into a yellowish mass called the corpus luteum, which announces pregnancy by secreting progesterone and a little estrogen. These secretions elaborate the uterine lining, making the luteal half of the estrous (or menstrual) cycle the beginning of pregnancy, whether or not a fertilized egg is present.

In some eutherians, such as the rat, every copulation signals a possible pregnancy to the pituitary. LH is released after every intercourse, even after one simulated with a glass rod in the hand of an experimenter. In other species (such as humans and sheep), the LH surge and ovulation are independent of intercourse. In either case, the environment suitable for early pregnancy is ensured by the corpus luteum, until either the embryo implants in the uterine lining and a placenta forms, or until no embryo arrives and the corpus is resorbed. In sheep, the uterus itself chemically informs the ovary when no pregnancy occurs. The chemical signal (prostaglandin, PF_2) causes breakdown of the corpus. If, however, the sheep's uterus is removed after ovulation, no signal can be sent to the corpus in the ovary, and it persists for 148 days, the normal gestation period of the sheep.

It is not clear what shuts off the corpus in humans when pregnancy does not occur. It cannot be the uterus, because hysterectomy (removal of uterus) does not prevent ovulation or the timely decline of the corpus luteum two weeks later. A cyclic alternation of pituitary and ovarian hormones seems to govern the rise and fall of the human follicle.

Every female whose ovulation is followed automatically by progesterone release from the corpus luteum, as ours is, experiences the very first stages of pregnancy, whether or not she has conceived, during the luteal phase of her cycle. In women, the uterine lining grows and its glands and blood vessels thicken and coil up; the breasts swell; there may be exaggerated hunger, nausea, extra fatigue, and tension. This "being a little bit pregnant" is also called the premenstrual syndrome.

If the signs of pregnancy persist or proliferate without the presence of a fertilized egg, the condition is called pseudocyesis or pseudopregnancy. In some species, such as ferrets, minks, ground squirrels, and rabbits, pseudopregnancy must occur if intercourse does not result in fertilization. But among these induced ovulators, the reflex release of an egg immediately after intercourse almost guarantees pregnancy. So pseudopregnancy occurs rarely—after copulation with an experimenter's probe, say, or with a single sterile male, a most unlikely event since these females usually mate with several males during estrus.

In species like our own that are *not* reflex ovulators, pseudopregnancy indicates either endocrine malfunction or unconscious mimicry of the symptoms of pregnancy, including cessation of menstruation. Among humans, males are occasionally pseudocyetic. Psychological causes make these men imitate a pregnant appearance by retaining solid wastes and gas and by subtly changing their posture.

After the initial luteal phase but before the formation of the placenta in true pregnancy, cells of the chorion membrane around the embryo begin to secrete a pregnancy-maintaining hormone, which in humans is called hCG (human chorionic gonadotrophin). This is the hormone that reveals conception in an early pregnancy test. Once formed, the placenta takes over the maintenance function by producing hCG and somatomammotrophin as well as steroids, which prevent rejection of the fetus. Placental estrogen promotes the growth of the muscle layer of the uterus, and progesterone suppresses uterine contractions before parturition. At the end of pregnancy, progesterone falls, allowing the uterus to contract in response to a rise in estrogen and oxytocin (another hormone from the pituitary).

Estrogen and progesterone also prepare the mammary glands for nursing. The former stimulates proliferation of the glandular tissue, and the latter prevents premature secretion of milk. When progesterone falls off and oxytocin rises at the end of pregnancy, contractile tissue in the breast can then expel milk, just as contractile tissue in the uterus expels the fetus. Sucking further stimulates the release of oxytocin from the pituitary, causing postpartum contractions of the uterus and the continuation of lactation.

Lactation is also a regulator of ovulation and pregnancy. Whereas LH, the corpus luteum, hCG, and the placental hormones inhibit ovulation *during* pregnancy, lactation either inhibits ovulation or delays egg implantation *after* pregnancy. Delayed implantation, or diapause, of a fertilized egg during the nursing period has been seen to occur in certain kangaroos and also in mice and rats. The length of the delay in these species is determined by the amount of nursing going on. Thus, more than five rat nestlings will be sufficient to suppress estrogen production and thereby prevent implantation and pregnancy. With litters smaller than five, one pregnancy can follow immediately upon another, because gestation lasts as long as the period up to weaning—twenty-one days. It is easy to see that with small litters a female rat can produce more than eighty offspring per year.

Delayed implantation also helps mammals that mate in late summer, such as roe deer, badgers, sea lions, seals, and (sometimes) beavers. Instead of giving birth in midwinter, females of these species "use" delayed implantation and give birth the following spring. The technique of freeze-thawing embryos, only recently used on humans, provides an artificial diapause. At the most opportune moment, embryos may be thawed and implanted in the uterus that will gestate them, which is not necessarily the uterus of their biological mother.

The foregoing are only some of the mechanisms for governing ovulation and pregnancy. There is much to be learned from the great diversity of endocrine control of female cycles among the four thousand or so species of our subclass, Eutheria. Knowledge gleaned from the wide range of systems offered by nature may help us to improve human birth control methods and devise ways to overcome infertility in particular individuals. Study of the ovulatory cycle and its hormonal control has already yielded the procedure, described at the beginning of this section, that produced the first so-called test-tube baby. Patrick Steptoe, one of the pioneers in the study of extracorporeal fertilization, reported (in a lecture at Oxford, 1980) that he found externally fertilized eggs, grown to blastocyst-sized embryos in vitro, grew best when transplanted into the uterus one day into the luteal phase. By this time the corpus luteum has prepared the uterine wall to accept the embryo. Optimal success of the procedure also demands that the embryo be inserted at night because progesterone levels are higher at night in most women, and this reduces uterine contractions, making expulsion of the blastocyst less likely.

In future, external fertilization and reinsertion of the embryo should allow many women whose blocked oviducts prevent sperms from meeting eggs in the usual way, to have babies. This procedure could also be used for foster-gestation of human fetuses, so that ovariectomized or postmenopausal women could have children. Foster-gestation has already been accomplished in other species and even across species lines. A mare, for example, can receive a donkey embryo in her womb via hypodermic syringe and successfully carry the embryo to term. While it is imaginable that a female of another species might foster-gestate a human embryo, it was a woman in Australia who became the first surrogate mother of an externally fertilized egg from another woman, carrying to term an embryo that contained none of her genes. The surrogate mother in this case was not destined to give the baby to another couple; she had been unable to produce an egg of her own and therefore had decided to receive an embryo formed from the egg of another woman and the sperm of her own husband. Amazingly, she was able to gestate and breast-feed the son who was no more genetically hers than an adopted child would have been. However, this unusual pregnancy did not mean that the baby was less hers or that she was less his mother. Her desire to produce and love a child was more important than the presence of her genes. With her magnanimous mothering she took more of a giant step for mankind—clear out of the selfish gene framework—than the man who first set foot on the moon. Try to imagine what the world would be like if none of us cared whether we were nurturing our own genes, our *own* children, but would be willing to love a child, to serve and deserve a child with love, rather than own it.

Eutherian and marsupial mammals are separated from other groups with amniote eggs—reptiles, birds, and monotremes—by possession of a placenta that is usually composed of the chorion and allantois, not just of the yolk sac membrane, as in most marsupials and viviparous reptiles. Evolution of a good placenta helped eutherians prolong pregnancy and transmit immunity, as well as sustenance, to the growing young. Since the placenta is also an independent secretory organ that supplies hormones to maintain itself and the pregnancy and to promote lactation, it is worth knowing something about how it evolved (its phylogeny) and how it grows (its ontogeny) inside the mother.

Because placentas do not fossilize, it is difficult to picture how they evolved. One evolutionary biologist, R. D. Martin, thinks it is likely that in early placentas all three membranes—chorion, allantois, and yolk sac—were involved in nutritional maintenance, with the yolk sac playing the most important role in nutrient absorption. Although the yolk sac layer seems to have been first to elaborate into a functional connection between mother and embryo, it is now the chorionic and allantoic membranes that are more important in eutherian placentas.

Considering its present diversity of form, the placenta probably began to evolve very early in mammalian history, soon after the hair and skin glands that differentiated the therapsids from other reptiles. However it may have come into being, the placenta is a compound of cells that act as lungs, liver, intestine, kidney, and gland.

In humans and many other eutherian species, the placenta takes over the pregnancy-maintaining function of the pituitary and the corpus luteum, which are active at the earliest phase of gestation. The corpus luteum may regress (and does so in humans), and the ovaries and pituitary might even be removed, without sacrificing the pregnancy, since the placenta will keep up the level of hormones needed to maintain the pregnancy. It can even continue its own gestation without the fetus and be "born" at term.

When the embryo first enters the uterus, it rests at one point on the uterine lining. There, some of the outer cells of the embryo, called the trophoblast, slightly eat away the endometrium, which then sustains the early embryo on glycogen, before the placenta forms. As the embryo grows, its surrounding membranes—amnion, allantois, and chorion—participate to different degrees, according to the species, to form the placental projections, which interlock with the endometrium. Both maternal and fetal blood vessels supply the placenta, but the bloodstreams do not mix.

Eutherian placentas come in many forms. Some, like that of the horse, are sacs that surround the embryo entirely and have diffuse attachments to the endometrium. Cattle typically form a patchwork placenta, in which the points of attachment to the uterine wall are like a scattering of seeds or large beans. The dog has a zonary placenta which girdles the embryo round the middle. The human placenta is the disc type, concentrated on one side of the fetus.

Closeness of connection between placenta and maternal tissues also varies from one group of mammals to another. Placentas of seals show the most slender separation of maternal and fetal circulations. This fine barrier, which is only four hundred-millionths of an inch in places, probably allows easy transmission of oxygen to the fetus during its mother's dives, when breathing ceases and heart rate slows. In some species, the placental projections, called villi, which latch onto the uterine wall, easily pull away from it at birth. However, in our species, the connection is so close that uterine material may be torn away with the placenta at birth.

All placentas, whatever their shape or form of connection, have evolved to actively transport substances, like amino acids (protein building blocks), against a concentration gradient. This means that even if the concentration of amino acids is higher on the fetal side of the placenta, more amino acids will be passed in. Immunity, in the form of gamma-globulin proteins, is also transferred to the fetus, and primate placentas can even transmit leukocytes (white blood cells) and blood platelets. Fetal wastes are carried over to the mother's bloodstream for elimination through her excretory system.

Most female mammals, even herbivores, eat the placenta, which is also called the afterbirth. Only human and sea mammal mothers regularly do not. Whales and dolphins are too busy ensuring that the newborn gets up to the surface for a breath of air. Seals give birth on land but also do not eat the placenta.

Humans have elaborated a variety of culturally prescribed behaviors connected with the afterbirth, ranging from burial to ceremonial drying for amulets to routine medical examination, which determines if pieces of it have remained in the uterus. There is even one progressive home-birth manual that records a recipe for afterbirth soup, and other do-it-yourself advocates recommend feeding the placenta to the family dog. An article in *World Medicine*, February 21, 1981, reports that a woman in Kentish Town, England, ate her placenta fried with onions, hoping it would relieve postpartum depression. A warning is in order, however, for those who might take up this idea: the placenta could be a reservoir for drugs used in delivery or taken during pregnancy.

While eating the placenta and fetal membranes, in nature, may simply be a quick meal for a very hungry mother after labor, it is also a way to clean up the birth area, doing away with the blood, tissue, and odors that might attract predators to the mother and offspring. In any case, the placenta is digested and its nutrients absorbed like those of any other food. It is a source of protein and iron, and the steroid hormones in it could possibly elevate the new mother's mood.

Creating a female that will eventually nourish her young via the placenta is a complex, species-specific process, which can be divided into two parts. The first is the growth of the female conceptus *in utero*, directed by the genes of her cells and the hormone environment created by her mother and her own developing organs. The second part of the process occurs after birth, as the female interacts with her mother and later with other species members; as she is influenced by the continuing growth and chemical changes of her own systems; and as she gives birth and learns to mother her young.

Whether or not *most* female mammals actually do become mothers is an important question for zoologists because the answer will influence ideas about female, as compared to male, mating and parenting strategies. For the time being, however, there does seem to be less *variation* in reproductive success (also called reproductive variance) among female than among male mammals (but see below). While females have similar limiters—fertility cycle and gestation period—that put a ceiling on their fecundity, male fecundity is, theoretically, limited primarily by female availability.

Due to the victories and defeats of male-male competition, however, there may be great variation in the number of offspring each male leaves, even while he retains the potential to leave many more young than any female. Moulay Ismail, a seventeenth-century emperor of Morocco, reputedly sired 888 children at a time when a peasant man might sire 5 to 10, and when many men left no viable offspring due to high infant and child mortality. In contrast, the greatest number of live births attributed to any woman is 69. This was the achievement of Mme. Vassilyev, a nineteenth-century Russian, who had sixteen pairs of twins, seven sets of triplets, and four sets of quadruplets.

But variation in number of babies born does not fully represent reproductive variance; variation in numbers of young reared to reproductive age must be taken into account. As Sarah Blaffer Hrdy and G. C. Williams say in *Social Behavior of Female Vertebrates*, "Can there be any doubt that a substantial fraction of Mr. Bloodthirsty's [Moulay Ismail's nickname] children died young? . . . that his favorite wives raised a larger proportion of their children than did his low-status concubines and lived to see a larger number of thriving grandchildren[?]" They go on to point out that differential access by females to essential resources not only creates variance in their reproductive success, it can be determined by natural selection acting upon women through the agency of culture, as in status and marriage customs.

Until recently it was assumed that the variation in reproductive success among females was minimal, all females presumably mating and becoming pregnant at maturity, season after season. But now it has been discovered that several (perhaps many) species have behavioral-biochemical ways of interfering with reproduction in certain females. For example, the mere proximity of a dominant female (that is, one that has won a fight with or simply frightened and displaced others consistently) may inhibit ovulation in a subordinate female, as among the tiny South American marmoset monkeys, or cause her to cannibalize her litter, as among density-stressed tree shrews. Lion, wolf, and baboon females vary sharply in their reproductive success, according to the dominance relationships within the group and the assistance they are able to obtain from males in the tasks of provisioning, baby-sitting, and protecting young from female kidnappers and male marauders. Among Richardson's ground squirrels reproductive success correlates with the sex ratio of the litters. Most females are unsuccessful in leaving progeny over several consecutive years, but those that do succeed have female-biased litters. Dominant female talapoin monkeys and gelada baboons may interfere with conception in subordinates by harassing them, especially during estrus. Harassment appears to cause eggless (anovulatory) cycles, which are associated with high levels of prolactin and cortisol, hormones that, respectively, inhibit libido and help the body cope with stress.

Reproductive variance is well documented also among women. In the United States in 1870, families with ten or more children were frequent, but at the same time about 25 percent of all women never bore any children. In 1909, according to Wilson and Daly, 23 percent of thirty-five-year-old women were childless; by 1960, however, only 12 percent were childless. While the percentage of women in the age group thirty-five to thirty-nine years who were ever married stayed the same from 1960 to 1975, the proportion of childless women continued to decline to about 6 percent by the end of this period. So, in spite of the most recent trend for some females of our species to disequate themselves from the mother identity, there is evidence that these same women are becoming mothers in droves, at least in the biological sense of having had a child. The reproductive variance among women in this particular society has almost disappeared.

Better nutrition, widespread health care and good housing, the welfare state, softer mores on illegitimacy, a better press for female sexuality have made it possible for almost all women to become mothers. The criteria—health, education, attractiveness, social and previous marital status—that once operated to narrow the field are now so generally adequate or so broadly defined that there is virtually no differential reproduction among American women anymore. No woman, on average, is doing that much better than any other in terms of numbers of healthy offspring she raises to maturity. There has been a great leveling off, through which all but the most severely handicapped have gained a roughly equal share of fitness, measured in terms of genes passed into the next generation. This could mean that there is less and less reason for conflict. Offspring of men and women in almost all parts of this society now have a good chance of surviving, and becoming more or less equally fit.

Repetition of this picture in other societies would bode well for world peace, were it not for underdeveloped countries where survival still fluctuates with environmental conditions and with the oscillations of internal politics and external assistance. Competition among parents for survival resources is now performed on a large scale. Through gifts of "aid," advanced countries act as competitive fatherlands or investing motherlands with respect to their adopted third-world wards. In spite of the fact that it has been achieved in relatively few places, the trend toward leveling off reproductive variance among women *could* be worldwide with the use of birth control. The social consequences of such leveling are dealt with briefly in the birth control section below.

The very first step in the formation of a female mammal occurs in the oviduct, where the egg is penetrated by an X-bearing sperm. Compared to reptilian or avian eggs, mammalian eggs are tiny—ranging in diameter from about 70 micrometers (μm) to 180 μm in placentals, to 240 μm in marsupials, and 15,000 μm in monotremes (1μm = 1/1000 mm). In spite of being smaller than eggs of other land vertebrates, mammalian eggs are still vastly larger in volume than their respective sperms. The head of the human sperm is only about 4 micrometers long. Even the smallest mammalian egg, produced by a fat, mouselike rodent called the vole, is larger than all other body cells, excluding long-axoned motor neurons. The vole's egg, about 70 μm in diameter, could easily hold, within its borders, a red blood cell, a connective tissue cell, a sensory nerve cell, a motor neuron cell body, *and* a sperm.

After several cell divisions, the female embryo is on her way to the uterus, still enclosed by the outer membrane of the egg, called the zona pellucida. In the uterus, the embryo of about one hundred cells hatches out of this clear membrane and is ready to begin the process of implanting in the uterine lining.

Before following the embryo from its first cleavages through its development into a female mammal ready to be born, the so-called sex chromosome pair, XX, deserves some consideration. Although it is the X-chromosome in double dose that is the signature of every *mammalian* female, it is not exclusively devoted to female sex determination. In fact, in humans, the traits that make a female female seem to be scattered over all her twenty-three chromosome pairs. In rare cases, the effects of the twenty-two pairs of non-sex-designating (autosomal) chromosomes run counter to the XX pair, resulting in an appearance or sense of sex that is more male than female.

The only known gene on the X-chromosome that has something to do with sex determination is a gene called Tfm, short for testicular feminizing mutation. This mutant gene actually affects males (XY) and not females. All the body cells of males that carry the Tfm gene are insensitive to androgens. Therefore, in spite of the fact that these males have an X-chromosome from their mother and a Y-chromosome from their father, like all normal males, they develop the external genitalia of females. When they reach puberty, the small amount of estrogen normally secreted by the testes makes them perfectly feminine in appearance. (Testes exist inside these androgen-insensitive males because they are formed early in gestation and are independent of androgen for their formation.) Tfm genetic males are raised as girls, and they can become healthy, well-adjusted but infertile women, who may be successful adoptive mothers.

It is possible to discern the sex of a normal XX female early in embryonic life, even before her ovaries or sex organs have formed. This can be done because the nucleus of each female cell has a concentration of dark-staining DNA, called a Barr body, that can be seen under a microscope. This dark spot, first noted by Murray Barr in the late 1940s, is one of the X-chromosomes encapsulated. In every female body cell (except mature red blood cells, which have no chromosomes) one of the two X-chromosomes is encapsulated. If the dark spot appears in the fetal cells taken from the amniotic fluid, the fetus is female.

The X-chromosome that is encapsulated in the Barr body may be from either the mother or the father. Since the encapsulation is apparently random throughout the body, and since encapsulation means inactivation of the genes on the X-chromosome, some cells in a female mammal will "print out" only the X-gene instructions from the mother, and others will "print out" only X-gene instructions from the father. In this sense, every female is a mosaic of traits from her X-chromosomes. This accounts for the mottled fur of the tortoiseshell cat and for the fact that identical twin females are less identical than identical twin males! Since the X-chromosomes of twin sisters' cells are encapsulated randomly, the overall expressions of the X-traits will differ between the sisters and may give them somewhat different appearances. Of course, this difference may be very slight because the human X-chromosome is only one in the total of forty-six chromosomes found in each cell, and therefore governs only a small fraction of all traits.

The fact that female cells with different X-chromosomes operating are slightly different from each other underlines the point that the two X-chromosomes are not identical. Although they contain genes for the same traits, the expressions of these traits may be different. Thus, the trait for one aspect of the clotting process is carried on both X-chromosomes. The gene for this trait on one of a female's X's may call for the hemophiliac expression of clotting, while the other X-chromosome may carry the gene for normal clotting. Since most of the hundred or so known traits carried by the X-chromosomes are recessive (that is, need to be present on both X-chromosomes in order to show up in the organism), women suffer much less than men from X-linked disorders, including hemophilia. Unless a woman takes the same "bad" X-gene from both her mother and father, she will always have a "good" X gene to offset the corresponding bad one. In addition, some of her cells will encapsulate the X-chromosome containing the bad gene in the Barr body and thus inactivate it. With the recessiveness of X-linked traits, the presence of two X-chromosomes that usually have different expressions of each trait, and the Barr body, female mammals are spared almost all manifestations of X-linked diseases.

In contrast, male mammals have only one X-chromosome, and any genes on it are usually given full expression. This is why Queen Victoria, who carried the gene for hemophilia, was untroubled by the disease, but her son, Leopold, Duke of Albany, died of it at thirty-one. There are more than thirty serious disorders of X-chromosome origin, and all of them are found almost exclusively in males. They include congenital cataracts, Duchenne's muscular dystrophy, hydrocephalus, scaly skin, certain forms of parkinsonism and mental retardation, and progressive deafness.

The small Y-chromosome, which is the signature of all mammalian males, carries almost no traits. The only known Y-linked trait, of the more than two thousand known human genetic traits, is the H-Y antigen trait. This antigen sticks to the surfaces of all male cells and causes the embryonic gonad to become a testicle. The only other trait that is Y-linked in *some* human groups is that for hairy ear rims!

Although the Y-chromosome is not a big trait carrier, it is vital to male differentiation of the embryo. Still, possession of the Y-chromosome is not always the guarantor of perfect maleness, because, as mentioned above, the Tfm gene on the powerful X-chromosome can make a male insensitive to his own androgens. Although, among humans, more Y-bearing sperms fertilize eggs (reason unknown) and although more male than female babies are born (about 106:100 worldwide), males die more often than females at every life stage, partly because they have only one X-chromosome. So the slightly higher male to female ratio at birth soon reverses.

Returning to the development of the female embryo, we see that the first divisions of the female zygote appear to be no different from those of the male zygote. In either case the fertilized egg cleaves vertically, as if it were an apple cut in half; then it divides horizontally, slightly above the equator, to form four cells. When such cleavages have formed a ball of about a hundred cells, the outer layer, called the trophoblast, begins to nip away at the endometrium, where it implants, and placenta formation begins. Soon the ball sinks in upon itself, forming a double cavity linked by a disc upon which the embryo grows.

There are three layers of cells in the embryo from which future tissues, organs, and systems arise. They are the ectoderm, mesoderm, and endoderm. From the last the gut wall forms, and cells that will eventually become eggs migrate to the site of the future ovaries. The female mammal has all her immature eggs in her gonads by the time she is born. Female rats have about 160,000; bitches (female dogs) about 700,000; and estimates of human female egg hordes at birth range from about 400,000 to 2,000,000 (lower estimate Money and Ehrhardt; higher estimate Wilson and Daly quoting Austin and Short, 1972). These numbers already indicate a decline from the maximum of about 7,000,000 that a human female possesses when she is a five-month-old embryo.

About six weeks after conception, the human male embryo shows signs of sex differentiation, with the beginning of testis formation. Ovary formation begins in about the twelfth week. We still do not know how the second X-chromosome stops the very early, undifferentiated gonad from turning into a testis. Without the second X (as in Turner's Syndrome, in which the individual has one X and no other X or Y) the ovaries will not develop normally, although the external genitalia and appearance throughout life will be female.

During the twelfth to sixteenth week of gestation of the human female embryo, the outer rind of her gonad begins to grow, as the inner core degenerates. The process is complete at about six months. Very rarely, a fetus will develop neither ovaries nor testes. When this happens, the external appearance of the individual is always female. The underlying blueprint for all mammalian fetuses seems to be female and will develop thus, even without the secretion of fetal estrogen. In fact, development of the human female normally proceeds without the influence of her ovarian hormones well into the fourth month of gestation, when the fetal ovaries begin to secrete estrogen.

In contrast, the fetus that is to become a male must form testes that begin to secrete androgens (principally testosterone) early in the second month of gestation. If this early androgen direction does not occur, the embryo will become female in spite of an XY chromosome constitution, as with the Tfm mutation. Thus, the mammalian embryo seems to be preprogrammed to become female in its gonads, ducts, genitals, and possibly even its behavior. Maleness appears to be a superimposed variation on this basic plan.

In the third month of gestation, while the gonads are still forming, the human female embryo begins to accentuate the Mullerian ducts, which arch down from each rudimentary gonad to the urogenital passage and develop into the oviducts, uterus, and upper part of the vagina. At the same time, the rudimentary Wolffian ducts, which elaborate only in the presence of androgens (normally from the testes of a male fetus), are resorbed. The uterus and oviducts (fallopian tubes) develop even in the absence of fetal ovaries, so long as there is no androgen to inhibit the transformation of the Mullerian and the resorption of the Wolffian ducts.

If the testes of a male embryo fail to develop or to secrete sufficient androgens to inhibit Mullerian duct development, then a male with a uterus may be the result. The male embryo with underactive testes may still turn out to look male, in spite of the formed uterus, if his testes become active later in uterine life and secrete enough hormones to stimulate the completion of male genitalia.

The incomplete disappearance or partial development of female structures in male mammals is not uncommon. Uterine rudiments have been found in male cattle, sheep, goats, beavers, and horses. Pockets off the male urethra (urinary canal), resembling the vagina, have been seen in guinea pigs, primates, and most carnivores. Among males of several tree shrew species the Mullerian ducts consistently develop into an accessory sexual gland, located at the base of the bladder. This gland, formed from female ducts, secretes a fluid that augments the ejaculate. This is an example of dimorphic preadaptation, whereby structures or behaviors generally used only by one sex are "reshaped" and used in new ways by the other sex.

There is no parallel situation in females. So far as is known, no special substance need be secreted by the ovaries to inhibit the Wolffian ducts; they simply degenerate without the added stimulus of androgens. There are no genetic females with male reproductive duct systems and female external genitalia. The ovary itself, however, may develop ambiguously and be streaked with testicular tissue. There are also very rare cases of females with one ovary and one testis. One thing that may go wrong with the differentiation of the human Mullerian ducts into tubes, uterus, and upper vagina is the misshaping of these structures. The uterus and oviducts may form a T rather than the usual Y configuration, and the vagina may be a shallow cavity that does not connect to the uterus. These malformations may or may not be compatible with pregnancy, and sometimes they resemble the shapes of the uterus and tubes of other mammals.

Human female external genitalia start to form in the eighth week of prenatal life. Until that time, the external appearance of the genitalia is identical for both sexes: a urogenital slit surrounded by a pair of skin folds, capped by a midline bump of tissue, called the genital tubercle, which becomes the body of the clitoris or penis. In the female the folds around what will be the urethral opening remain separate and become the small and large labia. In males, the same structures fuse to form the urethral tube in the penis and the scrotum, respectively. Again, differentiation of these masculine structures requires testes; differentiation of the feminine structures requires only that there be *no* testes.

There are at least two mammals in which masculinization of the female external genitalia is normal: the spotted hyena (*Crocuta crocuta*) and the spider monkey (*Ateles geoffreyi*). There are a few other South American monkeys in which the female genitalia are always partially masculinized. Our species also shows variation in this feature. For example, the Hottentot apron, an elongation of the labia minora (usually 2 to 4 inches, rarely up to 7 inches), has been confused, at first glance, with male genitalia. The apron may or may not be associated with higher prenatal levels of androgen (male hormone), as is masculinization of the genitalia of female spotted hyenas (see pp. 203–204). In this species the clitoris is pierced by a urogenital canal, and is therefore the channel for intercourse and birth. Drawings of hyena genitalia in L. Harrison-Matthews' 1939 monograph show that the young female is indistinguishable from the male.

Two abnormal states can more fully masculinize the human female embryo's genitalia. In one condition, too much androgen is put out by the fetal adrenal glands. In the other condition, the fetus is exposed to too much androgen, either from a maternal tumor or from a drug used (twenty to thirty years ago) to prevent miscarriages. This drug contained synthetic progesterone (progestin), which mimicked the action of a male hormone and masculinized the female fetus's external genitalia. In these cases, surgery was performed early to make the external genitalia consistent with the genetic and internal sex. However, since doctors and parents sometimes mistook the true sex of the babies of progestin-treated mothers, the infants were not surgically corrected and were raised as boys. This was most unfortunate, because at puberty the intact ovaries began to put out female hormones, which called forth the body changes for a pubescent girl, making the sex identity of the boy ambiguous and his psychological adjustment difficult. If, on the other hand, surgery had been performed early, the life history of the genetic female with masculinized genitalia at birth scarcely differed from that of a normal female; she could menstruate, conceive, even give birth depending on the extent and type of surgical correction she had had.

In the condition where female fetuses were masculinized by their own malfunctioning adrenals, surgery was also used to correct the external genitalia, and cortisone administered throughout life counteracted the androgenlike hormone from the adrenals. This allowed the girls' ovaries to feminize them in the normal manner at puberty. A remarkable side effect of excess progesterone or adrenal androgen *in utero* is a significant increase in intelligence (IQ) and academic performance; this applies to both females and males, as reported by Katherine Dalton in 1968 and John Money in 1971.

The gestation of the female, naturally, is not just restricted to the formation of her reproductive system. Certain areas of the brain also differentiate sexually, under the influence of fetal hormones. For instance, the hypothalamus, the crescent of midbrain tissue in direct communication with the pituitary, apparently changes permanently after exposure to fetal androgens. If it receives an early dose of male hormone, it will not be able to cyclically release factors that trigger ovulation. Only the female hypothalamus, *unexposed* in fetal life to androgens, will be able to do this.

Geoffrey Raisman and Pauline Field showed that giving a female rat male sex hormones in the first few days of her life makes nerve connections in a tiny area near the base of her brain (the preoptic-suprachiasmatic area) look like those of a male rat. It is not yet clear to what degree the prenatal fixing of the brain influences behavior apart from the fertility cycle with its attendant activities and thoughts. Just as the female baby's external genitalia can be masculinized to varying degrees *in utero*, depending on the time and amount of exposure to androgen, so her brain and hence her future behavior may be masculinized to different degrees.

The social behavior, or role, assumed by a mammal is a composite of her structure and physiology, but it is also more than that. At this level of organization, the influences of experience come into play, making a general description of role formation more difficult than one of corporeal gender formation.

Adding the influences of self-consciousness to structure, physiology, and experience brings us to the level of organization known as gender identification, which is the human verification of sex role performance. For most of us, performance is so natural that verification seems superfluous, but the fact that there are people who do not feel themselves to be the sex which they are, genetically, physically, and socially, highlights the difference between gender role and gender identification. While all mammals have a gender role, it is not yet possible to tell which of them may reflect upon their gender identity.

Let us review a few attempts to assess the relative importance of structure and physiology versus experience in the developments of gender identification in humans.

In the 1960s and early 1970s, John Money and Anke Ehrhardt matched twenty-five prenatally masculinized girls to twenty-five normal girls of similar age and social background. The prenatally masculinized girls had been treated surgically, and fifteen of the twenty-five had been given cortisone to counteract improper adrenal function. In spite of being raised as girls and having the full effect of their functioning ovaries at puberty, prenatally masculinized girls were found to be significantly more tomboyish. The researchers define tomboyism as taking more interest in boys' games and vigorous outdoor play than in girls' games and rehearsal for motherhood and housekeeping; preference for utilitarian clothes and an aversion to feminine dress; plans for career with marriage secondary; and objectification of the opposite sex in visually erotic imagery. Although, by today's standards, these criteria would scarcely differentiate girls from boys, let alone girlish girls from boyish girls, Money and Ehrhardt believe that they detected a slight but consistent difference in the behavior of their two groups of girls. The subjects were too young to assess for frequency of marriage.

Another group of females was also assessed. These were adrenally masculinized girls who grew up before it was discovered that cortisone could halt the action of defective adrenals. These girls were, therefore, postnatally as well as prenatally masculinized. It was found that, when they became adults, ten of the twenty-three girls in this sample had homosexual as well as heterosexual *fantasies* and that three reported bisexual experiences. Although these androgenized girls and women did not think they were wrongly assigned as females, only thirteen of the twenty-three married, and eleven of the thirteen marriages occurred in girls who eventually received cortisone therapy, the efficacy of which was discovered in 1951. While the desire for marriage is declining as a conditioned feminine trait, a group of twenty-three women in which just over half marry, and the majority of those only after hormone treatment, would be extremely atypical, even today. But perhaps it was their high intelligence, caused by fetal exposure to adrenal progesterone derivatives, and not masculinity that steered these women away from marriage. Indeed, Money and Ehrhardt point out that some of the women in this group were not masculine in their behaviors and goals by any of the tests applied.

Thus, it is difficult not only to weigh the relative inputs of endocrine secretions and experience, it is difficult to find behavioral criteria for femininity that stand the test of time. Although we intuit that there are some females who are more masculine than others, it is hard to quantify the difference, given the sliding scale of gender definition in our society.

Another approach to the problem of teasing apart the biological and social influences on the making of a female is to compare the behaviors of individuals of the same genetic and hormonal sex who were raised in opposite genders. Cases like this are rare, but Money and Ehrhardt report on three matched pairs of hermaphrodites in which one was raised as a boy and the other as a girl.

In every case, in spite of similar genetic, gonadal, and fetal hormonal inheritance, the pairs split apart when it came to gender identity. All six subjects had ovaries, had been exposed to too much androgen from the adrenals *in utero*, and were born with masculinized genitalia, but those raised as boys felt like and wanted to be boys, and those raised as girls wanted to be girls.

Two of the pairs of hermaphrodites were bolstered hormonally at puberty, and surgically early in life or at puberty, to make their genitalia consistent with sex of rearing. Girls received cortisone at puberty or even before, so that their ovaries would not be inhibited by their adrenal androgens. Boys were ovariectomized (had ovaries removed) and sometimes were given extra androgens to augment masculine development at puberty.

The third pair of hermaphrodites did not receive their surgical and hormonal treatment as early as the other four subjects, and this necessitated late sex reassignments at eleven to twelve years of age. Because their parents and doctors had not recognized the adrenogenital syndrome when these youngsters were infants, their identities until puberty were sexually ambiguous. By leaving notes on crumpled bits of paper, these embarrassed children finally gave clues about which sex they felt they were or could be. One said she wanted to be a girl like her sisters, and the other emphatically indicated that he wanted to be a boy.

The subject who "became" a girl then received cortisone, which disinhibited her ovaries, and underwent surgery to remove an enlarged clitoris and construct a vagina. The subject who became a boy was ovariectomized; prosthetic testes were inserted and the incompletely fused urethral canal of the penis was corrected. While he would be able to function as a male sexually, the absence of gonads would leave him sterile. Testosterone was prescribed to ensure the continued masculinization of his physique, which was already clearly male due to the effect of his unchecked adrenal androgens. Although this boy was chromosomally XX, this made no difference to his gender identity as a male. He thought of himself as a male and began dating girls at age fifteen.

These cases show that it is a totality of delicately balanced endocrinal, anatomical, and social factors, above and beyond the chromosomal sex, that create gender identity and make a female (or male) look, act, and feel her (or his) sex.

Parturition is the complicated and often dangerous passage between the uterine and postnatal phases of the making of a female. For most other primates the process is shorter than it is for women and larger mammals. Elephants, for example, suffer a long and painful delivery, which is the culmination of nearly two years of pregnancy. They may be attended by other members of the herd, especially their sisters and grown daughters. The elephant baby weighs about forty pounds, and about one in a hundred births is twins. The elephant delivers about four to five young in her fifty-to-seventy-year life span, and she suckles each youngster for several years. Another mammal that has great difficulty giving birth is the otter. Her young are born large and mature, and after their delivery her death is not uncommon.

The size of the baby is rarely proportional to the size of the mother. For instance, polar bears have one to four tiny young (3 to 6 inches long), and the black bear's young, which are born and suckled during her winter hibernation, weigh only 8 to 13 ounces at birth. Each of her two or three cubs is only about 0.25 percent of her weight. In contrast, the lesser horseshoe bat, weighing only 0.2 ounces, will have one baby of about 0.06 ounces, 30 percent or more of her total weight. The blue whale, which weighs ten million times more than the bat, has a baby that weighs only 2.5 percent of her nonpregnant body weight.

Although human babies are born quite immature, the delivery is often traumatic for both mother and offspring. The difficulty is the result of a conflict between two evolutionary trends: one to maximize the volume of the skull for the enlarging brain and the other to maintain pelvic proportions necessary for upright walking. Beyond a certain point the female pelvis could not broaden to accommodate the enlarging infant's head because this would interfere with her easy bipedal gait. This problem was partly solved by the birth of an embryonic human infant with a small head (relative to that of a year-old child); a brain one-quarter of its adult size; and partially formed bony skull plates. The human brain and skull are still growing rapidly at birth and continue to do so for at least two years after. It seems that the maximum rate of brain development was selected for within the limits of our typically hominoid gestation period; any faster rate or longer gestation period would have produced a head too large for safe delivery.

Offspring so immature at birth helped the mother during parturition but burdened her afterward with an infant that could not even see clearly or cling to her. So the human female was obliged to hold and be more attentive toward her baby than most mammalian mothers.

(It should be noted that the immaturity of human newborns may not have been selected for only or mainly because of the development of upright walking. The great apes, who move around with the assistance of their arms and do not show the pelvic alterations of humans, also have immature infants, which, compared to mother's body weight, are relatively smaller than human babies and have smaller heads. The newborn human is about 5.0 percent of its mother's nongravid weight, and the newborn gorilla about 2.5 percent.)

As hominid infants were evolving toward being born extremely dependent, hominid culture was evolving toward cooperative support of the woman during the early postpartum months. Without this support the hominid would have been obliged, like other mammalian mothers that have no huge store of subcutaneous fat, to leave her baby periodically to forage or hunt. But as hominids moved into colder areas, the danger of hypothermy for the furless infant, compounded with the danger of predation, made it adaptive for our ancestors to feed and protect the mother and child. Groups of hominids that could cooperate to this extent survived better than those that could not, and they, therefore, passed on any genes or traditions that ensured mothering of the mother. In this way, mothering qualities also came to be shared with and instilled in men.

Incorporation of mothering behaviors in the male repertoire was a great boon to the development of certain human societies (including ours), and has contributed to the success of other mammals, such as the wolf and beaver. Mothering the mother is a method of integrating males into the troop or nuclear family. It is another example of dimorphic preadaptation, in which one sex advantageously uses structures or behaviors normally found in and used by the opposite sex.

In most mammals, birth is preceded, sometimes for days or weeks, by self-stimulation and signs of sexual arousal. Manual or oral self-stimulation of the nipples and genital region seems to be directed toward relief of sexual tension, as libido increases in the late stages of pregnancy, and it may also serve to prepare the breasts for lactation and the reproductive system for parturition by strengthening and regularizing uterine contractions in the early stages of labor.

Lorises, vervet and talapoin monkeys, baboons, and macaques are only a few primates that show intense self-grooming, examination, and stimulation of the genitalia just prior to and during parturition. They will massage the pubic area, examine the vulva, and probe the vagina with their fingers, grooming, rubbing, and exploring the area sometimes for days before the birth. Cats, rats, and mice add licking the nipples and perineal area to this list. Self-licking of the rows of nipples by pregnant rats helps prepare their mammary glands for nursing. For many female mammals licking behavior also carries over to the grooming of the young, as babies often need licking and stroking to stimulate their eliminative functions.

Arousal near parturition is often mixed with too much discomfort and vulnerability for sexual interaction, and most mammalian mothers seek privacy as birth approaches. Still, there is great variation from species to species and many females go into an estrous state at the time of parturition or just after, and they do copulate. Even the placid cow sometimes experiences a false estrus (that is, without ovulation) in the late stages of pregnancy. Just as in true estrus, she swishes and raises her tail, tries to mount or solicits mounting from other females in her group, and may even seek a male. She is sniffed with interest by other females in the group, indicating that her altered hormone balance has changed her scent.

The existence of self-stimulation and sexual restlessness around parturition are related to the fact that birth, lactation, and coitus are not only linked as aspects of reproduction but also as behaviors based on similar hormonal and nervous patterns. P. J. Hogarth states in his monograph on viviparity that estrous behavior, ovulation, and birth are all associated with a sharp peak in estrogen release. This explains the rise in sexuality before parturition in many mammals and the postpartum estrus of several rodents, insectivores, and marsupials.

Estrogen magnifies the effects of oxytocin, the other hormone present during birth, lactation, and coitus. Since oxytocin is released whenever certain mechanical stimulation is applied—distension of the vagina (as in birth and intercourse); manipulation of the nipple and breast (as in nursing and foreplay)—and since estrogen is usually high at these times, oxytocin is able to have a strong effect on its target tissues: the smooth muscle lining the uterus and the milk reservoirs. It is oxytocin's release that causes these muscles to contract in orgasm and labor and makes the breasts eject their milk during feeding and sometimes during foreplay and orgasm.

The interaction of these hormones and behaviors was nicely illustrated in an experiment performed by Debackere, Peeters, and Tuyttens. They made pairs of sheep share the same blood circulation by connecting their jugular veins with plastic tubing. With this arrangement it was possible to show that a blood factor, released upon sexual arousal of either a ewe *or* a ram, caused milk letdown in an attached lactating ewe. When the vagina was distended or the scrotum massaged, a factor (probably oxytocin) was released into the blood and traveled to the attached ewe, causing her udder to fill within thirty seconds. It is interesting to note that sexual excitation of the male also caused the release of the lactation factor, showing that male and female hormones are structurally close and may overlap in biological function.

Without knowing anything about the underlying hormones, many peoples have utilized the triple connection between birth, lactation, and sexual arousal through oxytocin and estrogen to assist childbirth. The Siriono Indians of Bolivia, for example, used intercourse to induce active labor in women whose contractions were intermittent. They also used breast stimulation to hasten and increase the strength of uterine contractions. In Asia the Lepcha also use this natural aid to childbirth.

The probable explanation of the consistent association of breast and genital stimulation with birth in humans and other animals is that these activities cause a reflex release of oxytocin (from the posterior pituitary) that helps the uterus contract and expel the fetus. Uterine contraction due to oxytocin was first observed in treated samples of cat uterus, by Henry Dale in 1906. Because of the contractile effect of oxytocin, doctors in Israel are able to stimulate labor predictably by having their patients use a breast pump in the last days of pregnancy. Naturally, oxytocin is also released when babies are born and begin to suckle, causing uterine contractions that some mothers experience as cramps and that help prevent hemorrhage and shrink the uterus close to its previous size.

Oxytocin and oxytocinlike hormones are found throughout the vertebrate subphylum and are, therefore, presumed to be very ancient phylogenetically. Although these hormones control mammary and uterine muscle contractions in mammals, they are also found in birds, amphibians, and fishes. The long evolutionary record of oxytocin points to the fact that it was probably used in other ways, possibly for water excretion regulation, but was also preadapted (that is, present and available to be used in a new way) for its role of assisting milk ejection, orgasm, and birth. Nowadays a synthetic form of oxytocin is used routinely in hospitals to induce or speed up labor. A mixture of this oxytocin with the alkaloid ergometrine, from the ergot fungus on cereals, helps prevent hemorrhage after delivery.

In addition to the hormonal link between birth, coitus, and lactation, Niles Newton points out that there are two behavioral links. First, all three processes are easily inhibited in their early stages and, second, they all trigger caretaking behavior under certain circumstances. She explains that early inhibition of coitus, labor, and lactation is adaptive because it helps the participants avoid interference at a time of complete vulnerability. Among New World monkeys, for example, early labor can stop at sunrise and resume after sunset, when the group has encamped for the night and the expectant mother will not be distracted by foraging and keeping up with the others. Because females can give birth in relative comfort and safety after dark, nighttime initiation of birth is common among mammals. For example, most normal human births occur between midnight and seven in the morning.

Because of the link between sex and birth and because of the consummate vulnerability of a female during either of these activities, fear and distraction can disrupt them. This is why an atmosphere as private and secure as would be sought for coitus is ideal for human birth. The hospital environment used for Western births has been criticized for lacking this atmosphere. But generally, the criticisms voiced by women wanting privacy are not because they are conscious of a sexual connection to labor; birth in our society is not defined this way and has not been a private affair for a long time. So, distress over the birth environment is presented as fear of gadgetry, bright light, and rough handling that might harm the infant. Even if they were aware of the sexual arousal element in birth, most women would hesitate to ask for the atmosphere they might prefer for "selfish" reasons: for fear that the desire for a sex-related experience in birth might be thought of as silly and lascivious by most doctors. The people who recognize why they want a different environment and are not embarrassed to say so may not want to give up the facilities of a modern hospital in order to get it.

Given the biosocial setting of Western birth, it is inevitable that the link between sex, parturition, and lactation will be played down, and that speed, athleticism of labor (my Lamaze coach compared it to a 12-mile hike), and emotional composure will be played up. We may regret that we have lost awareness of and ability to uninhibitedly use the connection between sexual arousal, birth, and lactation, but until the physical and moral atmosphere for the safe expression of this connection exists, it is impractical for most women to try to capture it in their birth experience.

In our society, birth is a difficulty to be passed over quickly, hopefully without breaking the connection to mothering or being too much of a nuisance to doctor, midwife, and nurse. This attitude is consistent with our tendency to deemphasize both the sexual aspect of parenting (especially lactation) and the parenting aspect of sexuality (partners mothering each other in courtship and marriage is now taboo and comes under the heading of neurotic infantilization). Still, in looking critically at our own birth practices, we must not make the mistake of romanticizing all non-Western techniques. Other cultures may also overdo intervention, in the desire to assist parturition. Herbs that strengthen contractions are used by the Baganda. Among them there is a high incidence of uterine rupture and death of the neonate by asphyxia, as mighty contractions clamp down on the placental blood vessels carrying oxygen to the baby. Another African tribe, the Hausa, give the laboring mother a salty mixture to suck on, and among them there is an extremely high incidence of cardiac failure and hypertension in new mothers. While both herbs, which strengthen contractions, and salt, which replaces that lost during a long labor in a hot climate, may help, they, like our good medical ideas, must be used with knowledge and restraint.

The benefits of modern science need not negate the benefits of millions of years of natural selection. With intelligent planning it should be possible to have the best of both. Evidence of insightful planning begins to show in the hospitals that create bedroom-type labor facilities and allow the father-to-be to attend and assist the birth. Once, these arrangements would have been considered totally impractical, but now they are being instituted (at least in the name of less traumatic first moments for the neonate and easier deliveries for the staff). What is really happening is women are being allowed to experience their mammalian heritage without being asked to forsake modern medicine. At the same time, men are being allowed to discover the caretaking, arousal, and self-enhancement experiences that have almost universally been restricted to females at the birth scene.

Who attends a birth varies greatly from species to species and from society to society. Many mammals give birth alone; they are particularly careful to avoid lustful or aggressive males. This is seen with cats, beavers, and chimpanzees, to mention only a few.

While, in general, involvement of male mammals in birth is extremely unusual, as far as observations in captivity and in the field have shown, the participation of male primates has been witnessed occasionally. Therefore the role of men as caretakers during parturition is not so surprising, especially in the more monogamous sectors of our species. Still, the nearly universal presence of midwives in human societies reflects the fact that primate birth attendants are almost always females and also that primates, including humans, are rarely monogamous.

Tree shrews (species of *Tupaia*), which are not primates but are believed to resemble the seventy-million-year-old common ancestor of all primates, will reject their males as parturition approaches. They build a nest of foliage, moss, and bits of food for seclusion during birth. Captive tree shrews housed with their males at this time will be annoyed by the males that become sexually aroused before and during parturition due to the females' changed hormonal and scent condition. After the litter is born, each baby taking about ten minutes, females go into a postpartum heat and will copulate.

Males of many species, including rhesus monkeys, gibbons, and orangutans find birth sexually arousing. The fact that men have almost always been barred from the birth scene implies that it may be sexually arousing to them and so be a source of annoyance or even danger to the laboring woman. A Lepcha tribesman's report that he would become too excited if he witnessed a birth contrasts with but may underlie the explanations of birth avoidance in which men of other cultures claim queasiness or observance of religious taboo. Because postpartum coitus carries the risk of infection and injury for the mother, peoples all over the world have deterred men by training them to believe in the magical danger of birth. Thus, very few societies have the custom of intercourse immediately after birth. However, Margaret Mead reported that certain groups in New Guinea followed this procedure, after both mother and child had washed in a cold stream.

Occasionally, husbands or close male relatives or friends of women did attend delivery. In fact, in Laos at one time, men and sexual arousal were put to practical use in childbirth, distracting the woman from her pain with licentious jokes and stories, illustrated with carved models of the phallus. Other occasions for male attendance at birth were cases of exceptionally difficult delivery. It was thought that the crisis called for the magical potency of a male shaman, and the extremity of the pain and the nearness of death on these occasions precluded his sexual arousal.

Because mammalian births generally occur at night and in seclusion, a comprehensive comparative field study of birth attendance would be difficult to make. Many isolated instances of female caretaking of the mother and neonate have been reported in a variety of mammals, but it is not known how regular this behavior is within each species. Elephants and sea mammals have special problems during delivery, and, therefore, they seem to be assisted on a regular basis by other members of their group. The dolphin, for example, is buoyed up by her schoolmates during labor so she can be near the surface to breathe.

Primates, like the rhesus macaque (*Macaca mulatta*) and the chacma baboon (*Papio ursinus*), have occasionally been observed being attended during birth. The laboring female usually moves some distance from the rest of the group, but another female or females may sit near her. Primatologist G. Mitchell reports that the attendants arch their backs and finger their vaginas as they watch the baby being delivered. But unlike any nearby males, who would try to mount the mother-to-be, females do not interfere with or endanger the parturient in any way.

New World marmoset (*Callithrix*) and tamarin (*Saquinus*) monkeys, which are the smallest monkeys in the world and look a bit like tiny lions or lynxes, are noted for their twin births and the devotion of their males to female and young. One marmoset was reported to have a mate who helped her deliver and clean the offspring. Males of these species regularly carry the young on their backs. Paternal attentions are consistent with the habit of monogamy in these species. However, monogamy is not always a sufficient condition for male involvement in birth and infant care. The gibbon (species of *Hylobates*) male is monogamous but takes no assisting role at birth. He only becomes aroused and tries to mount the laboring female.

Male proboscis monkeys (*Nasalis larvatus*) and male orangutans (*Pongo pygmeus*) have been seen attending deliveries. In the latter case, the male ape, observed in captivity, became sexually aroused while witnessing the birth of his eighth offspring.

Pain is certainly a better known commonality in primate parturition than sexual arousal or caretaking behavior. The grunts, screams, moans, and cage-clutching shudders of primates delivering in captivity testify to pain in parturition. Sometimes the signs of discomfort appear days before the delivery; decline of appetite and an inability to sit or stand in one position for more than a few minutes at a time are the primary signals that birth is approaching. Rejection of males, intolerance of touching, and writhing show that labor has begun.

The duration of labor among primates varies greatly. In certain monkeys, it can be as short as twenty-three seconds, and in many human deliveries longer than twenty-four hours. Most New World monkeys deliver in sixty to ninety minutes, or 10 to 350 contractions. The average human birth range is from 300 to 1000 contractions.

Fortunately, for many primate females, and especially women, the caretaking ties of birth to lactation do make some supportive intervention likely. Many cultures capitalize on the preadaptive content of the infant-mother bond by rewarding both females and males for showing concern for pregnant women and their young. In our society the compassionate interest we take in laboring women and in other vulnerable beings is that collected upon the initial nursing investment of our mothers.

Even when a mammalian mother, such as a marmoset or night monkey (*Aotus*), does not care for her young in other ways, she still must suckle them. The only exception to this rule is the bottle-fed baby of our species, and the few in captivity that must be hand reared.

When lactation begins, sexual activity declines, even if there has been a postpartum estrus. This decline is based on hormonal mechanisms, directly related to nursing, which inhibit ovulation and the sex drive that usually accompanies it. In many human societies this tendency toward lowered libido is reinforced by taboo. The adaptive advantage of postpartum sexual prohibition is twofold: it allows the mother to focus her energy and attention on her young rather than her consort, and it spaces pregnancies. So, relative abstinence during breastfeeding is perfectly normal, but, paradoxically, it does not eliminate gentle, sexual feelings associated with suckling, which reinforce the vital connection between mother and newborn.

Lactation also benefits the mother by helping her uterus almost regain its prepregnancy dimensions—(in humans) down from more than 1 foot in length and 2 pounds in weight, with a volume of 4 to 5 quarts back to about 3 inches in length, 1 ounce in weight, and an internal volume of about half a teaspoon! Lactation, obviously, benefits the offspring by providing species-tailored nourishment, disease immunity, and a primal period of care that may carry over to adult relationships—courting, mating, parenting, and altruistic behaviors.

As mentioned at the beginning of this chapter, lactation very likely predates gestation in the evolutionary sequence. The mammal-like reptiles were probably supplying their hatchlings with milk three hundred million years ago. With all this time to specialize, mammalian milk is now available in forms suited to the needs of the approximately four thousand species of our class.

Sea-mammal milk, for instance, has little or no sugar but is rich in fat, the insulator against cold seawater. Whale milk, which is up to 50 percent fat, is essentially cream with only 12 percent protein and not more than 2 percent sugar. On this a baby blue whale is said to double its birth weight of 1 to 2 tons in a week (compare the human baby that doubles its weight in 120 days).

Human milk is very sugary. In fact, it is sweeter than any other mammalian milk. It has one-quarter of an ounce of lactose, or milk sugar, in every 3 ounces compared to only one-sixth of an ounce of lactose in a similar quantity of cow's milk. The sugar and fat in human milk are important for the rapid development of the brain, which grows fastest in the last trimester of pregnancy and the first three months after birth.

Despite specialization of milk, it is possible for certain species to cross-feed. Thus, women have occasionally suckled puppies in ancient Hawaii, piglets in New Guinea, and deer in Guyana. Naturally, other female mammals have been used to foster human babies. Goat, cow, and llama milk supplement or replace human milk at times, and, in the tale of Romulus and Remus, a wolf's milk sustains the human twins.

Some mammals regularly share the nursing of young in their group. Brown hyenas bring their three-month-old cubs to a communal den, where any female may suckle them until they are fourteen months old. Mexican free-tail bat babies, clinging by their toenails to the ceilings of maternity caves, nurse from any lactating female within reach. Elephant cows without young of their own may start to lactate and suckle when there are several infants in the herd. These examples suggest that genetic relationships among the females in these groups are close, if it is true that altruism in infant care, as with birds, actually improves the helper's fitness.

Duration of lactation varies from a few weeks in small mammals to up to eight years in elephants. In addition to the variable duration and nutritive composition of milk, there are different immune factors in it. Human milk, for example, contains interferon, immunoglobulin A, and the bifidus factor (*Lactobacillus bifidus*); the last two help prevent fatal infantile diarrhea. An enzyme found in the eye, lysozyme, is also found in human milk, which may be why breast milk, used as eye drops, has been noted as a folk remedy for conjunctivitis.

Offspring of many mammals, including man, would become less fit for survival and reproduction without the nursing female's contact, even if all nutrients and immunities were mechanically supplied. This was best shown with bottle-fed rhesus monkeys that were denied all contact with their mothers. They were not only more fearful and less able to explore their environments, they showed mating aberrations. When impregnated by normal males, they neglected and rejected their young. Because the rhesus mothers who had not been nursed as infants were arbitrary and brutal in their punishment of their young, these young also grew up to be inadequate mothers. Thus, even the grand-children of the monkey that was not nursed showed certain aberrations. They were more introverted; they cooed and mouthed themselves, and played alone more than the young of normally reared mothers. The male young were especially aggressive, as judged by the number of unprovoked attacks they made on stuffed animals and on other young. One male bit off an infant's finger; another killed a female.

Lactation begins after the placenta is delivered because placental progesterone largely inhibits production of the enzyme alpha-lactalbumin, needed for the synthesis of milk sugar. When the placenta is passed, the progesterone block is removed, and the benefits of milk begin to flow. Incidentally, eating the placenta does not bring back the progesterone block because the placenta is broken down in the stomach and intestine.

At one time, the beginning and end of lactation defined the spacing of children for all women. Now there are few places where the use of some form of birth control and artificial feeding does not alter this pattern. In the Kalahari Desert, where Bushwomen lived until recently with their men and children in gathering-hunting bands, four to five children were born to each mother, spaced at approximately four-year intervals by the demands of lactation set against the background of seasonal variation in caloric and protein intake. As Rose Frisch's re-search on body fat and menstruation implies, lactation in the context of a relatively low caloric diet and a high energy output (as in Bush-women) could, along with endocrine changes, delay the resumption of menstruation and ovulation.

The reliable lactational birth control of Bushwomen began to break down when they moved to trading posts and started to eat more cal-ories. Babies then arrived every two to three years, instead of every four. But diet is not the only thing that changes when village living is chosen. Work habits change, the amount of time per day spent breastfeeding declines, and early weaning becomes the norm.

The amount of time spent breastfeeding each day may be just as, or more important than, diet in determining the efficacy of lactation as a contraceptive. Substituting bottles and intermittent breastfeeding breaks the almost continuous relay of messages along chains of nerves connecting the nipple to the hypothalamus. As the frequency of the messages is reduced, the hypothalamus secretes less of the factors that order the pituitary to release prolactin. A drop in prolactin, in turn, promotes pituitary secretion of gonadotrophin, the hormone that stimulates ovulation. Thus, low-frequency breastfeeding means ovulation may resume, and pregnancy during the nursing period becomes possible.

Frequent short nursing periods, used by gathering-hunting women, chimpanzees, and other primates, are a more effective form of birth control than the four-hourly feeds of our regimes. Still, diet and feeding patterns fluctuate and prolactin secretion declines over a period of months, regardless of which feeding schedule is used, and therefore people have always sought ways to back up lactational regulation of birth spacing. The two most prevalent ways to do this have been sexual interdictions for the nursing mother, and infanticide. If the mother produces too little milk; has a sick child that cannot suck enough; is depressed or incapacitated for other reasons and gives her baby to a wet nurse, coitus taboos or infanticide (where sexual relations resume soon after birth without contraceptive or lactational protection) will help prevent there being too many children too closely spaced.

If cultural changes mean cessation of these taboos and of infanticide and that women must work *under high pressure for productivity* precluding breastfeeding on demand throughout the day and night, a circular pattern arises: the more the lactating woman works, the less she is protected from pregnancy, and the more children she has, the more she may need to work. Therefore, if old breastfeeding patterns are taken away, modern contraception should be made available, or the population will rise rapidly. If this happens where the diet of the community is poor, many children will die of malnutrition.

Wherever formula milk is introduced to help support children that are being breastfed less during the day and weaned earlier, sterile water, refrigeration, and adequate instruction for use of mother's milk substitutes are essential. Otherwise, the use of contaminated or diluted formula milk may become *de facto* infanticide. In *The State of the World's Children* (1982–83), UNICEF estimated that a million babies die each year from infant formula abuse. This ghastly "solution" to the problem of overpopulation and undernutrition may be the only one available to women caught in the bind of uneven cultural change. While women in transitional societies can establish priorities for themselves in accepting cultural changes, it is also true that unwise promotion of milk substitutes and poorly planned programs of "aid" can confuse and push them into maladaptive decisions.

This is why biology must be brought into all considerations of social and economic change. Where women work and no longer have the benefit of traditional methods of birth spacing but also have no access to modern birth control and adequate bottle-feeding, means must be sought to reestablish lactation as a reliable birth control. Women should be able to feed their babies on demand, even every fifteen minutes for two minutes at a time, if necessary; thus, facilities for nursing and keeping babies nearby at work are required. Women should be able to sleep with their baby at the breast and to comfort with the breast instead of pacifiers. When solid foods are introduced, they should be given after breastfeeding, not before. All these recommendations, made by reproductive biologist R. V. Short, will increase the amount of nipple stimulation, ensure more prolactin secretion and, thus, better contraceptive protection.

Changing societies cannot afford to neglect this solution, because although many children die from improper bottle-feeding, rapid reproduction due to the loss of lactational birth control quickly offsets these infant deaths. D. B. and E. F. P. Jeliffe, world authorities on lactation, estimate that there will be a 20 percent rise in population due to replacement of breast with bottle. Such a spurt can deter social development and weaken the social order.

When a woman and her growing child can drink milk, cultural development is not so tortured. People of northern European and northern Asian background almost never consider that the ability to regularly drink milk past infancy was an adaptive advantage, and it is not seen in any other species or in any other part of our own species, except for certain pastoral groups in Africa. The unusual ability to drink milk is based on the availability of and terrain for dairy animals, a climate in which milk can stay sweet for some time, and (most important of all) enough of the enzyme, lactase, to break down milk sugar (lactose).

Sufficient production of this enzyme in humans past infancy depends on the possession of a genetic mutation or, as some say, the continued use of milk from other mammals in childhood, adolescence, and adulthood, which conditions cells lining the intestine to produce lactase. In having had this mutation (or conditioning), certain peoples were most fortunate. They had another source of protein and carbohydrate for themselves and their weanlings. Thus milk drinkers raised relatively more offspring, since more closely spaced births could be achieved without malnutrition.

Milk drinkers further improved their diets by trading some of their fermented milk products, such as cheese and yogurt, for other foods. (People who lack lactase can eat only these cultured milk products.) Drinking sweet milk may also have afforded some advantage in brain development in childhood, since lactose is metabolized to galactose, which becomes part of the galactolipids (sugar-fats) in the brain and spinal cord. In childhood the supply of lactose would not have to be interrupted upon weaning because the child could drink milk from other mammals.

The modern non-milk-drinking cultures are now trying to imitate what the milk-drinking cultures did over a very long period of time: take one aspect of the female animal (her milk) and "bottle" it. But without the mutation or dietary conditioning for lactase in the adult, the introduction of bottle-feeding captures none of the adaptive advantages of the milk drinkers because neither pregnant women, nursing mothers, nor their weanlings drink the reconstituted cow's milk or any fresh milk.

Perhaps companies that advertise the adequacy (or superiority) of formula milk do not realize that for bottle-feeding to be at all advantageous, it must be part of a larger biosocial picture that includes the continuation of milk drinking or a highly nutritious diet after weaning. Children weaned off inadequate bottle-feeding onto an inadequate solid diet cannot prosper, especially if the bottle itself, as destroyer of lactational contraception, means that there will be more children. It would be better if the weaned children drank the milk instead of the babies.

Without very sensitive planning for rapid change, which would compensate for all the missing pieces (such as absence of lactase mutation or dietary conditioning for the enzyme), babies drinking formula milk from other mammals stands now as a distinct disadvantage for all concerned. It deprives infants of their mother's milk; it makes mothers have too many children too closely spaced; it causes overpopulation; and, where the milk is reconstituted with dirty water and left to stand in hot weather, it causes disease, suffering, and death.

In addition to the health and demographic problems that such a misunderstanding of our mammalian nature has brought to parts of our species, there are the psychosocial disadvantages to be considered. Ideally, the extension of infantile milk drinking into later phases of life should reiterate ties to the female and to a period of gentle care, thereby helping people form more stable mating, family, and societal bonds.

It is said that the kiss, as a greeting, comes from the shape that the mouth takes during nursing in many species. The "kiss"—mouth to mouth, or to mammary or genital region—is a greeting and parting gesture among many mammals: hunting dogs often lick the female's teats before departing on the hunt, and Indian flying fox bats do the same as part of courtship; rodents, insectivores, and primates mouth-lick each other upon meeting. Emphasis on the mammary, mouth, and genital areas as social communicators is reinforced by the presence of scent glands in the chest, chin, armpit, and groin.

While all mammals need the nursing female's contact for development of normal courtship, mating, and parenting behaviors, none of them seems to have taken up the preadaptive potential of lactation the way we have. For all their backsliding, cultures that hold up the image of a nursing mother and child as their ideal, their idol, and have the insight to recognize the connection of this symbol to the creation of a working and fulfilled human society (even without admitting the evolutionary basis of the symbol!) confirm that the mammalian heritage of lactation and mothering may be a potent force in shaping the social order.

Just as evolution has given all lactating females the ability to make food for and bestow essential security upon their young, so it has provided them with an assortment of birth control mechanisms and tactics. Lactational contraception is connected to the evolution of short annual estrous periods separated by long periods without ovulation or estrus. During the anestrous intervals, females neither desire sex nor inspire male interest, and the sexes therefore form separate groups. This is true of wild grazing mammals, such as red deer, and of domestic mammals, such as horses, pigs, sheep, and cows. It is also true of small hibernators, such as ground squirrels. Several females may hibernate in the same burrow, but males spend the winter alone.

While long intervals of separation of the sexes is not the pattern for most primates, seasonal anestrus and seasonal birth peaks are evident in many species. That women mate regardless of season or ovulatory state may reflect the cultural achievement of a relatively high level of survival for newborns at any time of year, but it does *not* demonstrate that monthly and annual peaks in sex drive do not exist in certain groups. As will be seen, much of sexual receptivity is feigned by primate females to promote the pacific integration of males into their (female) groups and to protect young from the murderous attacks of males.

For many species of prey animals, such as mice and rabbits, spontaneous abortion, resorption of fetuses, cannibalism, and other forms of infanticide are also reliable mechanisms of birth and population control. For us, they occur, but not reliably.

Abortion or resorption of abnormal fetuses often prevents the birth of offspring that would die before reaching maturity. In these cases, cessation of an early pregnancy spares the female an unnecessary investment in gestation, birth, and lactation. Spontaneous abortion can also occur under adverse nutritional or social conditions. Snowshoe rabbits, for example, resorb litters within two days if they are overcrowded.

In mice (and probably other species too), resorption even of normal fetuses is provoked by the odor of a strange male's urine. This reaction, known as the Bruce effect after its discoverer Hilda Bruce, prevents a female's investing in young that would probably be devoured by the stranger. This male may also benefit by getting to breed with the female he caused to miscarry.

The Bruce effect occurs more often in young females than in older ones. Younger females may not have reached the levels of prolactin or progesterone present in older females that have been repeatedly pregnant or lactating, a theory supported by the observation that prolactin or progesterone injections will block resorption.

Failure of embryo implantation and consequent resorption appears to be prevalent in our species too; estimates range up to 50 percent of all conceptions. It is not known whether any pheromonal (scent) mechanism is involved. If it is found to be, then the adolescent period of reduced fertility might be better called the adolescent period of nonimplantation.

When birth controls fail to prevent the completion of a pregnancy, the most common mechanism of population control is the swift killing of the young just after they are born. Particularly when conditions of overcrowding exist, a nesting mother may allow other adults to enter the nest and eat the young. Her own cannibalization of the young occurs under a range of stress situations, including too much handling before or interference during parturition.

The best-documented response of a female to density stress is that of the tree shrew (*Tupaia belangeri*). Used to living with her male in a scent-demarcated and defended territory in the dense foliage of southeast Asian forests, the female tree shrew undergoes a multifaceted decline in fertility in overcrowded captivity conditions, where she meets other mature and threatening females.

Tree shrews look like squirrels with rat's tails, which fluff up like proper squirrel's tails only when the shrews are under stress. By observing the proportion of time per day that the tails of his subjects were fluffed up, D. von Holst made direct correlations between amount of stress and reduction of the shrew population through reduction of individual fertility. Since lower population density reduces stress caused by the proximity of others, the tree shrew's birth controls work as a stress-stat and population-stat.

Normally, in captivity, a pair of tree shrews produce one to four young every forty-five days. Once the young have been fed enough to increase their birth weight by 50 percent, the mother leaves them in the nest and feeds them only every forty-eight hours. Her male and other adults will not normally enter the nest. However, things go awry if she is disturbed by the repeated confrontations that occur in over-crowded cages. If her tail is fluffed up for 20 percent of the day over a period of weeks, she will continue to give birth every forty-five days, but she will remove the young from the nest and eat them. If her tail if fluffed for 50 percent of the day over a period of weeks, a more fundamental birth control mechanism comes into play: the ovarian follicles degenerate, and sterility is the result. Both cronism and stress sterility are reversible; so, although the overcrowded situation may be abnormal for the tree shrews, their response to it is normal and adaptive.

Both sexes of the young of these crowded nesting mammals are cannibalized equally. However, among human societies that practiced infanticide, the young often were killed differentially—usually more female babies than males. Whenever the object has been to control the growth of a group that is pressing hard on available natural resources, the curtailment of female numbers has kept the birthrate down. In the words of astute eco-anthropologist Marvin Harris, "the most widely used method of population control during much of human history was probably some form of female infanticide."

The tactic of infanticide is only one step removed from abortion, which most peoples did not have the skill to perform on the scale required to stabilize population. From a woman's fitness point of view, infanticide was preferable to an abortion in which a twig might be inserted into her cervix as an inducer. Infanticide, after a normal birth, left her well and able to care for existing children and to have others when conditions permitted.

Harris points out that villages and bands that practiced frequent female infanticide were often also caught up in small-scale warfare for women. Infanticide plus the skirmishes were a double population control. So vital was the pattern of warfare-infanticide to population control and so completely absorbed were people by the proximate reasons (such as vendetta) for their activities that the illogicality of fighting wars to obtain women in a society that produced its own scarcity of females was either not recognized or not admitted. Because males were needed and prized as warriors, female rather than male infants were killed. Because female babies were killed, there was a scarcity of women. Because of this scarcity, men fought. The cycle was never broken because the people did not or could not address its first cause: crowding.

Female infanticide was also favored in societies where males were prized for dangerous tasks that required much strength. This was true among the Eskimos, who did not have warfare but had male dominance built into their ecological and economic situation. The muscle of males was necessary for the hunting on which all members of the society depended. Male deaths and disabilities from hunting were analogous to male deaths and disabilities from skirmishes. The position of females was analogously low, as reflected in female infanticide and absence of decision-sharing status for adult women, wife-lending, casual rape, etc. Any society that fundamentally depends on war or any other activity requiring male brawn will devalue daughters and make the choice of female infanticide more likely.

As our society stands now, so far from exclusive dependence on lactational or taboo-enforced birth control, it is difficult to imagine the need for warfare and female infanticide to minimize population pressure on resources. But, denied the more reliable birth control devices of other female mammals, such as long anestrous intervals, lactational inhibition of ovulation or delay of implantation (diapause), or regular spontaneous abortion and fetal resorption, girls and women have had to pay the price of devaluation and death whenever the birthrate surpassed the habitat's carrying capacity.

With modern methods of birth control and safe abortion, things change. For the first time, birth/population can be controlled without differentially sacrificing females. Sex ratios can remain virtually even. Female-controlled contraception means the loss of all rationale for male supremacy. With modern agriculture and animal husbandry as a background to modern human birth control, there need no longer be excessive pressure on the land. The group can survive without an excess input of male strength for hunting, heavy farming, or warfare. Male contribution is still needed, but not differentially. In fact, there is now a differential need for female input: that is, for the maternal trait complex of endurance, patience, and intelligently used strength.

We turn now to the subject of contraception because it describes human attempts to extend or emulate some of the birth controls of other mammalian species, particularly alterations in the fertility of cycles and prevention of embryo implantation or growth. Of course, it would probably be even more effective for us to harness methods that occur outside our class: the pheromonal contraceptives of social insects (also known to occur in at least one mammal, the mole rat, discussed in chapter 2); and the spermatheca, which, although not technically a contraceptive, could be used to allow a female to determine when and *if* her egg is to be fertilized.

The diaphragm and condom are simply rubber barriers placed between the egg and sperm, but the pill and IUD (intrauterine device), as well as sterilization, actually disrupt some part of the female reproductive system. As of 1979, worldwide there were about 54 million women on the pill, about 55 million using an IUD, and another 60 million had been sterilized for contraceptive purposes. However, recent statistics for China indicate that the IUD figure is too low, as it is their most frequently used contraceptive method, with 94 million inserted between 1971 and 1978 (as reported in 1982 in Johns Hopkins Population Report J25). The sterilization estimate could encompass China because during the same period of time only 20,330,000 women (and fewer than 14 million men) were sterilized. Sterilization is the second most popular contraceptive method in China. In spite of the enormous use of modern contraceptives that these statistics indicate, the older barrier methods are also widespread. (In China, however, due to problems with their manufacture, condoms account for only 6 percent of total contraception.) These methods can be almost as effective as system-disrupters, and they are safe, less painful, and less dangerous. Most important, the diaphragm is totally female-controlled (apart from renewal of manufactured stores), and therefore it is less vulnerable to male-controlled legislation governing contraceptives than any other method.

The hormones contained in the pill—usually a combination of estrogen and progesterone—allow it to shut off ovulation and place the body in the postovulatory, or luteal, phase. In other words, by taking the pill for three weeks per month, a woman tricks her body into thinking it has already ovulated. During the one week per month when the pill is not taken, the menstrual flow occurs, just as if an unfertilized egg were being passed along with the sloughed endometrium. In fact, this menstruation is just for show; it makes the woman feel normal, but since there is no ovulation or pregnancy, she could take the pill every day and skip menstruation altogether. Obviously this is an unnatural situation that carries with it advantages and disadvantages. There is some evidence that the chances of contracting breast, ovarian, and uterine cancer are reduced, but this must be weighed against the added risk of blood clots that may cause a stroke or heart failure.

There are also estrogen-free pills that do not shut off ovulation but work by altering the endometrium (uterine lining) so that it secretes a mucous block to sperms at the opening of the womb. This form of the pill sometimes interferes with embryo implantation in the uterus and is therefore associated with a higher risk of tubal (ectopic) pregnancy.

Intrauterine devices have been used since Cleopatra's day, when Arab camel traders inserted stones in their mare camels before commencing long journeys, and, it is alleged, the great queen herself carried pebbles in her uterus to prevent conception. It is still not known how they work. The modern loop, squiggle, or 7-shape of plastic, with its bit of fine copper wire coiled round it, may prevent implantation of a fertilized egg. This is why antiabortionists protest IUDs; they say the devices are not stopping conception but causing an abortion by interfering with implantation of a living embryo.

It must be mentioned, although it should be obvious, that the only male method of contraception that I have referred to—the condom— is easier, cheaper, and less dangerous for the user than any of the female methods. Still, women seek contraceptives and use them more often than men. Women also undergo sterilization far more often than men, although it has always been a safer and simpler operation for men. Of course, the fear and danger of numerous pregnancies has always affected women differentially, so they naturally have sought their survival with contraceptives, abortion, and sterilization. To me this gross imbalance in use of contraception is the greatest indication of the truth of the concept that evolution resides at the level of the individual—each fighting for her own survival even in apparently cooperative arrangements such as marriage. Remarkably, knowing that the condom is the only method of contraception that also prevents serious diseases—syphilis, gonorrhea, herpes, urinary tract infection, cervical cancer, etc.—was not sufficient inducement to make it the number one contraceptive. Only now as a protector against the dread AIDS is the condom becoming more popular.

There are two methods of sterilization, apart from hysterectomy performed for reasons other than contraception: the tying and cutting of the fallopian tubes (oviducts) and the removal of the ovaries. It is only the latter that shuts off most of the production of female hormones—estrogen and progesterone—along with all basis for ovulation. Of all forms of birth control (other than a regime of pills for every day of the month), only hysterectomy also ends menstruation. All other forms of man-made contraception maintain the monthly cycle.

Continuation of monthly cycling without frequent, long breaks for pregnancy and lactation is a recent development for women. It means that women using any modern method of birth control, other than removal of the ovaries, are exposing themselves to estrogen more continuously than other female mammals. While estrogen is secreted throughout pregnancy and especially just before delivery, the lactating period is one of lower estrogen. Traditionally, lactation lasts longer than gestation. So, when there are many pregnancies followed by lactation, there is, cumulatively, much less estrogen exposure. Without repeated pregnancies and lactation, it is possible for a woman to experience a maximum of about forty years of cycling; modern Western women approach this limit. By comparison non-Western women, or women of sects within the Western world that do not practice birth control, may have, totally, only about four years of cycling. This means a nine- to tenfold increase in cycling for birth control users.

If, in addition, the pill is the method of contraception chosen by a woman, estrogen exposure may be raised even further, as almost all pills contain estrogen. Exposure of the breast tissue to estrogen, month after month, for twenty-five to thirty years may contribute to high breast cancer incidence in women who have had no pregnancies or a late first pregnancy. Only time will reveal the impact of this huge increase in amount of menstrual cycling and reduction of lactation in one portion of the human species. However quietly they may creep into our biology, however normal they may seem to us, changes like these are not small. They are potentially equal in magnitude to the vertebrate "decisions" to lactate and gestate, taken some 250 million years ago.

Another change which has taken place in the last twenty-five years is an enormous increase in induced pregnancy terminations. Although statistics for many non-Western countries are not available, it is estimated that thirty-five million women per year undergo legal abortion. If another twenty to thirty million have illegal abortions, the total abortion figure is somewhere between one-third and one-half the total number of live births, estimated at 120 million per year.

Acquisition of anesthesia and asepsis have enabled us to enter the age of abortion, but many other things besides the simple fecundity of women necessitated the use of abortion to the degree that it is used today. These things include the introduction of enough medical know-how to reduce child mortality without introducing modern contraception in many parts of the world; entry of more women into the wage-earning ranks and their consequent loss of lactational contraception; widespread removal of traditions forbidding education of women and regulating marital and extramarital pairing.

Luckily, abortion is now a procedure with less than 0.001 percent casualties when performed under modern hospital or clinic conditions. Before the twelfth week of gestation, an embryo can be removed by gentle suction through the dilated cervix. Even abortions required after the twelfth week of pregnancy, as are those recommended after amniocentesis, can be performed safely. Injection of soap or salt solution into the uterus can cause expulsion of the fetus, and in the past five years, an even safer procedure for fourth- to sixth-month abortions has been found. Chemical factors called prostaglandins, which are normally produced in many body tissues, are injected intravenously and cause uterine contractions that expel the fetus and placenta.

Whether or not abortion is seen as an ethical method of birth control, because it is applied after rather than before conception, it is still an effective depressor of population growth rate. Abortion halved the birthrate in Japan and helped cut population growth in eastern Europe. The putative unethicality of taking an unborn life must be weighed against the demonstrated immorality of permitting overcrowding, with its attendant diseases and social disorder.

The best way to enhance human birth control, whichever method is used—all the way from abstinence to abortion—is to find out what is behind the female desire to have babies and try to curb that pressure: Do women gain prestige by having children? Are children needed to help their mother run a household, farm, or business? Are women assured a more secure old age if they have children? Behind all these proximate motivators is there the ultimate driving force for all evolution: production of viable young, who in their turn reproduce? If so, then it should be extremely difficult to persuade women to reduce their individual fitness by having fewer children for the good of society, especially before they possess new ways to live, new ambitions and priorities.

About twenty years ago, women in Taiwan towns wanted four children; in the country villages, they wanted slightly more. After four or five children had been born, they were interested in birth control. The individual female's fitness needs were clearly inconsistent with the fitness needs of the larger society. On mainland China, a similar conflict existed; what was good for the individual and the rural family caused the Chinese population to grow to its present one billion.

Now an attempt is being made by Chinese social planners to counteract the culturally ingrained (and some say biologically innate) drive to have as many offspring as can be successfully raised to maturity. Encouraging as many young couples as possible to have only one child, they are moving their society one step closer to the peaceful hive, the smooth-running societal organism. In so doing, women are taken another step away from the general female mammalian condition: years of bearing, birthing, and suckling young.

When a society intends to remove economic and educational disparities as much as possible, it must control female fertility by reshaping attitudes and offering practical inducements. Since one-child families help homogenize hope, planners offer cash bonuses, preferment in housing, priority in health care and schooling for an only child, plus social approval. Women come to see other members of the community and the state in roles once filled by their children: indispensable helpers in home and farm, providers of old-age security. But if new attitudes and inducements do not affect the majority of women, then a single-child elite may be produced rather than a decline in population and a more uniform society.

In the West also, the prevalence of small families and single-parent-one-child dyads forces people to turn to non-kin and state where once they relied upon their grown-up children. Society moves toward greater uniformity with the reduction in fecundity and reproductive variance among women. It also produces women who are freer of their procreative identity than all other female mammals. From this change in the human female will follow changes in mating and parenting strategies for both sexes.

Battles, violent or devious, for mates or breeding space; danger of injury during courtship and sex; possibility of death during pregnancy, parturition, or baby care make mammalian reproduction a risky business. Because it is so often contrary to individual survival, the compulsion to reproduce seems to arise from a source less transient and less "concerned" with individual survival than is the individual herself. Most animals, including humans, behave as if they were ordered by their genes to proceed, at whatever cost, to create another vehicle for the genes' passage through time—the old a-chicken-is-an-egg's-way-of-making-another-egg story.

Because, in this pursuit, each individual acts as if it were seeking to maximize its reproductive profits in relation to its reproductive costs, these behaviors are called strategies. Mating strategies include an animal's decision to participate in courtship and copulation, its way of choosing partner(s), and its frequency of mating and length of association with consort. Parenting strategies refer to an animal's decision to bear young, to help rear or desert the young, to cooperate with and sometimes help feed the mate and young, or to abandon the mate at some point after copulation.

The partner that has invested less in reproduction is always the one more likely to desert. By deserting and going on to mate again, the smaller investor acts as if it has estimated that the larger investor's stake is too great for it to abandon the embryos or young. The deserter is usually the male, simply because, by physical design, there are less ways for him to invest in the young and, thereby, improve his fitness. Also by physical design, the female mammal is literally bound (by her placenta) to invest in her fertilized eggs, and so is likely to carry out her rearing responsibilities, even if she is abandoned. If she were to desert her young before they were weaned, she would lose her entire gestational investment, and she might not have another opportunity to mate for a long time, depending on the frequency of her ovulation.

Since female mammals other than women cannot escape the gestational and lactational costs of mating, and since males cannot contribute more to their own reproductive profits by directly investing in the young during gestation and lactation, females will tend to stop mating abruptly after fertilization, and males will tend to continue to hop from female to female in quest of new eggs to fertilize. In most species, however, male promiscuity is curtailed by the restricted mating period—sometimes only hours, more commonly a few days or weeks per year—in which females are fertile and receptive.

Gestation and lactation mean that the strategies of mammalian sexes are more apparently polarized than they are among birds. As Devra Kleiman states, 90 percent of bird species are monogamous, but only about 3 percent of mammals are. In fact, mammalian monogamy does not remove but only covers up the biological opposition of the sexes. The stability of the truce of monogamy depends on the ratio and distribution of the sexes and of resources and on all the factors affecting the frequency of female cyclicity.

The more help the females of a mammalian species need to survive during the gestation-lactation period and the more prolonged the helplessness of the young after birth, the more possibility there is that the mating and parenting strategies of the sexes will converge. In a sample of forty species of birds and mammals, anthropologists Melvin and Carol Ember did not find that length of dependency of the young predicts male-female bonding but that, where bonding already exists, length of dependency of the young positively predicts the length of the bond. So, dependency seems a necessary, but on its own an insufficient, condition to cause bonding with male assistance.

In order to narrow down the permissive condition to the predictive condition for pair-bonding with male care, the anthropologists postulated that where the female's food gathering interfered with her baby tending, a male would mate exclusively with (that is, bond with) a female through one or more estrous, menstrual, or breeding periods. This they found to be true for their sample. In other words, females that could fast or feed without being separated from their young (such as grazing animals) showed significantly less bonding with a male than did females that had to leave their young to hunt or forage.

In predatory species, such as hyenas, lions, wolves, and raptorial birds, in which a female's hunting interrupts her baby tending and in which a male can conceivably improve his fitness by provisioning a den or nest filled with young that he is likely to have sired, he is found in close association with female(s) and young. The adult females will still dominate the group (that is, there will be more of them, and they will be doing more: nursing, hunting, threatening outsiders, teaching the young), and there will still be more wandering than group-integrated males, but the hunting way of life does seem to dispose the sexes toward pair-bonding, sharing of parental duties, and, in gregarious species, integration of males into the group.

Human females may have started to bond with males for the same reason: whether hunting, fishing, herding, or just gathering heavy vegetable material from a distant foraging area, the food-getting activities of early women could have interfered with their baby tending and made bonding very adaptive. Bond-males would have been useful both as part-time provisioners and baby-sitters.

While attention of males to offspring is sometimes beneficial—as when the male marmoset carries his twins on his back or the male baboon staves off a kidnapper—it may also be detrimental. Proximity of males can mean females and young must share food resources with them, and this can be disadvantageous in certain environments. In addition, some male mammals have evolved enormous bodies and weaponry for seasonal duels over space and females. For example, the dagger tusks of male walruses plus their great weight and extreme pugnacity make it possible for them to harm females and kill young accidentally. Each year walrus and sea lion nurslings are killed when big bulls roll over on them. Fred Bruemmer describes how a female made an indifferent bull move off her smothering baby by nibbling on his neck and presenting herself for mating—a bit of estrous trickery which, as described below, is a standard ploy of some primates.

There are two general conditions under which males can assist more with parenting:

1. When the young remain dependent for some time after weaning and cannot immediately take up the way of life of the adults.

2. When roving males outside the group (troop, pack, clan, pride, etc.) threaten to invade, kill resident males and their offspring, and mate with the group females.

Prolonged dependency of young is known in many carnivore and primate groups. Invasion and baby killing by males has been recorded among langur monkeys, and at least the baby-killing part of the pattern has been recorded among chimpanzees. But invasion, takeover, and infanticide are best illustrated among the social carnivores.

George Schaller, who studied lions (*Panthera leo*) for many years in Serengeti National Park, Tanzania, saw three males of one pride taking over another while the lioness was out hunting. The invaders killed one of the pride males and chased the other away. Then they ate one of the cubs, killed the other two, and carried one away. The lioness returned to ruin but lay down to eat a dead cub. Thus, a female's fitness (measured in numbers of young that she can raise) is influenced by male guarding ability.

In another pride, with only one male to guard the young, only two out of twenty-six cubs born in two years survived. A pride with three adult male guards raised twelve out of twenty cubs in the same span of time.

Using males as baby-sitters, lionesses do most of the hunting for the pride. They hunt individually and in groups. When there is plenty, females share the game they catch with each other, with their communal consort(s), and with the weaned juveniles. Females also share lactating duties. Schaller says, "Lactating lionesses permit small cubs of any litter to suckle on them, almost indiscriminately, and the cubs in turn respond to the calls and leadership of any such female . . . cubs of several litters may occupy the four teats of one lioness. Lionesses sometimes give their own cubs preference in suckling either by withdrawing with them from the group or by chasing other young away."

The Indian langur (*Presbytis entellus*) also illustrates several reproductive strategies of females that live in groups. Langurs allow a male (or males) to be integrated into their sisterhood. If their resident male is attacked, they band together to fight the invader(s). If he is killed or ousted, however, females may shift quickly from resistance to solicitation.

Because these monkeys are considered sacred in India, they multiply without interference from humans and have come to overpopulate their space. While at the high density of 130 monkeys per square mile the possibility of invasion and aggression toward young increases, reproductive advantage, not crowding, is the ultimate cause of these behaviors. For males, invasion and non-kin infanticide are generally adaptive because dislodging or killing unrelated males and their unweaned young always leaves an invader at a genetic advantage; he may then sire young of his own with the females that come into estrus soon after their babies have been killed. While females with nurslings must fight these males, young and pregnant females must seduce them: the young to avoid incest with the resident male, the pregnant to trick the invader into thinking their fetus is his. Thus, the langurs supply a parody of conditions in our own species: the aims of group females and their bond-males so strikingly opposed to those of male outsiders.

Defensive solicitation, both by pregnant and nonpregnant females, occurs in our species, especially in crowded, highly competitive situations, the extreme example of which is war. Although individual women may experience amenorrhea (lack of menstruation) and loss of libido under stress, neither of these is a guarantee of inability to conceive. Since women do not have any built-in birth control mechanisms that function under stress, they must try to spare the unborn baby with sexual bribes to hostile males.

Female mammals that live in groups lower their reproductive costs also by sharing rearing with their daughters and sisters. Mutual aid can consist of baby-sitting, cross-suckling, and assistance and guarding during parturition. The continuous, mutually altruistic association between closely related females, litter after litter, permits females to intensify their genetic and experiential input in clusters of young. Their input into the population is much greater than that of the single males that may become incorporated in the group.

Wolves (*Canis lupus*) demonstrate female cooperation particularly well. Not only do females cross-suckle, but all members of the pack, including males, help feed the weanlings. Meat is regurgitated for the pups when they mouth the adult's muzzle. It seems that a wolf pack consists of related individuals—one or more breeding couples that may be related as siblings, their young, and their yearlings (which look like adults). Close genetic relationship between the members of a pack means that cooperation boosts the fitness of all concerned.

In the past, when parenting strategies have been looked at, they have usually been evaluated from the viewpoint of the parents (as has been done here) and not from the view of the offspring. In a parallel way, mating has most often been looked at from the male's view. To illustrate the parallelism between the parent-offspring and the male-female interactions, a passage describing some of Robert Trivers's thoughts on parenting is quoted from Roger Bingham's "Trivers in Jamaica." When rewritten, replacing the word *parent* with the word *male* and the word *offspring* with the word *female*, the congruity of the female and child positions becomes clear. (It must be emphasized that none of the activities described below for males, females, or offspring are conceived to be occurring normally at a conscious level, not even in humans.)

Classically, parent-offspring relations have been viewed from the standpoint of the parent. Trivers championed the offspring, arguing that they were not simply "passive vessels into which parents pour the appropriate care." What is appropriate to a parent may be inappropriate and inadequate to a child. Conflict develops as a result.

The parent-offspring relationship is clearly asymmetrical: parents have a monopoly on resources and physical strength. But, Trivers argues, the offspring have a battery of psychological weapons at their own disposal.

Consider weaning. When the benefit to the offspring begins to be outweighed by the cost to the parent [that is, the mother], she will opt for weaning. A dissatisfied offspring cries for more food. Suppose that an offspring has been selected for its ability to "cheat." The offspring knows how hungry it is; the parent can only guess. Are the child's screams genuine cries for hunger or deceitful manipulation?

In essence, parents want their offspring to be more altruistic [that is, tolerate the parents' withdrawal of some attention to focus on their own survival and production of new young].

The passage above provides similar insight about male-female relations when rewritten using the parent = male and offspring = female equations. A few other changed words are shown in italics.

Classically, male-female relations have been viewed from the standpoint of the male. *I emphasize* the females, arguing they are not simply passive vessels into which males pour the appropriate *gametes*. What is appropriate to a male may be inappropriate and inadequate to a female. Conflict develops as a result.

The male-female relationship is clearly asymmetrical: males have a monopoly on resources and physical strength [in many mammalian and some avian species]. But . . . the females have a battery of psychological weapons at their own disposal.

Consider *mating*. When the benefit to the female begins to be outweighed by the cost to the male, *he* will opt for *mating with other females*. A dissatisfied female cries for more *loyalty* [that is, assistance and attention to herself and the young; protection, food, "love," the same things that a weanling cries for]. Suppose that a female has been selected for *her* ability to "cheat" [that is, suppose natural selection has worked, through time, to allow females who can deceive males into thinking their needs are greater than they really are to reproduce more efficiently, due to the extra male help they manage to get]. The female knows how *needy she* is; the male can only guess. Are the female's screams genuine cries for *help* or deceitful manipulation?

In essence, males want their females to be more altruistic [that is, allow them to mate with several females and sire many young].

Until just recently, and in a few small areas of the world, women, like some other social primates, have been more similar to avian females in their childlike position with respect to males. In fact, our social grouping and that of certain monkeys and possibly gorillas is founded upon males possessing the "mothering trait complex." Sometimes the incorporation of the complex is so complete that an astounding mimicry of the mother-child picture is achieved by the male-female consort pair. This can be seen clearly among the hamadryas baboons (*Papio hamadryas*), in which a young male adopts a juvenile female. He hugs and carries her around and protects her from aggressors for a year or more, until she is ready to mate. Seeing them without knowing that the larger animal is a male and the smaller his intended consort, one would conclude that it is a female, protecting a cowering little one. The male hamadryas is the archetypal big-mother-male.

Many women now reject the asymmetry in male-female relationships that parallels the asymmetry in parent-child relationships. The single-parent (usually single-mother) family and the polygamous commune are manifestations of this rejection. The pattern of the male as jealous protector of his female or females is one that served human societies for a long time, both in the form of sanctioned and illicit polygyny. The pattern is now changing. While most of the Western world still functions with a monogamous mask on somewhat polygynous activities, polygamy for both sexes through open marriage or serial monogamy is making strong headway. Education and work for women, and woman-controlled contraception, have removed the necessity for human females to function with childlike dependence on males, and new mating and parenting strategies are forming in direct reaction to these innovations.

7 | PRIMATES

This final chapter of the tale of the female animal, unlike the others, does not focus on a class-sized leap made by female animals. There are no more classes of vertebrates left to leap to. Fishes, amphibians, reptiles, birds, and mammals have all been considered, and now the focus must resolve to a smaller category: the order.

There are seventeen orders of modern eutherian mammals. Ours is called Primates because there are species in it that resemble the primitive or prime placental mammals, which lived some seventy million years ago at the start of the Paleocene, or first epoch of the Tertiary period. The animals living today that probably most resemble the primitive mammalian ancestor are the rat-sized tree shrews (species of *Tupaia*). While they have frustrated human classification, being labeled Insectivores, then Primates, then Scandentia (an order of their own), and again Insectivores, they bear several characteristics that recall our Paleocene beginnings. First of all, arboreality, or tree dwelling. The earliest primates are thought to have been arboreal because the oldest fossilized primate limb bones show adaptations for living in trees. These adaptations are deduced from the shape of the bones, modeled by the relative tensions of the muscles used in life. And just as musculature leaves its mark on limb bones, foods shape and mark the surfaces of the teeth. Fossilized primate teeth suggest a seed and fruit diet, which also makes a tree-dwelling existence in tropical rain forests highly likely.

In just such a leafy environment the modern tree shrew and her male defend a territory. Clinging to branches with claw-capped fingers and toes, she vociferously warns intruders away from her area. Perhaps because of the claws and imperfectly opposable grip, she does not carry her young or nurse and comfort them in a vertical position, as do almost all primates. She leaves them, with their eyes tightly shut, in a nest, as the early placental mammals probably did and as most other small mammals and birds still do.

Modern species of primates that share some characteristics of the tupaiidlike stock, from which all eutherians arose, belong to the prosimian division. This "half" of our order includes lemurs, lorises, galagos, and tarsiers. While some of these tree dwellers have specialized and evolved far from the Paleocene ancestor, they retain, in most cases, exclusively nocturnal activity, primary dependence on the sense of smell, imperfect body-temperature control, and, in some cases, nesting of the young.

Primates are closely related to the other two primitive placental orders, Rodents and Insectivores, but in spite of the strong "primitive" streak in our order, there are species in it that have a tremendous ability to learn. These species include some of the monkeys, the great apes, and humans, forming the anthropoid division of the order. Recent, successful attempts to teach chimpanzees, gorillas, and orangutans sign language have shown that these primates stand on a precipice of symbolic potential, which will be discussed later in this chapter.

The first evolutionary "decision" of primates, which seems to have set them apart from all other mammals, was to master the arboreal environment with an opposable thumb and big toe. Even when they came to the ground, primates continued to make good use of the opposable grip, which held the great preadaptive key to environmental control. Through thousands of millennia, it had been selected by pressures favoring the coordinated use of eye, hand, and brain during the mandatory survival activities of clinging to mother's fur, arboreal acrobatics, and grooming.

The second decision was a further accentuation of mothering. Mammals mother, and primates mother most outstandingly. The opposable grip changed the way primates used their habitats, and therefore, as will be discussed, it changed primate mothering. Because the opposable grip provided better support and therefore permitted feeding in new positions and from new food sources, a larger body could be supported.

Increased size is generally favored by natural selection in environments that will sustain larger animals. That is to say, if you can get the food, it is better to be bigger. Greater size is not only advantageous in predator confrontation, it also leads to a longer life span. A larger animal generally lives longer than a smaller animal because the metabolic rate of a big animal is relatively lower than that of a small one, and therefore internal organs are subject to a much slower rate of wear. (The metabolic rate of a larger animal is relatively lower than that of a smaller one because while basal metabolic rate increases with increased body weight, it does so only to about three-fourths the power of body weight. This lag may be related to the fact that the larger animal loses heat more slowly, since its surface area is relatively smaller [compared to its body weight] than the surface area of the smaller animal [compared to its body weight].) In primates, longer life span also meant a longer period for learning in infancy.

Larger size is advantageous for individual females in a species. The larger female will probably produce more surviving young. Due to her relatively lower metabolic rate, she can divert more of her food stores to milk. In addition, a larger mother may produce larger than average offspring compared to other young in her species. Size alone can give a survival advantage to these offspring, and the probability of more and better milk from their larger mother and her likely superiority in defense and carrying abilities make their chances better still. Largeness, translated into height in our species, has been noted frequently as a reproductive asset. The World Health Organization and other observers have reported that tall women are more efficient reproducers than short women.

The slower-paced body clocks of larger animals are usually also associated with relatively long gestation and single birth. Both these features plus relatively slower maturation were shown, by M. Kay Martin and Barbara Voorhies, to be characteristic of primates. In *The Female of the Species*, they paired seven primates (tarsier, galago, rhesus macaque, chacma baboon, chimpanzee, human, and gorilla) with nonprimates of comparable weight (chipmunk, rat, beagle, lynx, wild hog, laughing hyena, Hampshire sheep). All the primates in the sample have one baby at a time, but only one nonprimate, the hyena, does. Gestation in the primate sample takes from 144 days (galago) to 280 days (human), whereas gestation in the nonprimate sample is much shorter: 25 days (rat) to 147 days (Hampshire sheep). In addition, the primates in the sample take three to ten times longer to reach puberty than the nonprimates.

The characteristic of prolonged pregnancy in our order was permitted by selection for improved design of the placenta (see chapter 6). Longer gestation meant longer exposure of the developing brain to progesterone, which has been shown (along with some of its androgenlike derivatives) to have a positive effect upon intelligence in humans (see pp. 164 and 166). Could progesterone, the hallmark hormone of gestation and mothering, have enhanced intelligence in our order, as it may in our species?

Single birth was probably selected for partly because it allowed the mother to abandon the nesting strategy and carry her baby everywhere, providing it with greater safety and herself with a broader feeding range. One major consequence of single birth, which strengthened its selection, must have been its contribution to intelligence. The carried primate baby, with its eyes open soon after birth, is in an ideal position to learn at her mother's (and sometimes her father's) side. (Interestingly, further perfection of the opposable grip was probably selected for under conditions of singleton-carrying because its strength and accuracy increased the survival chances of the clinging youngster. Thus the selective cycle turned again: grip ◊ larger size ◊ slower growth ◊ longer gestation ◊ single birth ◊ infant-carrying ◊ grip.)

Single birth created a situation of paramount investment in each offspring that, in turn, demanded strategies of competition and cooperation between females and associations with males that were preadapted to short-term and long-term monogamy and gynopoly. Although monogamy is found in only a minority of primate species, it is, as Sarah Hrdy has pointed out, more than four times as common in our order as in other mammalian orders. In gynopoly, several females share one or a few males for mating and have more control over group composition than they do in harem polygyny (see sections on langurs and macaques, pp. 210 and 221).

The paradoxical protection/subjugation treatment of many primate females by males, which appears most consistently in harems but is also seen in gynopoly and monogamy, is a result of the inseparability, in male eyes, of the female from her single offspring. Males vie so keenly for potential mothers to "raise their genes" that they may kill the offspring of another (usually unrelated) male to release the female for use in their own reproductive projects (remember, after lactation ceases menstrual cycles begin again).

Naturally, male as well as female primates experience being mothered and so learn mothering techniques. Females may demand that males apply such techniques to females and young in order to remain in the group. A male benefits from group membership through immediate and reproductive survival. Bachelors, loners, and subordinates are on the outside looking in, and, as certain langur monkeys have shown, the desirability of joining the female group is great enough to be served by violence. A few species have been fortunate to find systems that group-integrate all or almost all males, for at least part of their lives, thereby solving the age-old problem of how to tap the energy normally wasted by male idleness. John Kurland, discussing Japanese macaques, says, "Prior to emigration [from the natal troop] subadult males spend increasingly long periods by themselves doing absolutely nothing." A field-worker, Kelly Stewart, mentions that she would find it exceedingly difficult to observe a lone male gorilla for eight hours because he does so little. Time may always weigh heavily on males; however, male freedom and energy can sometimes be channeled into group structuring activities, such as ritualized power displays and herding; baby-sitting; cooperative hunting (chimpanzees, baboons, humans); and occasional or habitual protective activity.

Having hit upon ways to incorporate males into the nuclear family, female primates entered new habitats—grasslands; semideserts; colder, snowy regions; and caves. They became tough and gregarious ground dwellers, giving rise to the physically, socially, and symbolically most manipulative organisms on earth.

Prosimians, as their name implies, resemble the ancestors of modern monkeys. At one time they were the only primates, and at least sixty genera lived in Europe, Africa, Asia, and the Americas. The principal evolutionary development among prosimians, during Eocene times (fifty-five to thirty-five million years ago), was enlargement of the brain and a gradual shift of emphasis from the olfactory to visual centers therein.

In addition, some prosimians and early anthropoids began to live in groups, just as certain prosimians and nearly all anthropoids still do today. The main cohesive element may well have been based upon attraction to mother, for as Alison Jolly points out in *The Evolution of Primate Behavior* the benign emotions that accompany grooming among modern social primates probably originate in mother-infant contact. T. R. Anthoney observed that the ontogeny (development through an individual's lifetime) of grooming behavior among captive baboons proceeds from suckling, to grasping and sucking the mother's fur, to parting the fur and picking off particles and parasites with lips or fingers, an activity essential to health and comfort.

Attraction, achieved through the body contact of grooming, and relief from discomfort may be two of the proximate causes of primate group formation, but safety derived from numbers is probably the ultimate reason for the continuation of gregariousness. Grouping helped certain primates enter more exposed habitats on the ground.

Lemurs, indrids, lorises, and the rare aye-ayes and tarsiers form the modern prosimian families. Their members often look like plush, fantasy toys with thick fur coats, which compensate for their imperfect temperature control as they seek food in the cool forest night. Their mating season is unusually short, less than one week per year, and they do not menstruate; the dead cells of the uterine lining are absorbed if no pregnancy occurs.

Large prosimians live on Madagascar, the big island off the southeastern coast of Africa, where they evolved without the competition of other primates and came to fill the niches of monkeys and apes, clinging vertically to trunks and boughs, leaping incredible distances with their long legs, and also coming to the ground. The largest prosimian, *Indri*, is about 4 feet high. One species, the sifaka (*Propithecus verauxi*), looks very much like a monkey and carries her single baby ventrally, clinging to her fur. Another species, the ring-tailed lemur (*Lemur catta*), looks a bit like a slender, long-legged raccoon, but with the addition of a long, long, horizontally black-and-white-striped tail.

Ring-tail and sifaka societies were compared by Jolly, who stressed that the "friendly behaviors" that characterize lemur troops are related to "mother-infant emotions of trust, dependence, and solicitude." She also pointed out that these species form troops with slightly more males than females, the reverse of the situation in most primate societies. Despite the excess of males, free ring-tailed lemurs and captive *Lemur macaco* form troops in which all females are dominant over all males. Females cuff or take food from any male, even the most dominant. But while males defer to females, they are far more aggressive with each other than females are among themselves. Thus, lemur grouping does not depend on male dominance or on recurrent or continuous female receptivity. Friendly behaviors such as sitting wedged together in train formation, games of foot-to-foot bicycling and wrestling, and grooming are the social glue of lemur society.

Lemurs have elongated lower incisors and canines that form an excellent comb with which they clean each other's fur. Licking, sniffing, and parting the fur with the fingers and scratching with a special "toilet claw" on the second toe are also part of the friendly service that typifies not only mother-infant relations but juvenile contacts and mating solicitation as well.

Although females are the primary groomers of their own babies, males sometimes take an active interest in grooming and playing with infants. Sifaka males groom the young as often as do females, but ring-tailed males ignore babies. Males of both species accept being groomed themselves, especially by a prospective mate, and they often groom females during courtship. Although lemurs have small brains compared to those of anthropoids, they have achieved stable societies, with the lifelong inclusion of males based upon behaviors derived from mother-infant interactions.

Social behavior probably preadapted primates to effective manipulation of objects. Carefully manipulating their infants and each other, during long hours of grooming, primates moved on to inspect, use, and modify objects in their environment. On a less concrete level of analogy, social manipulation—for example, a female getting a male to attack her female superior by presenting her hindquarters to the male while threatening the female—is what primatologists Michael Chance and Hans Kummer believe predisposed our ancestors to technical manipulation. From social tools to material tools, using the same "ability of predicting combined effects" is what Kummer thinks may have liberated the primate potential of reasoning. Social intelligence, gained from handling in infancy, enhanced by hours of peer-group play, and exercised in adult assemblies, opened the door to the handling of tools, and, later, ideas.

The social grouping was perhaps both a cause and an effect of the evolutionary development of anthropoids. Social formations of lemurs on Madagascar and monkeys in other parts of the world developed independently but in parallel. Unlike the sheltered lemurs on Madagascar, little prosimians in other parts of the world met sharp competition and were confined to solitary, nocturnal niches by the larger and brainier tree champions: the monkeys. Perfected stereoscopic color vision and thumb-forefinger precision grip enabled monkeys to pluck the plum of primate ascendancy from the prosimians.

Today free species of Old World monkeys live only in Africa, India, Southeast Asia, and Japan. New World species are found only in Central and South America. Elimination of monkeys from most of the northern hemisphere indicates how the spread of human culture, especially agriculture and cities, removed the trees that most monkey species depend on. Urbanization and industry coming into the equatorial belt will probably mean that monkeys will lose their last evolutionary battle and end as relics in zoos and game reserves.

New World monkeys are divided into two groups: the callithricids and the cebids. Callithricids are the kitten-sized marmosets and tamarins, active during the day but seldom seen by human eyes. The females regularly give birth to twins, are about the same size or slightly larger than the males, and fight one another more than do males. A breeding marmoset will not tolerate another potentially breeding female in her territory. Some species are monogamous, and even have a sort of honeymoon when the bonding couple mate frequently. Later, sexual behavior is infrequent but the pair groom and sleep together. Still later, the male may carry the twins on his back.

Enduring monogamy is shown by two or three species of titi monkey (*Callicebus*), also called pygmy marmosets. When faced with a same-sex competitor, females pay less attention to their mate, but males pay more attention, a reaction also familiar in our species. Although it is often said of such asymmetrical reactions to competition that the female is less jealous than the male, it is simply that females profit by following strategies different from those of males. Female expressions of jealousy will depend on species patterns, such as seasonal synchrony of estruses in a group, frequency of estrus through the year, and on individual conditions, such as pregnancy, estrus, and menopause (which occurs in some Old World and possibly some New World species).

Cebids are the larger New World monkeys, and some of them look very much like some of the Old World species. However, their skull and tooth structure reveal a thirty-million-year differentiation between them and the Old World group. Where New and Old World monkeys are similar in structure and social behavior, primatologists ascribe it to convergent evolution—similar solutions to similar ecological problems. Cebids are familiar to us as zoo inmates, especially the squirrel (*Saimiri*), the spider (*Ateles*), and the howler (*Aloutta*) monkeys. The cebids also boast the only nocturnal species in the anthropoid division: the night monkey (*Aotus*). Like marmosets and the lesser apes (siamangs and gibbons), the night monkey relies on her male to carry infants, a rare pattern among primates and mammals in general.

The spider monkey is also unusual, for she possesses a mock penis, formed from the elongated labia minora and clitoral hood, which is more pendulous than the male organ. She completes her disguise with a false scrotum formed by fused, adipose-filled labia majora. A few other South American monkeys have elongated labia, but none imitate the male so accurately as the spider monkey. To find another male-mimic with even more astonishing organs one must look in the order Carnivora, at the spotted hyena (*Crocuta crocuta*). In this case, however, the clitoris not only looks like a penis, it also houses a common urinary-genital canal, through which intercourse and birth take place. In contrast, the spider monkey's mimicry is only skin-deep, and beneath the tubular cloak over the clitoris there are separate urinary and vaginal openings.

The reasons for the spider monkey's structural imitation of males remain mysterious, but an increased level of androgens during fetal life may be responsible, as it has been shown to be in the spotted hyena. (Extra androgen, as noted in chapter 5, is also the immediate explanation of nonmaternal behavior in the polyandrous phalaropes.)

The adaptive advantages of female mimicry of male genitalia have been guessed at—intimidation of aggressive males, species recognition, use in greeting and in hierarchical identification—but these putative advantages are probably due to opportunistic adjustments made by both sexes rather than to prior natural selection for any intrinsically adaptive quality in male mimicry. In other words, organisms may be "making the best of" a hormonal quirk in their species. As Hans Kummer says, "Discussions of adaptiveness sometimes leave us with the impression that every trait observed in a species must by definition be ideally adaptive, whereas all we can say with certainty is that it must be tolerable since it did not lead to extinction." There is no reason to reject the idea that what appear to be adaptations are often just products of massed individual acceptance of and adjustment to burdensome change. Such dubious adaptations may be selected for only in the sense that they "hitch a ride" with organisms that survive in spite of or perhaps, after behavioral adjustments, with the marginal help of those adaptations.

For female spider monkeys, part of making the best of male mimicry means having a convenient organ for depositing scented urine, which males find attractive. While not monogamous, they have very cordial and equable relations with their males. Mounting and presenting (that is, showing hindquarters) are not used for purposes of dominance and submission, only for intercourse. Spider monkeys live in large groups without clear-cut dominance of one sex over the other.

Howler monkeys also live in groups, but they are not outstanding brachiators (under-branch swingers) like the spider monkeys, and they do not have the spider monkey's fifth limb—a long, strong, gripping tail with sensitive skin at its end, like a fingertip. The howlers are, however, the most outstanding primate vocalizers of the South American jungles and have a deep lower jaw that hangs a bony protection over their precious voice box. Although the average heights and weights of the sexes are very close, males vocalize more than females and lead groups through the trees slightly more often than females. The latter are not herded by the males, however, and although they do not fully mimic the shape of male genitalia, they, like the males, have flashy yellow sex organs.

While the two sexes of howler monkeys do not differ in color of genitalia or in coat color, which is red or black according to species, they are dimorphic (showing sex-related difference) in size. Howlers are also the largest New World monkeys. It is a recurrent theme throughout the primate order that the larger species are the more sexually dimorphic. It is not known why larger-bodied species show sharper size differences between males and females, but it may have something to do with the direct correlation between larger size and amount of time spent on the ground. It seems that the more terrestrial the species, the larger and more dimorphic it is. Whether certain primate species came to the ground because they got too large to live gracefully in trees or they got large because they came to the ground and had to fend off terrestrial predators is difficult to say. Whatever the order of events, both ground dwelling and relatively larger body size seem to dispose primate species toward sharp sexual differences in appearance, size, and behavior. Still, there are exceptions: the rather dimorphic howlers are arboreal, as are the extremely dimorphic orang-utans.

The tendency for female primates to live in groups, both in the trees and on the ground, also disposes toward dimorphism, for grouped females mean fiercely competing males, which means selection will usually favor larger, more dangerous males. The stakes are high when females cluster because the winner male may take all: the females and the resultant young. This pattern is seen in hamadryas baboons, Indian langurs, and mountain gorillas. In contrast, chimpanzees, who are at home on the ground or in the trees, show dimorphism and social arrangements that are intermediate between those of the ground-dwelling, gynopolous and polygynous species just mentioned and those of the tree-dwelling monogamous marmosets and lesser apes.

Trying to explain why and predict when the sexes will look and act the same or differently has been a focus of primate research for a long time. No definitive answers have been found yet. Researchers and theorists often accuse each other of overgeneralizing from too few species or too few studies of one species. There are also the almost unavoidable pitfalls of ethnocentrism and sexcentrism in interpreting data. Obviously, the only solution to these problems will be more studies of various species by researchers of both sexes from various cultural backgrounds. Also, a public that is aware of the embryonic state of primatology and is willing, therefore, not to assign the status of absolute fact to extrapolations from nonhuman primate behavior to human behavior will be helping in the task of assessing our species' gender flexibility.

Some Old World monkeys live primarily in the trees, others live on the ground. Ground dwelling in open areas is said to make life more precarious. Predators, such as carnivorous cats, make tight group structure, intolerance of strangers, and mutual warning and defense highly adaptive. Arboreal species also face danger, chiefly in the form of predatory birds, and falls that expose them to ground hunters like the boa constrictor. However, their social relations seem calmer, with less energy spent on dominance competition and less sexual dimorphism of structure and behavior than among ground dwellers. Of course, it must be added that ground species are easier to study than tree species, and as more is learned about the latter, the picture of their pacific existence may change.

What is being learned by primatologists is that a female's physiology, the speed of her maturation, the tempo of her ovulatory cycles, pregnancies, and lactation periods may far outweigh predator presence in shaping the social unit and adding emotional colors to the behavior of both sexes. Female competition for food and the resultant spatial arrangements and cooperative ties that arise among females are also critical to primate group organization. This is not to say that predator pressure, food and water availability, and climate changes are unimportant; they are the elements that shape female physiology and patterns of deployment.

Full- or part-time ground dwelling is something that only a minority of primates achieve. Examples are, among the prosimians, the ring-tailed lemur, and among the anthropoids, only certain monkeys (langurs, baboons, macaques), the chimpanzees, gorillas, and humans. Biologists are particularly interested in ground-dwelling Old World monkeys and apes because it is thought that they hold answers to questions about early human social structures.

While not everyone agrees about what the two sexes in terrestrial species of primates are doing, they do agree that the dangers peculiar to ground dwelling have made the sexes behave differently toward young, each other, and enemies. In almost every ground-dwelling primate species, the female is smaller than the male. The only exception seems to be ring-tailed lemurs, which are slightly larger than their males but which are only partially terrestrial. Ground dwellers weigh less and are less strong than their males. This means they face a formidable enemy within their own ranks. Before summarizing the field findings that show how females deal with this problem, a brief review of some of the possible reasons for sexual dimorphism is in order.

The contrast in size between females and males of ground-dwelling primates shows that different selective pressures have been at work upon the two sexes. Females may be smaller than males for several reasons:

1. Since skeletal maturation is partially governed by attainment of puberty, the earlier sexual maturation of females relative to males can mean smaller size for females. (For example, female baboons mature at three to four years, compared to males at five to eight years. Female baboons are on average one-half to three-fourths the size of males.) In competing with other females of her species, an early maturer may have an adaptive advantage in being able to complete more pregnancies. Thus, earlier maturation may have been the trait selected for, bringing smaller size in its wake.

2. Females, if much smaller, may exist on less or different foods from males; this is a way of sharing what the environment has to offer.

3. Females may have been subjected to eons of natural selective pressure to be more delicately muscled than males in order to achieve optimum handling of infants. This would not necessarily have made females smaller, just lighter.

4. Females may have been sexually selected to be small. That is to say, if males of a species consistently mate with smaller females more often than with larger ones, larger females will produce fewer young, and pass on "genes for largeness" less often than small females pass on "genes for smallness." However, unless large size is sex linked (that is, carried as a recessive trait on the X chromosome and therefore usually seen only in males) or is primarily under the ontogenetic control of diet, it is hard to see how selection *against* large females could succeed if, simultaneously, large males were being selected for by female preference. After all, large fathers should produce large daughters as often as large sons.

Sexual selection against large females may be particularly strong where males try to control groups of females for long periods of time (as among hamadryas baboons). The single male, trying to defend a harem, would face less opposition from small, fragile females; he could have more energy to ward off male competitors. One way in which male "preference" for small-sized females is operationally expressed is through the selection of immature females over older ones. This may have contributed to the pressure upon females to mature at an early age. The hamadryas female shows the bottom-swelling sign of puberty by two years, which is one to two years earlier than savanna baboons, who do not normally form harems.

It would be interesting for someone to study variation in sexual dimorphism for size as it may relate to different social systems in our species. In societies with long histories of male dominance or harem formation, it might be expected that women will be relatively much shorter than men and have earlier menarche than women released from this social structure. Of course, the differential effects of diet would have to be corrected for, as improvement in diet might well be correlated with disruption of female subordination. Correction for the factor of diet could be achieved by making indexed comparisons:

$$\frac{\text{Height of female from culture A}}{\text{Height of male from culture A}}$$

compared to

$$\frac{\text{Height of female from culture B}}{\text{Height of male from culture B}}$$

Thus, it might be ascertained how much of the fantastic increase in height in Japan over the past fifty years was due to an increase in height of women. The only human groups in which there may have been a long history of reduced size dimorphism are found in Polynesia. Here, particularly among the rulers of Hawaii, there is record of extremely tall females who enjoyed an unusual degree of sexual and political parity with males.

G. Mitchell reports on a study by M. E. Hamilton that suggests that sexual differences in size are related to method of subsistence. Hamilton measured the bones of five American Indian populations and found that there was more dimorphism in tribes dependent on hunting and less dimorphism in tribes dependent on agriculture. While there is no one-to-one correlation between method of subsistence and social systems, the more dimorphic specimens would appear to come from hunting societies in which male and female roles were highly differentiated, and the less dimorphic from horticultural societies with greater role equality.

Discussion of langurs, baboons, and macaques will now focus attention on the behavioral adaptations of ground-dwelling female primates. But there are two warnings that must be attached to the presentation of any primate findings. One is that no broad generalizations are valid; every species has its own ovulatory rhythm and, therefore, its distinctive pattern of coping with the environment and reproduction. Even slight variations in the birth interval from species to species may completely change the tactics that females will follow. Differences in climate and terrain can affect when females of a species will give birth and, hence, the strategies that both sexes will employ in living together or apart, in mating, and in treatment of the young. My rough guide to female cyclicity in our order is:

Prosimians and New World monkeys do not menstruate. They ovulate at intervals during only part of the year. Although some anthropoids, like the rhesus macaque, also ovulate seasonally, most Old World monkeys, apes, and humans ovulate cyclically throughout the year. Old World monkeys, apes, and humans also menstruate visibly.

This guide is paralleled by a division in the overall amount of sexual dimorphism seen in these two groups:

Prosimians and New World monkeys are *generally* less dimorphic than are the Old World monkeys, apes, and humans. Of course, there are some New World monkeys, such as howlers, in which there is some sexual dimorphism, and there are Old World species, like the monogamous Mentawei Island langurs, in which the sexes do not differ much at all.

The second warning attached to primate findings is that there is no consistent approach to studying primates. Consequently, the same species may be approached by one observer behind a blind, by another in a Land-Rover, or by another with tempting supplies of extra bananas. Naturally, all these observers gain totally different views of the same species.

In addition, primate studies sometimes suffer from sexcentrism. Until the past ten to fifteen years, the most familiar published and filmed reports on monkeys had been prepared by men. A male primatologist, Masao Kawai, in Japan, lamented this one-sided perspective in the following words:

The social behavior of adult male monkeys is essentially understood. By contrast, study of female monkeys was begun later and many aspects of their behavior are still not understood. We had always found it more difficult to distinguish among females as we could not see any particular differences among them. However, a female researcher who joined our study could recognize individual females easily, and understood their behavior, personality and emotional life much better than that of male monkeys. I was very taken aback by this revelation. There were many puzzles about female behavior and I revealed that I could analyze males' activities much more easily than those of females. Sometimes I was aggravated by such things as females taking advantage of their dependent rank and activities like masturbation.

The reason why the study of female monkeys has lagged behind is that the researchers have all been men. I never before thought that female monkeys and women could immediately understand each other but there has been some barrier between female monkeys and male observers. (Pamela J. Asquith generously supplied this translated quotation from M. Kawai's *Life of the Japanese Monkey*, 1969, p. 292.)

First let us consider langurs. There are more than thirty species of them (*Presbytis*) living from India and Sri Lanka, across southern Asia, to Borneo. They live in gynopolous groups—that is, groups of about ten females, usually with their infant, juvenile and subadult offspring, to which one male is admitted. It is only during very extended droughts that they may congregate in groups of one hundred or more near possible sources of water.

Langurs have long, light fur of gray, white, or golden hue, according to species and season. The fur contrasts with their black-skinned faces, hands, and feet. Males and females do not differ in appearance, except for size and genitalia. A fully adult male can weigh twice as much as a young adult female. In Borneo, where langurs have snub or pendulous noses, males are strikingly larger than females.

While langurs are as adept as baboons and macaques on the ground, they are also supremely adapted arborealists. Lithe and energetic, they bound up trees, ricochet off trunks and branches, and jump gaps up to 30 feet, even while carrying an infant. In addition, the langurs and their African cousins, the colobus monkeys, have another adaptation that makes the trees their consummate domain. They eat leaves. With this staple diet, they need not descend to parched ground and can survive several months without a drink of water. In fact, langurs give birth and nurse during the driest season. This means that their young will be weaned in the wet season, when there is an abundance of food.

In spite of this seasonal birth peak in many langur groups, some give birth at any time of the year. If a baby dies, its mother will come back into estrus within a few weeks and have another baby after six months, a fact that has ominous meaning for relations between the sexes, as will be shown below.

In addition to six months of pregnancy, females are responsible for ten to twelve months of nursing and weaning. In all, it has been calculated that a langur spends 70 percent of her adult life involved with motherhood, less than 5 percent in a state of sexual receptivity, and less than 1 percent of her time in active sexual relations.

Not surprisingly, all studies of langurs show that females are greatly interested in newborn young. If there were not something intrinsically attractive and compelling about infants, females could not devote so much of their time to them. This does not mean that we know precisely what that something is. Since babies *almost* inevitably release female caring, cases of infant neglect or abuse are all the more striking, occurring when females kidnap and mishandle non-kin infants, possibly as a form of reproductive competition.

There are many speculations about kidnapping. It could be a way for mothers in a troop to protect their own young from the practice sessions of juvenile females. The kidnapped baby becomes a doll when handed over to the youngsters and adolescents. It could be a retaliatory tactic in a series of troop-troop clashes, especially in crowded areas, where groups of females compete for short resources. In most cases, the mother crosses troop lines to retrieve her baby. If she does not, it dies for lack of milk and from rough handling.

As is quite common among primates, including humans, a female's status rises with the arrival of her baby. This is one of the rewards through which holding the baby becomes part of the female repertoire. While the langur mother's status does not rise as sharply as in certain other primate species, she does become the center of solicitous grooming which barely cloaks the selfish curiosity of the crowd. Her reward may also come from the sensations of seeing, touching, and smelling the infant. A new langur mother can retrieve her infant from any other troop female, regardless of her age or status.

The rank of a female langur does not seem to be influenced by the rank of her mother, as it is among Japanese macaques, but seems to peak during the years of her reproductive vigor. A female's survival does, however, depend on her mother's experience and temperament. Phyllis Jay observed clear differences in the ability of langur females to mother. Those that made quick and unpredictable movements irritated their babies and had difficulty keeping them calm.

When a langur is born, its mother inspects its head, hands, and genitals. As soon as it is dry, she allows other females to do the same. They hold and touch the neonate gently, and lick, smell, and stroke it without disturbing its sleep. The intensity of female attraction to babies is confirmed by Jay's statement that *apparently* bereft, childless females (or just kidnappers?) have been known to steal a baby. A mother may carry her dead infant for two or more days.

A langur's control of sexual relations is as consistent as her greed for infants. A female is never mounted unless she solicits the male by dropping tail, presenting hindquarters, and flashing her head from side to side. Langurs do not show an estrus swelling, like macaques, baboons, and chimpanzees, whose massive, vermilion cushions sometimes prompt zoo visitors to query their disease. Because female langurs' sexual invitations are actions, rather than swellings, they are sometimes able to make males think they are in estrus when they are not, a tactic applied to males that try to take over their groups and kill their infants.

In her masterpiece of modern field primatology, *The Langurs of Abu*, Sarah Blaffer Hrdy gives a detailed account of the strategies used by Hanuman langurs (*Presbytis entellus*) in the face of male takeover challenges. From 1971 to 1975, Hrdy and her assistants witnessed fourteen takeovers, eleven of which were accompanied by infanticide.

Weaned juveniles are not killed by invading males during a takeover because they do not interfere with their mother's estrous cycling, as do nursing young. So only nursing young are killed. Another reason weaned young are not killed is that weaned females will be ready to mate one to three years after the takeover; thus the invader may get the chance to mate with some of these females before his reign is ended by another invasion. This may be why very young juvenile females have been seen soliciting an invader. Although, at eleven to thirteen months, these females are too young to be mating, they will pretend to be in estrus. As best they can, they will shudder their heads and present tail-down, as if to say to the male that might kill them, "I'm not a baby, but a female—willing to pass your genes to the next generation. I am of value to you, so don't kill me." This could also be incidentally altruistic behavior, for by distracting males from their mother, who may be about to wean an infant, juvenile females may help spare a sister or brother.

Pregnant females also employ the tactic of solicitation. Behaving as if they realize that they may make an invader believe they are in estrus, they produce the appropriate signals. If he mates with them, chances are the new male will accept their future offspring as if they were his own. Since males cannot detect early pregnancy and do mate with estrus-shamming pregnant females, young born several months after a takeover are not killed.

Lions, hippos, bears, wolves, wild dogs, hyenas, rats, rabbits, and more than a dozen species of primates, including most of the leaf eaters, chimpanzees, gorillas, and humans are some of the species which Hrdy lists as regularly infanticidal and homicidal. Most of the killing is of and by males as a direct result of reproductive competition, and most of that competition is dictated by the needs, groupings, and preferences of females.

In our species this pattern has been extended and distorted through numerous cultural mangles, but institutions of murder—feud, battle, mass execution, and warfare on every scale—all derive from the same basic struggle among males for differential fitness (reproduction) through access to resources and females. As in other species in which males are larger and stronger than females, our species has been subjected to a history of selection that powerfully differentiated the modes of struggle of the two sexes, making the male strategies more offensive and the female ones more defensive. Females, to reiterate, need not strive as openly for fitness as males because they will probably pass on their genes regardless of which males win. Still, the evidence is beginning to mount for the case that female competition is fiercer than once thought. A thorough and convincing discussion of this point is presented by Hrdy in chapter 6 of *The Woman that Never Evolved*. Her observations have contributed to the discussions here of kidnapping, harassment during estrus by dominant females, and inhibition of ovulation in subordinates.

Among langurs, the pressures that have favored male competition for female monopolization include the clustering of related females and their young in stable groups; a birth interval of fifteen to thirty months; the ability of females to cycle throughout the year and to regain estrus shortly after miscarriage or death of an offspring; and the departure of immature males from the natal group.

While females stay in the troop in which they were born for the twenty or more years of their life, males leave at about one to three years of age. This departure may occur peacefully, with brothers and male cousins forming a bachelor band or joining an already existing one. Alternatively, young males may leave their troop under the pressure of attack. A detailed description of the expulsion of a resident male, along with the subadult and juvenile males of a troop, has been made by Sugiyama, who watched a takeover struggle that lasted for two weeks. The resident challenged the invader twice without success and then went into exile with the younger males, most of whom were probably his sons. The cohort of male invaders were repelled by their own leader once they had helped him oust the resident male.

Females, especially the older ones, do not submit meekly to the invader's plans. Mothers, grandmothers, aunts, and great-aunts resist singly and as allies. The older females fight even harder than the mothers and younger females. Although they may be childless at the time of a takeover attempt, they behave as if they were defending their own young when they fight for the infants of the troop. They behave as if they realize their own relative expendability, and so their strategy works to protect both the juveniles and their mothers who are in their reproductive prime.

If defensive fighting does not help stop an invader's attacks, nursing females may leave the troop until their babies are weaned. If the baby is injured, the mother will not abandon it, but if it dies or is very near death, she will rejoin the troop, where she has no choice but to mate with the new resident male. He is the only source of another baby.

In contrast to the ferocious resistance of mothers with unweaned young and of the elder females, young females in estrus may solicit nearby males, practically enticing them to invade. While such behavior may bring havoc to their mothers, grandmothers, lactating sisters, and infant siblings, young females seem to prefer to be served by nontroop males rather than by the resident male, who is most probably their father. Such outmating may be of more importance to a female than to the resident male, since she stands to lose more by gestating a stillborn or handicapped infant through inbreeding.

In Abu, gynopolous langur troops experience a change of resident husband about every twenty-seven months. As the relationship between females in a langur troop is estimated, by Hrdy, to be approximately that of first cousins (that is, one-eighth of all genes are shared), it is to their long-term advantage to have different partners at regular intervals. So, while grandmothers and mothers will fight an invader that attacks babies, they are not resisting his sexual takeover as much as protecting their current investment in the newest crop of youngsters. Indeed, the females that fight an invader will mate with him after a short time.

While the strategies described here may apply to other leaf-eating monkeys, no complete generalizations can be made even within this family. The West African red colobus, for instance, shows a pattern in which females switch troops. Although both females and males are ejected from their natal troop, males find it more difficult to enter new troops because resident adult females, sometimes assisted by a resident male, can and do kill single males.

In the other great Old World monkey subfamily, the cercopithecines, females have found ways to live in more permanent alliances with males. Their habitat is more terrestrial; their diet more varied;

and their sexual dimorphism more marked than among the leaf eaters. Cercopithecines or cheek-pouched monkeys socialize their male young for long periods of time. Perhaps this is one reason males of these species acquire extensive mothering repertoires, which they sometimes apply to juveniles and females. The temporary husband of the langur troop and the insecure male drifter of the red colobus contrast with the permanent harem masters of the hamadryas and gelada and the multimale troops of the various savanna baboons.

Baboons and macaques are the only thoroughly ground-dwelling monkeys. They and we are the primates best adapted to live in a wide variety of terrestrial habitats. Chimpanzees and gorillas, by comparison, spend most of their time in restricted forest ground zones. Baboons live throughout Africa, in forests, savannas, on barren cliffs, and in semideserts, where they must sometimes dig for water in empty riverbeds to survive, yet baboons have not forgotten how to climb trees, and take to them each night.

Medical researchers, psychologists, space scientists, and primatologists of both sexes have studied baboons in detail because they are closer to us than any primates except the great apes, and they are easier to keep in captivity than apes. The fact that antibodies to placental secretions are being tested on baboons as a potential birth control method for humans underlines the biochemical similarity of these species.

Data on baboon behavior has been the source of interpretive flights about the origin of our species. The accentuated sexual dimorphism of baboons and their troop structure once seemed excellent models of what early people must have been like, until male scientists realized that these species simply mirrored their own ideas of how men treat women. Too many conclusions had been drawn from provisioned groups in the wild and from zoo colonies. High aggressivity, the rapacious sexual appetites of male baboons, and their incessant quarrels over females turned out to be artifacts of provisioning and captivity.

Now it is known that the relations of free baboons are generally placid. In troops of ten to one hundred individuals, they arrange themselves in a fairly constant hierarchy, with subordinates giving way more or less gracefully to dominants on issues of place, food, and sex. Not only do baboons have organized tribes with male and female leaders but they can also cooperate to hunt prey in relays. Add to this picture the antics of the young, their mother's retrieving them by the tail and carrying them jockey-style, their fathers' and uncles' solicitous baby-sitting, and it is easy to see why humans have identified with baboons since ancient times.

Savanna baboons are only half the size of their males, who weigh about one hundred pounds. They have smaller canines than males and no mantle of long hair on their neck and shoulders. It is thought that the danger of ground dwelling selected for largeness and masculine features like manes and dagger canines, which might equip the males to defend the troop. Kummer has suggested that the juvenile hamadryas may transfer her attraction for her mother's fur directly to the male's great, bushy mane and so transfer easily from her mother's protection to his and bond to him by grooming his abundant fur. Also the biggest, hairiest, sharpest-fanged males probably forced other males to wait in line for estrous females and, so, put more gene copies for big, hairy, fanged males into the population. Hopefully, when danger stalked, the bullies were in the front line of defense, but it may have better served their reproductive fitness to nudge forward an underling or granny, as dinner for the cats.

The obvious question is, Why didn't the females grow larger and fight their own battles? Probably it was not genetically or hormonally possible, because of the continuous selective pressures for delicacy of musculature (without too great a sacrifice of strength) and relative mildness of manner (without loss of courage), as distinct advantages in mothering.

Hrdy asks the same question about female langurs at the end of *The Langurs of Abu*. She answers it by saying, "a female who 'opted' for larger body size in order to fight off a male might not be so well-adapted for her dual role of both survivor (of drought and other climatic fluctuations) and childbearer. An oversized female might produce fewer offspring than her smaller cousin." This is not a contradiction of what was said above about the general advantages of largeness for mothering because langurs may live in marginal environments, where the general rule does not hold. Thus, as Hrdy states in *The Woman that Never Evolved*, "Droughts and food shortages, meanwhile, are recurrent hazards of the langur's environment; under these circumstances, the smaller the female, the better adapted she is at converting the available resources into offspring."

The smaller, more childlike female, however she may have evolved, is the basis of harem formations among the hamadryas and gelada baboons. Usually one to four, sometimes as many as nine, hamadryas baboons (*Papio hamadryas*) stay with their male at all times. Hans Kummer, who studied and experimented with this species in captivity and the wild, maintains that the severity of their semidesert environment favored the "invention" of harems, which are small enough to forage efficiently where food is sparse. Adding support to this explanation is the fact that South African chacma baboons (*Papio ursinus*), which normally live in large troops with several adults of both sexes, splinter into harems when food is short.

Among hamadryas, juvenile females and males from all harems play together. In the course of this play, a female is picked up, held, and mothered by an older *male* playmate. By one to three years of age most females have found their consort in this playmate and stay with him and the few other young females he may catch, carry, and court. Together they begin a harem. Their playful hugging gives way to sexual relations over the following eighteen months.

The continuity of the group's association depends on the male's ability to cradle, protect, and herd the females. If they stray from him, he stares hard at them over his shoulder and may pull them along or bite them in order to make them follow him. Kummer says, "This herding technique, reminiscent of a baboon mother controlling her infant, apparently was the best means available to baboons for a small, stable foraging unit."

The evolution of harems, as constant social units among the hamadryas and as temporary crisis units among other baboons, is founded on three preadaptations present in the genus at large: dominance hierarchy formation, sexual dimorphism (marked difference in size and/or appearance of the two sexes), and exclusive access bonding. Exclusive bonding in baboons exists between temporary consorts and between mother and infant. The baboon mother is less tolerant of other females taking her baby than is the langur and may prevent other females from holding her infant, especially if she outranks them.

Male baboons, of all species, also want to hold infants. This interest drives the young hamadryas male to fondle babies and acquire female playmates. Sometimes babies cling to the bellies of males, just as they do to their mothers for the first four or five months of life. Male olive baboons (*Papio anubis*) may even adopt sick or orphaned young. Baboon males of all species often carry babies when other males, particularly strangers, approach. Since infanticide now seems to be much more of a danger than primatologists first believed, carrying is probably the way males protect their sons, daughters, nieces, or nephews. Clearly, the mothering aptitude of *male* baboons must be considered the fourth preadaptation for harem formation.

In addition to being objects of fascination and compassion, babies are cherished by males for another reason: babies protect males. An infant may inhibit male aggression and, thus, act as a living shield against a threatening fellow. But offspring are not automatically tools of peace. The prerequisites for them to function as such seem to be adequate space and food for all group members and a strong tradition of exposing males to the mothering process, both as juveniles and as adults. It is not sufficient for a male to have been mothered for a short time in infancy; he must have contact with females and their young and be part of their group. The infanticidal langur males, for example, who are normally repelled by their mothers within the first year of life, have had little time to be socialized by females. They take up residence at an early age in bachelor groups, in which interaction with females is so minimal that some males take the sexual role of females.

Still, the potential for males to gently handle infants exists even in the infanticidal langur genus. In captivity, the male spectacled langur (*Presbytis obscuris*) has shown solicitude toward juveniles. He may carry, embrace, kiss, and even sleep with the infant. He has been observed grooming a male juvenile and pushing him into a "present" posture, as if he were teaching him the polite form of langur greeting.

Kummer's experiments with olive and hamadryas baboons reveal that females of both species are more flexible in their behavior than males. If transferred, females soon adopt the customs of the other species' troop. Thus, olive females will allow themselves to be herded by hamadryas males, and hamadryas females will take one or successive olive consorts.

A male's herding behavior is more resistant to change than a female's following behavior. He will herd only his harem or females that are alone. The male hamadryas that has seen another male in the company of a particular female will not go near that female, even if a previous confrontation with the paired male has shown the unpaired one that he is stronger. He will look at the sky, stare off into space, and shuffle pebbles rather than peek at his friend's wife.

Harem formations are also found among gelada "baboons" (a different genus [*Theropithecus*] from the savanna and hamadryas varieties, which are *Papio*). Gelada harems graze on the Ethiopian highlands and sleep on the craggy cliffs below. Their groupings are achieved in a very different way from that of the hamadryas. Gelada females form a dominance hierarchy within the harem and then herd each other. Only the first consort is herded by the male, and she is the one that eventually permits the harem to grow by accepting another female's bid for admission.

The female that wishes to join the gelada group presents hindquarters to the *female* already paired with the male. The paired female mounts the newcomer, just as a male would mount a female during intercourse. Then the paired female allows the newcomer to groom her. This method of establishing harems was observed in a primate research center in which none of the geladas in an enclosure knew each other. So, it is possible that the female-created harem is a distortion of the natural system. However, the behavior of wild gelada, in the Ethiopian highlands, seems to confirm this arrangement.

Gelada harems are held together by the threats of females. Only rarely does the male gelada go out and round up a distant female with a frightening charge, the way a male hamadryas does. When a strange male approaches one of the females of a troop, he is not only challenged by the male of the group but by all the females as well. Kummer suggests that this group action permits gelada harems to disperse and mix with other harems and unattached troop members. In contrast, hamadryas harems must remain discrete because their integrity depends exclusively on one male's vigilance. He must hold tighter rein, since the females do not herd one another. The gelada male will, however, exert his control in trying to prevent a pubescent female from meeting males of other groups, in order that he may be the one most likely to mate with her during the first estrus of her life. While most female geladas remain in their natal troop for life, they sometimes change after the birth of a first offspring, sired by the harem master.

In gelada harems, females of higher rank reproduce significantly more often than those of lower rank. Robin and Patsy Dunbar demonstrated that this difference was not the effect of differences in female age or size of troop. High-rankers apparently reduced the fecundity of low-rankers by harassing them during estrus, which seems to either suppress ovulation or cause an abortion soon after fertilization. High-ranking females do not, however, interfere with solicitation and copulation; so, low-rankers have just as many consorts with just as many ejaculations as their superiors; they just do not have as many pregnancies.

Similar suppression of fertility occurs in female marmosets, talapoin monkeys, and tree shrews when they are exposed to the stress of a dominant female. Prolactin, which is one of the hormones that becomes elevated in "nervous" females, seems to interfere with the surge of luteinizing hormone needed for ovulation, thus blocking pregnancy just as it does during lactation, when suppression of ovulation and libido are normal.

The space devoted here to the baboons, while insufficient to do them and their investigators justice, is relatively extensive because baboon societies have been thought to reflect early human social formations. It may or may not be true that early hominids lived in open

grassland or semidesert environments and traveled together in organized troops. It may or may not be true that prehistoric humans sub-
divided their groups into a core of females and young, surrounded by
defending or expendable males as among savanna baboons, or into
harems as among hamadryas and gelada. But since women have
sometimes found themselves in similar constellations with men and
young in historic times, it is important to explore the convergences
further.

If females of our nearest phylogenetic relatives can herd or be herded,
can be protected or ignored by males, can attack or entice males, then
their ability to vary their behavior is clear. If different environments
favor different group sizes, compositions, and birth patterns, then
females must alter their behavior accordingly. Do the various patterns
of human marriage also reflect the fine-tuning of female rhythms and
partner choices to the demands of habitat?

Perhaps the variable success of human cultures in socializing males
away from aggressive confrontation, frequent adultery, and murder is
due to the wide variability in exposure of boys and male adolescents
to females with young and to opportunities to practice mothering, just
as mothering of and by males varies from the Hanuman langur to the
hamadryas baboon.

Did female primates select big-mother-males (see p. 195) by mating
preferentially with those males that were attentive and defensive to
females and young? And could such a selection pattern have led to
extremely powerful, defensive, and dominating males, who then steered
and manipulated females with the same strength and determination
that was originally "meant" to protect them and their young?

Unfortunately, baboon fieldwork at present cannot answer these
questions or shed a clear light on human beginnings. Indeed, there is
conflict about what baboon activities mean for their own species, let
alone for ours. The early primate-observers, K. R. L. Hall, I. DeVore,
S. L. Washburn, and H. Kummer, were all men and came away with
the impression that group cohesiveness was due to male interactions:
threats and short fights, which created an understructure called the
dominance hierarchy. The strongest males were called alpha-males
and were seen as group defenders.

More recently, female observers, such as T. E. Rowell and S. Strum,
among others, have gone baboon watching and come back with the
impression that females and their babies form the understructure of
groups, and males are more transient figures. For instance, in the
"Pumphouse gang" of baboons, watched by Strum, females did not
leave the group, but males did. Their shifts were influenced by the
approach of new males and the maturation of younger males, by bat-

tles, deaths, and, not insignificantly, female acceptance of them as sexual partners, friends, and baby-sitters.

Thelma Rowell found that the baboons she watched preferred forest areas, in a habitat that offered both open grassland and trees. She suggested that the shelter provided by the forest might explain why there was no rigid male hierarchy or placement of males around females and young in the groups she observed. Far from seeking the protection of males, pregnant females took paths away from the group.

People who have hesitated to grant animals a large portion of behavioral flexibility have been surprised to discover that some Old World monkeys are capable of modifying their social structure, including relations between the sexes, according to the physical setting and variations in group composition. Certain savanna baboons can form harems when living in semidesert instead of grassland. In forest, they are more loosely structured than on the plain. Males do not guard females and young in forests as they do on the plain. Hamadryas females can function as members of harems or as independents when they are put in savanna baboon troops. The only bedrock of primate association is that between mother and nursing infant, followed by uneven strata of mother-juvenile and female-female ties. Recognition and knowledge of female hierarchies is just being gained. The ways in which high rank, within and among female lineages, affords fitness advantages have been explored most among species of the next Old World genus to be considered: *Macaca*.

No discussion of Old World monkeys, even one as abbreviated as this, can overlook the macaques. These monkeys have so long been cohabitants with us of Europe, India, and Asia that it is practically impossible to find a totally feral population. As far back as 1938, more than fifteen thousand rhesus macaques were shipped annually to the United States for research. By 1959, fourteen thousand rhesus juveniles were exported from New Delhi each *month*. These have been the primate martyrs of the development of polio vaccine, the discovery of the red blood cell factor Rh (for rhesus), the testing of the birth control pill, and the search for a malaria vaccine. They are truly worthy of their Japanese title, *o-saru-sama*—"very honorable monkey." It is from the macaques that we gain the clearest knowledge of the nonhuman primate female's individuality, perspicacity, and authority.

There are more than a dozen species of macaques and many more subspecies or races, but even geographically well recognized species, such as the Indian rhesus (*Macaca mulatta*) and the Japanese monkey

(*Macaca fuscata*), may not be species in the biological sense: that is, unable to mate with each other and produce fertile young. Linda Wolfe reports that a fertile female hybrid was produced by rhesus and Japanese macaque parents. She had five daughters, one son, and two grandchildren.

Macaques are the most widespread of all Old World monkeys—from the Rock of Gibraltar to the islands of Japan. Surviving on crabs in mangrove swamps, sugi evergreens in the forest, and human handouts and crops near villages and temples, macaques are supreme opportunists and the most worldly-wise ground dwellers next to humans.

Remarkably like the human inhabitants of Japan, the indigenous macaques are always alert to technical breakthroughs and cultural diffusion. The now legendary habits of sweet potato washing and separation of wheat or unhusked rice from sand by throwing the mixture on water, allowing the sand to sink, were both the documented brainchildren of a three-year-old female. The only novel custom I have found that was the inspiration of a male was snowball rolling. In a troop of Japanese macaques, translocated to Oregon, a juvenile male rolled a snowball, and then a high-ranking female did the same. Experimenters have found that female concentration surpasses that of males in tasks like finding peanuts buried in sand.

In Japan all macaque troops live in primate parks where they are provided with some of their food. The Japanese see restriction of the ranges of these monkeys as a fourfold blessing.

a. macaques are prevented from disturbing local cash crops
b. they serve as a tourist attraction and hence a source of money
c. they can be observed in seminatural conditions
d. they can be skimmed, as populations grow, for experiments.

Thus, the sweet potatoes, wheat, rice, and peanuts were all supplied by the humans: the monkeys, especially the females and the young, supplied the wit!

On Gibraltar, the only primate besides man is the Barbary "ape" (*Macaca sylvanus*), which probably would not roam on the Rock if it had not been carried there, as a pet, by Roman soldiers crossing the straits from North Africa. Perhaps it has been the warping effect of accommodating to humanity that exposes modern Barbary macaque females to very unusual treatment by their troop mates. Unlike all other macaques and baboons, they are rejected by and isolated from other troop members during their adolescence. They do not hold and help socialize youngsters because males grab the young. This aberration appears to be very recent. In 1940, Barbary subadult females were observed to be much more involved with infant socialization. Something has happened on Gibraltar, an odd case of female liberation that is probably the result of struggles among individuals to remain fit under changing conditions.

Kuster and Paul observed pregnancy even in lactating Barbary apes. Except for females nursing their firstborn, mothers regularly continue to nurse one baby throughout the 5.5-month gestation of the next. Here a male strategy of killing a nursling to impregnate its mother is unnecessary.

Macaques differ from baboons in the way they court and mate. While female baboons show marked estrous swelling of the perineum, female macaques only swell markedly in adolescence, when they are just beginning to cycle. In Japan, where the mating season extends from December to March, *both* sexes show a reddening of the sexual skin. This is consistent with the fact that there is less dimorphism among macaques than among baboons. Female rhesus macaques weigh about 15 pounds when full-grown, and males weigh about 25 pounds. Females are ready to mate at 3.5 years; males have their first successful matings at about 5.0 years.

While male langurs and baboons are dutiful and attentive when females solicit them for mounting, male macaques sometimes attack estrous females. This *apparently* maladaptive behavior has been seen only in certain free-ranging groups in India and Japan, and in some zoos. Therefore, it has been labeled a "cultural difference." Michael Chance and Clifford Jolly explained the strange habit of males attacking estrous females in London Zoo as retaliation upon females that had "solicited by threatening."

Roberta Kurland made a more perceptive observation about this unusual courtship. She noticed that when estrous females were threatened and attacked by males, their muscles contracted involuntarily and with such force that they expelled the semen and the copulatory plug of mucus inside them from any recent mating. Those males that hit upon the attack-the-estrous-female strategy could be clearing the way for their own sperms, improving their chances of inseminating an egg. No wonder female macaques in the London Zoo "solicited by threatening their *prospective overlords*"! (quote from M. R. A. Chance and C. J. Jolly, 1970, p. 59; emphasis mine)

As among langurs, male-male competition is exaggerated in densely populated areas. So, the rougher male strategies of infanticide and assault courtship are seen in zoo colonies and provisioned troops, such as the Takasakiyama troop, which grew from 220 to 770 members in ten years.

Macaques, like baboons, are jealous mothers. They do not give up their babies easily to other troop members, the way langurs do. Because female macaques are organized in a tight hierarchy, they not only guard their offspring but provide them with a precarved niche in the social order. A Japanese monkey falls into position just below her mother. Any little sisters, interestingly, squeeze in between mother and next highest ranking sibling. In the end, the last is first but still one rung down from mother. Variations of this pattern have been seen in laboratory and semiwild troops, where one offspring may come to outrank its mother. Male offspring will also be influenced by their mother's rank, but they may change troop and therefore enter new hierarchies.

The benefit of high maternal rank has been attributed to many things: a leading mother's connections with other high-ranking members; the model of her demeanor; her tendency to allow her young to play more frequently and further from her than low-ranking mothers; her greater ability to defend her young with effective threats or active attacks. One group of researchers noted that in captivity over a twenty-year period, high-ranking rhesus mothers produced more daughters than low-ranking mothers. This may be a reflection of female reproductive competition in rhesus troops. Females other than the high-rankers may pass more genes to the grandchild generation through sons than through daughters, if upon leaving the troop the sons produce more offspring than the daughters, who remain low-rankers in the natal troop. No one knows how skewing toward one sex is achieved.

The protectiveness of macaque mothers carries through as a disregard of orphaned young. Females devote themselves exclusively to their own young; they will not adopt. If anyone cares for an orphan or just-weaned juvenile, whose mother is busy with a new baby, it is a subadult sister, brother, or elder male. Adoption customs vary from species to species and troop to troop. Judith Breuggman, who studied free-ranging rhesus macaques in India, found it was not unusual for an old male to care for a one- or two-year-old female and later begin to treat her more like a consort and demand grooming from her, an echo of the adoptive tactic of the hamadryas harem-master.

Macaque troop formation in the wild resembles that of the savanna baboons. At the center of the group are females with new babies, weaned yearlings, and juvenile females. In a schematic drawing of Japanese monkey troop formation, Imanishi shows the word "LEADERS" and below it "ADULT ♀ ♀" (adult females). It is assumed that the reader will understand "LEADERS" to mean dominant males. This 1957 view of things has changed, and primatologists have shown that male proximity to females with young at the core of a troop has less to do with leadership of the troop than with the forbearance of high-ranking females. Even Imanishi admits, "it is necessary for males to be accepted by females, especially by dominant females, in order to enter the central part [of the troop] from outside."

The core males are the ones most likely to take over care of juveniles when they are weaned. Perhaps females make sure that their "LEADERS" have fostering qualities. According to the observations of John and Roberta Kurland, the female Japanese macaques of Kaminyu seem to cooperate in choosing resident males. Females resist males entering the feeding ground and sometimes even evict resident males. The latter change troop about every two years, a periodicity similar to that of Hanuman langur husbands. The Kurlands conclude, "female alliances may, in effect, screen out the potentially superior males" (that is, choose the best ones).

It is still debated whether core males, as compared to solitary, young, or subordinate males on the periphery, always have first privilege with estrous females. While females try to share their favors fairly, even visiting the edges of a troop to do so, some males (perhaps the older, more experienced ones) seem to recognize the high point of estrus. Possibly by assessing a female's behavior, odor, or, in the case of adolescent females, swelling, the "clever" male mates just when fertilization is most likely.

While females remain in the center of their natal troop, males drift to the edges as a matter of course. Some males come back to the center of the troop as they mature and replace their elders; others remain solitary, and others enter neighboring troops. Rarely, the son of a high-ranking female may remain at the center and never experience contests for power. The only fluctuations of female position, in contrast, are within the core area—high-rankers at the center, low-rankers slightly off center. Female macaques may grow old in their own troops and, in the case of rhesus, even experience menopause at about age twenty-eight.

For other female anthropoids, troop life was to be transmuted. Ancestors of the apes evolved and came to occupy a wide range of habitats that required different relationships between the sexes. Modern species of apes can be found in various relationships with males, some of which we have already encountered: monogamy, harem, solitary, and diffuse, or variable. The first apelike creatures came swinging through the apparently secure simian empire in the trees thirty million years ago. With arms and hands specialized for quadrupedal locomotion on the ground, as well as brachiation in the trees, the early apes could feast on grasses, roots, seeds, *and* fruits. New resources permitted the ever-present selective pressure for large size to operate, and apes made the quantum leap in size past the monkeys, as the monkeys had once passed the prosimians.

Gibbons and siamangs, long-armed inhabitants of India, southern China, southeast Asia, Borneo, and Sumatra, are the best brachiators of all the apes and probably of the entire primate order. Only spider monkeys can approach the rapid brachiation of the lesser apes, so called because of their small size compared to chimpanzees, gorillas, and orangutans. The gibbons (species of *Hylobates*) and siamangs (*Symphalangus*) form a separate family, seen as a "link" between the Old World monkeys and the great apes.

While the lesser apes spend their lives in the highest, slenderest branches of 100-foot-tall trees, they still share some outstanding similarities with humans. First, they are habitually erect; that is, they hang and sit upright. Second, they are monogamous, the way humans sometimes are. While human couples are estimated to be monogamous 20 to 50 percent of the time, lesser ape couples are always monogamous. They live in small, stable families—no circle of aunts as among langurs, no fostering male "leaders" as among baboons and macaques—just mother, father, and children (usually an infant and a juvenile or subadult of six or more years). Third, a female and male usually share baby-carrying and cuddling responsibilities with each other, not with subadults of either sex. In fact, gibbon and siamang parents "encourage" their subadult progeny to move away from the family unit, just the way human parents may encourage young adult offspring to get a job or get married. Ejecting adolescents ensures that density will remain low, families small, and resources adequate.

In addition, there are a few anatomical coincidences between lesser apes and humans. Gibbons, siamangs, and humans all retain the labia majora. Although this feature develops in all apes and humans during fetal life, it persists into adult life only in the lesser apes and humans. Oddly, the lesser apes and humans do not show marked enlargement of the perineum during ovulation, while chimpanzees, regarded as our closest primate relatives, usually show striking estrous swelling.

We also share with the hylobatid apes a flatter facial profile than that of the great apes, probably due to the reduction of jaw size. This, in turn, causes humans and gibbons to have similar dental problems: crowded, twisted, or impacted teeth, and the occasional congenital absence of the last molars (wisdom teeth), especially in females.

In perfecting brachiation, lesser apes were able to move into an exclusive niche of the forest: the upper canopy. Here groups, shielded by foliage, sing loudly to their unseen neighbors. Every morning, vigorous choral and acrobatic displays establish each family's possession of about a tenth of a square mile of forest.

Among the white-handed gibbons (*Hylobates lar*), it is the female that gives the morning "great call" (an elaborate song specific to each species), after an overture of wailing hoots from her male. While in most species the male produces the dawn reveille, male-female duets and whole-family choruses take place at intervals throughout the morning or every few days, according to species. Juveniles learn the great call at their mother's knee, and it has been observed that younger couples are not as synchronized in their duets as longer-mated pairs.

Siamang females use their inflatable, pink throat pouch to resonate and amplify their song. Males do the same and also produce shattering booms and screams that punctuate the female's bark-chatter at its crescendo. The interwoven calls of the two sexes can express alarm, define territory, and embellish border confrontations with other families. The calling increases with food availability, dry season reproductive activity, and environmental disturbances like human timber felling.

Cooperative vocalizing is so much a part of gibbon and siamang life that lone captive females will try to reproduce the male part of the calling sequence. Elliott Haimoff suggested one possible explanation for this. When widowed, a wild gibbon with an infant was heard trying to sing her dead mate's song. Perhaps this imperfect rendition prevented another male from joining her and possibly killing her offspring. Adding strength to this hypothesis is the fact that a widowed female *without a baby* gave only her part of the duet call, possibly allowing the absence of the male part of the song to signify that she was at liberty and her territory could be safely entered by a male.

During the mating season, subadults advertise their increasing separation from their families by singing loudly on their own. Young females find young males and start new families. The "married" pair become more dependent upon each other than most other couples in the mammalian class. They eat in the same tree all day long and sleep in the same tree at night. Sharing of all activities, including baby carrying and adolescent shooing, is reflected in the minimal physical dimorphism of the sexes. Both sexes are similar in size and in dentition, including the extra-long canines typical of the lesser apes. In fact, the diminished dental dimorphism of gibbons can only be compared with that of modern humans.

As in other egalitarian or female-dominant species, such as the spider monkey and the spotted hyena, certain gibbons (such as *Hylobates hoolock*) mimic the male in genital form. Therefore the Hoolock gibbon sexes are best distinguished by coat color, males being dark brown and females lightening to yellow-brown at puberty (six to seven years). Coat color is not, however, a reliable way to sex most other lesser apes, as their hue varies with age from dark brown or black to golden. Gibbons are usually some shade of brown or gold, and all siamangs are black.

Both sexes share the ability to eat while suspended and to reach for foods at the tips of branches. Terminal branch foods include new leaf shoots, flowers, and buds. The bulk of the diet is fruit and leaves, with figs, mangoes, grapes, and plums generally taken in the morning and vine leaves in the afternoon. Occasional bird's eggs, caterpillars, and termites provide protein. Although fruit trees are shared by a couple and their offspring, each gathers food independently, and there is no need for exchange. No member feeds any other, except, of course, the lactating mother.

One thing mated siamangs (*Symphalangus syndactylus*) do not share equally is leadership of the family. The adult female almost always leads, and if another member takes up a new direction, she races forward to assume the lead or to follow closely. When she wants everyone to proceed to a new spot, she moves several yards away from them, looks toward another part of the forest, and then back at the others. No one knows why female siamangs consistently lead their families (gibbon [*Hylobates lar*] couples often share group leadership), but it is a demanding role, especially during pregnancy or lactation. It has been suggested that this role is one reason females eat faster and for about thirty minutes longer each day than males. They need extra food, in spite of the fact that males weigh slightly more. Both sexes of siamang weigh about twenty-five pounds, and gibbons about half as much.

Female siamang leadership may indirectly dictate that the adult male carry the weaned or almost weaned infant. His position at the center of the group, between the female and the juvenile or subadult, is safer than hers. Of course, this would not explain why females lead even when they are carrying the baby, during its first nine months.

Females are not necessarily pregnant or nursing a new infant when males begin to carry the weanling. In this respect, the lesser apes differ from Japanese macaques, in which males tend juveniles only when females are nursing new young. While the female siamang may continue to night nurse the juvenile until it is eighteen months old, the male carries the youngster during the day, from the time it is about nine months until about three years of age. For most of this period, the male is just a part-time carrier, and by two years of age the juvenile needs assistance only for the boldest crossings.

Although the life cycle of gibbons and siamangs is not well known, it seems they mate infrequently—only during several months every three years—in spite of the female's twenty-eight-day cycle year-round. In their abstemious sex lives, lesser apes resemble the other monogamous, arboreal primates: marmosets and tamarins. They seem to use abstinence, both during and after the lactation period, to ensure birth spacing of at least two to three years. This helps budget resources and makes baby care easier. But the longer birth interval and private living arrangements of lesser ape families mean juveniles are isolated from playmates. The older sibling begins to detach from the family just when the juvenile is ready to start frolicking confidently among the branches.

Safety of infants and juveniles must be the overriding pressure in gibbon-siamang life, considering the speed of their locomotion and the height of their habitat. According to Sarel Eimerl and Irven DeVore, in *The Primates*, a gibbon can pluck a bird out of the air in midjump without breaking pace. In order to stay stuck to each other through this kind of action, both mother and baby must be very skillful. The skill of clinging to their mother's fur is highly developed in lesser ape young. (Reflex clinging is also seen in other primates, including humans. The human baby's grip is strong enough after birth to permit it to hang from a bar without support, but the reflex is lost after three or four weeks of age. Many think it is a vestige of our arboreal past.)

Gibbon authority J. O. Ellefson says, "clinging is greatly facilitated by the density and structure of gibbon fur. It is my contention that the long, dense fur of the gibbon was selected for by the pattern of early clinging by a very underdeveloped neonate." The importance of fur for baby survival means that a mutation for loss of fur could have grounded our arboreal forebears. No matter how good a brachiator she was or how well her baby could cling, a naked or partly naked ape would not win any fitness contests in the trees. Her infant would soon lose its grip and fall. While loss of body pelage is thought to postdate our descent ("fall"?) from the trees, if it were the other way around, then females with their babies (soon followed by the males) would have been forced to descend.

Something like this may be happening to the near-extinct orangutan. Orangutans' orange fur is scraggly and falls out in patches; it is inadequate for a baby to cling to, so a mother must constantly support and shift it. Orangutans usually move slowly through the trees, and so can handle their babies carefully, but if trying to escape human harassment, they may easily lose their grip on an infant. Barbara Harrisson reported two cases of a mother orangutan dropping her infant when startled by the gunfire of men hunting wild pig.

Although I would not want to lay too much stress on the point of our ancestors of thirty million years ago having been somewhat like gibbons in form and behavior, I suppose that I have unexpectedly found my pet model for our progenitor. Grounded for lack of fur, walking erect with her too-long arms wrapped around her baby, a gibbonlike ancestor would have found her habits of fruit eating and sharing baby protection with a male helpful in the new terrain. Abundant new food in the form of grass seeds could have been gathered as she sat on her toughened posterior and her long arms described a conveniently wide circle for foraging. In fact, seed eating as a hypothetical stage in human evolution was proposed by Clifford Jolly, who visualized a gelada-type ancestor.

(Incidentally, Bornean native lore has it the other way around: something like a gibbon did not come to the ground and turn into a human, but a human took to the trees and became a gibbon! The folk explanation for this retreat to the trees tells that a person was making a fire, none too skillfully. With hands and face all covered in soot, the disgraced one sought shelter in the high branches and wailed mournfully for shame. This explains how the gibbon got its black face and hands and loud, sad song.)

It is really no obstacle that the brain of a gibbon-type ancestor was rather small and its intelligence no greater than a monkey's (which, in my opinion, is far from minimal). Intelligence and brain expansion arrived late on the scene, about twenty-five million years *after* our arboreal ancestor was grounded. As anatomist John Fleagle says of our four-million-year-old ancestor "Lucy" (the most complete australopithecine skeleton ever found): "[She] had a brain that was no bigger than an orange."

The last point that elevates the lesser apes to ancestor candidacy for me is their complex duetting. What better preadaptation for speech than the learning of songs from mother! Also, the vocal cords and larynx of gibbons and siamangs strongly resemble our own. Still, it *is* a long way from a stereotyped song to verbal communication, and as A. F. Dixon wisely warns, "it is not advisable to treat any [single primate species] as a prototype ancestor."

Asserting the shape and habits of our apelike ancestors leaves one on spongy ground that sinks with contradiction at every step. For example, orangutans (*Pongo pygmeus*), the other southeast Asian apes, whose devoted observer John MacKinnon nominates as "the best ape ancestor for man," are extremely intelligent but very solitary. This does not fit the usual picture of the gregarious anthropoid ancestor. In fact, orangutans do not seem to regularly form pair-bonds, in spite of having the longest period of infant dependency apart from our own.

The orangutan not only appears not to want or need a husband, she does not even want female friends. This is particularly true in Borneo, but in Sumatra there is more sociality and a truncated form of monogamy. MacKinnon, who studied orangutans both in Borneo and Sumatra, attributes this to a difference in predation. He suggests that Sumatran orangutans hang together more often than their Bornean relatives because Sumatra is the home of tigers, panthers, and aggressive families of siamangs. He reports that Sumatran orangs signal each other with "squeaks, grunts, or loud *lork* calls" if a predator approaches.

No one knows for sure whether the shyness of orangutans is an ancient or modern condition. Some theorize that competition with people has made orangutans melancholy and antisocial. Certainly solitariness as a feature of adult females is remarkable among higher primates. Only siamangs and gibbons show this trait, but they, after all, each have a loyal, helpful husband.

MacKinnon believes that solitariness is an old characteristic and social contacts, as between Sumatran consorts, are recent accommodations to local conditions. The orangutan, he maintains, prefers her own company because she is a large animal dependent on an erratic food source: ripe fruit. The female weighs about 88 pounds, and the male about 165 pounds. Both need a lot of food, and that means they require a private domain of fruit. However, when one part of the forest comes into abundant fruit, especially in Sumatra, several adults may feed in the same area, but it would be most unusual for more than one male to be in the company.

Another solution to the food requirements of orangutans is nomadism. Adults of either sex that do not find or successfully defend a territory may move continually through the territories of others. In either case, nomad or property holder, the individual tries to remain solitary to survive.

Great intelligence is required for solitary survival. An orangutan must know her territory and remember the pattern of fruiting for approximately five hundred different species of trees. MacKinnon believes it is within the orangutan's capacity to remember which trees are seen with immature fruit and accurately estimate the time of ripening. There are no other troop members to follow, so she must be quick to employ cues from other fruit-eaters, such as the hornbill and various pigeons, monkeys, and gibbons. Observation, memory, foresight, and possibly mental maps allow the orangutan, whose fruit needs are three to six times that of a gibbon, to exist in one-quarter the territory secured by a gibbon family.

The size of the adult male orangutan, almost twice that of a female, has been a prime factor in spacing out the species, because they tax the middle-canopy niche to its limit. But why are the males so large? Why are they so visibly different in form from the females?

The extra size of orangutan males and their fearsome features, which include enormous flattened jowls, an even longer beard than females have, and a huge throat sac that resonates their long call, probably helped them compete with each other for females. However, too little consideration has been given to the idea that larger males were fitter because they could battle females into sexual submission. The four-to-seven-year period of infant-juvenile care may be the reason why females have been seen, both in the wild and in zoos, strongly resisting intercourse. Another pregnancy might endanger their enormous investment in an existing offspring.

It was the combination of fruit eating and large size, necessitating broad ranges, that forced the orangutan species to take the precarious turn toward solitariness. The addition of the triple curse of human curiosity, chauvinism, and competition soon turned what was once a bold and successful creation of nature—large, enemy-free primates, with enough acumen to support an energy-costly life of swinging their great bulk from branch to branch—into the remnant of today.

Still, it is important to study the orangutan in details because she, along with the chimpanzee and gorilla, shares with us the profits and problems of intense mothering. Although orangutan mothering may have brought great intelligence to the species, it has brought an incredible burden to each female. She, like the woman, must gestate for eight to nine months and then go through a long, painful labor. But, in addition, the orangutan mother must carry her infant daily through the trees for *four* years. She nurses steadily until the baby begins to move away from her in its fourth year, and she may continue to suckle it part-time until weaning at age *seven*.

These remarkable facts were recorded by Biruté Galdikas, who with her husband, Rod Brindamoor, accumulated twelve thousand observation hours of wild and partially forest-rehabilitated orangutans during nine years in southern Borneo. Until Galdikas undertook her long-term study, information about basic female orangutan patterns was ambiguous. Like Barbara Harrisson, Galdikas tried to implement a practical apology from our species to the orangutan by rescuing babies, which had been kept as pets or in bad zoos, and gradually accommodating them to the rain forest.

It was found that, apart from occasional short consortships of up to ten days, a female orangutan is on her own. No male helps her carry the youngster; no friends or relatives are around for grooming comfort or advice. No one but she builds the night nest.

Not only does the orangutan nurse and carry her infant up to the fourth year of its life, not only does she build sleeping nests and defend against harassing siamangs and leopards, she acquaints her baby with the foods of the forest and trains it to hang freely and move independently. She teaches it the safe pathways through the trees, the reliability and elasticity of different branches and vines. The juvenile follows her precisely through the forest, branch for branch, and sleeps in and uses her nests as models for its own. (Note, sleeping nests are not the same as nests built to leave nestlings in.) The orangutan must convey to her young which species of tree to use for nests, the way to bend and break branches for support and leaves for comfort and protection from rain.

Zoos report that orangutans educate their young to hang securely by holding them around the waist with one arm and placing the infant's hands and feet around the bars of the cage. They may leave a baby alone on the floor of the cage, knowing it will try to approach and thus learn to move independently. They feed their infants premasticated food, and in the wild, continue to share foods with their weanlings. Orangutan mothers also clean the baby's fur with water or urine, groom its coat by hand, and bite its fingernails and toenails short. Cleanliness may also be the aim when zoo mothers allow their babies to dangle freely from the bars. Frightened, the infant screams and defecates. If this procedure is followed by an immediate rescue and cuddle, a very useful conditioned reflex can be established, keeping both mother and infant cleaner.

The mother orangutan in the wild has little energy left to play with her baby. Finding her daily food, carrying the infant, nursing, and nest building make her very tired. She can rarely engage in more than a brief tickle with her youngster. Few orangutan young have a sibling playmate, and usually there is no adult male around. (The orangutans of Sumatra are exceptions, and a young adult male may travel for months at a time with a female and the offspring.) So, in spite of the high level of maternal care, orangutan young are isolated. If their mothers happen to be feeding in the same part of the forest during a time of plenty, youngsters will race to each other for maximum contact and play, although the females will ignore each other. MacKinnon believes that "unused to making friendly social relationships, orang-utans grow up to be shy, solitary, antisocial adults."

An orangutan is not fully grown at age seven, but she may be impregnated from about that time. She is free in the forest for only a short period before her life of constant motherhood begins. Contrary to the estimates of birth intervals at two to three years by David Agee Horr and John MacKinnon, and a later estimate of three to four years by MacKinnon, Galdikas, whose study continues, found the interval to be eight to nine years. It must be emphasized, however, that birth spacing can be altered by environment. In the part of his study range that was adjacent to timbering operations, MacKinnon extrapolated an eight-year birth interval from the numbers of females seen with infants. In contrast, an area of the range that was "totally undisturbed by man" produced a mean birth interval of about three years.

Shorter birth intervals and almost continuous female receptivity are observed in zoo orangutans. There can be many different reasons for this: abundant food, higher fat portion in the body weight, more contact with males, even artificial insemination. But one factor frequently overlooked is light.

When the orangutan is taken out of her shady jungle and put into a well-lit cage, something happens to her ovaries. It seems that the pineal gland, at the center of the brain, inhibits ovarian activity so long as it is not exposed to too much light, but when it picks up stimulation from increased light exposure, under artificial conditions, it ceases to inhibit the ovaries and mating begins.

An increase in exposure to light is also partly responsible for the springtime courtship urge in land mammals of temperate and arctic latitudes. As days lengthen in spring, the pineal inhibition of the ovaries is overcome. Eskimos once vividly illustrated the courtship urge brought on by increased daylength. During Perry's expedition to the North Pole in 1894, Dr. Cook noted that menstrual cycles and sexual desire, interrupted during the four months of winter night, returned with spring and its accompanying light (and possibly better diet).

In lush equatorial zones there is less seasonal variation in daylight (and in resources), and variation in moonlight may set up a monthly rhythm. Thus, equatorial mammals are more likely to be polyestrous, and mammals in higher latitudes monestrous, with an annual rather than a monthly cycle. Just as increased light for captive orangutans may mimic conditions causing spring disinhibition of ovaries and sexual drive, so the move of our ape ancestors from forest to open grassland may have increased light exposure and changed their sex life to a more active one twenty-five to thirty million years ago.

Galdikas' study in Borneo and laboratory studies in Yerkes Primate Center in Atlanta, Georgia, show that there is a midcycle change in female orangutan behavior, which amounts to an estrus around the time of ovulation. This approximately ten-day period of "heat" is surrounded by neutral days, completing a twenty-five-day menstrual cycle. At most times in her life, a female is pregnant or lactating and carrying an infant, so she is probably acyclic most of the time. This explains the female orangutan's almost uniform lack of interest in sex and her inclination to leave a tree that is approached by an adult male.

During the midcycle heat, however, the normally shy female may answer a male's call, approach, and sometimes try to groom him.

As Galdikas describes it, estrus is an out-of-character experience for one of the females in her study area:

> Beth had always been a mild, retiring individual. . . . Yet here she was moving right up to Ralph, shaking a vine in his face, slapping his stomach, and tweaking a certain part of his anatomy. . . . He did not react but stared and stared. When he finally moved, she followed. . . . Beth and Ralph consorted for ten days and mated several times, each time seemingly at Beth's instigation.

In Sumatra this type of consortship characterized all young orangutan couples, with and without babies. MacKinnon sees the female's extended (or sham?) receptivity in these pairings as a strategy that holds the presumably protective male near her in this dangerous habitat.

Ironically, the future looks bleakest for these primates who so resemble people in their extreme maternalness, high intelligence, sparse hair, and ability to walk erect on the ground. The hope of habituating illegally captured babies to the forest, while enormously noble, cannot revive this species if its habitat disappears. Since human population and mercantile logging are not declining in the orangutans' part of the world, it would take an act of superior imagination (and limitless money) for humans to carve a new niche for the orangutan. Maybe there could be a place for orangutans, no longer as "people of the forest," as their Malay name denotes, but as primates given the chance to explore and use their intelligence in a new setting. This might happen were they to acquire, and later transmit to each other, a human language, for orangutans learn signs as fast as chimpanzees and gorillas. The intelligence of orangutans is not unexpected, however, when the pressures of food finding and mothering are considered as selectors for association and memory.

Language, of course, is not just a possible means of forestalling orangutan extinction. It is the keystone of self-identification and self-consciousness necessary to survival for all primates. (The first chimpanzee to learn American Sign Language for the Deaf, when asked whom she saw when she looked in a mirror, replied, "Me, Washoe.") As it is virtually the exclusive responsibility of the mother to help her child simulate a self, communication has probably been the domain principally of female primates for the past twenty-five million years. By this view, human language, both gestural and vocal, would have its roots in the Miocene, with the appearance of the open-ground, woodland apes. Perhaps this is one reason *female* apes were chosen by researchers to be the first nonhuman subjects to learn to speak through sign.

The female gorilla Koko was thirteen months old when Penny Patterson began to teach her to speak, using the hand signs of American Sign Language for the Deaf (Ameslan). With several assistants, she trained and cared for the infant gorilla at Stanford University, California. In six years, Koko learned 375 signs and used them to express her needs and emotions. In so doing she joined the ranks of the other pongid pioneers—chimpanzees Washoe, Lucy, Sarah, and Lana, and orangutan Rinnie—who also learned to communicate with humans.

Seven-year-old Koko was able to define objects; she explained that a stove is to cook with and an orange is a "food, drink." She remembered events and correctly ordered them in time, using words like "first," "then," and "later." Koko saw a picture of the albino gorilla, Snowflake, resisting a bath and said, "Me cry there," meaning she hated to be bathed too. She saw a Pinocchio doll and dubbed it an "elephant baby," and she signed to her young, male gorilla companion, who was not yet as adept at signing as she, to encourage him to find the words that would make his human teacher release him for a play session: "Do visit Mike hurry, Mike think hurry."

Now at age thirteen, Koko understands some one thousand Ameslan signs. She regularly uses more than five hundred of them to express her needs and feelings. She said "Love that" when shown a litter of kittens and laughingly signs "obnoxious" when her pet kitten nips. Language is not forced into the young gorillas' behavior repertoire by massive doses of stereotyped rewards because once they experience the insight of the connection between object, feeling, or idea and sign, language becomes its own reward. Koko will even sign to herself when she is alone, thinking or looking at pictures. She and Michael sign to each other. Someday they may try to communicate to their offspring.

Why don't gorillas in the wild make signs for objects, feelings, and ideas? The answer to that question might be given by paraphrasing Booth Tarkington's deceptively simple statement: "Man could always fly, he just did not know how." That is to say, gorillas could always sign, they just did not know how. Or they just did not know how in a way that humans could understand!

How deep the preadaptive stream of language runs in the great apes can only be measured when it is known if they continue to use language for long periods away from human contact; if they continue to invent and add to their vocabularies; and if they teach language to their young.

In the wild, gorillas make about twenty different vocalizations. Of these, George B. Schaller reports that eight are used frequently and can be associated with particular activities—the soft grunting of contentment while feeding; the staccato grunt of annoyance; the harsh bark and scream of a quarrel; and the screech of an infant in danger. In his exhaustive survey entitled *The Mountain Gorilla*, Schaller states that "females emitted the largest variety of sounds, and the panting *ho-ho-ho* during their own displays appeared to be peculiar to them alone."

Another sound that all gorillas make is the hollow *pok-pok* produced by chest beating. This sound is the result of resonance from inflated laryngeal sacs, which are unusually developed in gorillas, extending up into the neck and down between the upper chest wall and rib cage to the armpits. (All other apes, except gibbons, also have inflatable laryngeal sacs, which are used to resonate their loud calls. People have two crypts in the larynx, which are vestiges of the laryngeal pouches.)

Both sexes may chest beat to intimidate other individuals: another group, a lone male, or a human observer. This aim is sometimes further accomplished by jumping down from a display position, usually a stump or log, charging toward the intruder, uprooting and throwing vegetation along the way. Without pursuing an attack to kill or maim, the male gorilla may strike and seriously wound any animal that stands in its path. The female's display is shorter and less furious than the male's. Her resonating pouches are smaller, and, therefore, the sound she produces does not carry so far.

Expressive as the chest-beating routine is, it is not linguistic communication. It is not even learned; gorilla infants in zoos will chest beat without ever having seen an adult do so. The only thing that young gorillas learn about the chest-beating display is to avoid the vicinity of performing adults.

In neither his thorough monograph nor his popular book, *The Year of the Gorilla*, does Schaller indicate that mother gorillas teach their offspring any element of vocal communication. In fact, the only examples that might be construed as direct teaching of anything were the removal of inappropriate food items: an unpalatable leaf, a flower, a piece of dung.

And yet gorilla infant and mother do communicate vocally. The earliest mewlings of the infant, combined with its rooting reflex, signal to the mother that the baby needs to be positioned so it can reach the breast. Under three years of age the infant expects to be carried by its mother, and if she moves too far away, its scream will halt her or even make her turn around. Dian Fossey, who so understood and used the gestural language of gorillas that she eventually achieved acceptance into their community, observed a mother vocalizing to her child. A dominant group member had harassed the mother, who then turned to her little one, grumbled, mock-bit, and pushed it off her back.

While there is vocal interaction between mother and young, there is nothing reported about communication in wild gorillas that would predict their striking ability to learn highly specific and grammatical language from human teachers. Also there is nothing in the apparently incurious behavior of gorillas in the wild that would indicate they could be alert and responsive to human requirements. However, Colin Groves's record of a young male gorilla raised by Alyse Cunningham in London from 1918 to 1921, does suggest this. One day, when Alyse wore a light dress, she prevented her ward from climbing up into her lap. Like a human child denied access to its mother, he fell upon the floor and began to scream. When his tantrum subsided, he fetched a newspaper, put it on Alyse's lap, and climbed up!

It may be inferred that the lack of varied vocal signals and gestural communication in wild gorilla groups and the absence of tool using is a consequence of the safety of their position and the easy satisfaction of their needs. Before the recent appearance of man as a gorilla hunter— for meat, trophy, zoo, and museum—the gorilla was unchallenged in the rain forests and bamboo-covered mountainsides of central Africa. Only the leopard can be regarded as a natural predator, and its attacks are infrequent. Food is at hand, never cooperatively stalked or vociferously guarded. So it is in nearly complete silence that the group pursues its eating, resting, sunbathing, and walking. And it is silently that a young gorilla learns, by imitating mother, to choose foods and prepare sleeping nests.

Baby gorillas not only learn which foods to eat, they learn how to eat them. Bark must be stripped with a mincing nibble, pith extracted from stems, and *Galium* vines wadded for easy chewing. That infants do closely watch their mothers and other adults was shown by the baby that pulled down a female's lower lip and removed a piece of *Galium* from her mouth in order to eat it. Gorillas also eat wild celery, goose grass, musk thistle, bamboo shoots, and wood nettle, but never have any of the three gorilla subspecies been seen eating meat in the wild.

A group usually consists of five to ten members, about 40 percent adult females and 60 percent infants, juveniles, adolescents, and adult males. Adult females outnumber adult males, but there is always one elder, silverback male directing the movements of the group. Some units have more than one silverback, but only one is the acknowledged leader. Because of their tendency to gray later and less than males, females are more difficult to classify by age.

As the male-female ratio is roughly equal at birth, the excess of females in the group is probably matched by an excess of males wandering between groups. These lone males occasionally join groups for short spells, or permanently, if they are still blackbacks under ten years of age. But lone silverbacks are males without females or young, and they may be a source of great danger to the established group. Dian Fossey records three instances of lone silverbacks killing infants while attacking and apparently trying to take over their mother's group.

In contrast, young females can change their allegiance to males peacefully, transfer usually occurring when two groups are in the same area. These meetings are fraught with tension, expressed in repeated chest-beating displays. There is the quality of a grudging wedding ceremony between two feuding villages. A. H. Harcourt noted that there were aggressive interactions between males in ten out of twelve female transfers, and that the young females that change group usually have not yet been pregnant. They are the precious daughters taking the genes of their parents to new ranges.

Sometimes a young female will join a lone silverback in a peaceful fashion, and they will begin a new clan. Sometimes a group of females with infants, juveniles, and adolescent blackback males will find itself without a leader due to disease or predation. They may join another clan. All in all, female movement accounts for more of the changes in group membership than does male movement.

While females are mobile when young and nulliparous (not yet having had a baby), it seems that they finally settle down permanently with one male and form the stable core of a stable clan. The gorilla harem seems to be a reliable structure in which the young can grow and form attachments to members they have known from infancy until they may depart to fulfill adult roles. Thus, for seven to twelve years, offspring mature in close contact not only with their mothers and siblings, which are spaced at approximately four-year intervals, but with the patient and protective silverback.

While older juveniles of both sexes cavort with infants and youngsters, adult females take little interest in each other's young. There was one remarkable exception to this generalization. Schaller observed a "kindly, old female" who played with a six-month-old male and even let him suckle on her dry breast. She may well have been his grandmother. Her patience and evident enjoyment as the infant lay on his back on her belly, playing with her hand and kicking his arms and legs, seemed very much like the patience and joy of a human grandparent. This is the sort of confidence and pleasure that female and young can experience only in secure groups.

In spite of the fact that gorilla groups are safe and peaceful compared to some other primate societies, there is still a high infant mortality rate: 25 percent in the first year of life. In the span to six years of age, 40 to 50 percent of the youngsters die from disease, accident, or attack by lone males. Normally this high death rate could be offset by the infrequent but efficient mating of adults at or around the time of monthly ovulation; but human poaching has made population stabilization impossible.

Although gorillas do not have large sexual skin swellings to announce their estrus, they do emit strong signals of their receptive state. Axillary and genital odors change, and all group members, especially juveniles, show intense interest in the estrous female and in copulation. During the three- to six-day preestrous and estrous period, females walk past silverbacks, giving them long, languid stares and presenting. They may even grab and fondle the male.

If females are denied access to males, as they may be in captivity, their sexual energy may be channeled toward each other or into masturbation. Adult females housed together and, therefore, free of pregnancy and the responsibilities of baby care, have been observed in long bouts of lovemaking and play. Such behaviors are virtually unknown among adult wild gorillas seen to date.

Heterosexual intercourse often continues after pregnancy and, in captivity, has been observed to run up to the week before birth. Could the estrous behavior and labial swelling that occur at intervals during early pregnancy be part of a complex of traits selected to protect unborn offspring from roaming silverbacks? Sometimes during her first pregnancy, a gorilla is taken by a roaming silverback or transfers to another group; her receptivity may protect her fetus.

From conception through approximately 260 days of gestation, to the end of lactation, a period of roughly four years, the female will be devoted to her youngster. After the baby reaches three years of age, the female is fertile and regularly receptive again. Even if she becomes pregnant, she generally maintains close contact with her juvenile through its sixth year. By age seven her daughter experiences her first periods of fertility, but she does not normally conceive until nine or ten.

It is only after age nine that the characteristic size disparity between the sexes becomes apparent. Males undergo a growth spurt that leaves them twice the weight of same-age females. They exceed females by about 20 percent in height, girth, and arm length. Why gorillas are so sexually dimorphic is difficult to say. Both sexes eat the same abundant forage, follow the same routines from sunup to sundown, and the female, although smaller, almost exclusively carries the baby for its first three years on her belly and back.

The great size and distinctive appearance of the silverback and his resonant chest pounding have been seen to function in group protection. He is one of the big-mother-males of our order, and to some extent his females are also his children. It is their certainty of his superior strength that enables him to quiet them when they are angry with each other. His power, paternally and benevolently disposed, keeps the females and young clinging to him. Fossey observed one silverback that adopted and mothered an orphaned three-year-old female. At night she slept in his ground nest, as she would have slept in her mother's. He groomed and cuddled her and was even more restrictive of her play than a natural mother would have been.

Mothering is equally important among chimpanzees (*Pan troglodytes*; *Pan paniscus*), and yet they have not developed big-mother-males or harem-style groups. Chimpanzee males "mother" neither juveniles nor adult females, but they do show gentle handling of both from time to time. A male may single out a female and baby to accompany for days or weeks, but this is unusual. Males normally keep male company, and females keep with their offspring.

The nuclear family of female plus young is the only consistently long-lasting unit in chimpanzee society. Other extended associations may include pairs of adult brothers, an older and a younger sibling (sometimes in the form of an adoption), an estrous female and her consort, and sometimes two mothers with their children. None of these associations is as constant or lasts as long as the mother-child tie.

While chimpanzees are occupied for at least four years with each of their youngsters, the males have no paternal responsibilities. They are free to forage, groom each other, indulge in knee-jerk sex (see p. 248) with the estrous female(s) of the moment, patrol the borders of the range, and give vent to flashes of rage or exuberance. Adolescent females of ten to thirteen years and young adult females without babies often travel with males on border patrols and in hunting parties. They are given meat by male hunters, but rarely make a kill themselves. In Gombe Stream, Tanzania, the chimpanzee study area established by Jane Goodall, only two out of ninety-seven kills observed from 1960 to 1970 were made by females. Two females simultaneously killed a bush pig each, and did not share their quarry with each other or call out and stamp on the ground to attract other community members. Ordinarily, after males have killed, their excited screaming brings others to the site to share. Mothers and infants approach, but estrous females are most successful in obtaining pieces of the prey. One feast, attended by fifteen, lasted for nine hours.

In contrast, females share their gathered insect and vegetable foods only with their young. Females strip and shorten grass-wand and twig tools to extract ants and termites, and they may also make sophisticated use of the springy quality of saplings to create comfortable perches from which to fish. Sitting above her chosen anthill on her sapling bench, the chimpanzee cannot be bitten by any spilled ants.

In contrast, males do not use tools during the hunt. In over one hundred instances of predation seen at Gombe Stream, tool use was observed only once. A male threw a stone at a group of bush pigs so that they fled, leaving a defenseless piglet behind. William McGrew, who measured and compared the foraging methods of male and female chimpanzees, came to the conclusion that females use tools more often and longer than males.

McGrew sees gathering as providing the bulk of nutrition for both chimpanzee sexes and speculates "that [early human] tool-use originated in solitary female-foraging activities rather than cooperative male hunting." More evidence for this view comes from the Tai National Park in the Ivory Coast, where researchers from Zurich University found females using heavy sticks or stones to break open hard-shelled panda and coula nuts nine times more often than males. The researchers suggest that the nonhunting female had to invent increasingly elaborate methods of tool use to acquire necessary protein. Like McGrew, they believe females must be considered the main tool users in species that evolved into man. Of course, this view opposes the prevailing one, which sees the stone tool kit of early hominid hunting and butchering as primary and disregards the importance of earlier gathering tools, which were probably made of perishable wood, grass, mud, and bone.

Perhaps male chimpanzees do not forage with tools so long or patiently as females because males apprehend that they can get their protein in a much less laborious way. Unencumbered by fetus, infant, or juvenile, they wander farther and may move quickly into a kill situation; capture and kill usually take less than five minutes. Eating and sharing may take hours. Still, the reward is immediate: mouthfuls of meat (usually baboon baby), prized brain, and blood sopped up with leaf wads. A good termiting session, in contrast, could take three to four hours, with a skilled female obtaining only about two termites every five minutes.

Perhaps this division of dietary methods between the sexes was the chimpanzee way of adapting to population pressure. Females and their young are secure in taking a larger proportion of the vegetable and insect resources, and males in taking the larger portion of the meat. Again, it is noted that although this division exists, both sexes eat both sorts of food. So, while adult males do most of the killing, adolescents, adult females, and youngsters do share in the meat bounty.

Food sharing is seen not only at a kill, but on a daily basis between mother and child. Adriaan Kortladt, who sat in a blind 80 feet above a pawpaw plantation to watch chimpanzees forage, saw mothers share the fruit with and hand-feed offspring up to six years of age. Food sharing to such a degree has not been observed among other species of primates, although it is well known among the social carnivores, such as wolf, hyena, and lion.

As the food sharing would indicate, the bond between mother and children is strong and long-lasting. However, not all mothers are equally generous or attentive. A mixture of compassion and firmness allows the chimpanzee mother to nurture and transform her offspring into capable adults. The proportions of the mixture are determined by the age, physical condition, intelligence, and fecundity of each mother.

In the early days at Gombe Stream, as Goodall narrates *In the Shadow of Man*, Flo was one of the most successful chimpanzee mothers. She had two adolescent sons and a six-year-old daughter, Fifi. By the time she was about thirty years old, Flo was middle-aged. Her estruses were becoming irregular in duration and spacing. But once, after a week of pink estrous swelling (the average period of maximum swelling is sixteen days in a thirty-eight- to forty-day cycle), she came back into estrus within five days and stayed so for three weeks. Pregnancy, the birth of another son, Flint, and almost four years of lactation followed.

Menopause, which would have halted Flo's intensely male-attracting estruses and her fertility, did not come soon enough to save her. She entered estrus again, mated with several briefly avid males, and after almost eight months of gestation gave birth to a daughter, Flame.

Flint, like many chimpanzee and human weanlings, was jealous of his new sister, and he jumped on his old mother's back while she carried the baby. He might have abandoned this phase, but Flo fell ill. Her baby, Flame, was lost and died in the forest. After that, Flint remained an unseparated "infant," sleeping in his mother's nest and riding on her back until she could no longer move. Flo was too weak to push Flint toward independence. When she died he was eight years old, and in spite of the attentions of his doting sister, Fifi, he could not be motivated to normal self-maintaining activities and died within three weeks. Thus, female assets of attractiveness and mothering may turn into liabilities if they are held too long: for Flo the unstoppable consequences of her endocrine cycles, for Flint the extended mothering abruptly ended by death.

Communication between mother and child is largely physical and gestural. Chimpanzees can be very vocal and, at times, like to make noise by stamping, breaking branches, and drumming on hollow tree trunks, but when they are mothers, they communicate by cradling, grooming, and gazing at their young. With these gestures they not only relay security but also achieve very practical aims: giving access to the breast, protection from rain, freedom from dirt and parasites, and the signal to jump aboard when it is time to move on.

On a dangerous part of the path, like a log over a ravine, a mother may tap her baby as a warning to hold tightly. The unusual quietness of maternal communication is part of the overall demeanor of caution, for females and infants are easy targets for attack. They must move more slowly than single members, and are attractive to both chimpanzee and human hunters. The former may want the female for mating and the latter the infant for a zoo or laboratory. In either case, it is usually the baby that dies. Mother chimpanzees behave as if they were aware of the dangers around them; they do not even call out to a separated child but return to the sound of its uninhibited cries.

Passion made an exception to this rule of retrieval. If her daughter, Pom, cried at being left behind, Passion did not return to her. Pom had to run after her mother. In other ways too Passion had shown unconcern for her youngster. She had forced Pom to ride on her back from the age of two months, whereas most babies ride clinging to their mother's belly for the first six to eighteen months. Passion seldom let Pom take shelter beneath her when it rained. In spite of her apparent callousness, Passion became a successful mother in terms of the number and strength of her children and grandchildren. By 1979, she had borne a son, Prof, and Pom had borne her a grandson, Pax. Both babies were large and rapid developers.

Perhaps Passion's biological fitness was the result of even more perverse behavior than her harsh mothering. She and Pom (and later, Prof) cannibalized three infants of two other mothers in the Gombe Stream area. It is likely they also murdered a fourth. Pom had learned to kill in the same way that other chimpanzee children learn to fish for termites: by watching her mother. The protein that mother and daughter consumed at these kills may have contributed to the favorable size and rate of development of their offspring.

There are too few long-term observations of free-living chimpanzee families (that is, mother plus young) to know if the behavior of Passion and her children is uniquely aberrant. It may be that their activities were just part of a communitywide trend toward more predation and greater aggressiveness, observed over the past twenty years at Gombe Stream. All of Passion's "crimes" were committed within the three-year period when males of the community were preoccupied with regaining a piece of territory to the south of the range. Perhaps their inattention and absences made Passion's gruesome successes possible, since ordinarily the males would have defended a community mother and infant under attack.

The murders and cannibalism by Passion and her young are the first reported *within* a chimpanzee community; the invasion and conquest of the southern territory (4 square miles) by the males of Passion's community (5 square miles) is also a first. David Bygott, one of many observers of the Gombe scene, theorizes that encroaching agricultural settlements on the border of the reserve squeezed chimpanzees into a smaller area. Consequent overcrowding caused the vicious attacks by the northern males in order to broaden their foraging range.

Goodall emphasized that the victims were the former friends of their attackers; all of them had once lived in the northern section, but some had emigrated to the south in 1970. By 1977, one of three females and all seven males in the southern community were dead (two of natural causes). The northerners had effectively exterminated the southerners and regained the territory.

In addition to attacks that were part of the three-year invasion, ten severe attacks on mothers or elderly females were recorded between 1970 and 1978. Three infants died as a result. This underscores that while adolescent and nulliparous females may wander about and even switch communities in relative safety, older females and mothers carrying babies are in extreme danger if found alone by noncommunity males. In the economic jargon of sociobiology, it may profit males to allow young, childless females into their range but others—alien males, mothers with young, and the elderly—would all be fitness losses: eating food but not producing babies. Given the rate of attack and murder in the Gombe Reserve, it is understandable that an adult chimpanzee gives up the wandering life of her adolescence once she becomes a mother, at about age fourteen.

Mothers are cautious and placatory, especially with males. Even well-known male members of the community can be unpredictable. They can flare up one minute and be kind the next. Sometimes they bully females into accompanying them for days. Male display-threats, the clamoring after a kill, not to mention the tournaments for receptive females and the routing of strangers, are all potentially lethal to females and their babies. The mother that happens to be too near a displaying male can be pummelled while holding her infant. In fact, the frustration aroused in males by an inexperienced mother when she refuses to allow them to see her newborn can provoke a dangerous outburst of temper, and while running for cover, she may drop or drag the baby by the umbilical cord if the placenta has not been delivered.

Barring such untimely confrontations with excited males, a chimpanzee spends the first thirteen to fifteen years of her life with or not far from her mother and siblings. She watches her mother mate with many males but not with her sons. There seems to be an inhibition against mother-son incest. Although sisters do mate with their brothers, Fifi was seen, in her early estruses, violently resisting being mated by her brothers. Like juveniles of many primate species, the chimpanzee harasses couples while they mate, by pushing, touching, minutely observing, and jumping on them as they have intercourse. She experiences her own first matings between ten and twelve years of age, at which time the first sex swellings and menstruation also appear.

Youngsters of both sexes may play-care for a younger brother or sister, but females are more interested in this game. If the mother dies, the game becomes serious, and the older must really care for the younger sibling. Goodall observed three older sisters and one older brother adopt younger siblings after their mothers had died. Only one of the four orphans survived, although three out of four were past three years of age and could manage without milk. Evidently, mother's milk is far less important than mother herself, her contact, her watchfulness, her example, and, it may be said of these primates, her love.

Usually there is some carefree time for every adolescent female, when she travels widely with male friends, visits or transfers to new communities, and has intercourse with many partners without conceiving. A one- to three-year period of infertility in adolescence is normally part of female chimpanzee (and human) development. The reasons for adolescent infertility may include insufficient hormone levels and consequent absence of ovulation. It is possible that some hormonal mechanism in response to the pheromones or actions of older, more dominant females also plays a part in preventing pregnancy in young females. Infrequent intercourse or intercourse with immature males that may not complete the mating sequence are other obvious reasons for fewer conceptions. (It is interesting to note that among certain Polynesian peoples who followed the pattern of sexual freedom for adolescent girls, many believed that a variety of partners prevented pregnancy. In other words, some people in Tahiti, Lau, and Rai'vavae saw teenage promiscuity as the cause rather than the effect of reduced fertility in adolescence. This idea is not so farfetched if a pheromonal mechanism, similar to the Bruce effect, operated in pubescent girls as it does in young mice [see p. 182]. Adolescent infertility is not as long or as reliable as it was, due to changes in diet and possibly in sexual customs, which once may have brought girls into greater contact with the pheromones of their consorts.)

If a female chimpanzee remains infertile, as did Gigi of the Gombe group, the pattern of her life differs strikingly from that of other females. While Gigi came into estrus regularly and was attractive to males when she did, her matings never resulted in a pregnancy. Consequently, she had the time, throughout adulthood, to continue to accompany males on border patrols. Like males, she sniffed leaves and branches along the trail, climbed trees to survey a wide area, and moved silently in pursuit of intruders. But like other adolescent and young adult females she walked behind the males and usually was not as alert and intense in tracking and examining abandoned nests as they were. She did, however, show male-type charging displays and attacks. Gigi might be thought of as the chimpanzee equivalent of an Elizabeth I—bold yet attractive, and occupied with challenges to the integrity of her society.

In contrast, mothers with infants and juveniles must be much more circumspect than Gigi. They travel in smaller core areas within the community range, which is about 2 to 4 square miles. They stay away from border areas unless accompanied by other adults. In 1973 alone, Goodall's students and assistants reported three attacks on lone females. In one case, the female escaped but dropped her baby, which was grabbed by two adult males that proceeded to tear it apart and eat it.

While the loose-knit social structure of chimpanzee communities, in which all inhabitants of a range know each other well but are constantly changing their associations, resembles our own social situation, and while there are many other similarities between chimpanzees and people, including nearly identical blood proteins and a full twelve-year-long, mother-bound childhood, one thing does seem different: the chimpanzee's sex life. On first consideration, it seems impossible that a chimpanzee experiences any enjoyment of intercourse, so brief is the male's service. Intercourse usually takes ten to fifteen seconds. In Goodall's words, "The most the female can expect of her suitor is a brief courtship display, a sexual contact lasting, at most, half a minute and, sometimes a session of social grooming afterwards."

While males are evidently strongly compelled to display for and mate with females showing estrous swelling, they are almost oblivious to the act as they perform it. One male was photographed resting his bunch of bananas on the female's back, unenthusiastically staring into space as he engaged her. This is what is meant by knee-jerk sex, and it is possibly the consequence of the females' extreme availability. Their repeated crouching in front of every nearby male during estrus is less an invitation than a demand, and the males seem to grow weary and distracted with the frantic appeals of several desirable females in heat at once.

The female's solicitation of partners in rapid sequence during estrus may be her way of achieving sexual fulfillment. While climax as a *regular* occurrence in species other than ours is still debated, the longer period of time required for female, as compared to male, gratification is not in doubt. Since chimpanzees and rhesus macaques (which have been stimulated to orgasm under laboratory conditions) have very brief intercourse with males in the wild, the probable aim of their repeated copulations is prolonged arousal and climax.

The five ape genera, reviewed above, have shown four very different ways for females to relate to males: gibbons and siamangs in pacific monogamous pairing, with long intervals between sexual contacts; orangutans normally in isolation, enduring rape or having estrous love affairs; gorillas in stable harem formations, which resemble some of the more contented human polygynous arrangements; and the chimpanzees in shifting associations, with periods of eager contact. Each of these patterns is set against a background of intense mothering.

Of course, everyone would like to know what the preceding descriptions of female animals may mean with respect to the emergence of human females. Trying to imagine the bodies and movements of our ancestors from fragments of skulls and jaws is difficult and controversial. Therefore, trying to visualize ancestral social relationships, based on nonhuman primate behavior, piles speculation upon speculation, but it may be more profitable to put forward some hypothetical picture than to forbid logic to mingle with imagination.

The view that I can offer of the earliest members of our superfamily (Hominoidea, containing species of apes and man) and family (Hominidae, containing extinct species of man and the only extant: *Homo sapiens*) is drawn from the labors of primate behaviorists, paleontologists, paleogeologists, and paleobotanists. Because such a composite can only be as accurate as present evidence and correct interpretation allow, the reader is invited to view the hominoid-hominid pictures of several of the authorities in the field, whose works are listed in the bibliography: Elwyn Simons, David Pilbeam, Richard Leakey, Sarah Blaffer Hrdy, John Fleagle, Owen Lovejoy, and Alison Jolly.

(In the discussion of early humans I will refer to all members of our genus, *Homo*, as hominid or human. However, it should be kept clear that, technically, "human" refers only to members of our species, *Homo sapiens* [sometimes called *Homo sapiens sapiens* to distinguish it from *Homo sapiens neanderthalensis*]. Likewise, in the next section, on modern humans, I refer to members of the species *Homo erectus*, *Homo sapiens neanderthalensis*, and early *Homo sapiens* as human or modern human. Technically, "modern human" refers only to members of our species after the decline of neanderthals thirty thousand to fifty thousand years ago.)

The roots of our superfamily, which includes all extinct and living species of apes and people, go back thirty to thirty-five million years to the Oligocene, or third epoch of the Tertiary period. Back then, a creature named *Aegyptopithecus zeuxis* roamed the high treetops of tropical rain forests in northeastern Egypt, an area called the Fayum, which is now part of the Sahara Desert.

Fossilized skulls of *Aegyptopithecus* show that it was apelike in certain features and monkeylike in others. It is possible that this early hominoid was ancestral to both chimpanzees and humans. With its long snout, almost completely enclosed bony eye sockets, "advanced" molars, and sagittal (skull midline) crest, *Aegyptopithecus* resembled the ancient prosimians and New World monkeys, which preceded it, and the forest-dwelling apes, which succeeded it some ten million years later. Elwyn Simons visualizes this protoape as smaller and more lightly built than modern apes. It may have had a tail, unlike modern apes. It moved on all fours most of the time but could also swing under branches, knuckle-walk, and leap from branch to branch. *Aegyptopith-*

ecus ate leaves and fruits, and was about the size of a modern gibbon. Other inhabitants of its moist, tree-filled environment included elephants, hippopotamuses, hyraxes, bats, rodents, and other primates.

Fleagle, Kay, and Simons present evidence that *Aegyptopithecus* and two other Oligocene anthropoids, *Propliopithecus chirobates* and *Apidium phiomense*, showed dental dimorphism similar in degree to some sexually dimorphic modern apes and monkeys. Analysis of all lower-jaw specimens shows one group (presumably the females) with canines that are 25 percent smaller than those of the other group (presumably the males). Sexual dimorphism of this degree would probably have been associated with either gynopolous or polygynous social groups. Knowing that our possible Oligocene ancestor had sexually dimorphic teeth and jaws cannot positively reveal the relationship of females to males other than to suggest that this relationship was almost definitely not monogamous; with very few exceptions (such as De Brazza's and simakobou monkeys) monogamous primates are not strikingly dimorphic in dentition or size.

Moving ahead fifteen million years to the end of the next Tertiary epoch, the Miocene, brings us to a time when the ancestors of the great and lesser apes thickly populated Africa and were spreading into the then forested areas of southern Europe, the middle East, northern India, and China. At this time, mastodons, tapirs, dogs, cats, and pigs diversified and also migrated throughout the Old World.

During the Miocene too, *Ramapithecus* and a similar African species, *Kenyapithecus*, the oldest known hominids, may have *walked* on earth. While *Ramapithecus* remains are only cranial, Simons briefly puts forward the thought that these earliest hominids were already walking. In a gratifying echo of my progenitor pipe-dream (see pp. 230 ff.), I have recently found Simons weighing up the features of *Ramapithecus*, the lesser apes, and pygmy chimpanzees (*Pan paniscus*) to conclude his *Primate Evolution* with the exclamation: "Our forebears could thus have been bipedal from the moment they left the trees!" All that is needed now is the right explanation for leaving the trees.

The attraction of another source of food for those Miocene apes bald (see p. 229) enough to have been forced to spend more time on the ground, in spite of their long arms, exposed them to selective pressures favoring adaptations for ground dwelling. Perhaps the general cooling trend of the following Pliocene epoch, during which *Ramapithecus* flourished, caused some of them to look for more food in their thinning forest habitats. Perhaps a female, dizzy with hunger, discovered that it was much easier to support her baby on the ground than on a swaying branch, much easier to rest the infant in her lap or beside her on the ground while she used both hands to pick up food around her.

Dental wear patterns and the reduced size of *Ramapithecus'* canines compared to those of Miocene apes (the dryopithecines) seem to indicate that the new source of food was hard seeds. Due to scarcity of specimens, it is difficult to say whether or not the ramapithecines showed sexual dimorphism in their small canines and premolar teeth. Based on the finding that the australopithecines (who were *Ramapithecus'* descendants ten million years down the road) all show dental dimorphism, M. H. Wolpoff predicts that *Ramapithecus* will eventually be shown to have been dimorphic. However, none of the species of *Homo—erectus, neanderthalensis*, or *sapiens*—show sharp differences between the sexes in the breadth of canines. Therefore, I think, there is the possibility that *Homo* descended from *Ramapithecus* (or *Kenyapithecus*) without ever having passed through a highly sexually dimorphic, australopithecine stage (which is, on average, dentally intermediate between the modern chimpanzee and gorilla). Never having been dentally dimorphic could have meant that early hominid females were not excessively subjugated by much larger males.

Since several primates have been successful on the ground in several different ways, it is impossible to say at this stage of fossil knowledge which evolutionary "experiments" linked ramapithecines to australopithecines or early *Homo* during the intervening ten million years of Pliocene. Whatever these experiments were, the result, at the dawn of the Pleistocene, was a female hominid about as different from the male of her species in size (and probably in secondary sex characteristics) as modern women are from men. She would almost definitely have associated with several males in her group, alternately soliciting and ignoring them, and, in turn, being both threatened and protected by them or their counterparts outside the group.

She would have maintained strong ties with her offspring, particularly daughters and their offspring. Because of these ties, I think that it was probably females who first became aware of their biological link to their young. It seems logical to me that the origin of survival-important kin-group knowledge and manipulation lay with females, since it was only through maternal lines that individuals could, at first, have been certain of their kin.

By four million years ago, the female hominid (variously named *Australopithecus afarensis*, late *Ramapithecus*, and *Homo habilis*) was an adept biped, able to make her living in a variable terrain of forest, patchy woodland, and grassy plain. She undoubtedly supported her baby with her arms when she walked. She gathered vegetable foods with hands as dexterous as our own. That she used a tool for gathering or fashioned some sort of carrier for her infant cannot be proved, but it is highly likely.

In the early Pleistocene, which is estimated to have begun from three to four million years ago, hominids (both australopithecines and *Homo*) probably bore their babies in a state of immaturity similar to that of modern great apes and humans. Upright posture made parturition more difficult for them than for their ape relatives because of a smaller pelvic outlet and probably a nonlinear configuration of uterus and birth canal, like that of modern humans. The forward angle of the birth canal in relation to the uterus counteracts the pull of gravity upon the developing fetus in an upright female. Quadrupedal primates, including the knuckle-walking great apes, do not have to worry about the baby "slipping out" because their posture resists the pull of gravity; therefore, their uterus and birth canal are arranged in a continuous line pointing backward.

Early *Homo* and *Australopithecus* probably had a birth brain-volume of about 400 cubic centimeters (cc), similar to that of an infant gorilla. Adult *Homo* of the early Pleistocene had a brain of about 750 cc, on average 250 cc larger than that of a modern adult gorilla. As the adult brain of hominids evolved to a larger size over the next four million years, bringing it to its modern adult average of about 1400 cubic centimeters, the baby brain weight simply did not get bigger. The result is (and probably has been for the past five hundred thousand to one million years) a baby born with only 25 percent of its adult brain volume (350 cc compared to 1400 cc). The infant gorilla, by comparison, is born with 80 percent of its adult brain volume.

The early Pleistocene female was between 4 and 5 feet tall. She was not dentally or muscularly so different from the male of her species. This suggests that the sexes shared a long history of similar diet and activities and probably also implies that group living was based not on a dominance order of the fang-mane-muscle variety but upon a network of responsibilities shared among kin, mates, and affines (relatives by marriage). A variety of female-male bonding patterns must have been tried over the millennia: gynopoly-polygyny, serial monogamy, static monogamy, and occasional polyandry (where females were temporarily scarce), all of which may or may not have been preceded by a testing period of adolescent promiscuity.

Lovejoy and others have proposed that even the australopithecines, who were numerous during Pliocene-Pleistocene times, were living in groups of monogamously mated couples with their children. Bipedalism is seen as established by then, having been selected during the preceding fifteen to twenty million years because of the advantage it provided in freeing the arms of both sexes to carry infants securely and to bring provisions to a base camp. Males are visualized as the providers for females with more than one dependent youngster. Not only did mothers share food with their young, adults shared both gathered and hunted foods. According to this scenario, bipedal-hominid groups that worked cooperatively, through monogamous subunits, propagated more rapidly than those that did not. The male-provider-female-homebody dichotomy is seen as an extremely ancient key to reproductive success.

But how did female primates that had been providing for themselves and their offspring for the previous sixty-five million years manage to get males to do some of their work for them? How did females come to live in long-standing, cooperative peace with males and not just in transient consortships? I think there were three important factors in obtaining successful integration of males, whether these integrations were of the monogamous-duo or the polygamous-group type:

1. lack of strong sexual dimorphism in the ancestral line that gave rise to both australopithecines and *Homo*
2. the ability to identify fathers and other kin, both visually and conceptually, an ability, that, I believe, was first possessed by females
3. the cultural delineation and control of female sexuality, including menstruation, ovulation, orgasm, chastity, and fecundity.

Knowledge of the biological basis of the parent-child connection is obviously not needed to permit both sexes to act in their best fitness interests. A female does not need a conscious awareness of the link between her sexual desire and the birth of her baby or, for that matter, of the link between herself and the baby via the umbilical cord and placenta, in order to carry, shelter, and suckle the infant. Likewise males need not know the ultimate genetic benefits of paternity, or indeed the fact of paternity, to be attracted to estrous females, to threaten or fight male competitors, and even to kill infants in order to gain sex with estrous females. Immediate stimuli and benefits are more than sufficient.

Still, the habiline Eve who was able to suggest paternity knowledge to her Adam offered him the fruit of rapid reproductive success. She could offer this knowledge by revealing the cycle of her egg. The insight that ovulation "faced" menstruation, the way the full moon "faces" the new, gave women the tool with which to construct deeply binding relations with men, who would then know themselves to be the fathers of particular children. Whether these relationships were monogamous or polygamous, an appreciation of paternity provided a positive pathway to channel male energies toward provisioning women and young, and away from seasonal rivalries with each other. Both sexes profited by the latitude in this system for adoption of orphaned kin.

Women of a community might even synchronize their ovulatory cycles and plan a birth peak. Recent studies have shown that women living together do synchronize. Whether this is due to similar exposure to light or, as one study suggests, the imposition of the pattern of one or a few regular cyclers through a pheromone in their sweat, or to some other cause remains to be shown. Many cultures use female cycle synchrony and say it may be achieved by regular exposure to all the light phases of the moon: full moon coming to be the time of ovulation (light canceling the pineal's "inhibition" of the ovaries?), and dark moon coming to be the time of menstruation (see Knight in Bibliography). Synchrony of female cycles would have meant that all young could be born in favorable season, a significant advantage when people moved to colder climates. Also, group migrations toward new resources could be planned with the knowledge that all children would be nearly the same age at a particular time. It was, of course, the beginning of rhythmic birth control.

The ubiquity of customs that identify menstrual periods—by forbidding women to prepare food or to have intercourse while menstruating, and enjoining them to have baths in water or smoke for purification after—implies that these are also important ways to identify fertile periods. By showing the time of manifest nonpregnancy, the menses, women are revealing its opposite, high fertility at the time of ovulation, easily calculated to be fourteen days after commencement of menstruation in those with a regular twenty-eight-day cycle.

While women may have wished only for a break from normal duties by establishing their own separation from the family at the time of menstruation, and only secondarily to suggest to males the link between the phases of the cycle and potential pregnancy, thereby, hopefully, gaining a greater measure of male allegiance and assistance, men saw in the exposure of menstruation unalloyed advantages to themselves:

1. Obviously, it made impregnation of particular women by particular men easier. Women do not always show (or know) their estrus (in other words, ovulation); they may even fake an estrus.

But they cannot hide menstruation. Being able to estimate when ovulation occurred removed some of the hazard of females shamming estrus, a strategy that could get a man to foster children not his own.

2. Once the twin insights of the opposition of ovulation to menstruation and the connection between coitus and impregnation had been given to men by women in hope of stronger alliance, men were in a position to blackmail women into guaranteeing them paternity knowledge and lifetime service: Make your fertility clear to me by revealing when you menstruate; offer that fertility only to me; become my slave; and I will be your ally. If you do not do this, I will not assist and protect you; I will not help nurture your infants or prevent other men from killing them and raping you afterward.

In other words, the gift of Eve's understanding had boomeranged, and she was forced to buy protection with chastity, fidelity, and the observance of ever more subordinating menstrual taboos. (That women in the West minimize their menstruation, make it invisible with the use of tampons, or make it disappear with the use of daily-dose contraception seems, to me, to show the urgency of women's attempt to opt out of the viciousness of sexual subjugation, which both sexes are coming to realize profits a few and destroys many.)

In the early Pleistocene, these and other abuses of paternity knowledge were still hundreds of thousands of years off. Malign polygynies of potentates; wholesale female infanticide; confinement of women and of their genitals by lock and key or surgery; the ransoming of kidnapped children were to occur in a future time, when conditions in the Garden would have so changed that the descendants of early hominids would have been forced to wander to all the cold caves and starved corners of the earth.

Of course I hear the objection: "How was this four-million-year-old female with her 750 cc brain supposed to have perceived the subtle notion of paternity, let alone convey it to her equally uncerebral male friends?"

I believe that female knowledge of the cycles of fruiting trees, which had been part of the female repertoire since the time of an arboreal-terrestrial existence back in the Miocene, not only helped the early Pleistocene hominid survive on plant foods but also helped her create an analogy between her own body in intercourse and the flowers visited by bees and other insects; between the subsequent ripening of the fruit and her own pregnancy. The idea that early hominids formed such analogies is not as improbable as it may sound. In *The Golden Bough*, J. G. Frazer illustrates the universality of various comparisons between botanical and human fertility by citing examples of scores of cultures in which women have sought the power of trees to remove barrenness and, conversely, have tried to stimulate the productivity of plants through their own fertility ceremoniously applied, as when a pregnant woman eats the first fruit of a tree in order to make it bear abundantly. Drawing an accurate analogy between seasonal renewal of plant food-sources and human reproduction must have been a long, erratic exercise, with biologically correct insights of women, based on their experience and observations, being repeatedly confused with homeopathic magical belief. Finally a more or less clear perception of the link between intercourse and pregnancy was achieved.

In addition to grasping the connection between intercourse and pregnancy, the early hominid female had noticed that when she was in estrus and the males had caught a rare and tasty monkey or fawn, they were more inclined to share its meat with her than when she was not in estrus. She had also noticed that male strangers were not as rough with her, if she were nimble enough to hide her baby and then sham the desire and climax normal to estrus.

In a small but very successful experiment in sexual competition, she could have put these facts together and marked all her days, for several months, with the signs of estrus (however modest these signs may have been compared to those of modern chimpanzees or rhesus macaques). In this charade she was much assisted by fantasy and masturbation that brought on a fair mimic of the arousal and genital changes which males found attractive. The extension of her receptivity was then, as I believe it is for women now, part act, part acquiescence, and part genuine desire. As a result of this experiment, the early hominid female found she was now eating better and wandering more safely with her consort(s).

Time spent together—sexually, cooperatively—brought the sexes, innocent as they were of any recognition of their gametes, closer to an understanding of the unseen mechanisms leading to parenthood. The future looked bright to the early hominid female with her Knowledge. How could she have foreseen that sharing with males the knowledge that intercourse, during the fertile period of her cycle, is the cause of pregnancy would engender the coercion of her daughters down the generations? Let us begin to see how it may have happened.

The Pleistocene, which began three to four million years ago and extended to the initiation of agriculture about ten thousand years ago, was a time of sharp weather contrasts, when the tropic, temperate, and arctic zones became distinct. During parts of the Pleistocene, 30 percent of the earth's surface was covered in ice. While glaciation usually affected less than 10 percent of the surface during this epoch, it incorporated much of the world's water, and the sea level dropped to reveal island chains and land bridges. People and other animals moved across these and, finally, confronted the stresses of cold, and food scarcity.

Even what we would classify as a mild winter in mid-Pleistocene Choukoutien (eastern China's famous site of *Homo erectus* cannibal activity) would have been an endurance challenge for early woman. Dietary decline, consequent reduction of body fat proportion, the stress of cold, and infections could have easily disrupted ovulation and menstruation. Under these conditions, it may have been difficult to retain the reproductive insights gained in an equatorial Garden. Indeed, it has been recorded that Australian Aborigines, living under conditions different from but almost as harsh as those of the Ice Age, did not recognize the connection between intercourse and pregnancy. Although I think this denial had more to do with their focus on the constitution of a new personality in the birth of a child (and thus was more sophisticated than our own focus on the constitution of a new body) than with a lack of biological acuity, it is easy to see how irregularity of female cycling and receptivity, which may have resulted from harsh conditions and marginal nutrition, coupled with the long interval between coitus and birth, could have led to a logical denial of the prime role of intercourse in conception.

In that Miocene-Pliocene Garden of mixed forests and grassy plains, there had been no thought of the Ice Age to come. Hominids formed small cooperative units—mother and offspring, sisters, cousins, and their husbands—tied by a growing awareness of kinship and paternity. They were tied also by the success they found in sharing food and in dividing labor among gathering-processing groups, made up of both sexes. Perhaps we can visualize this situation best through the modern Hadza of Tanzania, who enjoyed sexual equality based upon economic independence of the sexes. There was sufficient plant food and small game in the East African Rift Gorge for men and women to forage alone. Meat was only shared in the rare instance of the men killing an impala, eland, zebra, or giraffe. Like the female chimpanzee and probably like the gathering hominids (from late *Ramapithecus* through *Australopithecus* and early *Homo*), Hadza women fended for themselves.

According to conditions, labor could also be divided by sex, with gathering-processing groups being more home based and female, and exploratory-hunting groups being mostly male but containing also childless young women.

By the time of Pleistocene, big-game-hunting *Homo sapiens neanderthalensis*, this equality had been disrupted. Examination of thirty-six neanderthal burials by Francis Harrold showed a difference in the way female and male bodies were treated. Judging from the grave goods, men were more honored than women. Eighty percent of the male burials contained offerings, but none of the female burials did. However, Harrold had only seven female burials, a very small sample for confident generalization. In later Pleistocene times, no sex-related distinctions in offerings occur. Perhaps neanderthal distinctions in prestige for the sexes had mellowed with the passing of the male hunters, who had helped bring about the extinction of their own quarry.

Development of brain and speech accompanied the formation of strongly bound, food-sharing hominid groups. Spoken language probably existed by Pliocene-Pleistocene times, three to five million years ago. No one as yet can prove this, and a few have tried to disprove it on the basis of supposedly inadequate speech apparatus in hominids before *Homo sapiens*, but an early origin for spoken language is argued for by the strong relationship between primate mother and child in which sounds may provide (1) a way for mother to comfort child, (2) a way for mother to find child and vice versa, and (3) a way to "name" child/mother.

Symbolic language would seem to have arisen from the realization that all things can be named, just the way the child is named with repeated use of the same call. Since the vital psychological task of separation of self from mother would have been assisted by the use of vocal names, the ability of the mother to name should have been selected for. Names also provided a way to verbalize knowledge about kinship and conjugal relationships, which would have helped identify appropriate targets for altruism and thus strengthen the bonds of the survival-adaptive extended family.

Facts about the vocal apparatus of two- to three-million-year-old hominids noted by Richard Leakey and Robert Lewin also suggest an early origin for speech. Upright walking, they say, made the larynx wider and positioned the tongue at the back of the throat, so that early hominids were able to make more different sounds than apes of that time. Also the faint imprint left by the brain upon the inner surface of the skull of the oldest supposed member of our genus *Homo* shows the Broca's speech center, which is one of three areas on the left side of the brain necessary for human speech.

One South African australopithecine skull also shows a small Broca's area, indicating that spoken communication was probably rudimentary even prior to three million years ago. Frank Livingstone offers the idea that australopithecines sang their personal or group identities, much as the lesser apes do today.

In a long essay arguing the gestural origin of language, Gordon Hewes emphasizes that speech and right-handedness are both controlled by the left side of the brain. If early hominids were right-handed and therefore held their baby's head toward the left breast, their free right hand may have been finger-writing on the baby or ground. This activity would have remained caressing or idle doodling until one mother noticed that designs-made-with-finger and sounds-made-with-voice could both be used to indicate baby . . . or anything else! Perhaps the designs and tribal brands that people throughout history have cut, burnt, or tattooed into the skins of their youngsters hark back to a profound discovery of symbolic meaning that mothers made long ago, when their soothing, examining, attending fingers marked the skins of their young with the first "written" name.

All through the Pleistocene, the development of the brain and of speech improved cooperation between members of hominid groups. Awareness and language helped people in their attempts to broaden their dietary range with more meat. As Leakey and Lewin point out, language allowed mental imagery to be shared—imagery not only of the hunt, but of the analogies between reproductive processes in plants and humans, imagery of things to be feared like thunderstorms and leopards, and of things to be shared like food, shelter, and sex. Apart from this practical, solidarity function, communication of mental images—vocally expressed in speech and song, visually in drawings and dance—permitted early people to see themselves doing the things that other animals do. This led to powerful forms of imitative learning. Imagine the lioness; dance the lioness; sing the lioness; become the lioness!

The emulation of predators was important in the middle and late Pleistocene and continued to increase in importance as hunting and the predator-family style of life took hold. By about one million years ago, hooved herbivores thronged the plains of Africa and Asia, and *Homo erectus* had radiated out from Africa to Europe and Asia. The gathering-plus-a-little-hunting way of life, which probably had prevailed for at least the previous five million years, gave way to big game hunting by five hundred thousand years ago.

The taste for meat gradually turned the once independently foraging and occasionally flesh-catching woman into a member of a more tightly knit family group. The fend-for-yourself, rarely share pattern that characterized (and still characterizes) vegetarian primate groups gave way to a pattern of sharing food and the duties attached to its collection and to baby care. Such familial closeness and cooperation are seen not among our nearest anthropoid relatives but among the social carnivores, such as lions, wolves, wild hunting dogs, and hyenas.

Progressively better techniques and tools made neanderthals superpredators between about seventy thousand and thirty-five thousand years ago. According to Valerius Geist's interpretation of *Homo* skeletal and tool remains from that period, two hunters working together, one to distract the prey by latching on to it and the other to kill with a wood-shafted, wide-blade knife, could have made short work of long-haired bison, mammoth, woolly rhino, giant deer, and horses. The risks had increased; the tracking took longer; and women had dropped out of the big game picture as hunters. They remained in the picture as flayers, butchers, tailors, cooks, and possibly as cave painters.

While hunting was more successful than it had ever been before, it was not a year-round activity. Only the winter months were dominated by trapping and hunting because fruit and vegetables were scarce. But even seasonal hunting was sufficient to exaggerate the differences between men and women.

The moderate dimorphism between the sexes of our species was magnified by the paraphernalia of the hunt: neanderthal thrusting knives and hand axes mounted in clay-resin mastic, and later the spears, clubs, and bows and arrows of *Homo sapiens sapiens*. It was the flaked rock spearhead and the arrow point that cut the activities of the human sexes asunder and made women appreciate the potential danger of male weaponry if turned upon them and their children.

Analysis of the status of women in modern hunter-gatherer cultures, with different ratios of hunting to gathering, shows the most devalued position for women in exclusively hunting societies. Then, as now, control of the main resources for survival brought men prestige and the power to control women. While few of the world's present three hundred thousand hunter-gatherers depend predominantly or exclusively on meat, as the Eskimos do (or once did), most of their societies reserve higher status for men, even when women supply more than 50 percent of the food in the form of gathered fruits and vegetables. This is because vegetable foods, being less concentrated energy sources than animal foods, are not so prized or shared beyond household boundaries, and therefore do not incur reciprocal obligations the way distributed meat does.

If hunting and meat are so important to status, why don't women hunt? Why did they never hunt as much, or as big, game as men?

Anthropologist Ernestine Friedl explains that childbearing, which begins as early as possible in small foraging groups, and childrearing are incompatible with long and frequent tracking of unreliable game. Childminding and carrying, however, are compatible with gathering, although they are by no means easier work than hunting. For example, the modern Dobe San of the Kalahari Desert carry fifteen to thirty pounds of food and a baby an average of 10 miles per day. Obviously lack of muscularity, endurance, or patience are not the reasons women are barred from the hunt. Rather, the absolutely essential reproductive and gathering functions of women cannot be placed in jeopardy or adjourned for hunting.

As women became more dependent on the foods supplied by men, they became objects that men deployed for work, reproduction, and alliance. By fifty thousand years ago, human societies probably had adopted the pattern of female transfer to strengthen ties between groups. Among primates, this appears to be an extremely rare pattern. So far as is known, females in only 6 out of 154 species in our order *regularly* leave their natal group: chimpanzees, gorillas, red colobus monkeys, howlers, and hamadryas baboons; gelada baboon females sometimes do.

Female transfer may be related to avoidance of extreme inbreeding, which in human populations threatens the viability of offspring. People may have become conscious of this possibility as they began to realize the male role in reproduction, and since there is always less certainty about who is the father of a child than about who is the mother, a young woman might end up mating with her father simply because she could not be certain who he was! Human female transfer, then, was one way to help avoid father-daughter incest and the undesirable consequences of inbreeding. Young men, on the other hand, knew who their mother was and, therefore, could avoid mating with her without leaving the group.

Although it is not known for certain when or why human females began to transfer, or, rather, be transferred, between groups, it was probably not until men had become highly skilled hunters and stone-tool makers. From the time it began, the practice of female transfer was probably a form of sale, and in this sense does not resemble the apparently independent female transfers in other primate species.

From what has been said above about the power and prevalence of contemporary female primates in groups, it may be imagined that extruding young women from a tight-knit human kin-group would have been a difficult pattern to achieve. The only way it was accomplished was by severing the mother-daughter bond and by predicating successful reproduction upon sale (in other words, a girl could have no babies before the marriage-sale was completed). Parents, especially mothers, had to be bribed by increment of status as well as by tangible goods or services in order to make them sever links with daughters. While grooms sometimes stayed temporarily with the bride's parents, possibly working off bride-service by meat contributions, a final return to the groom's locality would have been likely. When hunting became as or more important than gathering, males who remained in or returned to their natal territories could be more reproductively successful because they knew their particular terrain and each other very well, and therefore could, through more efficient hunting, better nourish themselves and their youngsters. In addition, hunting coalitions were preadapted to the activities of taking and breaking land for horticulture and agriculture.

People were beginning to form settled communities ten to fifteen thousand years ago. In some places, like Anatolia, Iraq, Iran, and Israel, village stability was not based on full-scale agriculture but on complete use of what the environment had to offer. People combined hunting, fishing, and sophisticated gathering. It was around this time that women, who were the chief gatherers, began to increase their wild harvest by weeding and watering the plants they knew so well.

In *Woman's Creation*, Elizabeth Fisher describes how gathering may have gradually shifted to farming. She mentions Jack Harlan's observation that in some parts of Australia and the Andaman Islands women understood the regenerative property of their staple yams and cut off and buried the tops so they might grow again. It was Harlan who used a prehistoric flint sickle to cut enough wild wheat, in one hour, to produce two pounds of grain, which had about double the protein of an equivalent amount of the domestic cereal. Protoagriculturalists, in well-endowed areas, needed only to note the cycle of ripening of the plants they relied upon and to have implements ready for rapid harvest. When Nature had been kind, women and men could gather more grain in three weeks than they and their families would consume in a year.

Ironically, it may have been women who were the first to sow seed, and men who were the first to mother herds. Women's familiarity with plants, through their immemorial occupation of gathering, probably enabled them to realize the crucial link between seed and mature, edible fruit. Hunting familiarized men with the habits of animals so that they could, first, guide them together and, later, pen, rear, and selectively breed them.

Of course, both sexes were and are active in "parental" manipulations of both plants and animals, and conversely, adults of both sexes cast themselves as children in relation to their crops and herds. Domesticators are sometimes nurtured by the milk of other animals and always by the fruits, cereals, and roots gestated in the earth. It is not surprising that "Mother" is our name for Nature and for Earth. We mammalian children understand that the gifts of the Mother are proportional to her satisfaction with our behavior, but there is more to this than metaphor or superstition. For instance, people who depend on dairy animals, whether they be cows, goats, buffalo, yaks, or mares, know that particular treatment of the milch female is required before she will actively eject her milk. The children who would be fed by the domesticated mother had to manifest a new sensitivity: they had to stop emulating the predator and start imitating the baby.

Off came the proud leopard and jaguar skins of the hunters. On went the calf's skins and the gentle, sometimes lascivious songs of the milkers, for not only is the connection between milk letdown and the sight of the offspring understood but the connection between sexual stimulation and milk letdown is also grasped. Thus, if the calf were dead or the conditioned reflex of milk-ejection to the sight and smell of the milker, disguised as the calf, were not yet established, then herdsmen (and sometimes women) would insert objects or blow into the cow's vagina (or rectum), causing milk letdown. Sometimes a spiral shell was used to assist this insufflation, and sometimes sticks, fat roots, or the hand and arm of the milker were inserted to directly distend and stimulate the genitalia for immediate effect. Ancient pictures and carvings from Ur and Egypt show that conditioning of the cow to calf decoys and direct stimulation of milk flow by sexual arousal were known at least three thousand years ago. Many peoples have used (and use) these techniques—Abyssinians, Wagogo, Hottentots, Somalis, Nuer and Dinka in Africa, as well as certain European (Hungarian, French), Arab, and Chinese pastoralists.

It is difficult to avoid the idea that men applied conditioning methods to women as they did to dairy animals. Conditioning people works in the same way that it works on cows and dogs. An unconditioned stimulus is presented—such as, meat to a dog; calf to a cow—and an unconditioned response is the normal result: salivation in the dog; lactation in the cow. Next a conditioned stimulus is presented with the unconditioned one, for example, a ringing bell with the meat; a milker with the calf. Soon the presence of the conditioned stimulus alone will release the response.

Analogously, the postdomesticator woman, when presented with the unconditioned stimulus of threatened harm from males, reflexed with submissiveness, which throughout our order is most frequently expressed in postures of sexual acceptance. (These postures, usually a lowering of the head and a raising or presentation of hindquarters, are almost as automatic a response to fear of attack from a conspecific as salivation is to anticipation of a good meal. In most primate species both sexes can elicit the response in a subordinate or offer it to a dominant individual of either sex. In our species, bowing, kneeling, and curtseying all originate from this source.)

Just as the bell ringing comes to mean a good meal will follow to the dog, so the offer of marriage came to mean cessation of institutionalized threat—threat of lack of means of survival, threat of low status in group, threat of rape, or murder of her offspring—to the woman. Since marriage was offered as a conditioned stimulus along with the threat, it could, in time, be sufficient on its own to elicit the desired response of submission, just as the bell ringing alone eventually elicits salivation.

It may seem strange to relate marriage to a threat, but consider that its absence meant (and means) in most cultures that a woman and any children she may bear will find survival difficult or impossible. Some cultures have removed this tacit threat behind the invitation to marry by arranging for brothers to assist their sisters and their sisters' children. The problem with this is that sometimes there are too few or no brothers or none of the appropriate age.

That women acceded to being "milked" for their work, bred for their sons, and traded as chattel (cattle) is, therefore, not surprising, when in exchange they were offered the sole means of survival for themselves and their offspring. Marriage in this sense is just another way of "buying protection"; its acceptance on these terms by women is the ultimate appeasement gesture.

It has sometimes been argued that women conditioned men in the same way, offering sex to elicit an unconditioned response of protection. But sexual offers only elicit sexual arousal in and mounting by males, nothing more. Nor could sex be used as the conditioned stimulus, the one paired with something stronger that would automatically release protective care. The female mammal is usually smaller and lighter than the male and cannot use physical threat as an unconditioned stimulus, and, in any case, threat would hardly evoke a protective response! The only thing that might elicit a reflex protectiveness from a male might be behaving like a baby. This strategy has been used (ad nauseam), but it only reinforces the threat-submission marriage tactic of males.

While the knowledge of domestication provided the basis for a reproductive boom—from an estimated ten million in 8000 B.C. to over five billion now—it was also the basis for the ecological and social bust which we are about to inherit. A spate of new economies and social orders was the result of plant and animal domestication: horticulture (hand farming with simple tools, sometimes called gardening); pastoralism; agriculture (farming with plough and/or irrigation); agriculture plus animal husbandry; and many mixtures of the above. All ancient and classical civilizations were founded upon agriculture and animal husbandry. Even the societies spawned by the industrial and high-technology revolutions arose from this economic base. The gross power skew away from women stems from an economic-social system that is only about 6000 years old and, therefore, is a relatively recent development for our 500,000-year-old species (considering neanderthals as a variation of our species, which, in its early days, overlapped the existence of *Homo erectus*).

A number of distinguished anthropologists, historians, and sociologists have tried to record and find causal links between ancient and modern forms of economy and the activities and status of women: Ernestine Friedl on the relevance of control and distribution of obligation-incurring commodities (such as meat) to status (for both sexes); Mildred Dickemann on the workings of societies in which women must "marry up" the social scale, with the result that most or all females born in the top class will have no one to marry and be killed in infancy; M. Kay Martin and Barbara Voorhies summarizing the work and treatment of women in hunting-gathering, horticultural, agricultural, pastoral, and industrial societies.

While there are and have been extreme contrasts in the male-female power ratios of different economies—women having the most power and independence in smaller foraging bands and sometimes in horticultural communities—the gist of the story in all systems that are based on agriculture and animal husbandry is that men dominate women. This is because surpluses can be accumulated and held by force. Extra food, animals, land, and later, money and trade goods are usually held by individual men or coalitions of men, who possess physical strength, competitiveness, and/or instruments of murder to secure their advantage.

It was not until agriculture enabled people to create concentrated working hives called stratified societies, which might drain an environment to the point of marginality, that female sexuality was reined in very hard—to control birth rate and to intensify the rule of certain men. It had become possible in such societies for a minority of men to monopolize a large number of women, produce the majority of surviving young, and cut off or redirect the sexual energies of other men by channeling them into warrior, slave, and ceremonial activities.

Men who possessed much saw the continuance of their possession in their sons, not in their daughters, who would be transferred to other men. Sons were reproductive success itself; they were the means toward future economic success, while daughters were sold for bride price (mostly in preagricultural societies); ransomed with a dowry in exchange for higher alliance (mostly in postagricultural, stratified societies); or slaughtered. Reproductive sweepstakes among men get higher, the more stratified a society becomes. Women are forced to arrange their reproductive strategies according to the options (or lack of such) for alliance with men at different levels of the pyramid. Whether a woman depends mainly on brother or husband for support of her children, she must accept alliance with a male.

So, in spite of the fact that women in mixed economies (that is, different combinations of gathering, horticulture, fishing, hunting, and herding) contribute most of the food, and sometimes control land, houses, and group decisions, the loss of ownership and authority becomes inevitable as men take over the resources and methods for survival. As the status and economic responsibility of women is reduced, their energies become available for consummate mothering.

This should have been, and in some cases doubtless was, a wonderful arrangement. It gave people an excellent diet and enabled them to settle in large communities with permanent shelters. Children could be produced in abundance and still be well fed. Men and women could feel fulfilled in their dimorphic tasks, so long as there was abundant arable land. Gradually, however, the land was drained. Men fought over unevenly divided resources, and women were caught in the cross fire.

The parallel between the hierarchical setup of social life after agriculture and the concept of evolution through survival of the fittest is immediately apparent. Consequently, it now appears that in order to fundamentally alter any systems in which men dominate women, the rule of perpetuation of the successful (or natural selection) would have to be denied, contravened, manipulated, or abolished. While religions may deny ("transcend") this rule, utopians try to contravene it, and science manipulate it, nothing, it seems, will abolish the rule of natural (including social) selection short of that which would abolish differential reproduction and differential death.

Wider availability of sufficient food, water, health care, and birth control have gone a long way toward this end, but they by no means abolish the rule. Patriliny and sharp differences in reproductive success still typify human life. Even where women enjoy marital freedom and nonmaternal prestige to a degree unprecedented in postagricultural societies, men worry about paternity, birth control, abortion, education and sexual freedom for women, single mothering, and serial marriage.

More than wealth and power are at risk when biological paternity is deemphasized. Changes like education and occupations for women, birth control, and women's choosing sperms from a menu of donor-fathers for artificial insemination (something that already occurs in Escondido, California, where a sperm bank called The Repository holds the seed of geniuses from around the world) may make it seem to men that they have less and less control over knowledge of who their children are and over women.

If experiments with clones and chimeras continue, it is only a matter of time before early cleavage cells from different human embryos are mixed to produce individuals with more than two parents, or separated into different egg envelopes to be gestated by different mothers and, nevertheless, to develop into identical twins, triplets, and so on to higher numbers of genetic carbon copies. For more than a decade, successful clones of frogs have been achieved by removing an egg's nucleus and replacing it with the nucleus of a donor cell (for example, an intestinal cell nucleus), which need not come from the mother (that is, the producer of the egg) or even a female. The embryo matures into a frog with the same genetic makeup as the donor. Successful chimeras, produced from mixtures of early embryos of two different individuals, have been achieved with sheep and goats; they are called shoats! Human cloning—using the mitotic poison colchicine to produce eggs without nuclei that might then be coaxed by Sendai virus particles to absorb a donor cell with its genetically complete nucleus—compounded with extracorporeal fertilization and foster gestation (and, who knows, maybe even extracorporeal gestation) appear to be in our near future. They challenge the very definition of motherhood.

It might seem that women would become the rulers of the world, were reproductive research to hit upon a way to unite the egg and polar body nuclei and trigger parthenogenetic development of females. But men would not tolerate biological redundancy and would probably be able to demonstrate that their own nuclei might also form a viable embryo, when placed in a suitable egg cytoplasm envelope. While parthenogenesis seems bizarrely remote to our species, it has evolved and worked for other species of vertebrates—fishes, amphibians, and reptiles—and is being studied as an inducible process in domestic fowl and laboratory mammals. If men ever controlled parthenogenesis, using their own nuclei placed in thawed, simulated, or nonhuman egg cytoplasm and gestated in artificial or nonhuman wombs, they could enjoy total domination. With their gametes alone they could produce either males or females—motherless all!

This would be a strange end to the world's most mothering female animal. But perhaps not so surprising, when it is remembered that since we became domesticators of plants and animals, we have been constrained to accede to the use of force, surveillance, infanticide, marriage, incarceration, infibulation, and social-psychological conditioning to ensure that the amniote-gestator-lactator legacy of female mammals be used at male behest. Perhaps it is time for a change.

AFTERWORD

"Time for a change!"

I hear my daughter's chirp and I leap out of bed. Before she cries, I whisk her out of her crib, hug her, and change the wet diaper, all in the amber light of the nightlamp.

Her large brown eyes swivel around to scrutinize me, as she approves the milk with a little nod. Although she is only four months old, her thick dark hair, in the medieval bowl style it has assumed from birth, makes her seem old and wise: imp from another age.

"Don't suppose I'm just a baby sucking milk. I mean to learn all about you, and I'm thinking all the time." Her glowing eyes speak the primate message so clearly, or am I half crazed with exhaustion? I wonder about her future.

By the time she grows up, will a woman still derive almost all her status from marriage and childbirth? Will she try some of the riskier forms of birth control? Or will she find a sensible, sensitive man who will protect both himself and her by using the safest form of birth control and later by undergoing the less dangerous sterilization procedure? Probably not. Worldwide, women are sterilized more than twice as often as men, at much greater expense and risk to health.

Will she lose her job when she has a baby? Well, at least she is very likely to have a job. A measure of dignity and security could be hers even if she were not to marry—that is, if she is clever and defends her rights. But what if she cannot?

Will she earn less than a man doing the same work and be passed over for promotions? Will she marry and try to pursue a career while being expected to shop, cook, wash up, vacuum, scrub the windows, floors, toilets, tubs, sinks, and woodwork, do the laundry and ironing, stay with preschoolers all day, chauffeur or walk school-age children to school and appointments, keep the accounts and prepare the tax returns, paint and decorate the house or apartment, do the gardening, and wash the car?

Still, in another society she might not dare to remain unmarried and might also have good cause to fear for her safety within marriage. Separated from parents and siblings, soon to be residing with hostile in-laws and an aggressive husband, she might be a twelve-year-old Pathan girl in Afghanistan, stoned by boys and men as she is carried in her draped litter chair to be married.

In India, a friend who runs a health clinic describes a case of harassment and death by immolation of a young wife, a not uncommon practice if the wife's family does not or cannot yield to pressure to supplement her dowry.

While these may be extreme examples of hatred of the bride, millions of women throughout the world must accept severe coercion, such as infibulation, sealing in black purdah, and strict limitation of mobility to the home compound. Millions more suffer restriction and threat just as real, if not as obvious, through discrimination in employment, enfranchisement, taxation, and marriage law. Pornography and prostitution are partly the result of such systematic restriction and threat to women. There are signs in almost every society that the unprotected woman is fair game for exploitation, torture, rape, and killing.

An anthropologist friend visits Sri Lanka with her husband. They are swept apart from each other by an all-male mob at a religious festival. Her dress is ripped by many hands, and the crowd seems to kick her feet from under her. She is a lone female past the border of her territory, and the men attack to injure, with the savage savor of male chimpanzees encountering an unfamiliar, stray female.

My daughter grows. She talks and walks. At Christmas time we drive through the gray East Anglian dusk to a fabulous chapel behind locked gates.

Angels' voices pierce the stone at Advent service. The distant voices of young women, I think. But then they file in, white surplices over red gowns: all boys and young men! Of course. I remember: the headmaster of the school that trains the choristers explained that female voices just were not right for this type of singing. I cannot work out why they try so hard to sound like females.

My thoughts float with the angelic voices. Could men displace us?

They sing like us. But no. They worship our ability to produce and nurture new life. Or do they envy it? Will they tear the babies from our hands, like male Barbary macaques, leaving us with a confused and vacant "liberation"? They have tried to make milk like ours, with formulas. No. It couldn't be.

Why, if women possess the biological means to supplant men— even now with the aid of sperm banks—do they not seem to contemplate it? Yet men have shut women out, and up, for centuries—out of these sacred universities and up in the home compound.

Have I read the signs correctly? Worldwide and throughout history, female infanticide has always exceeded male. Chinese boatdwellers still tie small float-barrels to the backs of little boys in case they fall overboard, but not to little girls. Will more female than male fetuses be aborted after prenatal sex determination with amniocentesis? Will this happen in the name of population control? Is the human female an endangered species?

But how can I think such things in this beautiful church, songs of love and mother-child adoration all around me? No, I must be wrong. Or am I?

Comparing our society to others, I decide, ethnocentrically, that my daughter is fortunate. This society is a descendant of those that bred love and moral altruism from the mothering trait complex, long ago. Here she will find a well-cultivated form of love, even if she cannot join the choir.

The service is over, and I return home to put my daughter to bed and to reread an old report by J. D. Watson to the U.S. House of Representatives' Committee on Science and Astronautics, entitled "The Future of Asexual Reproduction." In it he outlines the research in cell biology that permitted John Gurdon to create the first clonal frog and that Watson predicts will produce a clonal mouse in the coming decade, a clonal human in twenty to fifty years. He mentions Edwards and Steptoe before their test-tube baby fame, and warns of the potential availability of excess eggs for experimentation, after they have been removed from primed ovaries for in vitro fertilization.

Watson spoke in 1971. In vitro fertilization has come to pass, many test-tube babies have been born, and, at least once, an excess egg from one woman has been fertilized in vitro by the sperm of a second woman's husband and then gestated successfully by the second woman, surely the ultimate adoption. The Warnock Committee have set the "pros" of recent reproductive research—which include helping infertile couples have babies, and insights into embryological processes and genetic diseases—against the ethical and legal "cons" of exploitative surrogacy, human embryo research, and potential human cloning. But there still has been no *international* agreement, as Watson called for, banning experimental work with human embryos.

The age of amniocentesis, extracorporeal fertilization, and surrogacy is fully upon us, but the females of our species still stand clothed in their fragile wiles. Behaving like children and shamming estrus, we justifiably cling to time-tested tactics for dealing with men, but will these tactics continue to work? It seems to me they are worse than useless, making us believe our situation with respect to the opposite sex is no more dangerous than it ever was.

Referring to the possibility of human cloning, Watson says, "There are already such widespread divergences as to the sacredness of the act of human reproduction that the boring meaninglessness of the lives of many women would be sufficient cause for their willingness to participate in such experimentation, be it legal or illegal." A more damning condemnation of women is scarcely conceivable—from original sin to final sin—in the view of a brilliant, modern, male scientist. Is this another indication that we are about to allow our gestator-lactator legacy to be used again at male behest, but with consequences more devastating than those in the past? The possible existence of the first human clone—with, say, the exact genetic makeup of its father—appears no more strange or intimidating than the existence of an identical twin, except that it also foreshadows the possible elimination of an entire sex, either male or female. And every sign, it seems to me, points to that one being the female. Why would the Nobel Prize–winning sex let the sex with the boring, meaningless lives eat up half the food if they are no longer needed for reproductive reasons?

My alarm may be so premature as to sound false. But having reviewed some aspects of the amazing female legacy, I sense the enormity of the frontier we set foot upon now. Throughout the animal world, female control of reproduction within groups is a great "given" that we have barely explored, and yet we females of the human species seem to have surrendered this control completely. What may we learn from the queens that control the fertility of colonies, both of insects and of mammals? What of the pheromones and behaviors of females that block ovulation, trigger abortion or resorption of fetuses in other females? What about the use of cell-fusion techniques to study egg/polar body parthenogenesis of females?

I wish we could record and analyze these phenomena before we take another step in the latest, male-conceived biological journey. But this sounds like another book. *The Female Animal*'s daughter!

CHAPTER READINGS

Chapter 1

Cohen, J. (1967) *Living Embryos*. Pergamon, London, pp. 4–7. A good short textbook with diagrams and descriptions of eggs.

Daly, M., and M. Wilson. (1978) *Sex, Evolution, and Behavior*. Duxbury Press, North Scituate, Mass., pp. 48–51. A paperback textbook. I am indebted to the authors for facts and examples and for their crystal-clear sociobiological exposition.

Dawkins, R. (1976) *The Selfish Gene*. Oxford University Press, New York. The great popularist presentation of sociobiology that should be read by everyone. This book can shake up your point of view and change your life; it changed mine.

Goldwyn, E. (1979) The fight to be male. *Listener* (May): 709–711. Summarizes the material in a BBC Horizon program of the same title, dealing with the work of Dr. Imperato-McGinley and her team on an unusual form of "protogynic" pseudohermaphroditism. The cases of a very rare hermaphrodite with one active ovary and one testis, and of a woman with undescended testes, are also described.

Imperato-McGinley, J., R. E. Peterson, T. Gautier, and E. Sturla. (1979) Androgens and the evolution of male-gender identity among male pseudohermaphrodites with 5-reductase deficiency. *New England J. Med.* 300: 1233–37. Dr. Imperato-McGinley describes her research into the causes and pedigree of the disorder that makes certain apparently female children mature into males.

Playford, P. E. (1980) Australia's stromatolite stronghold. *Nat. Hist.* 89: 58–61. Short article with color photographs.

Smith, R. L. (1980) Daddy water bugs. *Nat. Hist.* 89: 56–63. Excellent article, inadvertently highlights the treachery of a sexcentric view of animal behavior.

Tatum, E. L., and J. Lederberg. (1947) Gene recombination in the bacterium *Escherichia coli*. *J. Bacteriol*. 53: 673–84. This article contains a photomicrograph of genetic exchange taking place between two bacteria.

Williams, G. C. (1966) *Adaptation and Natural Selection*. Princeton University Press, Princeton.

———. (1975) *Sex and Evolution*. Princeton University Press, Princeton. Both of these are required reading for those who wish to delve further into evolutionary theory.

Chapter 2

Gould, J. (1979) Do honeybees know what they are doing? *Nat. Hist*. 88: 66–75. Article on learning vs. preprogrammed behavior in bees.

Gould, S. J. (1976) So cleverly kind an animal. *Nat. Hist*. 85: 32–6. This article examines the connection between acts of altruism and the genetic relationship between the actor and recipient. Implications for human behavior are also considered.

Jacob, F., and E. L. Wollman. (1961) *Sexuality and the Genetics of Bacteria*. Academic Press, New York, pp. 114–17. Section on conjugation in *E. coli*.

Malogolowkin, C., and D. F. Poulson. (1957) Infective transfer of maternally inherited abnormal sex-ratio in *Drosophila willistoni*. *Science* 196: 239–40. Describes how normal female flies can be injected with a "factor" from strains that can only produce females. After injection previously normal females can also only produce female offspring.

Marais, Eugene N. (1937) *The Soul of the White Ant*. Methuen, London. Classic study of the life of the termite mound.

Trivers, R. L., and H. Hare. (1976) Haplodiploidy and the evolution of the social insects. *Science* 191: 249–63. This article describes the experiments that literally weighed altruism.

Wickler, W. (1972) *The Sexual Code*. Doubleday, New York. A popular book with the thesis that courtship patterns are derived from social interactions early in life.

Chapter 3

Atz, J. W. (1964) Intersexuality in fishes. In *Intersexuality in Vertebrates*, C. N. Armstrong and A. J. Marshall ed. Academic Press, New York, pp. 145–223. A long article treating a complex area with great clarity. Atz describes hermaphroditic fishes.

Breder, C. M., and C. W. Coates. (1932) Population and sex ratio of *Lebistes reticulatus*. *Copeia* 3: 147–55. An article that explains how cannibalism by the mother maintains the guppy sex ratio of two females to one male.

Daly, M., and M. Wilson. (1978) *Sex, Evolution and Behavior*. Duxbury Press, North Scituate, Mass., pp. 145–46. These pages describe the female impregnating the male seahorse.

Dröscher, V. (1976) *They Love and Kill*. E. P. Dutton, New York. A popular book with a section of photographs and easily read text on the natural history connecting these extremes of excitation.

Dawkins, R. (1976) *The Selfish Gene*. Oxford University Press, New York, p. 168. This is the page on which Ms. Carlisle's explanation of why male fishes often tend broods is noted.

McCormick, H. W., T. Allen, and Capt. W. E. Young. *Shadows in the Sea*. Sidgwick and Jackson, London. Very readable book about sharks, skates, and rays. Some amazing photographs.

Reid, M. J., and J. W. Atz. (1958) Oral incubation in the cichlid fish *Geophagus jurupari Heckel*. *Zoologica* 43: 77–87. An article that explains one of the many unusual patterns of reproduction in fishes.

Robertson, D. R. (1972) Social control of sex reversal in a coral reef fish. *Science* 177: 1007–9. This article describes the transformation of the top female into a male when the lone male in a group of females is removed.

Zahl, P. A. Dragons of the deep. (1978) *Natl. Geogr.* 153 (June): 840–41. Vivid color photographs depict some species of seahorses.

Chapter 4

Cole, C. J. (1978) The value of virgin birth. *Nat. Hist.* 87: 56–63. A description of the life history and ecology of parthenogenetic lizards.

Garrick, L. D., and J. Lang. (1977) The alligator revealed. *Nat. Hist.* 86: 54–61. A look at the breeding behavior of alligators. Good text and photographs.

Goin, C. J., and O. B. Goin. (1974) *Journey onto Land*. Macmillan, New York. A fascinating work detailing the facts and theories that form our understanding of how vertebrates came to live on land.

Griffiths, M. (1978) *The Biology of the Monotremes*. Chapter 2. Academic Press, New York. A definitive text in which it is possible to see the karyotypes (chromosome arrangements) of certain monotremes.

Hadorn, E. (1974) *Experimental Studies of Amphibian Development*.

Springer-Verlag, New York. The grafting experiments that helped reveal the chromosomal sex of certain amphibians are described.

Neill, W. T. (1971) *The Last of the Ruling Reptiles*. Columbia University Press, New York. A standard but nonetheless readable text dealing with contemporary species of reptiles.

Ohno, S. (1970) *Evolution by Gene Duplication*. George Allen & Unwin, London. Exciting but detailed and difficult text dealing with the role of extra sets of chromosomes in evolution.

Savage, R. M. (1961) *The Ecology and Life History of the Common Frog*. Pitman & Sons, London. A lifetime of painstaking field research is contained in this text, which manages to combine solid science with enthusiasm and humor.

Villee, C. A., and V. G. Dethier. (1976) *Biological Principles and Processes*. W. B. Saunders, Philadelphia, pp. 390, 410, 423, 654. Standard text.

Chapter 5

Barash, D. (1976) Male response to apparent female adultery in the mountain bluebird: An evolutionary interpretation. *Amer. Nat.* 110: 1097–1101. Title is self explanatory.

Brambell, F. W. Rogers. (1930) *The Development of Sex in Vertebrates*. Sidgwick and Jackson, London. This book is the source of the fifteenth-century French rhyme about birds that change sex.

Carr, D. E. (1970). *The Sexes*. Doubleday, New York. A good book for beginners in the field of sex differentiation.

Erickson, C. J., and P. G. Zanone. (1976) Courtship differences in male ringdoves: Avoidance of cuckoldry? *Science* 192: 1353–54. Can male birds avoid investing time and effort in young that are not their own by detecting whether or not a prospective mate contains fertilized eggs?

Everett, M. (1975) *Birds of Prey*. Orbis, London, pp. 43, 78, 80. This book deals with the natural history of raptors and contains material about sex differences in hunting.

Gordon, S. and his wife [sic]. (1927) *Days with the Golden Eagle*. Williams & Norgate, London. An antique book with clear text and photographs of fieldwork. Apparently there was then a taboo about mentioning the name of the second author.

Hohn, E. Otto. (1967) Observations on the breeding biology of Wilson's phalarope (*Steganopus tricolor*) in Central Alberta. *Auk* 84: 220–244. Like *Dotterel* (p. 277), this article treats the habits of polyandrous birds.

Knopf, F. L. (1979) A pelican synchrony. *Nat. Hist.* 88: 49–57. Excellent text and photographs dealing with the mating and rearing of young in a colony.

Nethersol-Thompson, D. (1973) *Dotterel*. Collins, London. A book about the life history of these unusual birds that produce broods with more than one male each season.

Ohno, S. (1976) The development of sexual reproduction. In *Reproduction in Mammals*, C. R. Austin and R. V. Short, eds. Book 6. Cambridge University Press, pp. 1–31. Contains information about parthenogenesis in birds.

Skutch, A. (1961) Helpers among birds. *Condor* 63: 198–221. Which birds help raise broods that are not their own, and why do they do it?

Snyder, N., and H. Snyder. (1974) Can the Cooper's hawk survive? *Natl. Geogr.* 145: 423–42. A popular article that describes the various threats to the species and details the attempt of one male to raise a brood. Photographs.

Storer, R. W. (1966) Sexual dimorphism and food habits in three North American accipiters. *The Auk* 83: 423–36. Deals with the differences in hunting between the sexes of certain species of hawks.

Chapter 6

Bingham, Roger. (1980) Trivers in Jamaica. *Science '80* (March–April): 55–57. This article is of interest to anyone who wants to know more about one of the leaders in sociobiology.

Buchanan, R. (1975) Breastfeeding: aid to infant health and fertility control. *Population Reports*: series J. Family Planning, no. 4 (July): J48–J69.

Bullough, V. L. (1981) Age at menarche: misunderstanding. *Science* 213: 365–66. Along with Rose Frisch's article, explains the various factors that influence when the first menstruation occurs.

Daly, M., and M. Wilson. (1978) *Sex, Evolution and Behavior*. Duxbury Press, North Scituate, Mass., pp. 290–91. Discussion of the decrease in female reproductive variance, i.e., almost every woman in certain societies has at least one child.

Davies, H. (1981) The woman who ate her placenta. *World Medicine* (February 21): 28–29. True story.

Frisch, R. (1980) Fatness, puberty and fertility. *Nat. Hist.* 89: 16–27. Easy article on the topic; more recent and more detailed article on the subject by the same author is listed in the bibliography.

Hogarth, Peter J. (1976) *Viviparity*. Edward Arnold, London. Short and clear monograph on the evolution of live birth.

Money, J., and A. A. Ehrhardt. (1972) *Man and Woman, Boy and Girl.* Mentor, New American Library, New York, Chapter 6: 97–121; also 94–95. Sections on the acquisition of sexual identity in cases of physical ambiguity.

Morris, Desmond. (1965) *The Mammals.* Hodder and Stoughton, London. Readable reference.

Chapter 7

Chance, M., and C. Jolly. (1970) *Social Groups of Monkeys, Apes, and Men*, chaps. 3, 4, 8. E. P. Dutton, New York.

Eimerl, S., and I. De Vore. (1965) *The Primates.* Time-Life Books, New York. Beautiful color photographic survey.

Friedl, E. (1975) *Women and Men.* Holt, Rinehart and Winston, New York. A short but scholarly work examining the social and economic background to relations between the sexes in different societies.

Galdikas, B. M. F. (1979) Orangutan adaptation at Tanjung Puting Reserve: mating and ecology. In *The Great Apes*, eds. D. A. Hamburg and E. R. McCown. Benjamin/Cummings, Menlo Park, Calif., pp. 194–233. This chapter summarizes some of Galdikas' observations. Many other chapters of interest to primate-lovers in this book.

Geist, V. (1981) Neanderthal the hunter. *Nat. Hist.* 90: 26–36. Describes the hunting proficiency of earliest human societies.

Goodall, J. (1971) *In the Shadow of Man.* Collins, London. This is the popular book that records the early years of Jane Goodall's observations of chimpanzees at the Gombe Stream Reserve. One of the great twentieth-century projects of primate observation, it reads like one of the great nineteenth-century adventure novels.

Groves, C. (1970) *Gorillas.* Arthur Barker, Ltd., London. Facts and anecdotes in an easy-to-read short book.

Haimoff, E. H. (1984) The organization of song in the agile gibbon (*Hylobates agilis*). *Folia Primatol.* 42: 42–61.

Hrdy, S. B. Male-male competition and infanticide among the langurs of Abu, Rajasthan. *Folia Primatol.* 22: 19–58.

Jolly, A. (1966) Lemur social behavior and primate intelligence. *Science* 153: 501–06.

Kurland, J. (1977) Kin selection in the Japanese monkey. *Contributions to Primatology* 12 (Basel, Karger). Field observations of the Japanese macaque.

Kuster, J., and A. Paul. (1984) Female reproductive characteristics in semi-free-ranging Barbary macaques. *Folia Primatol.* 43: 69–83. The unusual pattern of limited involvement of subadult females with young.

Lovejoy, C. O. (1981) The origin of man. *Science* 211: 341–50. Also includes some observations on early woman!

Martin, M. K., and B. Voorhies. (1975) *The Female of the Species*. Columbia University Press, New York & London. A comprehensive text including biological and sociological data.

McGrew, W. (1979) Evolutionary implications of sex differences in chimpanzee predation and tool use. In *The Great Apes*, eds. D. A. Hamburg and E. R. McCown. Benjamin/Cummings, Menlo Park, Calif., pp. 440–63. This chapter presents the idea that early human female gatherers, like chimpanzee counterparts, made more sophisticated tools than the first male hunters.

Patterson, Francine. (1978) Conversations with a gorilla. *Natl. Geogr.* 154: 438–65. Good text and photographs describe the teaching of American Sign Language for the Deaf to a juvenile female gorilla.

Schaller, G. B. (1965) *The Year of the Gorilla*. Collins, London. A popular book based on extensive fieldwork.

Starin, E. D. (1981) Monkey moves. *Nat. Hist.* 90: 36–43. This article describes the transfers of red colobus males and females between troops. Female efforts to prevent male entry into troop are dealt with.

Strum, S. (1975) Life with the pumphouse gang. *Natl. Geogr.* 147: 672–91. An article with good photographs and a female point of view on the savanna baboons.

Afterword

Arditti, R., Duelli-Klein, R., Minden, S. (eds.) (1985) *Test-tube Women: What Future for Motherhood?* Pandora Press, London. Opens the Pandora's box of reproductive evils in a high-tech, low-ethic world.

Watson, J. D. (1971) The future of asexual reproduction, *Intellectual Digest*. (October) 69–74.

GLOSSARY

See *Oxford Companion to Animal Behaviour*, ed. David McFarland, Oxford Press, 1981, for other definitions.

ADAPTATION–an organism's becoming and/or being well suited to the demands of its environment. (see NATURAL SELECTION; PREADAPTATION)

AN ADAPTATION–a physical or behavioral feature or complex of features that helps an organism survive and/or reproduce.

ADAPTIVE ADVANTAGE–the fitness benefit afforded by an adaptation.

ALLANTOIS–the membrane, laced with blood vessels, that grows out of the gut of reptilian, avian, and mammalian embryo(s). It functions in the absorption of nutrients and the exchange of carbon dioxide for oxygen. In reptiles and birds, the allantois holds the embryo's nitrogenous wastes in the form of uric acid crystals. In mammals, the allantois contributes blood vessels to the placenta. (see CHORION)

ALTRUISM–in sociobiological terms this is the performance of acts that confer an adaptive advantage upon other members of the species, usually close kin, and that may reduce the performer's fitness. (see SOCIOBIOLOGY)

AMNION–the membrane that surrounds the embryo(s) of reptiles, birds, and mammals. It holds the liquid in which the fetus floats.

AMNIOTE–describing the eggs of reptiles, birds, and mammals, in which the growing embryo floats in the fluid-filled amniotic sac.

ANTHROPOID–a member of the suborder Anthropoids, which includes all monkeys, apes, and people. Usually applied adjectivally to apes, extinct or extant. From *anthropos*, which means "person" or "man"

in Greek, and is also the root for "anthropology" and "anthropomorphic."

ARBOREAL–tree-dwelling, adapted for life in the trees.

BENTHIC–deep-ocean habitat.

BIFID–divided in two by a median cleft or notch.

BIFIDUS FACTOR (*Lactobacillus bifidus*)–the bacterium in human milk
that protects against infantile diarrhea.

"BIG-MOTHER-MALE"–a male that protects, restrains, and generally shows
maternal behavior toward the female(s) he mates; a male that is
gentle and tolerant with young and that may adopt an orphaned
juvenile.

BILATERAL SYMMETRY–showing similar structures on either side of a
midline, e.g., an eye, a forelimb, and a hindlimb on each side of
the body.

BIOLOGICAL FITNESS–see FITNESS

BISEXUAL–see GONOCHORISTIC

BLASTOCYST–in placental mammals the modified blastula, which has
an outer envelope of cells (the trophoblast) and an inner cell mass,
at one pole within the trophoblast, that is the precursor of the
embryo. (see BLASTULA; TROPHOBLAST)

BLASTULA–an early stage of a noneutherian embryo, when it is just a
hollow cavity surrounded by a single layer of cells.

BRANCHIAL–the gills and surrounding region; also structures derived
from the same embryological tissues as gills, in animals that do not
have gills.

CETACEANS–members of an order of mammals, including all whales,
dolphins, and porpoises. Usually marine but certain species of dolphin live in rivers.

CHIMERA (chimaera)–an organism with cells derived from different
zygotes, as when different embryos are experimentally grafted together. (see ZYGOTE)

CHITIN–hard, protein material that forms the exoskeleton of insects
and crustaceans.

CHORION–the membrane, laced with many blood vessels, that surrounds the embryo(s) and fetus(es) of reptiles, birds, and mammals. In mammals, it and the allantois form the placenta. (see AL-
LANTOIS)

CHROMOSOME–the thread-like bodies composed of DNA and protein,
primarily in the nucleus of a cell. (see DNA)

CICHLIDS–members of a family of mostly tropical, spiny-finned, fresh
water fishes. Many species are aquarium specimens.

CLASS–the taxonomic category of animals that is above the order and
below the phylum or subphylum. Thus, the class Mammals contains

the orders Carnivores, Primates, Cetaceans, etc. and is included in the phylum Chordata and the subphylum Vertebrata.

COELACANTH–a member of the family of lobe-finned fishes. Extinct species of this family are believed to have been the ancestors of the land vertebrates. Extant species have been identified only since 1939.

COITUS–sexual intercourse; copulation (adjective: coital).

CONSPECIFIC–a member of the same species (also used adjectivally).

CORPORA ALLATA–two small endocrine glands in the head of an insect that control metamorphosis and reproductive activity by secreting juvenile and other important hormones.

CORPUS LUTEUM–a yellow glandular mass in the ovary formed by the cells of an ovarian follicle that has discharged its egg. (see FOLLICLE)

CYCLOSTOMES–members of a class of vertebrates, including hagfishes and lamprey eels, which have a jawless, sucking mouth, no scales, and no paired fins. They are parasitic upon other fishes, like cod, flounder, and lake trout. They attach to and bore through skin with their teeth in order to suck blood.

DIMORPHISM–see SEXUAL DIMORPHISM.

DIPLOID–having two full sets of all the different chromosomes found in a cell. Thus, if there are N different chromosomes, the diploid number of chromosomes is 2N. This is the number of chromosomes in most body cells, but it is double the number found in mature gametes. (see CHROMOSOME; HAPLOID)

DNA–abbreviation for deoxyribose nucleic acid, the chief component of chromosomes and the carrier of chemically coded instructions for cell functions and other inherited characteristics.

ECOLOGICAL NICHE–the place in the habitat that an organism or species occupies in relation to other organisms and/or species. (see ECOLOGY)

ECOLOGY–the study of the interrelationships between organisms and their physical and biotic environments.

ELASMOBRANCHS–members of the class of fishes, Chondrichthyes, which includes sharks, skates, and rays.

ESTRUS–period of sexual receptivity in female mammals that occurs around the time of ovulation. (adjective: estrous)

ETHNOCENTRIC–consciously or unconsciously seeing the world from the point of view of one's cultural background. Also tending to regard one's culture as superior to others. (noun: ethnocentrism)

EUTHERIAN–a mammal in which the embryos and fetuses are nourished by a placenta and in which young are born after a much longer gestation than that of monotreme and marsupial mammals. (see MARSUPIAL; MONOTREME)

EVOLUTION–the theory that presently existing organisms are the modified descendants of preexisting organisms. Also specifies the process of adaptation by natural selection as the mechanism for change. (see ADAPTATION; NATURAL SELECTION)

EXOSKELETON–the horny, chitinous covering on the bodies of insects and crustaceans.

EXTANT–currently existing.

FALLOPIAN TUBES–a pair of tubes (also called oviducts, especially in nonmammals) that carry eggs away from the ovaries and to the uterus, uteri, or cloaca. Eggs are fertilized in the tubes and conducted down them by ciliary and peristaltic action.

FAMILY–the taxonomic group of animals above a genus and below an order. Thus, the Pongid family contains the genera *Pongo*, *Gorilla*, and *Pan*, and is contained within the Primate order.

FITNESS–an organism's state of superior genetic survival (i.e., differential production and/or sustenance of young and siblings) through the possession of particular adaptations.

FOLLICLE–the sac (or "nest") of cells in the mammalian ovary that contains the maturing egg.

GAMMA-GLOBULIN–a blood protein rich in antibodies.

GAMETES–sperms or eggs; sometimes called germ cells or sex cells.

GENUS–a category for plants or animals that are related by common ancestry and characteristics. It is the category above species and below family. Thus, the genus *Homo* contains the species *habilis*, *erectus*, and *sapiens*, and is contained within the Hominid family. (adjective: generic)

GONADS–gamete-producing glands.

GONOCHORISTIC–describing species with two sexes; also called bisexual or dual-sex.

GONOPODIUM–appendage (leg, tentacle) used in fertilization.

GYNOGENESIS–a form of parthenogenesis in which sperms are needed only to trigger the development of a new organism from an egg (usually a triploid egg—3N). Gynogenetic species exist in the fish and amphibian classes. The Amazon molly is an example and produces only female offspring.

GYNOPOLY–multi-female groups (particularly among primates) which admit a male or males into their company for reproductive purposes. (adjective: gynopolous)

HAPLOID–one-half the diploid number of chromosomes. That is to say, one-half of 2N, which is N, the number of chromosomes found in mature gametes. (see DIPLOID)

HERMAPHRODITE–an organism possessing both female and male gametes.

HETEROGAMETES–differentiated gametes; eggs and sperms. (see ISO-
   GAMETES)

HOMEOTHERMY–the property of maintaining constant body temperature.

HOMINID–a member of the family Hominidae, containing all species
   of people, extinct and extant.

HOMINOID–manlike. A member of the superfamily, Hominoidea, containing all apes and humans. (see ANTHROPOID; HOMINID)

IMMUNOGLOBULIN A–an antibody found in human milk that provides
   protection on the surface of the infant's gut.

INFIBULATION–a culturally prescribed operation performed on millions
   of young girls, in Africa and Asia Minor, in which the external
   genitalia are wholly or partially removed and the urethral and vaginal
   orifices are obliterated, except for a tiny opening, by scar tissue.
   Often the area must be incised for intercourse and childbirth.

INTERFERON–a protein, formed during the interaction of animal cells
   with viruses, that can confer immunity upon animal cells of the
   same species; also found in human milk.

IN VITRO–in a glass tube or jar.

ISOGAMETES–gametes that are similar in appearance, not differentiated
   into eggs and sperms.

KARYOTYPE–separation and arrangement of chromosomes of a cell in
   descending size order, for study and cross-species comparison.

LARYNX–the upper part of the trachea of air-breathing vertebrates that
   is modified to form a voice box containing the vocal cords. (adjective:
   laryngeal)

MANDIBLE–the lower jaw. (adjective: mandibular)

MARSUPIAL–a mammal in which the young are born as embryos and
   migrate to the mother's abdominal pouch for further development
   while attached to a teat.

MONOTREME–an egg-laying mammal.

NATURAL SELECTION–the theory that adaptation comes about through
   a competition among individuals in a species for the requirements
   of survival and for the survival of their young, and that the winners
   of the competition are those that leave more viable offspring containing the genetic codes that, presumably, enabled their parents
   to survive and reproduce differentially.

NEONATE–the newborn, especially up to one month of age.

NEOTENY–the characteristic of resembling the juvenile form in the
   species.

NULLIPAROUS–describing a female that has never given birth.

ONTOGENY–the development of an organism through its lifetime. (adjective: ontogenetic)

ORDER–the taxonomic category of animals that falls above the family and below the class. Thus, the order Primates contains the Lemurid, Cercopithecid, and Pongid families and is contained within the class of Mammals.

OVIDUCTS–see FALLOPIAN TUBES.

OVIPAROUS–egg-laying.

OVOTESTES–gonads that contain both ovarian and testicular tissue.

OVOVIVIPAROUS–describing a female that retains her eggs until the embryos develop fully and hatch inside her; embryos do not get nourishment via mother's bloodstream but from yolk.

OXYTOCIN–a hormone, produced in the hypothalamic region of the brain and stored and secreted by the posterior pituitary gland, that stimulates contraction of uterine and milk duct muscle, secreted at parturition and during milk ejection.

PARTHENOGENESIS–the development of an organism from an egg alone; may occur without sperm triggering, as in certain insects and lizards, or with sperm triggering, as in the Amazon molly. (see GYNOGENESIS)

PARTURITION–the birth process.

PASSERINE–a perching bird.

PELAGIC–open-sea habitat.

PHYLOGENY–the evolutionary development of a group of organisms. (adjective: phylogenetic)

PHYLUM–one of the major taxonomic categories of the animal kingdom, usually containing subphylums and classes. Thus, the phylum Chordates contains the subphylum Vertebrates, which contains the classes: Fishes, Amphibians, Reptiles, Birds, and Mammals.

PITUITARY–the gland that extends off a stalk from the base of the midbrain and secretes hormones, like melanocyte-stimulating hormone, growth hormone, and gonadotrophins, which control a multitude of processes including change of pigmentation, increase in size, and production of gametes, to name just a few. (also known as the hypophysis)

PLACENTAL–see EUTHERIAN.

POLYANDROUS–describing societies in which a woman may have more than one husband; also used to describe analogous mating patterns in other species.

POLYGAMOUS–having more than one mate.

POLYGYNOUS–describing societies in which a man may have more than one wife; also used to describe analogous mating patterns in other species.

POLYPLOID–more than two full sets of all (or some) of the chromosomes in a cell. Thus, if there are three sets (3N), the cell is triploid; if there are four sets (4N), the cell is tetraploid, and so on.

PONGID–a member of a family of the suborder of Anthropoids that includes the three genera of great apes: *Pongo*, the orangutan; *Gorilla*; and *Pan*, the chimpanzee.

POSTPARTUM–the period immediately following birth.

PREADAPTATION–a physical or behavioral feature or complex of features that may come to help an organism survive and/or reproduce, if used in a new and useful way. (compare: AN ADAPTATION) For example, the lower incisor teeth of a lemur ancestor were preadapted to be used as a comb to groom the fur. The benefits of such a novel use of teeth—presumably cleaner coat, less parasites, better survival—gave the users an adaptive advantage over nonusers. Competition between users then refined the shape of the teeth into the true comb of modern lemurs through natural selection of the most effective dental variants.

PRECOCIAL–describing avian young that are able to move about and sometimes feed themselves soon after hatching. Also used to describe a relatively high degree of independence in certain mammalian young.

PREHENSILE–able to grasp and grip, as does the trunk of an elephant, the tail of a spider monkey, and the hand of a person.

PUPA–the immobile, nonfeeding stage of an insect's metamorphosis between the larva and the adult (imago), most often in a cocoon.

SEX-CENTRIC–consciously or unconsciously seeing the world from the point of view of one's sex. Also, tending to regard one's sex as superior.

SEXUAL DIMORPHISM–differences in appearance and/or behavior between the two sexes of a species. Also called dimorphism.

SOCIOBIOLOGY–a set of explanations of structure and interaction in animal societies, based on biological laws of inheritance and natural selection, that emphasizes that behavior, as well as structure, is subject to the process of genetic evolution; the title of E. O. Wilson's definitive text.

SPECIES–the taxonomic category of animals, below the genus, in which the sexes are able to mate and produce viable young. Each species may be designated by a Latin genus and species binomial, e.g., our species is *Homo sapiens*. (adjective: specific)

SPERMATHECA–a sac for sperm storage in the reproductive tract of certain females, especially among insects.

SPIRACLE–a respiratory opening, usually in a series along an insect's side, or as a modified gill opening in sharks, skates, and rays.

SYMBIOSIS–mutually beneficial biological interaction between two or more organisms.

STOOPING–a hunting technique of raptors in which the bird drops swiftly from a height; technique may also be used in courtship display.

TRIPLOID–having three full sets of all the different chromosomes found in a cell of a particular species. Where N equals the number of all the different chromosomes in a cell, 3N is the triploid (or simply tripled) number of chromosomes.

TROPHOBLAST–the outer layer of cells of the mammalian blastocyst, which secretes enzymes that erode a small area of the uterine wall, permitting a point of union to develop. This cell layer plus the adjacent uterine cells form the placenta and fetal membranes (i.e. allantois, chorion, and yolk sac). (see BLASTOCYST)

VAS DEFERENS–a duct that runs from the sperm-storage tubes in the scrotum through the inguinal canal into the body cavity, over the bladder, and down to merge with the urethra.

VIABLE–the quality of being able to survive and produce young, which, in their turn, produce healthy, fertile young.

YOLK SAC–a membranous sac, containing yolk, which is connected to the digestive tract of most vertebrate embryos. The sac digests the yolk and makes it available to the embryos of most fishes, amphibians, reptiles, and birds. In mammals, the sac is almost vestigial.

ZYGOTE–the united egg and sperm; the first cell of a developing organism.

BIBLIOGRAPHY

Alcala, J. R., and C. H. Conway. The gross and microscopic anatomy of the *uterus masculinus* of tree shrews. *Folia Primatologia* 9 (1968). 216–45.

Alcock, John. *Animal Behavior: An Evolutionary Approach.* 2d ed. Sunderland, Mass.: Sinauer Associates (1979) 462–63.

Alexander, Richard D., and Katherine M. Noonan. Concealment of ovulation, parental care, and human social evolution. In *Evolutionary Biology and Human Social Behavior*, ed. N. Chagnon and W. Irons. North Scituate, Mass.: Duxbury (1979) 436–53.

Altmann, Jeanne. *Baboon Mothers and Infants.* Cambridge, Mass.: Harvard University Press (1980).

Amadon, A. Significance of sexual differences in size among birds. *Proceedings of the American Philosophical Society* 103 (1959) 531–36.

Amoroso, E. C. *Viviparity, Cellular and Molecular Aspects of Implantation.* ed. S. R. Glasser and D. W. Bullock. New York: Plenum Press (1981).

Amoroso, E. C., R. B. Heap, and M. Renfree. Hormones and the evolution of viviparity. In *Hormones and Evolution*, ed. E. J. W. Barrington. New York: Academic Press (1979).

Amoroso, E. C., and P. A. Jewell. The exploitation of the milk-ejection reflex by primitive peoples. In *Man and Cattle*. Proceedings of the Royal Anthropological Institute (24–26 May 1960).

Ando, Akihiro, Hideo Nigi, Toshio Tanaka, and Nakaaki Ohsawa. Routine measurement of urinary total estrogens of the female Japanese monkey as an index for estimating time of ovulation. *Primates* 17 (January 1976) 89–94.

Arditti, R., Duelli-Klein, R., Minden, S. (eds.) (1985) *Test-tube Women: What Future for Motherhood?* Pandora Press, London. Opens the Pandora's box of reproductive evils in a high-tech, low-ethic world.

Ardrey, Robert. *The Territorial Imperative*. New York: Atheneum (1966).

Armstrong, C. N., and A. J. Marshall, ed. *Intersexuality in Vertebrates Including Man*. New York: Academic Press (1964).

Ashton, E. H., and R. L. Holmes, ed. *Perspectives in Primate Biology*. Symposia of the Zoological Society of London, no. 46. London: Academic Press (1981).

Attenborough, David. *Life on Earth*. London: Collins (1979).

Atz, James W. Intersexuality in fishes. In *Intersexuality in Vertebrates Including Man*, ed. C. N. Armstrong and A. J. Marshall. New York: Academic Press (1964).

Austin, C. R. *The Mammalian Egg*. Oxford: Blackwell (1961).

———. *Reproduction in Mammals*. Cambridge University Press (1976).

Austin, C. R., and R. V. Short, ed. Sex differentiation and development. *Memoirs of the Society for Endocrinology*, no. 7. Cambridge University Press (1960).

Baker, John R. *Sex in Man and Animals*. London: Routledge (1926).

Balin, J., and S. Glasser, ed. *Reproductive Biology*. Amsterdam: Excerpta Medica (1972) 71–114, 645–46, 877–918.

Barash, David. Some evolutionary aspects of parental behavior in animals and man. *American Journal of Psychology* 89 (June) 195–217.

Barlow, George W. Contrasts in social behavior between Central American cichlid fishes and coral-reef surgeon fishes. *American Zoologist* 14 (1974) 9–34.

Barrington, E. J. W. *Hormones and Evolution*. London: English Universities Press (1964) Chapter 5. New York: Academic Press (1979) 1–72, 493–523, 925–89.

Baum, M. J. Progesterone and sexual attractivity in female primates. In *Recent Advances in Primatology* 1, ed. D. J. Chivers and J. Herbert. London: Academic Press (1978) 463–74.

Bielert, C., J. A. Czaja, S. Eisele, G. Scheffler, J. A. Robinson, and R. W. Goy. Mating in rhesus monkey (*Macaca mulatta*) after conception and its relationship to estradiol and progesterone levels throughout pregnancy. *Journal of Reproduction and Fertility* 46 (1976) 179–87.

Blackwell, Antoinette Brown. *The Sexes throughout Nature*. 2d ed. New York: Putnam, Hyperion Press (1875, 1976) 16–17, 1976 edition.

Bligh, John. *Temperature Regulation in Mammals and other Vertebrates*. Amsterdam: North-Holland Publishing (1973) Chapter 19.

Booth, Janet E. Sexual differentiation of the brain. In *Oxford Reviews of Reproductive Biology*, I, ed. C. A. Finn. Oxford: Clarendon Press (1979) 58–158.

Bowman, L. A., S. Dilley, and E. B. Keverne. Suppression of estrogen-induced LH surges by social subordination in talapoin monkeys. *Nature* (London), 275 (1978) 56–58.

Brandt, E. M., and G. Mitchell. Parturition in primates. In *Primate Behavior*, I, ed. L. A. Rosenblum. New York: Academic Press (1970).

Breder, C. M., and D. E. Rosen. *Modes of Reproduction in Fishes*. Garden City: Natural History Press (1966).

Breneman, W. R. Reproduction in birds: the female. In *Comparative Physiology of Reproduction and the Effects of Sex Hormones in Vertebrates*, ed. I. Chester Jones and P. Eckstein. *Memoirs of the Society of Endocrinology*, 4, Cambridge University Press (1955) 94–113.

Breugmann, Judith Ann. Parental care in a group of free-ranging rhesus monkeys (*Macaca mulatta*). *Folia Primatologica* 20 (1973) 178–210.

Breummer, Fred. The gregarious but contentious walrus. *Natural History* 86 (November 1977) 52–61.

————. Sea lion shenanigans. *Natural History* 92 (July 1983) 32–41.

Brown, J. L. Alternate routes to sociality in jays. *Amer. Zool.* 14 (1974) 63–80.

Brown, Margaret E., ed. *The Physiology of Fishes*, 1, 2. New York: Academic Press (1957).

Bullough, V. L. Age at menarche: misunderstanding. *Science* 213 (1981) 365–66.

Burns, George W. Cytoplasmic genetic systems. In *An Introduction to Heredity*. New York: Macmillan (1980) 479–98.

Burtt, Harold E. *The Physiology of Birds*. New York: Macmillan (1967) 181–89.

Caldecott, Julian D., and Elliott H. Haimoff. Female solo singing by a wild lar gibbon in peninsular Malaysia. *Malay Nature Journal* 36 (1983) 167–73.

Campbell, Bernard, ed. *Sexual Selection and the Descent of Man 1871–1971*. Chicago: Aldine Publishing (1972).

Cann, Rebecca, M. Stoneking, and A. C. Wilson. Mitochondrial DNA and human evolution. *Nature* 325 (January 1987) 31–36.

Caplan, Arthur L., ed. *The Sociobiology Debate*. New York: Harper & Row (1978).

Carter, C. Sue, and William T. Greenough. Sending the right sex messages. *Psychology Today* (September 1979) 112.

Chapman, R. F. *The Insects*. New York: American Elsevier Publishing (1969).

Cherchez la femme: Some mouse ova repair sperm mutations. *Bioscience* 29 (May 1979) 324.

Chikazawa, Dennis, T. P. Gordon, Carol A. Bean, and I. S. Bernstein.

Mother-daughter dominance reversals in Rhesus monkeys. *Primates* 20 (April 1979) 301–5.

Chivers, D. J., and J. Herbert, ed. *Recent Advances in Primatology*, 1. London: Academic Press (1978).

Chivers, D. J. *The Siamang in Malaya*. Basel: Karger (1974).

Chivers, D. J., and Sarah Chivers. Events preceding and following the birth of a wild siamang. *Primates* 16 (June 1975) 227–30.

Cloudsley-Thompson, J. L. *Spiders, Scorpions, Centipedes and Mites*. London: Pergamon Press (1958).

Clutton-Brock, T. H., and P. H. Harvey. Mammals, resources, and reproductive strategies. *Nature* 273 (1978) 191–95.

Clutton-Brock, T. H., P. H. Harvey, and B. Rudder. Sexual dimorphism, socionomic sex ratio and body weight in primates. *Nature* 269 (1977) 797–800.

Cochan, Doris M. *Living Amphibians of the World*. London: Hamish Hamilton (1961).

Cohen, Jack. Maternal constraints on development. In *Maternal Effects in Development*, ed. D. R. Newth and M. Balls. British Society for Developmental Biology. Symposium 4. Cambridge University Press (1979).

———. *Reproduction*. London: Butterworth (1977).

Crook, J. H. On the integration of gender strategies in mammalian social systems. In *Reproductive Behavior and Evolution*, ed. J. S. Rosenblatt and B. R. Komisaruk. New York: Plenum Press (1977) 17–38.

Crump, Martha L. The many ways to beget a frog. *Natural History* 86 (January 1977) 38–45.

Dalton, Katharine. Antenatal progesterone and intelligence. *British Journal of Psychiatry* 114 (1968) 1377–82.

Daly, Martin, and Margo Wilson. *Sex, Evolution and Behavior*. North Scituate, Mass.: Duxbury Press (1978) 75–86.

Darwin, Charles. *The Descent of Man and Selection in Relation to Sex*. London: John Murray (1871).

———. *The Origin of Species*. New York: Mentor Books, 1958 (first published 1859).

Davidson, Eric H. *Gene Activity in Early Development*. New York: Academic Press (1976) "Quantitative Aspects of Protein Synthesis in Early Embryos: The Role of Maternal Components," 87–135; "Transcription in Early Embryos," 139–85.

Davidson, Julian. Hormones and reproductive behavior. In *Reproductive Biology*, ed. H. Balin and S. Glasser. Amsterdam: Excerpta Medica (1972) 877–918.

Dawkins, Richard. *The Selfish Gene*. New York: Oxford University Press (1976).

Debackere, M., G. Peeters, and N. Tuyttens. Reflex release of an oxytocic hormone by stimulation of genital organs in male and female sheep studied by cross-circulation technique. *Journal of Endocrinology* 22 (1961) 321–34.

De Beauvoir, Simone. *The Second Sex*. Middlesex: Penguin Books (1972; first published 1949).

De Vore, Irven, and K. R. L. Hall. Baboon ecology. In *Primate Behavior*, ed. I. De Vore. New York: Holt, Rinehart & Winston (1965), 20–52.

Dixson, A. F. *The Natural History of the Gorilla*. London: Weidenfeld & Nicolson (1981).

Dickemann, Mildred. Female infanticide, reproductive strategies, and social stratification: a preliminary model. In *Evolutionary Biology and Human Social Behavior*, ed. N. A. Chagnon and W. Irons. N. Scituate, Mass.: Duxbury (1979) 321–67.

Douglas-Hamilton, Oria. Africa's elephants—can they survive? *National Geographic* 158 (November 1980) 572–73.

Downhower, J. F. Darwin's finches and the evolution of sexual dimorphism in body size. *Nature* 263 (1976) 558–63.

Doyle, G. A., and R. D. Martin, ed. *The Study of Prosimian Behavior*. New York: Academic Press (1979).

Droscher, Vitus B. *They Love and Kill*. New York: E. P. Dutton (1976).

Dunbar, R. I. M., and E. P. Dunbar. Dominance and reproductive success among gelada baboons. *Nature* (London), 266 (24 March 1977) 351–52.

Ehrankranz, Joel R. L. A gland for all seasons. *Natural History* 92 (June 1983) 18–23.

Eisenberg, J. F., and R. E. Kuehn. The behavior of *Ateles geoffroyi* and related species. *Smithsonian Miscellaneous Collection* 151, no. 8 (November 1966) 1–63.

Ellefson, J. O. A natural history of white-handed gibbons in the Malayan peninsula. In *Gibbon and Siamang*, ed. D. Rumbaugh. Basel: Karger (1973) 1–136.

Ember, Melvin, and Carol Ember. Male-female bonding: A cross-species study of mammals and birds. *Behavior Science Research* 13 (1978) (read in typescript).

Emlen, Stephen T., and Lewis W. Oring. Ecology, sexual selection, and the evolution of mating systems. *Science* 197 (15 July 1977) 215–23.

Epple, Gisela. The behavior of marmoset monkeys (*Callithricidae*). In

Primate Behavior, 4, ed. L. A. Rosenblum. New York: Academic Press (1975) 195–239.

Farber, Seymour M., and Roger H. L. Wilson, eds. *Man and Civilization: The Potential of Woman*. New York: McGraw-Hill (1963).

Feder, H. H., and R. E. Whalen. Feminine behavior in neonatally castrated and estrogen-treated rats. *Science* 147 (15 January 1965) 306–7.

Fischer, Robert B., and Ronald D. Nadler. Affiliative, playful and homosexual interactions of adult female lowland gorillas. *Primates* 19, no. 4 (October 1978) 657–64.

Fisher, Elizabeth. *Woman's Creation*. London: Wildwood House (1979).

Fleagle, John G. In the beginning. *Wilson Quarterly* 6 (1981) 50–62.

Fossey, Dian. Development of the mountain gorilla (*Gorilla gorilla berengei*): the first thirty-six months. In *The Great Apes*, ed. D. A. Hamburg and E. R. McCown. Menlo Park, Calif.: Benjamin/Cummings (1979) 139–84.

Fox, Michael W. *Behavior of Wolves*. London: Jonathan Cape (1971).

French, Jeffrey A. Individual differences in play in *Macaca fuscata*: The role of maternal status and proximity. *International Journal of Primatology* 2, no. 3 (1981) 237–46.

Friedl, Ernestine. *Women and Men*. New York: Holt, Rinehart & Winston (1975).

Frisch, Rose E. Body fat, puberty and fertility. *Biol. Rev.* 59 (1984), 161–88.

Galdikas, Birute M. F. Indonesia's orangutans. *National Geographic* 157 (June 1980) 830–53.

———. Orangutans, Indonesia's "people of the forest." *National Geographic* 148 (October 1975) 444–73.

Gardiner, Mary S. *The Biology of Invertebrates*. New York: McGraw-Hill (1972) 790.

Gartlan, J. S. Sexual and maternal behavior of the vervet monkey *Cercopithecus aethiops*. *Journal of Reproduction and Fertility* Suppl. 6 (1969) 137–50.

Ghiselin, Michael T. *Economy of Nature and Evolution of Sex*. Berkeley: University of California Press (1974).

———. Evolution of hermaphroditism among animals. *Quarterly Review of Biology* 44 (June 1969) 189–208.

Gladstone, Douglas E. Promiscuity in monogamous colonial birds. *American Naturalist* 114, no. 4 (October 1979).

Goin, Coleman J., and Olive B. Goin. *Introduction to Herpetology*. San Francisco: W. H. Freeman (1962, 1971).

Goldfoot, D. A., and Kim Wallen. Development of gender role behavior in heterosexual and isosexual groups of infant rhesus monkeys. In *Recent Advances in Primatology*, 1, ed. D. J. Chivers and J. Herbert. London: Academic Press (1978) 155–59.

Goodall, Jane. Life and death at Gombe. *National Geographic* 155 (May 1979) 592–621.

———. Some aspects of reproductive behavior in a group of wild chimpanzees. *Journal of Reproduction and Fertility* Suppl. 6 (1969) 353–55.

———. New discoveries among Africa's chimpanzees. *National Geographic* 128 (December 1965) 802–831.

———. My life among wild chimpanzees. *National Geographic* 124 (July 1963) 272–308.

Gould, Stephen J. Hyenas: myths and realities. *Natural History* 90 (February 1981) 16–24.

———. The first forebear. *Natural History* 89 (May 1980) 20–28.

Gould, Stephen J., and R. C. Lewontin. The spandrels of San Marco and the Panglossian paradigm: a critique of the adaptationist programme. *Proceedings of the Royal Society* (London) 205B (1979) 581–99.

———. Women's brains. *Natural History* 87 (October 1978) 44–50.

———. *Ontogeny and Phylogeny*. Cambridge, Mass.: Belknap Press (1977).

———. The advantages of eating mom. *Natural History* 85 (December 1976) 29–31.

Grant, James P. *The State of the World's Children, 1982–1983*. Oxford University Press for UNICEF (1982).

Greenwood, P. H. *J. R. Norman's History of Fishes*, 3d ed. London: Ernest Benn (1975).

Hafez, E. S. E., ed. *Reproduction in Farm Animals*. London: Bailliere Tindall & Cox (1962).

Hamburg, David A., and Elizabeth R. McCown, ed. *The Great Apes*. Menlo Park, Calif.: Benjamin/Cummings (1979).

Hamilton, W. D. Extraordinary sex ratios. *Science* 156 (28 April 1967) 477–88.

———. The evolution of altruistic behavior. *American Naturalist* 97 (1963) 354–56.

Harris, C. J. *Otters*. London: Weidenfeld and Nicholson (1968).

Harris, Marvin. *Cannibals and Kings: The Origins of Cultures*. New York: Random House (1977).

Harrison, R. J., and Judith E. King. *Marine Mammals*. London: Hutchinson (1980).

Harrisson, Barbara. *Orang-utan*. London: Collins (1962).

Hartmann, F. An annual aphid cycle. *Natural History* 88 (1979) 86–89.

Herbert, J. Hormones and sexual strategies of primates. *Symp. Zool. Soc. London* 46 (1981) 337–59.

Herrenkohl, Loraine Roth. Prenatal stress decreases fertility and fecundity in female offspring. *Science* 206 (30 November 1979) 1097–99.

Hewes, G. W. Primate communication and the gestural origin of language. *Current Anth.* 14 (1973) 5–24.

Hoar, William, and D. J. Randall, ed. *Fish Physiology* 6, Chapters 4 and 5. New York: Academic Press (1971).

Hohn, E. Otto. Observations on the breeding biology of Wilson's phalarope (*Steganopus tricolor*) in Central Alberta. *Auk* 84 (April 1967) 220–44.

Horney, Karen. *Feminine Psychology*. New York: Norton (1967).

Horr, David Agee. Orangutan maturation: Growing up in a female world. In *Primate Biosocial Development*, ed. Suzanne Chevalier-Skolnikoff and Frank E. Poirier. New York: Garland Publishing (1977) 289–321.

Horwich, Robert H. Development of behaviors in a male spectacled langur. *Primates* 15 (September 1974) 151–78.

Hrdy, Sarah Blaffer. *The Woman That Never Evolved*. Cambridge, Mass.: Harvard University Press (1981).

————. *The Langurs of Abu: Female and Male Strategies of Reproduction*. Cambridge, Mass.: Harvard University Press (1977).

Imanishi, Kinji. Social behavior in Japanese monkeys, *Macaca fuscata*. In *Primate Social Behavior*, ed. Charles H. Southwick. Princeton, N.J.: Van Nostrand (1963) 68–81.

Jelliffe, D. B. World trends in infant feeding. *The American Journal of Clinical Nutrition* 29 (November 1976) 1227–37.

Jelliffe, D. B., and E. F. P. Jelliffe. *Human Milk in the Modern World*. Oxford University Press (1978).

Jenkins, P. F. Cultural transmission of song patterns and dialect development in free-living bird populations. *Animal Behavior* 26 (1978) 50–78. (*N.B.*: Dateline at top of this article is misprinted in the journal and reads: *Anim. Behav.* 25 [1977].)

Jolly, Alison. *The Evolution of Primate Behavior*. New York: The Macmillan series in physical anthropology (1972).

————. *Lemur Behavior*. University of Chicago Press (1966).

Jolly, Clifford. The seed-eaters: A new model of hominid differentiation based on a baboon analogy. *Man* 5 (1970) 5–26.

Jones, Howard W., and William Wallace Scott. *Hermaphroditism, Gen-*

ital Anomalies and Related Endocrine Disorders. Baltimore: Williams and Wallace (1971) 200–201, 335–48.

Kawai, Masao, ed. *Contributions to Primatology: Zoological and Sociological Studies of Gelada Baboon*, Vol. 16. Basel: Karger (1979) 125–54.

Knight, Chris. Menstruation as medicine. Talk delivered to conference of British Medical Anthropology Society, Bristol, 1 October 1983.

———. Levi-Strauss and the Dragon. *Man* (N.S.) *18* (1983) 21–50.

Koestler, Arthur. *The Case of the Midwife Toad*. London: Hutchinson (1971).

Kortlandt, Adriaan. Chimpanzees in the wild. *Scientific American* 206 (May 1962) 128–38.

Kummer, Hans. *Primate Societies: Group Techniques of Ecological Adaptation*. Chicago: Aldine Publishing (1971).

Lack, David. *The Natural Regulation of Animal Numbers*. Oxford: Clarendon Press (1954) 112–13.

Lagler, Karl F., John E. Bradach, and Robert E. Miller. *Ichthyology*. New York: John Wiley & Sons (1962) 1–5, 285–300, 348–49, 404–05.

Lamming, G. E., and E. C. Amoroso, ed. *Reproduction in the Female Mammal*. London: Butterworths (1967) 478.

Laws, R. M. Aspects of reproduction in the African elephant *Lopodonta africana*. *Journal of Reproduction and Fertility* Suppl. 6 (1969) 193–217.

Leakey, Richard, and Roger Lewin. *Origins*. New York: E. P. Dutton (1977) Chapters 9 and 10.

Lee, Patrick C., and Robert Sussman Stewart, ed. *Sex Differences*. New York: Urizen Books (1976) 133–50.

LeMaho, Yvon. The emperor penguin: A strategy to live and breed in the cold. *American Scientist* 65 (1977) 680–93.

Levine, Seymour. Sex differences in the brain. *Scientific American* 214 (April 1966) 84–90.

Levine, Seymour, and Richard Mullins, Jr. Estrogen administered neonatally affects adult sexual behavior in male and female rats. *Science* 144 (10 April 1964) 185–87.

Livingstone, Frank B. Did the australopithecines sing? *Current Anthro*. 14 (1973) 25–29.

Lloyd, J. E. Aggressive mimicry in photorius fireflies: Signal repertoires by femmes fatales. *Science* 187 (1975) 452–53.

Lofts, Brian, ed. *Physiology of the Amphibia*, Vol. II. New York: Academic Press (1974).

Lowry, Thomas P., and Thea Snyder Lowry. *The Clitoris*. St. Louis: Warren H. Green, Inc. (1976).

Luft, Joan, and Jeanne Altmann. Mother baboon. *Natural History* 91 (September 1982) 30–39.

Maccoby, E. E., and C. J. Jacklin. *The Psychology of Sex Differences*. Palo Alto, Calif.: Stanford University Press (1974).

MacCormack, Carol, and Marilyn Strathern, ed. *Nature, Culture and Gender*. Cambridge University Press (1980).

MacKinnon, John. *The Ape Within Us*. London: Collins (1978).

———. *In Search of the Red Ape*. London: Collins (1974).

Marshall, D. S., and R. C. Suggs, ed. *Human Sexual Behavior: Variations in Ethnographic Spectrum*. New York: Basic Books (1971).

Marshall, N. B. *Explorations in the Life of Fishes*. Boston: Harvard University Press (1971) 11, 130–31.

Martin, M. Kay, and Barbara Voorhies. *Female of the Species*. New York and London: Columbia University Press (1975).

Martin, R. D., and Simon K. Bearder. The evolution of reproductive mechanisms in primates. *Journal of Reproduction and Fertility* Suppl. 6 (1969) 49–66.

Matthews, L. Harrison. *The Natural History of the Whale*. London: Weidenfeld and Nicholson (1978).

———. Reproduction in the spotted hyena. *Philosophical Transactions of the Royal Society* (London) 230, Ser. B (July 1939) 1–78.

May, Robert M. Human reproduction reconsidered. *Nature* 272 (6 April 1978) 491–92.

McKay, Francis E. Behavioral aspects of population dynamics in unisexual-bisexual *Poeciliopsis*. *Ecology* 52 (1971) 778–90.

McWhirter, Norris (compiler). *Guinness Book of Records*. London (1976, 1983).

Mead, Margaret. *Male and Female*. London: Victor Gollancz Ltd., 1949.

Mech, L. David. *The Wolf: The Ecology and Behavior of an Endangered Species*. Garden City: Natural History Press (1970).

Mertens, Robert. *The World of Amphibians and Reptiles*. London: George G. Harrap (1960).

Michener, Gail R. Differential reproduction among female Richardson's ground squirrels and its relation to sex ratio. *Behavioral Ecology and Sociobiology* 7 (1980) 173–78.

Mitchell, G. *Behavioral Sex Differences in Non-Human Primates*. New York: Van Nostrand Reinhold (1979).

Mittwoch, Ursula. Sex differences in cells. *Scientific American* 209 (July 1963) 54–62.

Money, J., and A. A. Ehrhardt. *Man and Woman, Boy and Girl*. Baltimore: Johns Hopkins Press (1972).

————. Prenatal hormones and intelligence: A possible relationship. *Impact of Science on Society* (Paris: UNESCO) 21 (October–December 1971) 285–90.

Montagu, Ashley. *The Natural Superiority of Women*. New York: Macmillan (1978).

————. *Coming into Being among the Australian Aborigines*. London: Routledge and Kegan Paul (1974).

Morgan, Elaine. *The Descent of Woman*. London: Souvenir Press (1972).

Morton, E. S., M. S. Gietzey, and S. McGarth. On bluebird responses to apparent female adultery. *American Naturalist* 112 (1978) 968–71.

Munoz, Juan. Chilean flamingo court and dance. *Natural History* 86 (December 1977) 72–78.

Napier, J. R., and P. H. Napier. *A Handbook of Living Primates*. London and New York: Academic Press (1967).

Newton, Niles. Interrelationships between various aspects of the female reproductive role. In *Psychosomatic Medicine in Obstetrics and Gynecology: Third International Congress* (London, 1971), ed. Norman Morris. Basel and New York: Karger (1972) 388–90.

Ogilvie, M. A. *Wild Geese*. Berkhampstead: T. Poyser and A. D. Poyser (1978).

Ohno, S. *Evolution by Gene Duplication*. London: George Allen & Unwin (1970).

————. Phylogeny of the X-chromosome in man. In *Cytogenetics of the Mammalian X-Chromosome*, Part A, ed. A. A. Sandberg. New York: Alan R. Liss (1983) 1–19.

Olson, E. C. Note: sexual dimorphism in extinct amphibians and reptiles. In *Sexual Dimorphism in Fossil Metazoa*, ed. G. E. G. Westermann. Stuttgart (1969) 223–25.

Orasanu, Judith, Miriam Slater, and Lenore Loeb Adler. Language, sex and gender: Does la difference make a difference? *Annals of the New York Academy of Sciences* 327 (1979) 1–121.

Ostrow, John H. *Archaeopteryx* and the origin of birds. *Biological Journal of the Linnean Society* 8, no. 2 (June 1976) 91–182.

Owens, Delia, and Mark Owens. Hyenas of the Kalahari. *Natural History* 80 (February 1980) 44–53.

Parker, G. A., R. R. Baker, and V. G. F. Smith. The origin and evolution of gamete dimorphism and the male-female phenomenon. *Journal of Theoretical Biology* 36 (1972) 529–53.

Petit, Michael G. Imperiled bats of eagle creek. *Natural History* 77 (March 1978) 50–54.

Pilbeam, David. *The Ascent of Man: An Introduction to Human Evolution*. New York: Macmillan (1972).

Ploog, Detev W. The behavior of squirrel monkeys (*Saimiri sciureus*) as revealed by sociometry, bioacoustics, and brain stimulations. In *Social Communication among Primates*, ed. Stuart Altmann. University of Chicago Press (1967) 207–219.

Ploss, Herman H., Max Bartels, and Paul Bartels. *Woman: An Historical, Gynecological and Anthropological Compendium*, Vols. I, II, III. London: William Heinemann (Medical Books) Ltd. (1935) (originally in German, 1885).

Pope, Clifford H. *The Giant Snakes*. London: Routledge and Kegan Paul (1961).

Porter, Kenneth. *Herpetology*. Philadelphia: W. B. Saunders (1972).

Porter, R., and J. Whelan, ed. *Sex, Hormones, and Behavior*. (Ciba Foundation Symposium no. 62) Amsterdam: Elsevier (1979).

Poulson, D. F., and B. Sakaguchi. Nature of "sex-ratio" agent in *Drosophila*. *Science* 133 (12 May 1961) 1489–90.

Raisman, Geoffrey, and Pauline Field. Sexual dimorphism in the preoptic area of the rat. *Science* 173 (20 August 1971) 731–33.

Racey, P. A., and J. D. Skinner. Endocrine aspects of sexual mimicry in spotted hyenas, *Crocuta crocuta*. *Journal of Zoology* 187 (1979) 315–26.

Ralls, Katherine. Mammals in which females are larger than males. *Quarterly Review of Biology* 51 (June 1976) 245–68.

Raphael, Dana. *Being Female*. The Hague and Paris: Mouton Publishers (1975).

Ray, G. Carleton. Learning the ways of the walrus. *National Geographic* 156 (October 1979) 564–80.

Reed, Evelyn. *Woman's Evolution*. New York: Pathfinder Press (1975).

Reiter, Russel J. The pineal gland. (*Extra-Reproductive Effects*, Vol. 3) Boca Raton, Florida: CRC Press (1982).

Reynolds, John E. The semisocial manatee. *Natural History* 88 (February 1979) 44–53.

Richdale, L. E. *Sexual Behavior in Penguins*. University of Kansas Press (1951).

Romer, Alfred Sherwood. *The Vertebrate Body*. Philadelphia: W. B. Saunders (1970) 93, 107, 116, 370–78.

Rosenblatt, Joy S. Reproduction in infrahuman mammals. In *Childbearing*, ed. S. A. Richardson and F. A. Guttmacher. Baltimore: Williams & Wilkins (1967) 245–301.

Rosenblum, Leonard A., ed. *Primate Behavior*, Vols. 1 and 4. New York: Academic Press (1970, 1974).

Rosenblum, Leonard A., and I. Charles Kaufman. Laboratory observations of early mother-infant relations in pigtail and bonnet macaques. In *Social Communication among Primates*, ed. S. Altmann. University of Chicago Press (1967) 33–59.

Ross, June P. Biological foundations of sexual dimorphism. In *Sexual Dimorphism in Fossil Metazoa and Taxonomic Implications*, ed. G. E. G. Westermann. Stuttgart (1969) 3–20.

Rowell, Thelma E. Effects of social environment on menstrual cycle of baboons. *Journal of Reproduction and Fertility* Suppl. 6 (1969) 117–18.

———. Female reproductive cycles and behavior of baboons and rhesus macaques. In *Social Communication among Primates*, ed. S. Altmann. University of Chicago Press (1967) 15–32.

———. Forest-living baboons in Uganda. *Journal of Zoology* (London) 149 (1966) 344–64.

Rumbaugh, Duane, ed. *Gibbon and Siamang*, Vols. I–IV. Basel: Karger (1973).

Sandor, T., and A. Z. Mehdi. Steroids and evolution. In *Hormones and Evolution*, ed. E. J. W. Barrington. London: English Universities Press (1979) 1–72.

Sauer, E. G. Franz, and Eleanore M. Sauer. Behavior and ecology of ostriches. *Living Bird* (1966) 45–75.

Schaller, George B. *The Serengeti Lion*. University of Chicago Press (1972).

———. *The Mountain Gorilla*. University of Chicago Press (1963).

Schopf, J. William. The evolution of the earliest cells. *Scientific American* 239 (September 1978) 110–38.

Selander, C. Sexual dimorphism and differential niche utilization in birds. *Condor* 68 (1966) 113–51.

Sellers, S. M., et al. Is oxytocin involved in parturition? *British Journal of Obstetrics and Gynecology* 88 (July 1981) 725–29.

Shaw, Evelyn, and Joan Darling. *Female Strategies*. New York: Walker (1984).

Sheehan, Elizabeth. Victorian clitoridectomy: Isaac Baker Brown and his harmless operative procedure. *Medical Anthropology Newsletter* 12 (August 1981) 9–15.

Signoret, J. P. Reproductive behavior of pigs. *Journal of Reproduction and Fertility* Suppl. 11 (1970) 105–17.

Simons, Elwyn L. *Primate Evolution*. New York: Macmillan (1972).

Skutch, Alexander F. Helpers among birds. *Condor* 63 (1961) 198–221.

Smith, J. Maynard. *The Evolution of Sex*. Cambridge University Press (1978).

———. Group selection. *Quarterly Review of Biology* 51 (June 1976) 277–83.

Southwick, Charles, ed. *Primate Social Behavior*. Princeton: Van Nostrand (1963).

Spencer, R. E. Primitive obstetrics. *Ciba Symposium 11* (1949–50) 1158–88.

Spotnitz, Hyman, and Lucy Freeman. *How to Be Happy though Pregnant.* New York: Berkley Publishing (1969) 53, 129.

Steptoe, Patrick. Experiences extracorporeal in the human. Lecture to the Society of Surgeons, John Radcliffe Hospital, Oxford, 11 March 1980.

Stevens, Vernon C. The use of female baboons for evaluation of immunological methods of fertility control. In *Recent Advances in Primatology*, ed. D. J. Chivers and E. H. R. Ford. London: Academic Press (1978).

Stewart, Glenn R. Sperm storage in a female garter snake. *Herpetologica* 28, no. 4 (1972) 346–47.

Stonehouse, Bernard. *Penguins.* London: Arthur Barker Ltd. (1968).

Symons, Donald. *The Evolution of Human Sexuality.* New York: Oxford University Press (1979).

Tarkowski, Andrzej K., Anna Witowska, and Jolanta Nowicka. Experimental pathogenesis in the mouse. *Nature* 226 (11 April 1970) 162–65.

Taylor, D. H., and S. I. Guttman, eds. *The Reproductive Biology of Amphibians.* New York: Plenum (1976) 73–86.

Teleki, G. The omnivorous chimpanzee. *Scientific American* 228 (January 1973) 32–44.

Tinbergen, Niko. *The Herring Gull's World.* London: Collins (1953).

Trivers, Robert L., and Hope Hare. Parent-offspring conflict. *American Zoologist* 14 (1974) 249–64.

Tudge, Colin. The best contraceptive in history. *World Medicine* 16 (29 November 1981) 22.

Urdy, J. Richard, and Naomi M. Morris. Distribution of coitus in the menstrual cycle. *Nature* 220 (9 November 1968) 593–96.

Uzzell, Thomas. Meiotic mechanisms of naturally occurring unisexual vertebrates. *American Naturalist* 104 (September/October 1970) 433–45.

van Tyne, Josselyn, and Andrew J. Berger. *Fundamentals of Ornithology.* New York: John Wiley & Sons (1976).

Vial, James L., ed. *Evolutionary Biology of the Anurans.* Columbia: University of Missouri Press (1973).

von Holst, D. Social stress in the tree-shrew *Tupaia belangeri.* Fourday Research Seminar on Prosimian Biology, 14–17 April 1972. ("Sozialer Stress bei Tupajas [*Tupaia belangeri*]" *Z. vergl. Physiol.* 63, 1–58.)

Voss, Gilbert L. Shy monster, the octopus. *National Geographic* 136 (November 1971) 776–99.

Walker, E. P. *Mammals of the World*. 3d ed. Baltimore: Johns Hopkins University Press (1975).

Watson, J. D. (1971) The future of asexual reproduction, *Intellectual Digest*. (October) 69–74.

Weismann, Marc. Social control of sex reversal as found in two coral reef fish. Student report courtesy of Dr. George T. Hemingway, Scripps Institute of Oceanography, San Diego, August 1973.

Welty, Joel. *The Life of Birds*. Philadelphia: Saunders (1975) 38, 133–34, 325.

Widdowson, Elsie M. Growth of creatures great and small. *Symposium of the Zoological Society, London*, no. 46 (1981a) 5–17.

———. *Feeding the Newborn Mammal*. Carolina Biological Readers no. 112. Burlington, N.C.: Carolina Biological Supply Co. (1981b).

Wigglesworth, V. B. *Insect Physiology*. London: Methuen (1934, 1961).

Williams, G. C. *Sex and Evolution*. Princeton University Press (1975).

———. *Adaptation and Natural Selection*. Princeton University Press (1966).

Wilson, E. O. The ants. In *Readings in Sociobiology*, ed. T. H. Clutton-Brock and P. Harvey. San Francisco: Freeman (1978).

———. *Sociobiology: the new synthesis*. Harvard: Belknap (1975).

Wolfe, Linda D. The reproductive history of a hybrid female (*Macaca mulatta* X *Macaca fuscata*). *Primates* 22 (1981) 131–34.

———. Behavioral patterns of estrous females of the Arashiyama West troop of Japanese macaques (*Macaca fuscata*). *Primates* 20 (1979) 525–34.

Wood, Gerald L. *The Guinness Book of Animal Facts and Feats*. London: Guinness Superlatives Ltd. (1982).

Wurtman, Richard J. The effects of light on the human body. *Scientific American* 233 (July 1975) 68–77.

Young, J. Z. *The Life of Mammals*. Oxford: Clarendon Press (1975) 469, 473–480, 491.

Young, William C. *Sex and Internal Secretions*. 3d ed. Baltimore: Williams & Wilkins (1961) 1060, 1355–56.

Zacharias, Leona, and R. J. Wurtman. Blindness: Its relation to age at menarche. *Science* 144 (1964) 1154–55.

Zuk, Marlene. A charming resistance to parasites. *Natural History* (April 1984) 28–34.

INDEX